ESSAYS ON INDUSTRIAL POLICY

ESSAYS ON INDUSTRIAL POLICY

R.K. HAZARI

CONCEPT PUBLISHING COMPANY, NEW DELHI

First Published 1986

Published by

Naurang Rai
Concept Publishing Company
H-13, Bali Nagar
NEW DELHI-110015 (India)

Printed in India by

Printway India
at New Suchdeva Press, Maya Puri,
NEW DELHI-110064.

PREFACE

SENILITY crept early and fast upon me after reaching 35. Till then, I had something to do with economic research, in particular the collection and analysis of primary data relating to joint stock companies. After that divide, circumstances exiled me from academe to assorted mundane activities. These enriched my experience but left me an antique piece of furniture listed in university catalogues, retrieved occasionally from hazy memories in ambiguous policy discussions, confused now as before by my findings and conclusions, which few actually consulted in the original.

Time and events have marched on. My publications of the 1960s have been out of print for more than a decade. Now past the half-century mark, conceit inspires me to believe that re-publication of these works has some merit, for reasons additional to personal vanity: it is useful to have a historical perspective as policy changes are debated. There has been advice and persuasion to update earlier studies or work afresh. Weak though I am now in flesh, mind and spirit, this is one temptation that I resist. Others, more competent and vigorous, should, if they so wish, carry on where I left off. I can only put the antiques on view again in their original shape with some trimming of edges.

This collection puts together:

(1) A lecture on Industrial Policy in Perspective delivered at the Administrative Staff College of India, Hyderabad, on 17 January 1983 which gave an overview of the evolution and continuity of industrial policy in the social and political environment from the 1870s till recent years.

(2) Chapter VIII in Volume III of the Gazetteer of India 1975 which I contributed in 1966 and which chronicles industrial policies from the Imperial era till the end of the Nehru era.

(3) Four chapters, that is, chapters 1, 2, 8 and 9 from *The Structure of the Corporate Private Sector—A Study of*

Concentration, Ownership and Control (Asia Publishing House) 1966, which defined business groups and studied 20 of them, representing a cross-section of the corporate private sector, on the bases of their published accounts and shareholders lists, and measured the concentration of economic power in this sector in 1951 and 1958.

(4) A review of the Report of the Monopolies Inquiry (Dasgupta) Commission which appeared in *The Economic Weekly*, 18 December 1965 which stated my views on the statutory regulation of concentration and monopoly.

(5) Volume I (Text) of the Final Report on Industrial Planning and Licensing Policy submitted to the Planning Commission in 1967.

(6) A paper on "Public Sector in India" contributed in E. A. G. Robinson and Michael Kidron (eds), *Economic Development in South Asia* (proceedings of a conference held by the International Economic Association at Kandy, Ceylon, in 1969), Macmillan, 1970.

I thank the Government of India, the Planning Commission and the Ministry of Education for permission to reprint (2), (3) and (5) and the International Economic Association to reprint (6).

Suhasini Ramaswamy and Sheela Bajaj of Concept Publishing Co. who went through the manuscript persuaded me to read my works again and cajoled me into preparing them for the press with minor editorial alterations. I appreciate their efforts to shake me out of lethargy.

A wide spectrum of colleagues and friends had assisted me when the studies were undertaken. Their help was acknowledged in the original publications. I reaffirm my gratitude to them.

R.K. HAZARI

BOMBAY
April 25, 1985

CONTENTS

PREFACE v
LIST OF TABLES xi
INTRODUCTION xv

PART ONE

INDUSTRIAL POLICY 1876-1964

Up to 1916	: Stores Purchase Policy, Foundation of Iron and Steel Industry, State Enterprises, Tariff Policy	6-17
1916—39	: Inter-war period, difficulties State Enterprises, Protection, Effects of Protection	17-36
1939—46	: Government Purchases, 1945 Policy Statement, Industries in Princely States	36-46
Summing Up		46-51
1947-66	: 1948 Statement, Second Fiscal Commission 1949-50, Industries Act, 1951, First Five Year Plan, Village and Small Industries, Summing up, 1956 Statement, Second Plan, Principal Deficiencies and Defects, Fiscal and Allied Developments, Evaluation, Industrial Licensing	51-92
Growth of Corporate Sector and Industrial Management	: Early History, Companies Act 1956, Managing Agents	92-118
Appendix I	: Government of India Resolution on Industrial Policy dated 6 April 1948 *119*	
Appendix II	: Statement made by the Prime Minister	

in the Constituent Assembly of India (Legislative) on 6 April 1949 *127*

Appendix III : Government of India, Industrial Policy Resolution, New Delhi, 30 April 1956 *129*

Appendix IV : List of Protected Industries as on 31 March 1963 *139*

Appendix V : Mukerji's Index of Industrial Activity 1900-01 to 1952-53 *141*

PART TWO

THE STRUCTURE OF THE CORPORATE PRIVATE SECTOR

A Study of Concentration, Ownership and Control

Economic Power 145

Preface *145*
Methods of Measurement *146*
Share of Leading Groups *148*
Definition of Corporate Group *149*
Inner and Outer Circles *152*
Controlling interest *153*
Classification of Joint Ventures *156*
Possibility of Error *158*
Managing Agents—a Polemical Digression *158*
Facade and Reality *161*

Change in Concentration 163

Choice of Aggregates *163*
Choice of Units *165*
Valuation of Physical Assets *166*
Ranking of Groups *167*
Increase in Concentration *171*
Policy Limitations of Study *172*
Appendix 182

Technical Note 196
Sources 196
Industrial classification 196
Composition of Complex 198
Lists of Companies 199
Accounting years 199
Combined balance sheet 199
Balance sheet items 200
Sources and uses of finance 201
Pattern of ownership 202
Controlling blocks 204
Techniques of control 206
Types of management 207

Statistical Summary 208
Representative Sample 208
Concentration of Economic Power 216
Occupational Diversification 217
Proliferation of Companies 218
Joint ventures 219
Financial structure 224
Preference capital 228
Ownership of share capital 228
Government and LIC holdings 232
Ownership of Public and Private Companies 233
Ownership Patterns by Industries 234
Inter-Industrial Corporate Holdings 237
Controlling blocks 263
Inter-Group Variations 257
Techniques of Control 272
Subsidiaries and Joint Subsidiaries 276
Managing Agencies 276

Policy Conclusions 290
Concentration of Economic Power 290
Managing Agency System 297
Inter-Corporate Investment 303
Diversification of Industrial Companies 308
Nominee Holdings 313

THE GREAT ESCAPE

Concentration Good, Monopoly Justiciable 320
Terms of Reference *321*
Analysis of History *324*
Product Catalogue *326*
Group Catalogue *326*
Definitions *327*
General Recommendations *328*
Expansion and Mergers *329*
Press and Managing Agency *331*
Note of Dissent *332*
Control over Resources *333*
Demarcation of Areas *333*
Superfluous Commission *334*

PART THREE

Industrial Planning and Licensing Policy 339

Framework and Policy *340*
Objectives of Licensing *344*
Analysis of Deficiencies *346*
Recommendations *349*
Project Preparation *359*
Coverage of Licensing *360*
Statistical Outline *373*
Limitations of Data *411*
Industrial House Code *414*
Product Code *416*

PART FOUR

Public Sector in India 425
The First Stage *425*
Post-1955 Policies *426*
Evaluation of the Public Sector *430*

Index 435

LIST OF TABLES

INDUSTRIAL POLICY 1876-1964

1 : Duties on steel *28*
2 : Dividends as per cent of ordinary capital (*Facing Page 36*)
3 : Interim Index of industrial production (1937=100) *38*
4 : Annual imports of machinery and millwork, 1899—1939 *48*
5 : Production of major industries, 1946 *49*
6 : Industrial establishments and employment in India 1945 *51*
7 : First plan: Public sector production *63*
8 : First plan: Private sector investment *64*
9 : First plan: Major industrial targets and achievements *67*
10 : Second plan: outlay on village and small industries *75*
11 : Second plan: major industrial targets and achievements *77*
12 : Second plan : Investment in industry *78*
13 : DGSD Purchases of equipment and stores *85*
14 : Outlay on village and small industries : Second and Third Plans *87*
15 : Government purchases of small industry products *87*
16 : Index of industrial production 1956-100 *89*
17 : Companies registered and at work in India 1900-1964 *93*
18 : Number and paid-up capital of companies in important industrial groups (as on 31st March 1964) *95*
19 : Public and private companies—1917-64 *95*
20 : Government companies at work—1951-61 *96*
21 : Foreign companies working in India *97*
22 : Managing agency commission *102*
23 : Distribution of directors by nationality in 1957 *106*

24 : Companies managed by managing agents—industry wise *111*
25 : Remuneration to managing agents—1950-63 *114*
26 : Remuneration to managing agents by size of companies—1959-1963 *115*
27 : Remuneration to managing agents by industry—1955 and 1959 *115*

THE STRUCTURE OF THE CORPORATE PRIVATE SECTOR

1 : Share capital of companies registered in India *164*
2 : Physical assets of non-government companies *166*
3 : Share capital and physical assets of 20 groups *168*
4 : Ranking of 20 groups *171*
5 : Share of 20 groups in corporate private capital *173*
6 : Share of 20 groups in corporate private capital *176*
7 : 20 groups : Physical assets by industry *209*
8 : 20 groups : Financial liabilities by industry *212*
9 : Structure of combined balance sheet of public companies *215*
10 : Ownership of public companies *216*
11 : Public companies in four top inner circles *217*
12 : Joint ventures 1958 *220*
13 : Combined balance sheet of public companies *225*
14 : Combined balance sheet of private companies 1958 *227*
15 : Ownership of companies in 1951 and 1958 *230*
16 : Government and LIC holdings in 20 complexes *233*
17 : Ownership of public companies in 1951 and 1958 *235*
18 : Ownership of private companies in 1951 and 1958 *238*
19 : Ownership of public companies by size ranges 1951 *240-41*
20 : Ownership of companies by size ranges—1958 *242-43*
21 : Ownership of companies by industry 1951 *244*
22 : Ownership of companies by industry 1958 *247*
23 : Inter-industrial corporate holdings 1951 (*Facing Page 250*)
24 : Inter-industrial corporate holdings 1958 (*Facing Page 251*)

25 : Change in inter-industrial corporate holdings 1951 to 1958 *250*
26 : Investment by industrial companies in financial companies *253*
27 : Controlling blocks in inner circles *255*
28 : Controlling blocks in inner circle public companies *258*
29 : Controlling blocks in public companies of 20 inner circles *260*
30 : Controlling blocks in inner circles by size of companies *262*
31 : Controlling blocks in inner circle private companies *263*
32 : Controlling blocks in inner circle banks and insurance companies *265*
33 : Controlling blocks in inner circle finance companies *266*
34 : Controlling blocks in inner circle industrial companies *268*
35 : Controlling blocks in inner circle service companies *270*
36 : Distribution of managing agencies by share capital *277*
37 : Distribution of managing agencies by size *278*
38 : Combined balance sheet of managing agency companies *279*
39 : Distribution of managing agencies by complexes—1958 *280*
40 : Ownership of managing agency companies *281*
41 : Managing agencies classified by ownership *282*
42 : Companies managed by managing agents *284*
43 : Public and private companies managed by managing agents 1958 *285*
44 : Industrywise classification of companies managed by managing agents, 1958 *286*

INDUSTRIAL PLANNING AND LICENSING POLICY

1 : CGC releases in Third Plan by years *351*
2 : CGC releases in Third Plan by sources *352*

3 : CGC releases April 1961—September 1964 by industries *366*
4 : Industrial licenses not covered by foreign exchange clearance as on Ist January 1964 *368*
5 : Licensing—a synoptic view (1959-June 1966) *375*
6 : Approvals by product groups (1959-June 1966) *377*
7 : Size distribution *380*
8 : Type distribution *382*
9 : Size distribution by type of applications (June 1964-66) *384*
10 : Distribution by foreign collaboration *386*
11 : Collaboration by type of licence approved 1959-60 and 1964-66 *387*
12 : Approvals by states 1959-June 1966 *388*
13 : Approvals by states and types (1959-June 1966) *390*
14 : Distribution of approvals by categories of applications (1959-June 1966) *392*
15 : Distribution of approvals to international combines (1959-June 1966) *394*
16 : Distribution of approved investment by states and categories of applicants *396-397*
17 : 28 Houses—applications and approvals (1959-June 1966) *398*
18 : 28 Houses—applications and approvals (1959-60 and 1964-66) *400*
19 : Type distribution of approvals to 28 houses (1959-June 1966) *402-403*
20 : Select products: applications and approvals to certain houses *405-409*

PUBLIC SECTOR IN INDIA

1 : Gross capital formation out of central government budgetary resources as percentage of GNP *427*
2 : Share of public sector in capital stock *428*
3 . Share of public sector in GDP (at current prices) *428*
4 : Sectorwise share of the public sector (non-departmental) in gross domestic product at current prices *429*

Introduction

INDUSTRIAL POLICY IN PERSPECTIVE*

ONCE UPON a time there was a feeling in this country that the wise people, who had either been elected to power or who were likely to be elected to power or those who had come into positions of authority and power by a process of careful selection and examination, were the people best equipped to decide upon the allocation of resources. The Fabian philosophy which formed the basis of much of our thinking, and even much of our political programming, made the basic assumption that one could not leave such an important matter as allocation of resources to the free play of market forces. There is, of course, no such thing as completely free play and no such thing as utterly free market forces, but even such as they were, they had to be fully subordinated to careful allocation under socially authorised decisions of the people in power. The generation to which I belong and an earlier generation were brought up on the intellectual cuisine of the London School of Economics and Cambridge and were greatly influenced by the success, during the thirties, of the Soviet planning mechanism. In simple terms, we were brought up to believe that policies should be at least regulatory. Now, it follows from the definition of policy that it has to do something either inconsistent with or different from how things would be if left to themselves. Otherwise, there would be no need for policy. So policy involves some kind of intervention. Even non-intervention is a policy, just as indecision is also a decision. While thinking of a regulatory framework, the generation to which I belong was keenly aware of the traumatic experience of the twenties and thirties during which it was found that the gold standard did

*Edited transcript of a lecture delivered at the Administrative Staff College of India, Hyderabad, on 17 January 1983.

not work; imperialism had to change its stance; Russia demonstrated that planning could achieve a large number of social objectives which had not been achieved by the market economies; unemployment came to be regarded an unmitigated evil, and all civilised governments accepted the proposition that a government had a lot to do with the creation and maintenance of employment. In this environment, the framework of the war economies between 1939 and 1945 and the subsequent efforts at reconstruction of Europe and Russia and China, all reinforced the belief that it was both desirable and feasible to have a large measure of intervention either by government authorities or by the duly constituted representatives of the community to achieve certain social objectives.

This whole spectrum of ideas was markedly different from the ideas of liberalism that had prevailed through most of the nineteenth century and in the early twentieth century, when it was believed that the economy should be liberated from various kinds of trade controls and internal and international barriers, restrictions on movement of personnel and of capital, etc. In the nineteenth century, the idea was that the invisible hand of the market was more efficient, more effective, more conducive to progress and growth than the visible hand of the sovereign. This liberalism came with a fairly large philosophical baggage. Just as Greek democracy was relevant only for citizens, not for slaves or women, who constituted the bulk of the population, similarly, most of these liberal ideas applied only to the masters of the world, mainly what are now considered the Western powers. For colonial peoples, the philosophy was certainly talked about but with some concession to the need for protection, advocated by the Germans and the French, for whom many of our intellectuals had great admiration. Dadabhai Naoroji, Gokhale and Ranade, who were our principal economic thinkers in the late nineteenth/early twentieth century, believed in political liberalism, but not in full economic liberalism as it was advocated in England. They wanted to protect the infant Indian industry against the competition offered by English goods, and a certain degree of positive government intervention.

In tracing the history of Industrial Policy, it is necessary to keep in mind that while there are certain important documents called Industrial Policy Statements, a more comprehensive and realistic view requires allowance for the fact that policies can also be made from day to day by a series of actions and by regulations rather than by laws, by interpretation and implementation rather than by statements.

The earliest that I can trace back the recorded history of Industrial Policy is to the 1870s when it was called Stores Purchase Policy, beginning with the purchases by the railways, whether of coal or local minor engineering goods required for the construction and operations of railways or, if you like, such things as the purchase of paper and stationery. By sheer force of circumstances, the railways required coal which could not be supplied from England, leave alone France, Belgium or Poland. Therefore, coalmines had to be opened. Similarly, the operation of the Post Office called for local purchases of such things as sealing wax, certain kinds of paper, bags of various sorts, and uniforms for the employees. Many letters were exchanged between the Secretary of State's office in London and the Government of India on such mundane issues. One can multiply these examples. Much later, this kind of demand spilled over into the purchase of pig iron and steel rails. It might interest you to know that the setting up of Tata Steel at Jamshedpur was initially made possible not only by Jamshedji's great enterprising ability but also by a firm order of one lakh tons of rails for the Indian railways. That is how the plant was made feasible. Later, the demand rose to three lakh tons and so forth and, accordingly, the size of the Tata Steel plant kept on expanding till, in the early 1950s, it was the largest integrated steel plant in the British Commonwealth.

A fillip of sorts was given by the First World War, when owing to disruption of transport and communications, the Government of India was compelled to appoint a Munitions Board in 1916, which started procurement of material not so much for the war in Europe as for the war in the Middle East: anything in the Middle East was very sensitive for the British Empire in India. As a historical footnote you might be interested to know that when, before the war, the Germans were extending the railway network into the Turkish Empire, they wanted to build it right up to Basra, at the head of the Persian Gulf. The British government intervened very actively to ensure that there was a break of railway gauge quite some distance before Basra, so that the railway line would not threaten the Indian Empire which, at that time, included Aden. In response to enlightened Imperial interest, the British government felt that some purchases had to be made in India. Some industry had, therefore, to be developed in India. This became all the more necessary, again from the Imperial viewpoint, because if the Indian market had been kept totally free, in the traditional nineteenth century meaning of the term, the beneficiaries would have been not just British industry but also German industry and, later, also the Japanese.

Some of the development on the ground got dismantled after the First World War, when war demands disappeared. In response partly to the Imperial interest, but also owing to the strident demands made by Indian political leaders, a Fiscal Commission was appointed in 1924. The burden of the Commission's recommendations was that a limited degree of selective protection should be given to Indian industry against foreign competition, including British competition, but British goods were to get preferential treatment as part of the Imperial arrangements. I deliberately refrain from getting into the textile question, because most students of history are familiar with it. I wish only to point out to you that while the British were naturally eager to promote the interests of Lancashire, they did not seriously attempt to throttle the Indian cotton mill industry. First, it served their interest in terms of export of yarn to China and Japan from India. Second, if Lancashire cloth was important, so was the export of British mill machinery.

To cut a long story short, during the twenties and thirties, we had limited protection (i) for textiles, more against Japan than against Britain ; (ii) for iron and steel, more against Germany and Japan than against Britain, and (iii) for sugar of which we were importing a lot from what was then called the Dutch East Indies, present day Indonesia, which led to a rapid growth of the sugar industry in U.P. and Bihar, where there was an urgent need to find a substitute for indigo, which had been replaced by synthetic dyes pioneered by Germany.

Industrial policy since Independence is essentially a continuation of the two strands of policies, namely, (i) Government purchases or public sector purchases or what you might in more sophisticated language call the investment or expenditure policy of the government under Plan and non-Plan outlays and (ii) import substitution by protection or otherwise. Much of Indian industrial history can be explained in terms of these two strands. Nearly two-thirds of the orders placed on the engineering industry come directly or indirectly from the public sector. Similarly, much of our growth has been determined by shutting out imports either by import licensing or by tariffs or by expanded or diversified production in one form or the other. The third strand which has acquired significance since the mid-fifties is the setting up of the public sector.

The public sector also is not an entirely new idea. There were attempts at setting up of a few government-owned and government managed industrial units in the nineteenth century, but most of these were closed down under instructions from London. The only large direct government intervention which survived was in the form of certain railways. Besides, owing to various events after the First World War, the British-owned railways started passing under government ownership. But, as you are well aware, this was not uncommon even in those countries which had a fervent belief in private sector development; even in the USA, where all the railways were privately owned and privately managed till a few years back, huge grants of land by public agencies greatly facilitated railway development and assured its financial viability: these lands used to be resold to farmers in order to raise funds. Then, there were the princely states, in some of which industries were set up as a manifestation of the enlightened policy of the rulers. This was particularly marked in Hyderabad, Mysore, Baroda and in Saurashtra where many of the smaller princes set up a cotton mill each in the 1920s and 1930s as a matter of prestige. But these were all mere drops in the ocean: anything done in India tends to be dwarfed by the sheer size of the country.

During the period of post-war reconstruction and planning, a number of amorphous ideas did float around, partly to take care of retrenched and demobilised war personnel, partly because some appreciation of the Indian contribution to the war effort had to be expressed, partly because we had accumulated large sterling balances and there had to be a programme for their gradual utilisation. The thinking at that time comprised, on the one hand, the official ideas based upon war-time British experience and, on the other, there was the very significant contribution of intellectual input made by the Congress National Planning Committee, of which Jawaharlal Nehru was Chairman and K.T. Shah the principal author. There was also a People's Plan prepared by M.N. Roy, a former distinguished colleague of Lenin and Trotsky, and an Industrialists' Plan. Regardless of the precise source, whether official, socialist or capitalist, there was a very large measure of agreement that (i) the government should be very active in economic activity by giving assistance as well as by participation in new industry ; (ii) efficient allocation of resources for definite purposes required a measure of government regulations and controls.

Please remember that, soon after Independence, the government was very small in relation to the overall economy, and it was busy with the problems of partition, Kashmir, threats of communal disturbances—and there were fears that the zamindars, the princes, the army, the civil service, the police, the whole inherited Establishment, was a danger to the new set-up. The new power structure felt itself threatened by the old power structure, but rather than seek to crush the latter, it sought to take the reins by persuasion and gentle pressure. The government did not have the confidence to take on much direct activity itself, but it had confidence enough—inspired by the inertia of inherited regulatory powers and contemporary wisdom—to continue with economic controls, after a brief premature experiment with decontrol initiated during the last days of Gandhji's life. So price controls continued, capital issues control continued and because it was believed that new industrial units must be consistent with social priorities about location, investment pattern and direction, and so forth, an Industrial Control and Regulation Bill was formulated. Later, this Bill became the Industries Development and Regulation Act, the change of name implying a more positive orientation of intentions to regulate private investment in order to make it consistent with social purposes, as interpreted by those exercising legitimate authority. *By and large, both the interpretation and the legitimacy commanded wide acceptance. Not much of a public sector was contemplated at that stage.* The emphasis was on regulated private investment.

It was only in the mid-fifties that the idea of the public sector emerged as the main vehicle for a positive allocation of resources and for the building up of an industrial base. The half-million-ton Rourkela steel plant as contemplated initially was merely a continuation of the old small-public-sector-investment concept. Russian aid for the Bhilai and heavy industry was a major catalyst for expanded horizons in steel and power. The progress (albeit slow) of river valley projects (Bhakra-Nangal, DVC, Hirakund) led to greatly enlarged government self-confidence. Meanwhile, food shortages and liberal imports depleted the sterling balances, bringing about the first of a series of foreign exchange crises in 1958. However, far from causing nervousness, the crisis gave a boost to import substitution and aid-financed infrastructure development. It also improved the social attractiveness of the Draft Planframe produced by Mahalanobis, then Director of the Indian Statistical Institute. This impressive theoretical framework offered the speeding up of growth through heavy industry, and balancing of the income thereby generated by getting consumer goods and employment from cottage and small industry, which were believed to be labour-intensive and capital-saving. This framework had many gaping holes, but it had the merit of being original as well as native, Leninist as well as Gandhian. If the Russian economic revolution had proved, as Maurice Dobb said, that growth was not limited by pre-existing savings but promoted by newly created savings, then what Mahalanobis offered went much further: the promise of more employment and consumer goods also at low cost. The Draft Planframe was the first economic *dharmasastra* in Indian history. True to tradition, it was elegant and attractive to intellectuals and rulers. Also, true to tradition, its acceptance was selective and subject to as many exceptions as looked useful or materially necessary. Philosophically, we appeared to synthesise Fabian, Leninist and Gandhian ideas. One quasi-ideological fall-out of this view was reinforcement of the regulation of large industrial units in respect of their prices, output, employment, location, investment, capacity and what have you, all for one good cause or the other. At the same time, demand was assured—till 1965 at any rate—by steep increases in government outlay, and near elimination of competitive supplies.

One of the chronic hangovers of the Fabian philosophy, however, was that the prices of essential goods and services, such as steel, cloth, cement, electricity and railway fares and freights should be kept down. This was meant to ensure that the general price level would thereby be kept down. It was also believed that, in the course of development, these commodities and services would tend to receive a disproportionate benefit of newly generated demand and their producers would, therefore, make excess profits. In order to prevent them from doing so, and to conserve resources for investment either in production of these commodities or for investment elsewhere, the resources should, it was believed, be canalised through official funds or similar means rather than be left in the hands of the producers themselves. In other words, the consumer of these essential goods and services was not to pay directly for their growth and development; that was supposed to be a charge upon the national economy as a whole.

This idea has a curious history which is worth dwelling upon. You might recall that in medieval Western Europe, if you travelled on a road (or turnpike as it was called in England) you paid a toll. You used a certain service and you paid for it on the spot. Then, as an integral part of nineteenth century liberalism, all these tolls and charges were abolished to free the domestic economies from restrictions. The theoretical basis of this abolition was admirably summed up in a famous article in 1926 by Hotelling. His theorem was fundamental to welfare economics till the late 1950s. This theorem demonstrated that if, for instance, you have a bridge and a charge is levied for its direct use, the welfare of all its users and of the entire society would be greatly reduced because of that charge. The argument was that the fixed cost of providing the bridge was a historical bygone, while the marginal cost of providing the bridge service was nil. Since maximisation of welfare required that price be equal to marginal cost, the price should be nil. The fixed cost would either have been recovered from a previous generation or could be recovered from present and future generations by means of a direct tax which, by definition, could not be shifted and which would not disturb the equality of price and marginal cost. This theorem was advanced in the heyday of pre-Keynesian economics but its influence on economic thinking and price policy in a welfare state survived long thereafer—ultimately to undermine the economic foundations of all welfare states; but that is a different story.

The 1950s was the first decade in many centuries when there

was positive growth in the economy. Only the sky appeared to be the limit—though food and foreign exchange were scarce towards the end, and there were nagging doubts about the increase in the concentration of economic power in the hands of capitalists.

But in the late 1950s, 1959 to be exact, troubles with China cropped up and came to a head in 1962. India's defence expenditure, which had come down to about 2.5 per cent of the national income, started rising till it reached nearly 6 per cent in 1965-66. This stiff rise ate into the development effort. From 1962 onwards, there was also a marked deterioration in the political climate. Politicians had set about their factional games in anticipation of Nehru's death and were collecting funds from dubious sources. Money used to be collected by politicians before also, but it used to be for a cause or a party, not for private purposes. Politics came to be rapidly monetised thereafter, especially in the seventies. Simultaneously, however, strong feelings were built up against further expansion of large private business units and groups, and policies were framed for imposing a variety of further controls over their expansion as well as current operations. Meanwhile, in the mid-sixties, Lal Bahadur Shastri's disenchantment with planning, the Indo-Pakistan war, subsequent devaluation of the rupee and near-famine conditions led to the abandonment of planning, except in name and ritual, with a lasting deleterious effect on advance action in respect of railways, power and steel. Fortunately, the momentum built up in agricultural research and extension produced a green revolution in some parts of the country. This positive development helped reinforce a shift of political power from the urban to the rural elite.

Towards the end of the sixties, there was no strong national leadership, no strong national political party, but a large defence expenditure. Bank nationalisation and the victory of 1971 generated a great euphoria, underwritten by large food stocks, though food imports continued. Privy purses of former princely rulers were abolished by an executive fiat after legislative effort was frustrated. Political and economic power became more broad-based, and many new elements secured entry into the power structure. The transition appeared smooth. Radicalism (with competitive populism thrown in) appeared to do no damage partly because of the green revolution, partly because bank funds were deployed more widely than ever before, more rural based politicians and white-and blue-collar workers acquired explicit muscle. Industries did not come to a standstill; far from it. Controls over the large units and groups created difficulties and caused delays, but small industrial units grew rapidly, and a lot of new industrialists came up who, it was believed, might not have grown to prominence, if the large houses had been allowed full sway.

It took some time for the negative side to loom large. The new elements that came to power, together with their *apna admis*, were neither familiar with nor did they care for what were essentially Victorian political values. The standards and norms of public conduct changed quite rapidly. Inflation undermined the middle class, which is the principal instrument of a welfare state—and of a bureaucrat-controlled economy. Nearly every segment of the political spectrum sought to misuse power for personal or factional gains—and, for that purpose, to abuse the police and administrative apparatus, followed logically by abuse of the instruments of economic and fiscal control to subserve partisan ends and by display of arbitrary power. Smuggling diversified and became rampant. Avoidance or evasion of income tax, which is a small part of total revenue, proliferated into avoidance or evasion of excise and sales taxes which are quantitatively far more significant. Price controls, MRTP, FERA, Company Law, the working of banks and financial institutions, all these have got tied in knots: first, because regulation has become so wide and deep that it has lost its purpose; second, it is widely believed to be a device for abuse; and third, given 'socialist' objectives, each round of deregulation involves circuitous navigation by politicians, administrators and businessmen. To make things worse or at least more complicated, the performance of the public sector has been, on the whole, uninspiring, often disappointing The abuses and failures are no longer, as the Italians say, mere *apertura*; they are wide-open doors. There has been, consequently, an undermining of the power of the state as also of the legitimacy of state controls.

I have deliberately spent some time on this question of ideas and legitimacy which I think are fundamental. Everything else is a matter of operational detail. The laws that regulate the economy, the parliamentary and executive controls that exist over the public sector, all these form part of this legitimacy of control. The private sector is accountable for its performance not only to the owners but also to the controllers representing the public at large. The public sector is run by professionals, not by owners, who are required to maintain certain standards of accountability. Where then have we gone wrong and how ? It is no use blaming the politicians alone, because most of us are parties to what has happened. Who puts the politicians in power ? We. Where and which controls have gone wrong ?

What are we seeking to control and for what purpose ? As in any particular firm, so for the country as a whole, there has to be a statement of objectives and a certain clarity of objectives in the light of which you can conceptualise a control mechanism. Nobody in his senses puts across the argument that there should be no controls at all. All of us want traffic controls. We want certain environmental controls. We do need town planning. We do need some controls over educational standards. All these are universally acceptable as necessary for the implementation of social objectives. One is familiar with the ABC concept of inventory control, namely, that 80 per cent of the total value would probably be in 9-10 items, maybe in only four items. For a control system, therefore, one has to concentrate on the few items which account for the bulk of the value. This elementary basis of a control system has, unfortunately, not informed the controls that we have had. Take investment control. All we need to do is only to control the bulky investments, not all investments. About half of the new investment outside agriculture is in the public sector, for which the kinds of control that are required are different. For the rest, is it necessary to have all the present far-ranging controls ? What I had suggested in my licensing report of 1967 was that you take the area or the projects that account for two-thirds of the total investment, and delete the rest from licensing.

We have sought to control capacity. Capacity is an undefinable concept. We all know that. Once licensing is done in terms of capacity, everybody has a certain theoretical capacity and since licences are issued in a bunch, there is pre-emption of capacity by those who are quicker on their toes, whether they are in the private sector or in the public sector. When the relative commodity will be produced in what quantity is a different matter. The basic question is ; are we seeking to have a monopolistic economy or a competitive economy? Licensing is a way of conferring monopoly of one sort or the other. If we seek to have pressure of competition to reduce costs rather than the pressure of parliamentary enquiries and issue of directives or circulars, then regulation of capacity by itself has no meaning.

Then, there is the question of location. When the IDRA Act was put on the statute book, policy for location was supposed to be one of its most important aspects. Now, in many ways, the location of public sector units does take some care of overall locational policy. Ideally, railway and power expansion should take care of locational policy. If, on the other hand, you wish to magnify the issue to the other extreme, you get the passion for no-industry districts. If you wish to untie the knots to which I referred earlier, you can keep on giving exemptions for Jammu and Kashmir or Sikkim or no-industry districts or backward districts and so forth. I am not objecting to this new passion. What I am questioning is the basis of the distribution of the cake over the country. When you locate industries in Jammu and Kashmir or Sikkim, there are high costs of transportation, power and so forth. Obviously, every district does not have a sound case for industrial location. Some districts do not even have water and many are not on the railway or power map. Rural electrification has already undermined the economics of the power system. If we are going to multiply these examples, are we in pursuit of economic policy or distribution of largesse? These are high-cost ideas. Similarly, when we go in for import substitution, regardless of comparative costs, that also lead to high costs. When, instead of licensing three or four economical units in a particular industry, we license 20 to please a larger number, this leads to high costs—and indefinitely high costs.

Earlier, I briefly explained the Hotelling theorem for pricing. Economic thinking has now moved towards the other extreme. It is believed that pricing of essential commodities should not only cover the full cost of production but also (i) provide for financing of growth, and what is more (ii) have a tax element so as to provide resources for growth elsewhere too. In other words, items such as electricity, petroleum, steel and cement should have a large tax element, apart from being subject to a pricing formula which covers full costs and also leaves a margin for re-investment of earnings. What is increasingly questioned in economic theory is whether price control is at all an economically efficient element of growth policy. This is a far cry from the thinking of 30 to 50 years back ; since then it has been found that price regulation is at best a cost plus formula, which militates against reduction of costs. Over time you get low productivity, obsolete technology and uneconomical units.

Let me take financing briefly. Whether in respect of banks or term-lending institutions, the ideas on control that came up in the late sixties and early seventies assumed that partisan politics would be kept out ; this was a brave assumption, which has not been borne out by actual events. Second, these ideas assumed that the public sector must occupy the commanding heights of the economy which, in turn, assumed that the public sector would yield expected results—better than unregulated private activity. Third, I was one of those who believed that credit and institutional controls would largely replace industrial licensing and controls on production and prices; this did not happen. The new controls merely got added to the old controls.

Talking further about commanding heights or command performance, the government alone now absorbs about 30 per cent of the national expenditure, a very large part of it in the form of administration, security or defence. Imagine the impact that this large chunk would have made had this expenditure been incurred on creating a genuine productive demand for goods and services. Furthermore, the real value of public sector capital formation tended to stagnate for more than a decade after 1966—even though, for statistical purposes, one-half of drought relief was included in capital formation. While the public sector as a whole keeps on drawing more from the national income, its contribution to further real capital formation and income generation has been disappointing. Take import substitution, which has been so important an element of our industrial policy. Most of the scope for import substitution was exhausted by the early seventies, with the exception of petroleum and petroleum associated products. High costs and low productivity have meant that income generation and re-investment have been depressed. Finally, the 'achievement' of a much higher capital-output ratio offset the advantages that could have accrued from the impressive increase in the ratio of savings to national income.

What I have sought to emphasise above has, no doubt, been

accompanied by a tremendous upgradation of skills, and of managerial capabilities. There has also been a great building up of our educational capabilities, notwithstanding all the criticism of the system that one encounters. Individually many of us can stand up to our competitors anywhere in the world ; it is as a totality or as a team that we get into or cause trouble.

Finally, before I end, let me emphasise that such of our industrial growth as has been on a competitive basis was based on cheap materials—not so much on cheap labour. Indian materials are no longer cheap. Our electricity is expensive when we get it. Our steel is more expensive than international steel. Now that we have a large debt burden, which we have to meet eventually out of exports, it stands to reason that we should be very much concerned about our material as well as labour costs and that in future industrial policy should be far more concerned with productivity than with the distribution of the cake.

PART ONE

INDUSTRIAL POLICY 1876-1964

This work* reproduces my contribution written in 1967 to Chapter VIII in Volume III of the Gazetteer of India published in 1975.

THE faint beginnings of an industrial policy in India under the British Crown can be traced to the report of the Famine Commission of 1880. The Commission attributed the frequency of rural distress to the decline of local industries brought about by imports from abroad, and recommended a policy of encouragement to local manufactures. However, no move was made in this direction. Laissez-faire remained the ruling philosophy, though it was more of a dogma than a complete fact. The bureaucratic mind accepted the dogma but was too pragmatic to accept wholly the norms of government policy derived from western economic thinking.

The desire to aid the merchant was an important factor in the drive in the 1860s to develop Indian public works. Investment in social overheads, state guaranteed investments in railway and irrigation schemes, extraordinary measures to extend the cultivation of raw cotton, remodelling of land regulations to suit European settlement and investment, expenditure of public funds to encourage European entrepreneurship—these were all examples of judicious intervention. On the other hand, laissez-faire principles were invoked against the infant industries argument in the 1890s over the tariff policy and intervention in food trade during famines; progressive taxation was avoided, and a positive role in industrial development was almost unthinkable,[1] though the state did set up a number of enterprises to meet its own requirements and, after

*I am grateful to the Government of India, Ministry of Education and Culture, for permission to reprint this work.

1908, undertook to enlarge its purchases of Indian manufactures.

Industrial development in the late nineteenth century was, to a great extent, a by-product of certain interrelated developments such as improved transport and communications, growth of foreign trade and consequent accumulation of commercial fortunes. Railway building and maintenance had effects more far-reaching than merely opening up of the interior and exposing of agriculture to the winds of commerce. It released some of the latent potentialities for industrial advance.[2] The coal industry could grow and expand; the development of engineering firms was geared to railway needs. Railway workshops had to be founded and these workshops subsequently developed as important centres of modern mechanical engineering and nuclei of skilled labour. The development and extension of the railways posed the question of the founding of iron works under the agency of the state, and when the Tatas embarked upon steel manufacture, they depended, in the initial years, to a considerable extent, upon government orders for rails. With the extension of the railway system, there arose the demand for bridged and metalled communications.

The strengthening of the British army after the Mutiny led to construction of barracks, founding of ordnance and army clothing factories and harness and saddlery workshops. In the interests of expanding trade, the government had to devote attention to the extension and maintenance of ports, harbours and docks. There was considerable building activity, and the decentralisation of powers to municipal administrations after 1870 and 1883-84 also generated a large demand for water, drainage and sewerage, and iron works.

The government became the largest single purchaser of iron and steel products and a big buyer of miscellaneous manufactures. The Railway, Military and Public Works Departments made the government a crucial factor in industrial development, handicapped as it was by the absence of fiscal protection and insufficient supply of entrepreneurs. In fact, some of the paper mills, woollen, leather, iron and engineering factories were founded in anticipation of government demand. The foreign rulers chose to pursue a laissez-faire policy but, even within that, there grew up a policy of purchasing local manufactures.

Under the Government of India Act, 1858 the Governor-General had to obtain the sanction of the Secretary of State for the indents prepared under the policy of purchasing stores. The India Office maintained a close scrutiny of and control over this policy. From 1858 to 1876 stores were imported exclusively through the India Office and were paid for in sterling. Following the silver depreciation, and rising pressure from Indian manufacturers, the rules were relaxed in 1876, 1880, 1883, 1909, 1912 and 1913.

During the second half of the nineteenth century, a modicum of public sector came into existence. State railways were the biggest undertaking. The government founded railway workshops, ordnance factories, canal workshops, postal workshops, harness and saddlery factories, cotton ginning factories, army clothing factories and printing presses. The possibility of developing iron resources could not be ignored when railways were being constructed and extended. The state engaged in iron manufacture and coal-mining. Government factories successfully undertook limited manufacture of iron, steel, building and engineering materials, coal, tools and plant, leather, chemicals and drugs, printing and lithographic materials, scientific instruments, woollen, cotton, linen and silk goods.

In contrast with the philosophy of laissez-faire in British India, the Mysore State Government took an active role in the promotion of industrial development. As early as 1881, its Dewan disputed the law of comparative advantage and promised to give every attention to suggestions for industrial development. By then, the state had already established a savings bank, financed 75 per cent of the cost of laying railways within the state, and created water supply and utility services. A hydro-electric plant was commissioned in 1902, which laid the foundation of future industrial development.[3] M. Visvesvaraya who was Dewan during the first world war gave a major fillip to industrialisation including the setting up of a steel plant at Bhadravati.

The evolution of industrial policy before independence can be divided in three periods : up to 1916, 1916-39 and 1939-46 and discussed under three broad heads, namely, purchases of government requirements (described as stores in earlier years), state enterprises and controls, and tariffs. The policy with regard to finance and management is dealt with separately under appropriate headings.

UP TO 1916

In the absence of fiscal protection or direct assistance, purchases of government stores could have played a key role in industrial development. The acceptance of this role, leaving aside its implementation, took a long time.

Stores purchase policy

In December 1862, the Secretary of State for India laid down that all articles required for India and manufactured in England should be procured only through the India Office. The question of purchases in India did not arise. The value of purchases amounted to £1.54 m. in 1875-76. Purchase of stores in India was first permitted in December 1876, subject to the condition that "nothing except articles of Indian origin shall be purchased or ordered in India unless it can be paid for on delivery after approval there (in India) and that no advances shall be made to any agent or firm for such service". In October 1877, local governments and officers were called upon to 'suggest and discuss' the steps to be taken to substitute Indian manufactures for European manufactures and to encourage local manufactures.

After the report of the Indian Famine Commission 1880, and the growing financial problems of the government following the depreciation of the rupee, and a number of disastrous famines, the Secretary of State amplified the objectives of relaxing the stores rules: (1) reduction of bills drawn upon the Government of India, (2) encouragement of local purchase and payment for anything which the local market could supply and (3) fostering the development of local industry. The Government of India issued new stores rules laying down that articles of Indian manufacture should be substituted for European articles "whenever it is possible to do, even at some temporary increase of cost". From 1879 to 1883, the Government adopted a number of resolutions recommending substitution of Indian for European manufactures, approving contracts for a term of years, listing the local firms which could supply specified and supplementary articles, and called for a careful scrutiny of indents for purchases abroad. As a result, purchases abroad fell slightly from £1.3 m. in 1881-82 to £1.1 m. in 1882-83.

In January 1883, a major policy resolution was adopted:

> The Government of India is desirous to give the utmost encouragement to every effort to substitute for articles now obtained from Europe, articles of bona fide local manufacture or of indigenous origin; and when articles of European and Indian manufacture do not differ materially in price and quality, the government would always be disposed to give the preference to the latter; and the Governor-General-in-Council desires to remind all officers of government that there is no reason why articles manufactured in India should not be obtained locally, even though the raw materials necessary for their manufacture may have been originally imported from Europe. It is most desirable to bear in mind the distinction between articles of European manufacture and articles produced or worked up in India from imported material; the former should not, save in exceptional cases, be purchased in the local market, while the latter should by preference be purchased locally whenever the quality is sufficiently good and the price not higher than the cost of laying down the imported article. There are many articles which may not be immediately obtained in the local market but which can be made in the event of government encouraging the manufacture.

With regard to iron and steel works, however, relaxation was slow in coming. Moreover, no special agency was maintained in India till as late as 1922 for the purchase and inspection of articles manufactured in India; the purchases were handled by officers of various departments. The value of stores manufactured and purchased in India by the Government of India rose from Rs. 39 lakhs in 1882-83 to Rs. 107 lakhs in 1891-92, to Rs. 202 lakhs in 1904-05 but declined thereafter to Rs. 119 lakhs in 1907-08. The articles purchased (including those from government establishments) included coal and coke, paper and paste-board, building and engineering materials, chemical products, drugs and medicines, cordage and rope, cotton, linen and silk goods, hardware and cutlery, leather goods, paints and colours, oils, scientific instruments and apparatus, wood, woollens, tools, canvas, iron and steel. The purchases of steel, machinery, agricultural implements, iron wire, steel wire, and glassware were insignificant.

Rigid rules were laid down for local purchases of imported stores. These purchases were more or less restricted to emergency requirements because inspection was difficult and costly. Such purchases were worth Rs. 41 lakhs in 1882-83, Rs. 36 lakhs in 1891-92, Rs. 46 lakhs in 1904-05, and Rs. 56 lakhs in 1913-14. Local bodies and private demand, rather than government orders, enabled the mercantile houses to flourish in this business.

The government spent £75 m. for import of stores through the India Office beween 1882-83 and 1913-14[4] against Rs. 338 m. spent in India during the same period. The objective of reducing payments in England for stores remained unfulfilled, mainly because the purchases for state railways continued to impose a heavy drain. The manufacture of iron work and machinery was the crux of the problem, as Lord Ripon, the then Governor-General, had recognised in 1883. In 1913, the Government expressed its satisfaction at having done all that could be done but noted the slow growth and inefficient standards of industrial enterprise in India.

Even the limited support received through government purchases proved invaluable. A committee appointed in 1902 to enquire into the paper industry and its supplies at alleged monopolistic prices to the government found that some of the mills could not have started or continued without government and railway orders. In the case of woollen mills, government purchases were 87 per cent of the total sales in 1885 (mills were exclusively European), declining to 8 per cent in 1905, but the difficult years of "infancy" had been taken care of.

During the second half of the nineteenth century, India became a large and growing market for the products of the British iron and steel industry, which were imported through the India Office. In 1863, the import duty on iron was reduced from 10 per cent to 1 per cent and machinery was placed on the free list.

Foundation of iron and steel industry: Bengal Iron and Tatas

Heath's pioneer attempt to produce iron failed in 1824; the East Indian Iron Works which functioned between 1853 and 1876 failed owing to shortage of capital and exhaustion of charcoal sources, and unwillingness of the government to accept any liabilities. The Bengal Iron Works at Barakar came up in 1876 but the government refused to pledge advance orders to them. The works were nevertheless purchased by the government in 1881. In 1882, Ripon's government "accepted as proved that India possesses the means of supplying all her wants in respect of cast iron, wrought iron and steel, and that such supply could be produced remuneratively on a strictly commercial basis". But the Secretary of State took a different view and the government of India was prohibited from giving any preference to Indian manufactures when entering into contracts for iron materials. In 1889, the Barakar Works were sold to Bengal Iron and Steel, a sterling company.

Though this company ran into difficulties in the 1890s and its requests for financial assistance were repeatedly turned down, it was able to secure railway orders and a reduction in the royalties payable on coal.

In 1896, the company was given a government contract for the supply of 10,160 tonnes of pig iron and castings annually for 10 years at rates 5 per cent lower than for similar materials obtained from time to time in England. This concession enabled the Company to do well and by 1901 its annual production of pig iron rose to 25,401 tonnes, of which 10,160 tonnes was supplied to state railways. This period coincided with the recovery of the English iron trade from the long depression which had begun in the seventies, and the fact that one-third of the iron and one-half of the steel imported into India were from countries other than the U.K. The coincidence was not a pure accident.

In January 1903, a contract was signed between the government and Bengal Iron and Steel, under which the former agreed to give a subsidy of £1,500 per year (3 per cent on a capital of £50,000) for 10 years to be reduced by Rs. 3 per tonne for every tonne of steel purchased by the government from the company. The plant was erected in June 1904 and commissioned in November 1904. It was, unfortunately, partially closed down in 1906 owing to inadequacy of orders from the government, railways and private buyers. Its pig iron production continued but when the 1896 agreement expired in 1907 the government refused to renew it. Its closure was attributed to low import prices, small orders for a wide variety of products, inferior quality of pig iron used and the necessity of importing firebricks and ferro-manganese.

The Tatas were more fortunate than the sterling company. In 1902, Tata asked for an assurance from the Secretary of State that "when making purchases, the Indian Government would be willing *ceteris paribus* to give preference to our manufactures over imported materials, especially iron and steel". Viceroy Curzon replied in January 1903 expressing the government's desire to give preference to local production provided the quality was not inferior to and the price not higher than similar supplies obtained through the India Office and that Tata's company and other manufacturing firms in India would have to stand on the same level. Nevertheless, Tata received government pledges almost straightaway: a guarantee in 1905 to purchase 20,321 tonnes of steel rails annually for 10 years, a promise in 1906 to purchase as much as possible of pig iron, reduced railway freight rates for carriage of construction materials and plant, and the opening of a new railway line to connect the plant to iron ore mines. The managing agents were satisfied with "the very generous concessions" from the government. The good quality of Tata products helped in securing orders from private railways and engineering firms in Calcutta and Bombay also.

The total capacity of the two iron works, Bengal and Tata, constitute, nevertheless, only a fraction of the total amount of iron and steel imported. A large part of the demand was met by mercantile houses (though their supplies were not always of the best quality), thereby promoting commerce, not industry.

Engineering stores

The engineering industry survived in the initial years mainly owing to port, municipal and private, rather than government, demand. The relaxation of the Stores Rules in 1876 did not help the engineering industry at all, since engineering stores were to be procured exclusively through London. In 1887, in fact, the Secretary of State pointed out the dangers of depending upon local engineering purchases and, in 1888, further asked the government to issue instructions "with a view to limiting to the utmost the local purchase of building materials not produced in India". Local purchases declined from Rs. 3 lakhs in 1882-83 to Rs. 45 thousand in 1887-88. In 1891 some relaxation was made on grounds of economy, not protection, for less important manufactured articles of iron and steel made up in India from unfinished imported articles, but railway supplies were again excluded. The intense memorialisation conducted during this period in order to achieve miniscule results indicates how difficult, if not impossible, it would have been for Indian industrialists to enter the engineering industry. From 1882-83 to 1898-99, the value of building and engineering materials, tools and plant, and machinery imported through London came to Rs. 437 lakhs and materials worth another Rs. 60 lakhs were procured from local agents of European suppliers.

Some relaxation in local purchases of engineering stores was effected in 1897 but initial equipment for railways and large engineering projects was again excluded. From 1899 to 1905, a series of relaxations were made: beginning with a careful scrutiny of indents before transmission to London via the decision in 1901 that "wheels, axles, springs and drawgear should be indented from the India Office", to the Railway Board orders in 1905 that 25 per cent of all goods stock required for state railways, would be called for in India.

In 1906, the British Government admitted that "local industries must frequently lean to some extent, in the first instance, upon the support of the government" and that "the system at present prescribed for the purchase of stores does not in practice result in the maximum amount of encouragement which the government could legitimately give". The matter was referred to a Stores Committee which sharply criticised the stores purchase policy especially in relation to iron and steel and engineering industries. The Committee found that Indian manufacturers were hesitant because of lack of assurance and continuity of orders, that officials suffered from a fear of infringement of the very precisely defined conditions under which purchases could be made in India, and that orders placed locally were largely rush orders. Indian manufacturers were expected to supply an article equal in quality to that obtainable in England "but the work allotted to them was too small to attain a pitch of excellence which had been achieved elsewhere after years of practice". Most engineering products were disqualified because they were inevitably dependent upon imported materials, such as plates for wagons. In a scrutiny of indents worth £3.3 m., placed on the India Office in 1904-05, the Committee found that orders worth £467,000 could have been placed locally.

In spite of insufficient and irregular orders from the government, Indian (mostly British-owned) firms succeeded in increasing their business considerably after 1882-83, thanks to the expansion of jute, cotton and tea industries, port and municipal requirements and demand for bridges for railway companies. Firms in Bombay and Calcutta depended mainly on private demand, those in Madras and Upper India on government.

In 1909, after some acrimonious debate between the Government of India and London, and the launching of the Swadeshi Movement, new Stores Rules were promulgated, in spite of a request for their suspension from the Secretary of State, who finally insisted on laying down that local purchases of electric power and lighting plant would not be permitted. The Rules prescribed that preference should be accorded to articles manufactured from imported materials and indents should be scrutinised before transmission to London. Local purchase of wheels and axles and springs of rolling stock was not permitted; railway bridges of spans up to 45.75 metres only could be purchased.[5] The list of approved firms in India was progressively enlarged, from 14 in 1897 to 40 in 1913. These relaxations notwithstanding, there was no appreciable increase in orders for stores produced in India. The value of European stores (engineering and building materials, tools, machinery and plant) procured in India rose from Rs. 15 lakhs in 1908-09 to Rs. 36 lakhs in 1913-14, while purchases of Indian stores rose from Rs. 9 lakhs to Rs. 20 lakhs only.

State enterprises

In a previous age, Indian industries had flourished round the thrones of the rulers and had looked to them for support; and the tendency was always to expect from the government a more positive regulation of activity than has been usual in those countries where individualistic ideals have been dominant. With the wave of nationalism which marked the first

> decade of the twentieth century, enthusiasm for industrial advance became general among the educated classes. The acceptance by government of the role assigned to it was not easily secured; and it was not until after the outbreak of war that Government, as a whole, accepted responsibility for giving active assistance to industries.[6]

The inhibitions of laissez-faire were most obvious in the setting up of state enterprises though they did not prevent the government from establishing assorted works to meet part of its own requirements. The principal advantages which the government had were its capacity to hire and retain high grade technicians and to generate its own demand for products. These advantages were barely utilised.

Iron-making was attempted in the 1850s and 1860s and culminated in the acquisition of the Barakar Works despite the opposition of the Secretary of State. From 1885 to 1889, when the Barakar Works were in government hands, local firms including Jessop and Martin petitioned against the unfair competition offered by the Works and requested that its production be confined to pig iron and cast iron sleepers for railways. In 1889, the Works were sold to Bengal Iron and Steel.

The number of railway workshops rose from 77 in 1901 to 96 in 1905 and persons employed therein from 60,000 to 79,000; they served as nuclei for the growth of mechanical engineering but few Indians received technical training in them.

There were already five ordnance factories in 1889, turning out products of a high standard; the Cossipore factory was the first to manufacture steel in India in 1905. The value of imported ordnance and miscellaneous military stores, nevertheless, came to nearly £10 m., between 1883-84 and 1913-14.

Pioneer factories were started in Madras for aluminium, chrome, tanning and weaving, and an Industries Department under the energetic Chatterton, a European civilian (later Controller of Munitions and a member of the Industrial Commission) was set up in 1906. Even these aroused the fury of local business; the Madras Chamber of Commerce unanimously and strongly opposed the floatation of industrial enterprises by the government.

Morley's infamous Despatch of 1910 cooled what little official ardour there was for state enterprises:

> The policy which I am prepared to sanction is. . . state funds may be expended upon familiarising the people with such improvements in the methods of production as modern science and the practice of European countries can suggest; further than this the state should not go and it must be left to private enterprise to demonstrate that these improvements can be adopted with commercial advantage.

Morley's Despatch was not the only discouraging factor. All the various interests were working at cross-purposes. British manufacturers opposed fiscal protection and relaxation of Stores Rules. European manufacturers in India urged relaxation of Stores Rules but opposed state enterprise and state control. Indian manufacturers were critical of laissez-faire and unanimously favoured protection, relaxation of Stores Rules, and pioneer (not permanent state) enterprises.

All that was attempted in pioneering enterprises, technical and industrial education and commercial and industrial information, was attributable rather to a few far-sighted individual officers than to any considered and general policy on the part of the government. On the eve of the First World War, four engineering colleges had been in existence for a generation but they produced civil engineers who were absorbed in the government and did little to foster industries. Technical schools were started in centres where there were no industries nor any prospects of development of industries; candidates, too, were often lacking.

Tariff policy

Fiscal protection could have played only a very limited role in industrial development during the late nineteenth century. Leaving aside the exceptional case of cotton mills (which got the reverse of protection but expanded and prospered nevertheless), protective tariffs would have in isolation done little to promote industries heavier than cotton under Indian ownership and management, without a definite policy for local purchases by the government of its requirements or for setting up of state-managed or state-financed and promoted enterprises, given the shortage of Indian capital and technical skill for mechanised enterprises. At best, protective tariffs on ferrous and engineering items, had they been imposed against the prevailing climate of opinion, might have brought about a somewhat larger influx of foreign capital into the industries concerned in order to pierce the tariff wall. Even that might have been worthwhile but it did not come about largely because returns from material-based extractive industries, cotton and jute, which required minimum imported skill and large cheap domestic labour were attractive enough to absorb most of the capital inflow.

Under the East India Company, the task of abolishing inland duties was taken up seriously in 1835 and completed in 1844. Though import duties were levied by the different provinces, a fairly consistent tariff was evolved by the late forties. Generally, the duties on raw produce were 3.5 per cent and on manufactured articles 3.5 per cent or 5 per cent; till 1848, these duties were doubled for goods imported in non-British ships. After 1848, the nationality of ships was ignored but, till 1859, the duty on non-British goods was double that on British goods. After 1859, revenue needs led to the abolition of differential rates, and the general rate of duty was raised from 5 to 10 per cent; the duty on cotton yarn was raised from 3.5 to 5 per cent. From 1862 onwards, financial exigencies no longer demanded a large revenue from import duties: the duty on cotton piece-goods was reduced to 5 per cent and on yarn to 3.5 per cent. In 1864, the general rate was lowered to 7.5 per cent.

Free trade as a matter of policy was ushered in from 1875, when the government found itself with surplus revenue. The general import duty rate was lowered from 7.5 to 5 per cent, but the duties on piece-goods and yarn were left untouched, which raised a storm in Manchester. The Secretary of State directed the government to abolish the cotton duties as soon as its finances permitted. These were partially abolished in 1878 and 1879, mainly on items which were being produced in India. In proposing these changes, the Finance Member laid down the following principles governing the tariff policy:

(a) "That no duty should exist which affords protection to native industry, and as a corollary, that no duty should be applied to any article which can be produced at home without an equivalent duty of excise on the home production; and also that no duty should be levied except for purely fiscal purposes.

(b) "That as far as possible the raw materials of industry and articles contributing to production should be exempt from customs taxation.

(c) "That the duties should be applied only to articles which yield a revenue of sufficient importance to justify the interference with trade involved by that machinery of collection".

In 1882, the government concluded that it could do without customs revenues and that "the duties still existing caused an amount of friction, scrutiny and interference with trade quite incommensurate with the net revenue they produced". From 1882 to 1894, no import duties were levied, with the exception of duties on arms and ammunition (for administrative reasons), liquor, opium and salt (which were complementary to excise policy), and a nominal revenue duty on petroleum which was imposed in 1888. Correspondingly, all export duties, except on rice, were also abolished between 1860 and 1882.

The sacrifice of customs revenues which was supposed to bring the classical benefits of free trade to the poor toiling masses of rural India succeeded only in increasing their misery. Local industries declined rapidly—the only major exception was handlooms which expanded owing to the greater availability of yarn—and land revenue grew more oppressive, particularly as silver depreciated and the rupee value of Home Charges mounted at an alarming pace. In 1894, import duties were levied again at the general rate of 5 per cent; railway materials and machinery were left free, and the rate was only 1 per cent on iron and steel; the Secretary of State declined to permit any duty on the chief import, namely, cotton piece-goods. By December of the same year, the revenue position necessitated the imposition of 5 per cent duty on cotton piece-goods and yarn; this was balanced by the infamous countervailing excise of 5 per cent on yarn counts above 20s. The limitation of excise to yarn failed to satisfy Lancashire. Accordingly, in 1896, the import duty on piece-goods was lowered to 3.5 per cent with an equivalent countervailing excise on Indian piece-goods, and cotton yarn was admitted free of duty. This level and structure of import duties remained practically unaltered till 1916.

On the eve of the First World War, the cotton mill industry (which was largely under Indian ownership and management) could hardly be described as an infant. In 1913-14, India had 271 mills with nearly 68 lakh spindles and one lakh looms. But there was no mill machinery industry. The explanation lay for the most part in the general absence of an engineering infrastructure, fairly consistent decline in the prices of British textile machinery from the 1870s through the 1890s, and lack of skill. The industry depended to a considerable extent for its prosperity on sales of yarn at home and abroad which implied a corresponding emphasis on preparatory and spinning machinery, rather than weaving equipment. Since the former was more complex and novel than the latter, the difficulties in undertaking its manufacture were greater. As new Indian entrepreneurs, unfamiliar with textile technology, entered the industry in rapid succession, they placed orders for what they believed was the best equipment available. British machinery suppliers such as Greaves and Cotton who went into cotton manufacture had no reservations or doubts about their choice of source.

INDUSTRIAL POLICY 1916-39

The outbreak of the First World War brought about a considerable change for the better in industrial policy thinking. But giving practical shape to this change was rendered difficult during the war owing to lack of engineering and chemical capacity and trained personnel, and later, in the twenties, by the appearance of severe international competition and consequent demoralisation of Indian capital, and pressure from British manufacturers to retain the Indian market. Tariff policy, at first for revenue and then for protective purposes, acquired much greater importance during this period though Indian middle class opinion continued to regard it as halting and inadequate. Government store purchase policies also became more explicitly helpful to industrial development and acquired greater significance as private railway companies were progressively acquired by the government. The consistent decline in the price of imported machinery after 1923 and piecemeal protection to individual industries, however, made entry into the machine industry unattractive. Barring sporadic attempts to finance some industrial units, most of which ended in failure, there was no policy for direct promotion of private projects or setting up of public enterprises to fill gaps in the industrial structure. Vocal Indian opinion, when not preoccupied with fiscal protection, seldom went beyond mute demands for pioneer factories. Constitutional reforms divested the Centre of responsibility for industry and vested it in the Provinces, which lacked the resources and perspective for sustained large scale interest in industrial development.

In 1912, the Atkinson-Dawson Committee was appointed to enquire into the means of bringing technical institutions into closer touch with employers of labour and, in 1913, the Morison Committee reported to the Secretary of state on the system of State technical scholarships established in 1904. A real change of policy, however, came about only in 1916 with the decision to set up a Munitions Board and the appointment of an Industrial Commission, both under a common chairman.

The functions of the Munitions Board, which came into being in February 1917, were to control and develop Indian resources, with special reference to the needs created by the war, to regulate contracts, to limit and co-ordinate demands for articles not manufactured in India, and to apply the manufacturing resources of India to war purposes, with the special object of reducing demands on shipping. The Board was responsible for the supply of all articles, except foodstuffs, medical stores and certain technical stores, to all armies in the East. At the peak of its operations, the Board was buying textiles worth Rs. 2 crores a month and hides and leather worth Rs. 1 crore a month. Besides, it scrutinised all indents for stores and could divert purchases from Europe to India. Priority was generally refused when a suitable substitute could be purchased or arranged for manufacture in a short time. The opportunities so created were brought to the notice of manufacturers with the result that a large number of new branches of manufacture were started. Expert assistance was made available in many cases. Ordnance factories were greatly expanded, and attention was paid to the manufacture of accessories for various industries. The Industrial Commission was so impressed by the working of its twin that it hoped "that care will be taken to preserve such features of this organisation (the Munitions Board) as are properly adaptable to peace conditions".

The Industrial Commission was appointed in May 1916 to examine and report upon the possibilities of further industrial development in India, particularly:

a. whether new openings for the profitable employment of Indian capital in commerce and industry can be indicated;
b. whether and, if so, in what manner the government can usefully give direct encouragement to industrial development:
    i. by rendering technical advice more freely available,
    ii. by the demonstration of the practical possibility on a commercial scale of particular industries,
    iii. by affording, directly or indirectly, financial assistance to industrial enterprises, or
    iv. by any other means which are not incompatible with the existing fiscal policy of the Government of India.

Questions of tariff policy were excluded from the scope of its enquiries. The Commission drew attention to the extra ordinary extent to which the country, with its great industrial possibilities and requirements, was dependent upon outside sources of supply for raw materials and manufactured articles. It found the cause in the fact that export and import trade and a large railway network had been created without an iron and steel complex to support it. Only the obvious need of having repairs done on the spot had led to the establishment of numerous engineering workshops, without any corresponding equipment for actual manufacture. The direction of industrial development had been predetermined by the existence of a large export trade in raw materials, and by the ease with which most classes of manufactured articles could be imported from abroad. The Commission attributed the import of boilers and prime movers to the absence of a complete system of engineering industries. Lack of familiarity with machinery accounted for the fact that the demand for agricultural machinery was limited to the products of a few small local manufacturers, supplemented by imports worth Rs. 2.5 lakhs in 1913-14. India produced 3 m. tonnes of raw sugar and imported sugar worth Rs. 15 crores, but the value of sugar machinery imported was only Rs. 4.5 lakhs. Similarly, oilseeds worth nearly Rs. 25 crores were exported but import of the crushing and refining plant was only Rs. 3 lakhs. Paper imports cost Rs. 160 lakhs while import of paper mill machinery was only Rs. 3.5 lakhs.

"These figures", the Commission said, "are significant of the exiguity of the efforts hitherto made in India to replace imported articles by the manufacture of indigenous raw materials. On the other hand, the very large value of the imports of machinery for the textile industry is due to the entire absence of any engineering works capable of supplying her needs". It also pinpointed the dependence on imported technologists and engineers and the preference of capital for a safe profit from trade or such well established industries as jute and cotton to a doubtful return from such ventures as metallurgical and chemical manufactures. "The industries based on technical science have been disregarded, because profits in other ways have been easy and assured. The neglect of applied science is, perhaps, the most conspicuous among our administrative deficiencies". Another contributory cause, according to it, was the absence of a stores purchase organisation to counteract "the tendency of indenting officers to place on some recognised authority the responsibility for price and quality".

The Commission listed the main deficiencies as being in metals, chemicals[7], rubber, superior textiles, leather finishing and cement. The Commission warned that "until they (the recommended industries) are brought into existence on an adequate scale, Indian capitalists will, in times of peace, be deprived of a number of profitable enterprises whilst in the event of war, which renders sea transport impossible, India's all-important existing industries will be exposed to the risk of stoppage, her consumers to great hardship, and her armed forces to the gravest possible danger". It recommended that the government should take special steps to facilitate the manufacture of such essential articles as magnetos, incandescent lamps, ferro-tungsten, high-speed steel graphite crucibles, porcelain insulators, chemical glass and certain heavy chemicals, rubber and vulcanite.

The Commission also recommended the creation of Scientific and Technical Service cadres, training facilities, and acquisition of lands for industrial enterprises. Regarding purchases of stores, it favoured the creation of an organisation for purchase and inspection under Imperial (Central) and provincial Departments of Industries, the meeting of all indents of the government and railways as far as possible in India, and the setting up of an agency for preparing specifications. As for cottage and small industries, it recommended familiarisation with the principles of co-operative credit, small loans from provincial governments, facilities for marketing, technical training, and education in the use of new tools and designs.

Inter-war period difficulties

In the post-war years, constitutional reforms, deterioration in economic conditions, attractions of protection and nationalist political opposition to the creation of new service cadres combined to distract attention from the Commission's recommendations.

The Commission's report was in favour of centralisation, but the Reforms of 1919 led to decentralisation. The general result was a separation of the spheres of influence of the central and provincial governments in regard to development of industries. The adoption of a policy of protection was, at a somewhat later date, to place the Government of India in a position to assist industries substantially. It was also able to exercise some influence on the development of industries by means of its purchasing activity. In all other directions, its power to advance industrial progress was restricted. Provincial governments, on the other hand, were unable to adopt protective policies and the comparatively small extent of their own requirements of stores made it difficult for them to make an impact with their purchases. They had to face serious financial difficulties and the two features which the Industrial Commission had regarded as the chief obstacles to progress, namely, "the lack of a definite and accepted policy and the absence of an appropriate organisation of specialised experts" remained unresolved after the reforms. "Much was achieved despite these difficulties" but, in the absence of a uniform all-India policy, the element "of co-ordination was necessarily weak and in consequence it was not always possible to secure the fullest results from the efforts which were made".[8] The idea that industry was to be a transferred subject but the administration would be in the hands of all-India services proved unpopular, especially since it was feared that the services would be manned exclusively by Europeans. The idea of industrial service cadres was finally abandoned in 1922.

The prospects of industrial development dimmed considerably before most of the new Industries Departments in the provinces could be effective. Retrenchment of expenditure and personnel after 1922 fell heavily on these Departments, since large industrialists did not need them and the smaller ones were not vocal. At the Centre, the Industrial Intelligence Section disappeared; inter-provincial conferences, publications and scholarships were discontinued. Fortunately, the stores branch was not disbanded as recommended by the Inchcape Committee on retrenchment.

A Stores Purchase Committee was appointed at the end of 1919 to recommend measures to enable the government to "obtain their requirements as far as possible in India". It recognised that the policy of purchasing Indian stores was defeated by the absence of an agency for purchase and inspection, and recommended the setting up of a department to purchase and inspect certain stores, particularly oils and paints, leather, textiles and timber and engineering stores for all central departments except military, railways and public works. Company railways, provinces and princely states, and municipalities could also employ the department. The Committee was divided on the question of local purchase of imported goods; the majority was in favour of purchasing imported stores through resident middlemen but the minority was against it.

New rules were published in 1924. The preamble stated that "the policy of the Government of India is to make their purchases of stores for the public services in such a way as to encourage the industries of the country, so far as is consistent with economy and efficiency". Instead of the prices being 'not unfavourable', the prices now were to be only reasonable. Subject to certain conditions, purchases of machinery manufactured abroad were permitted in India from branches of approved manufacturing firms. This formed an exception to the principle followed hitherto that Indian goods should be purchased in India and foreign goods in London. The Legislative Assembly passed a resolution calling for a system of rupee tenders for delivery in

India, but this was not accepted in principle till 1927. The new rules did not apply to the provinces.

In 1928, new rules were drafted giving preference, first, to articles produced in India from Indian materials, second, to articles wholly or partially manufactured in India from imported materials, and, third, to articles held in stock in India. With certain exceptions, all stores were to be purchased in India and tenders were to be for supply in India against rupees.

In spite of the halving of its budget in 1922 by the Legislative Assembly, and an embargo on its expansion recommended by the Inchcape Committee (which the government did not accept), the Indian Stores Department dealt with textiles and leather, engineering, hardware and miscellaneous articles. It also looked after intelligence, a metallurgical inspectorate at Jamshedpur, and the Alipore Test House and had inspecting offices at Calcutta, Kanpur, Bombay, Karachi and Madras. Its purchases, mainly textiles and leather, went up from Rs. 165 lakhs in 1922-23 to Rs. 373 lakhs in 1927-28, and stores inspected during the same period from Rs. 142 lakhs to Rs. 574 lakhs. But these represented only a fraction of the purchases of the government and railways.

State enterprises

In the twenties, the government continued to supply a large (though unquantified) part of its own needs. About 10 per cent of the factory population in the mid-twenties was employed in public factories. (Incidentally, a considerable number of minors worked in government-owned coal and salt mines.) The Government of Madras, as before, took the lead in pioneering enterprises and its Industrial Institute conducted a number of experiments, some successful and others unsuccessful; projects for ink, soap, fish canning and bone-meal succeeded while those for adhesives and fruit canning failed; the Institute also demonstrated the successful use of power-driven sugarcane crushing. In Bombay, fish trawling and oil extraction failed, mainly because the fish refused to co-operate; alleged interference with private enterprise led to the closure of a semi-commercial porcelain factory in the J.J. School of Art. Bihar and Orissa failed to set up a projected sugar factory, and their forays into blankets and matches proved unsuccessful. The Punjab model tannery made heavy losses and was closed down in 1927. In the United Provinces, the state turpentine factory did extremely well after the transfer of its majority control to private hands, while a bobbin factory had a chequered career even after such transfer. Clow's expert comment on the situation was: "It seems probable that, with the increase of industrial enterprise in India, the field for successful state pioneering factories has contracted and will contract further".

In 1927, the Railway Board was attacked for having ordered too many wagons and it became evident that orders for wagons would be small for some time. This was an industry which had received a guarantee from the government in 1918 of purchase of a specified number of wagons subject to conditions regarding price and quality. This undertaking was withdrawn in 1924 when the industry received protection but continued to remain dependent upon the government. In the course of negotiations with two exclusive wagon manufacturing companies which had been formed as a result of the guarantee, one was taken over by the government.

Some of the progressive princely states, however, seemed to have taken the recommendations of the Industrial Commission rather seriously. Mysore, Hyderabad, Gwalior, Baroda and many of the Kathiawar states actively financed several large industrial ventures in British India and some of them made special efforts to attract entrepreneurs with offers of assistance and concessions.

Mysore followed up its earlier pioneering efforts with the establishment of an iron and steel works based on charcoal in 1923, and factories for sandalwood oil, buttons and experimental industries such as power-driven crushing mills and jaggery manufacture. In addition to outright ownership, the state offered loans, gave guarantees, provided research and technical assistance, and participated in the share capital of private enterprises. During 1917-22, according to the Mysore State Gazetteer, the state department of industry "stimulated private initiative and private effort in the installation of machinery for deepwell pumping, in the more efficient utilisation of agricultural production by means of power-driven machinery, and the establishment of a number of small organised industries in various parts of the State". These enterprises lost very little money over the years prior to the depression. In the thirties, the state set up a sugar factory and a paper mill as government companies, carried out preliminary surveys and investigations for a number of projects, and participated in the share capital of a silk factory and granted various kinds of concessions, such as free or cheap land, power and materials for a number of engineering enterprises.

Hyderabad started an Industrial Trust Fund with a capital of Rs. 1 crore in 1929 for aid to industries, for improvement and development of small and cottage industries, industrial experiments and demonstrations, and economic and industrial enquiries; and for the provision of grants-in-aid for research work and scholarships for industrial training. Its funds were also used for investment in leading public companies outside the state.

Baroda took some interest in industrial development within the state from the 1880s but most of the assisted enterprises failed. Consequently, the state confined its assistance to financial participation in banking, and in several well-known public companies such as Tata Chemicals, etc.

The larger and coastal states of Kathiawar also took a keen interest during the inter-war years in the setting up of cotton mills and various miscellaneous activities, like pottery. This interest was more for prestige, than for purely business or economic considerations, though many of these enterprises did well during the Second World War.

Protection

If the reforms made it difficult or impossible for the Government of India to assist Indian industries by direct methods, they were destined to provide the central legislature and the central government with a method of granting state assistance hitherto untried. India became fiscally autonomous in 1919. The Montagu-Chelmsford report said:

> Desiring industries which will give him Indian-made clothes to wear and Indian-made articles to use, the educated Indian looks to the example of other countries which have relied on tariffs, and seizes on the admission of even free traders that for the nourishment of nascent industries a tariff is permissible. We do not know whether he pauses to reflect that these industries will be largely financed by foreign capital attracted by the tariff, although we have evidence that he has not

> learned to appreciate the advantages of foreign capital. . . . So long as the people who refuse India protection are interested in manufactures with which India might compete, Indian opinion cannot bring itself to believe that the refusal is disinterested or dictated by care for the best interests of India.

The Fiscal Commission 1921-22 was unanimous in its finding that the adoption of a policy of protection was in the best interests of India, but was divided on the extent and scope of protection. The majority favoured discriminating protection for industries subject to three main safeguards: (1) the industry should possess natural advantages, (2) without the help of protection it is not likely to develop at all or not so rapidly as is desirable, and (3) it will eventually be able to face world competition without protection. Claims for protection were to be examined by a Tariff Board independent of political influence. While recommending protection, the Tariff Board was to keep the following six broad principles in mind:

1. Industries that are subject to the law of increasing returns as well as those which are capable of supplying the entire home market should be regarded as possessing additional claims to protection.
2. Even though the protection of a particular industry should involve injury to the interests of other related industries, the Tariff Board should not withhold protection from that industry, provided that such protection is calculated to result in an economic advantage to the country.
3. While protection should ordinarily be granted to what are called infant industries, it may also be extended to industries that are in a state of temporary deterioration or atrophy and even to a strong and prosperous industry which might thereby be induced to develop a new branch.
4. Tariff protection should not ordinarily be granted to new industries.
5. The rate of protection should be neither too low nor too high, and should be determined primarily in the light of comparative costs.
6. The Tariff Board should be directed to review periodically

> the protection given to different industries so as to indicate the desirability of the continuance, or modification, or withdrawal, of protection.

The Chairman and four members did not endorse these safeguards and desired that no safeguard be laid down other than "such discrimination as may be considered necessary by the Government of India and the Indian Legislature". They wanted the Tariff Board to be semi-political and semi-commercial.

Among other main recommendations, the Commission also suggested abolition of the cotton excise duty (on political grounds), levy of customs duty on government imports (accepted in 1924), and restriction of government monopolies or concessions of foreign capital to firms registered in India with rupee capital and having a reasonable proportion of Indian directors and willing to train Indian apprentices. The minority wished to impose these conditions by legislation on all foreign firms establishing industries behind the tariff wall.

The Commission also recommended that raw materials and machinery be ordinarily admitted free of duty and that semi-manufactured goods used in Indian industries be taxed as lightly as possible. Industries essential for national defence and for the development of which conditions in India are "not unfavourable" should "be adequately protected if necessary". Regarding Imperial preference, it suggested that no such general system be introduced but the question of preferential duties on a limited number of commodities could be considered by the legislature on the recommendation of the Tariff Board. No such preference should diminish the protection required by industries or involve on balance any appreciable economic loss to India. Any preference to be given to the U.K. should be granted as a free gift but, in the case of other Empire countries, preference should be granted only on the basis of mutually advantageous agreements. It unreservedly condemned the cotton excise duty and called for the regulation of excise policy solely in the interests of India.

Though the government was agitated "over the harm that protection would do to the inarticulate agricultural masses", the necessity of raising revenue had already led to large increases in customs duties so that some industries were already enjoying a fair measure of protection. Annual revenue from import duties had gone up from Rs. 8 crores in the period 1909-10 to 1913-14 (average) to Rs. 12 crores in 1917-18 and Rs. 28 crores in 1921-22. As a proportion of total revenue, import duties rose from 12 per cent in the pre-war years to 24 per cent in 1921-22. These increases had not been made uniformly nor had they been made solely with regard to consideration of revenue. To some extent, therefore, the new policy involved the substitution of a tariff scientifically designed to assist industries for one which was arbitrary and irregular in its effects on industries.

The Commission had recommended first priority for protecting the iron and steel industry which was facing severe competition from imports after enjoying the prosperity brought about by war orders. The first Tariff Board made a detailed investigation into the costs of Tata Iron and Steel and the effect of protection on steel-using industries and recommended substantial increases in import duties on iron and steel in various forms and the grant of bounties on steel rails and fishplates and on railway wagons. The burden was estimated at Rs. 1.5 crores per year, over a third of which would be borne by the general consumer, the remainder by public bodies, railways and larger industries. The alternative was extinction of the industry and severe damage to industrial confidence, besides loss of employment of trained personnel and severe loss to the coal industry. When the recommendation came before a special session of the Legislature, members discussed, for the first time, the pros and cons of protection, nationalisation and advisability of confining protection to grant of bounties. The Assembly deleted the proposal for duty on agricultural implements, but approved protection for three years. Within two months, the company applied again for further duties because of dumping by European producers. In January 1925,

TABLE 1 : **Duties on steel**

	Duty before April 1924	Duty approved June 1924	Duty proposed November 1924
		Rs. per ton	
Galvanized sheets	30	45	78
Steel bars	14	40	75
Tinplate	40	60	104
Black sheets	17.5	30	52

the previous duties were left intact but the additional protection recommended was given in the form of bounties.

The duties generally represented 50 to 75 per cent in *ad valorem* terms. Further proposals for bounties were approved in 1925. The cost of protection could not be estimated but the bounties totalled Rs. 2.26 crores over the three years 1924-25 to 1926-27. In 1927, the Tariff Board gave the verdict that "the decline in steel prices and the expansion of the market indicate that the protective duties have not proved burdensome, that the trade of the country has not suffered, and that no serious hardship has been caused to the producer of steel or to the general public". The new duties agreed to in 1927 were generally lower, the bounties were discontinued, and preferential rates were allowed to imports from Britain. The duties were levied for seven years by which time it was hoped that Tatas would be able to withstand British but not Continental competition. In 1931-32, Tata, Indian Iron and Mysore Iron, the three principal manufacturers of pig iron, entered into an agreement to fix prices, regulate output and allocate markets.

The most publicised fiscal measure of the twenties was not the imposition but the removal of a duty as an article of faith. Tariff changes in 1917 and 1921 had made the import duty on cotton piece-goods substantially higher than the excise (though the duty exemption for mill machinery and stores had been withdrawn) but this failed to make any impact upon business sentiment and organised political opinion. The government proposal in 1922 to raise the duty on imported piece-goods (as part of the general revision in order to cover the revenue deficit) from 11 to 15 per cent was conditional upon raising the excise from 3.5 to 7.5 per cent, which the Legislature declined to accept. Consequently, no change was made in either import or excise duty but a 5 per cent duty was levied on imported twist and yarn (which had been on the free list since 1896) over the protests of handloom interests. In 1925, when Bombay millowners made the withdrawal of a proposed wage cut conditional upon repeal of excise duty and received the backing of the provincial government, the duty was suspended by an ordinance. The remission amounted to Rs. 2 crores but did not substantially help the industry particularly in Bombay, which suffered at least as much from internal as from external competition. The Bombay mills had frittered away their resources during the war boom by distributing Rs. 50 crores as dividend between 1915 and 1922, an average of 53 per cent on paid-up capital.

Encouraged by their success over the excise issue, the Bombay and Ahmedabad millowners pressed their demand for protection against Japanese competition. The Tariff Board was divided in its recommendations on the subject in 1927, and initially the government confined the relief to restoring the duty exemption on mill machinery and stores. Within a few weeks, however, the government agreed to subordinate its concern for handlooms and granted blanket protection till 1930 to mill yarn of counts 40 and below against Japanese competition, which was actually concentrated in the count range of 30 to 50 only. In 1928 and 1929, the piece-goods market became acutely competitive for Bombay and Ahmedabad and demands were made for protection to cover piece-goods as well. The government, too, was looking for revenue and did not look kindly on Japanese imports which cut into the market for Lancashire. In 1930, after the receipt of the Hardy report, a combination of specific and *ad valorem* duties was levied on imported piece-goods with a slight preference for British goods. Dey[9] estimated that the new duties were equivalent to a dividend of 11 to 12 per cent on the then paid-up capital of the entire industry and that about one-half of the total sum paid by the tax-payers went as bonus to mill-owners. These rates were further enhanced twice in 1931, and raised steeply from 20 to 50 per cent on non-British goods in 1932. An industry which had grown vigorously and profitably for nearly sixty years in spite of official apathy or antipathy, thus, came to depend upon protection, at least partly, because Bombay and, to a lesser extent, Ahmedabad mills, were not able to withstand competition from other internal centres and which, therefore, found Japanese supplies a convenient scapegoat for covering up their mismanagement of finance and labour. Evidence of mismanagement came soon with the break-up of the Currimbhoy Ebrahim group in 1933 and the transfer or liquidation of several other mills in Bombay shortly thereafter.

Protection to the sugar industry came about largely as a result of heavy revenue duties, but the industry developed only after the Tariff Board recommended their conversion into protective duties. The import duty on sugar was 5 per cent from 1894 till

1916 when it was raised to 10 per cent, and further to 15 per cent in 1921 and to 25 per cent in 1922. Three years later, the duty was made specific and was raised fairly consistently for revenue reasons through 1931, when Dey[10] estimated it as equivalent to 190 per cent *ad valorem* at current prices. In spite of the heavy duty, imports nearly doubled over the twenties to about 9 lakh tons. The revenue from import duty rose from Rs. 53 lakhs in 1900-01 to Rs. 870 lakhs in 1929-30, in which year the government encouraged the industry to seek protection. The Tariff Board recommended that the revenue duty (which stood at 120 per cent at the end of 1930-31) be transferred to the protective schedule for 15 years, the rate for the first seven years to be 135 per cent and for the next eight years 101 per cent. The government, without committing itself to the conversion, raised the rate of duty in 1931 to the level recommended by the Board. The policy underlying sugar protection was not designed primarily to help the sugar industry but to protect the interests of farmers growing sugarcane, the cultivation of which fetched the highest monetary return among all staple crops. In 1929-30, there were only 29 sugar factories producing 91,444 tons of white sugar. The import of sugar mill machinery in real terms increased thirtyfold between 1928 and 1933. Sugar production was 5.69 lakh tons in 1932-33 and reached self-sufficiency in 1935-36 when there were 135 factories.

Protection to other industries

In 1924, the import duty on sulphur was abolished in order to help chemical manufacturers. The Tariff Board reported on paper in 1925 and concluded that *sabai* paper was not an infant industry; protection could be given only for bamboo paper along with net non-tariff concessions as protection of process and patents and state guarantees for debenture issues. The government agreed to grant only protective duties for seven years but the industry was saved.

Among other industries that received protection between 1923 and 1939 were printer's ink, matches, salt, heavy chemicals, sericulture, magnesium chloride, plywood and tea chests. Protection to heavy chemicals hardly served any purpose because the period of protection was only one and a half years. Magnesium chloride and plywood received only a small measure of protection.

Among the industries that were denied protection were cement (in 1925, though the conversion of *ad valorem* duty into specific in 1926 enabled the industry to satisfy 95 per cent of demand by 1936), glass and worsted woollens (because their essential raw materials were not available locally), kerosene and coal. Another industry, locomotive manufacturing, was denied protection in 1924 on the ground that the home market was not large enough.

As viewed by the Second Fiscal Commission, the basic defect in the approach of the First Fiscal Commission was that "protection was not visualised as an instrument of general economic development but was viewed as a means of enabling particular industries to withstand foreign competition". The conditions laid down by it were, moreover, interpreted rather rigidly. The result was lack of attention to the development of basic and ancillary industries.

Effects of protection

While protection did impose in some cases rather avoidably high costs on the consumer, mainly because it was not aimed at general industrial development, it succeeded to a considerable extent in safeguarding the existence and expansion of the protected industries and also developed some interest in allied industries. Between 1922 and 1939, the production of steel increased eightfold from 1.32 lakh tonnes to 10.57 lakh tonnes; the production of tinplate, wire, wirenail, engineering and agricultural implements was also encouraged. Cloth production went up from 1,554 million metres to 3,658 million metres, matches from 16 to 22 million gross, paper and paperboard from 24,385 tonnes to 68,075 tonnes and cane sugar from 24,385 tonnes to 945,942 tonnes.

Employment in protected industries grew by 47 per cent between 1923 and 1937, from 580 thousand to 881 thousand while in unprotected industries the increase was only 24 per cent, from 870 thousand to 1051 thousand. None of the protected industries suffered any setback in production during the thirties when other industries were passing through difficult times. The area under cotton and sugarcane expanded considerably.

Going by the record of protected industries, the Second Fiscal Commission observed that "the policy of discriminating protection, within its limited scope, has achieved a fairly large measure of success and that, on balance, the direct and indirect advantages to the community of protection to these major industries offset the burden on the consumers".

External capital

Since the mid-nineteenth century industrial enterprises had been dependent to a considerable extent upon the supply of capital from abroad and those responsible for providing the capital had naturally secured a large measure of control. At the same time, the demand for industrialisation was closely associated with nationalistic aspirations. As industry developed, there were apprehensions that the power of foreign capitalists was increasing.[11] The question was discussed at length by the First Fiscal Commission which was divided on the issue; it was referred to an External Capital Committee in 1924, consisting of the Finance Member and some members of the Legislature. The Committee concluded that external capital was a valuable factor in assisting economic development and that general measures discriminating against it or penalising it by way of taxation or control would be definitely injurious to both the development of Indian resources and the interests of Indian investors. It also recommended that where investment carried with it the control of an undertaking, certain conditions (stated below) should be applied provided that discrimination was feasible. But it considered that, where a general concession was given, for example, by a tariff, it was impracticable to effect any discrimination. On behalf of the government, Sir Atul Chatterjee stated in the Assembly on 2 March, 1922, that:

> No concession should be given to any firms in regard to industries in India unless such firms have a rupee capital, unless such firms have a proportion at any rate of Indian directors, and unless such firms allow facilities for Indian apprentices to be trained in their works. This has been mentioned more than once, and I can only repeat this declaration.

The problems created by the setting up of foreign-controlled enterprises, both before and after the adoption of high revenue duties and discriminating protection, were highlighted in the thirties with the entry of international combines into the "new" industries and the frequent non-co-operation of such enterprises with the Tariff Board, in the enquiry into the woollen industry, for example.

Unbalanced and inadequate growth

In 1939, there were only 11,600 factories (each employing 20 persons and above) and the number of persons engaged in them was 17.5 lakhs. About one-half of these workers were in cotton and jute mills; engineering (including railway workshops), metals and chemicals together accounted for less than one-fifth, and government factories employed about one-tenth. The 1931 Census disclosed that, over the preceding 20 years, the working population had expanded by 4 per cent but persons employed in industry had decreased from 17.5 million to 15.3 million or by nearly 13 per cent. The decline was marked in the traditional handicrafts but the advance of modern factory industries failed to compensate for it. What were the reasons for this stagnation or arrested growth?

What little data there are of income trends in the inter-war period indicate that per capita income hardly increased during the period; probably it declined. The total production and per hectare yields of food crops, especially rice, remained constant or declined in British India excluding Burma. The terms of trade were adverse to agriculture. Gold exports, representing dissavings, totalled Rs. 321 crores during the seven years 1931-37. Between 1928-29 and 1932-33, the value of exports fell from Rs. 339 crores to Rs. 135 crores and of imports from Rs. 260 crores to Rs. 135 crores. Budgetary policy was orthodox, not contra-cyclical: direct and indirect taxes were raised and expenditure was reduced. The total revenue expenditure of central, provincial and local governments declined from Rs. 365 crores in 1928-29 to Rs. 325 crores in 1934-35; capital expenditure of central and provincial governments went down from Rs. 44 crores to Rs. 5 crores over the period. Aggregate public sector outlay in 1934-35 was Rs. 345 crores against Rs. 412 crores in 1928-29.[12] Decline in purchasing power and minimization of government purchases dimmed the prospects of industrial development which came to be based largely on substitution of imported light consumer goods behind a tariff wall which helped to create and maintain a gap between the prices and costs of finished goods.

The tariff wall had a large window in the shape of Imperial Preference during the thirties, and it was partial in the sense that it was extended piecemeal and never covered the import of machinery and stores on the ground that tariffs on them would raise industrial costs. Cotton, sugar, cement and steel expanded under the umbrella of protection, statutory or informal. Their ex ansion did not lead to any marked growth in engineering and chemicals. The growth of the engineering industry was arrested by severe retrenchment in the railway[13] and other public expenditure, and decline in coal and jute output. What demand there was for capital and intermediate goods (mainly from protected industries) was satisfied from imports which were substantially cheaper than in the early twenties; this demand was in any case subject to a ceiling set by the possibility of short-term import substitution in terms of quantity and/or select items. The cement glut in the thirties brought out the dangers of piercing this ceiling too rapidly.

Setting up of non-traditional industries required—understandably to a greater extent than in the planned fifties and sixties—foreign capital and skills, which were not forthcoming. British private capital was attracted to India when profits were fabulous in the jute industry during a few post-war years (Table 2). The annual export of British capital to India increased from £14.7 million (9 per cent of total) in 1908-10 to £29 million in 1921 and further to £36 million in 1922 when it was about one-fourth of total British capital exports. The annual figures dropped to about £1 million between 1924 and 1926 and to less than £1 million in 1927. There was some revival of British investment in the thirties but the new investment was almost wholly in consumer goods—and it came from international combines:

> In some important cases, notably the manufacture of cigarettes, matches, rubber tyres, soa-, paints, and certain chemicals, these industries are branches of important firms in the United Kingdom which have decided that it is to their advantage to meet the Indian demand from works situated inside the tariff wall, and also to be in a position to claim

the status of Indian origin when tendering for the requirements of government purchasing departments.[14]

As the depression took its toll of British prosperity and employment, the liberalisation of policies that had been evident soon after the First World War was gradually diluted till, in the thirties, one missed any reference to the importance of basic industries and assurance of government purchases which the Industrial Commission had stressed. Protection to politically influential industries sweetened the pill of Imperial preference. No attempt was made to extract a *quid pro quo* from protected industries in the form of rationalisation of management and location or to bring about backward linkage of production to intermediates and capital goods. It is fair to add, at the same time, that the few Indian business groups in existence were, on the one hand, debilitated by their misadventures and decline in profitability during the twenties and, on the other, their energy and resources were exhausted in the large expansion of sugar and cement and maintenance of cotton mills on an even keel. Not till the late thirties could Tatas, for example, recover sufficiently from their post-war setbacks to go into chemicals and heavy engineering. Filling up of the structural gaps which the Industrial Commission had pinpointed required considerable government initiative and assistance. Instead, the government was concerned exclusively with balancing its own budget.

1939-46

The Second World War found India somewhat better prepared and equipped than during the First World War but, as compared with the level and variety of demands imposed on the economy, the situation was not very different. Cotton, jute and steel remained the principal items of war procurement, though large orders for ammunition shells gave engineering factories and railway workshops some useful experience of mass production.[15]

The Second World War gave a considerable impetus to the development of industrial potential; the actual expansion was far from impressive. In 1940, the government announced that industries started during the war would be adequately protected if they were organised on sound business lines. After an initial setback caused by stoppage of trade with enemy countries and disruption of shipping, an uptrend was established which lasted till 1945 and then petered out the very next year.

Those industries which were already in existence worked to full capacity, often in more than one shift. New plants were added in several cases and a few basic industries were established in spite of the extreme difficulty of obtaining capital equipment. A rapid expansion of small-scale industries created new sources of supply; a variety of goods, such as cutlery, skewers, hand tools, taps, drains and camouflage nets and many other consumer and intermediate goods were manufactured. No precise information is available regarding the output of these small units, some of which disappeared soon after the war. The index of industrial production (1937=100) rose only from 102.7 in 1939 to 120 in 1945. The major increases were under steel, chemicals, paper, paints and liquors (Table 3), while jute, matches, sugar and wheat flour remained depressed. The production of major industries could not, on the whole, be said to have increased substantially though higher prices and profit margins conferred unprecedented prosperity on industrial enterprises and their managements. Capital equipment was exposed to considerable wear and tear; maintenance and replacement were neglected. Coal and transport bottlenecks remained a serious threat to output expansion through the war.

Some of the important new industries set up during the war were: (a) ferro-alloys such as ferro-silicon and ferro-manganese; (b) non-ferrous metals and metal fabricating industries such as aluminium, copper, copper-sheets, wires and cables; (c) mechanical industries such as diesel engines, pumps, bicycles, sewing machines, machine tools and cutting tools; (d) a few items of textile, tea and oil processing machinery; and (e) chemicals such as sulphuric acid, caustic soda, chlorine, superphosphates, photographic chemicals and bichromates. Some of these new articles were produced in very small quantities.

Between 1939 and 1945, the volume of factory employment expanded from 18 lakhs to 31 lakhs while in government factories it expanded from 132 thousand to 419 thousand (in 1944). The number of ordnance factories trebled and the number of employees increased from 15,000 to 100,000; the number of workshops capable of supplying engineering components rose

TABLE 3: **Interim index of industrial production (1937=100)**

	General index	Cotton textiles	Jute	Steel	Chemicals	Paper	Cement	Matches	Paints	Sugar	Wheat flour	Distilleries and breweries	Petrol
1938	105.4	109.0	98.3	108.0	84.4	121.6	124.8	85.1	130.1	88.7	100.6	102.6	123.0
1939	102.7	104.3	92.4	125.0	103.9	135.1	152.9	87.0	147.1	62.5	100.0	100.0	120.5
1940	109.9	103.6	96.1	125.5	133.3	169.7	152.1	90.0	165.6	106.0	97.8	114.5	157.1
1941	117.8	114.8	92.4	131.1	153.2	185.4	185.8	76.4	241.9	108.2	114.0	140.5	174.9
1942	111.2	102.0	99.5	136.7	138.7	180.9	194.5	60.0	233.5	78.4	90.3	144.1	168.3
1943	117.0	117.0	84.4	141.5	138.6	179.2	188.4	68.8	251.3	95.3	70.3	176.0	200.0
1944	117.0	122.9	86.7	139.6	126.3	192.7	182.1	68.1	259.3	97.1	89.2	197.8	197.7
1945	120.0	120.0	84.4	142.9	134.1	196.5	196.5	90.2	232.4	85.5	103.5	220.4	164.8
1946	109.0	101.9	84.6	130.0	111.2	193.4	181.1	90.5	177.8	80.5	64.8	211.7	134.7

Source: *Report of the Second Fiscal Commission*, 1949-50, p. 21.

from 600 to 1500. Output of guns and ammunition rose manifold. The monthly production of machine tools expanded from 100 in 1939 to 350-400 in 1945. By September 1941, 54 firms were licensed to manufacture machine tools and lathes, furnaces, power blowers, sand blasting plant, etc. Over 280 new items of engineering stores were manufactured for the first time by 1941, ranging from small tools and machine tools to heavy-calibre guns, torpedo boats and degaussing cables. Wire mesh, benzol, rubber goods, disinfectors, binoculars, lubricating oils, lead pipes and sheets, chloroform, carbonic acid, oxygen apparatus, stoves and heavy chemicals were produced for the first time. Aluminium alloy drop forgings and various high speed and stainless steels were produced for the air force. Power alcohol manufacture was taken up. The number of heavy automobile units assembled in Bombay rose from 11,000 in 1939 to 47,000 in 1942; armoured plate vehicles were produced in Jamshedpur, but their output was limited by the necessity of importing chassis.

Till the Japanese invasion of Burma and Assam, there was no serious attempt to develop aircraft, ship-building and automobile manufacture on the ground of certain "serious difficulties" which the invasion, nevertheless, helped to overwhelm. An official technical training programme was introduced in 1941 and then it only provided for training spread over one year of 7,300 persons at all levels including semi-skilled workers. There was no policy for large-scale training of manpower and its utilisation to the maximum advantage.

"Never within recent years", noted Tyson in 1942, "has there been any lack of capital in India or a reluctance to stake it on new and sometimes speculative projects." But the engineering industry was, not surprisingly, found to be organised on a jobbing and servicing basis; mobilizing it for mass production created problems, especially because there was a severe shortage of technicians, skilled labour and machine tools. Control of capital issues was introduced in 1943. There was no control over imports from sources other than enemy countries until May 1940; 117 commodities were under control by May 1941, but a comprehensive import control was introduced only in June 1942, and the tendency even then was to cut down all imports in the same proportion. The value of machinery imported declined from Rs. 20 crores in 1939 to Rs. 11 crores in 1943. Shipping was a severe limiting factor, before American entry into the war further cut down the available supply of machinery.

As Prest pointed out :

> India was called upon to produce more manufactured goods and grow more food despite the wartime lack of raw materials, fertilizers and machinery which inevitably made these tasks even more difficult than they had been before. The major part of the industrial expansion was in a few industries, engineering, iron and steel, textiles and chemicals, most of which were highly localised. In 1939, 400 out of 800 engineering works, 37 out of 157 foundries and rolling mills, 17 out of 26 chemical works and nearly all coalmining were in the Bay of Bengal area. This meant that the local resources of skill and even unskilled labour were exhausted soon.

The Japanese entry and evacuation and flight, together with demand for local military construction, aggravated the scarcity of labour. Many of the lacunae were the result of lack of foresight. The "Government thought in the first year of the war that the maximum force for which India could supply equipment was 1 lakh, an Air Force of nine planes with Indian pilots was thought ambitious and the production of ships, automobiles and aircraft was dubbed impossible".

Government purchases

Unlike the First World War, when the creation of the Munitions Board took more than two years, a Supply Department was set up as soon as the war broke out in September 1939. It was concerned as much with production as with purchases. The Department acted as the executive agency of, first, the War Supply Board and, later, the War Resources Committee, which directed the industrial war effort in collaboration with the Eastern Group Supply Council. The Director General of Supply was at first responsible for all supplies from ordnance factories and purchases from private industry, but some of his functions were later diverted to other directorates, principally the Directorate General of Munitions which looked after metals. The general method used by these agencies until 1941 was the peace-time one of competitive tendering, but later this disappeared and contracts were placed with industry on the basis of ascertained cost and profit margins. Competitive tendering was continued for small industries. Just before the war, the Charfield Committee had recommended a capital expenditure of Rs. 7 crores on the expansion of existing ordnance factories at the expense of the British Government. These went into production by 1942. The Roger Mission of 1940-41 surveyed the whole field of industry and recommended capital expenditure in India by the British Government of Rs. 1,235 crores on expansion and rational integration of production.

From 1939-40 to 1944-45, total defence expenditure amounted to Rs. 2,738 crores, of which Rs. 1,389 crores was recoverable from the British Government. The value of contracts placed between 1938-39 and 1942-43 exceeded Rs. 560 crores including a little more than Rs. 11 crores on small industries. Non-munitions industries also benefited from contracts. Between 1939 and 1945, the Supply Department absorbed, among other things, 3,566 million metres of cloth out of a total output of 23,774 million metres, 43 per cent of paper output, and the entire production of woollen mills. Textiles and engineering stores accounted for 43 per cent each of Supply Department purchases between 1939 and 1941. In the first year of the Eastern Group Council's existence, India supplied 60 per cent of total war demands in the region, 64 per cent after the fall of Hong Kong and Malaya. The high proportion of war procurement to industrial production, together with the shutting out of imports caused acute distress to the consumer.

1945 Policy statement

As in the First World War, the government was eagei to give assurance of various kinds of assistance for post-war industrial development. In June 1941, a high-level Reconstruction Committee of the Viceroy's Executive Council was appointed to draw up plans for post-war reconstruction. So n after the publication of the Bombay Plan in 1944, one of its signatories, Ardeshir Dalal, was appointed to head the newly-created Department of Planning and Development at the Centre. The Department established a number of industrial panels consisting of officials and non-officials and, on 23 April, 1945, issued a statement of industrial policy. The declared objectives of industrial development were stated to be: to increase the national wealth by the maximum exploitation of the country's resources, to make the country better prepared for defence, and to provide a high and stable level of employment. The highlights of the policy statement were as under:

1. About 20 major industries would be brought under the control of the central government.
2. Basic industries of national importance, namely, aircraft, automobiles, tractors, chemicals and dyes, iron and steel, prime movers, electric machinery, machine tools, electro-chemicals and non-ferrous metals, could be nationalised if adequate private capital was not forthcoming since it was essential in the national interest to promote such industries. All other industries would be left to private enterprise under varying degrees of control. Coal would be handled as a special case.
3. In order to regulate industrial development, the government would have to take power to license industrial undertakings. Industrial workers would be enabled to secure fair wages and reasonable living conditions. Controls would be utilised to prevent excess profits and to ensure the quality of industrial products, and so on.
4. The government would have the primary responsibility for assisting industrial progress through the development of transport, power and facilities for scientific and industrial research and technical education. The government might also assist industry by helping to raise capital by tariff and taxation policy and by the procurement of capital goods from abroad.

In 1945, the government realised the importance of assisting or protecting industries during the transitional stage pending the formulation of a long-term tariff policy. An interim Tariff Board was set up for two years to investigate the claims of various industries seeking protection or government assistance. To qualify for such cover, an industry had to satisfy the Tariff Board that:

a. it is established and conducted on sound business lines;

b. having regard to the natural or economic advantages enjoyed by the industry and its actual or probable costs, it is likely within a reasonable time to develop sufficiently to be able to carry on successfully without protection or state assistance; or

c. it is an industry to which it is desirable in the national interest to grant protection or assistance and that the probable cost of such protection or assistance to the community is not excessive.

The criteria laid down were more liberal than in pre-war days; the power to make recommendations on matters other than protection gave the Board considerable flexibility of inquiry and evaluation. Besides protection and other forms of assistance, the Board was empowered to:

a. maintain a continuous watch over the programmes of protected industries and advise the government on the modifications of protection or assistance required;

b. report to the government on factors which lead to higher costs of production in India as compared with other countries;

c. enquire into the cost of production of commodities and determine their wholesale, retail or other prices;

d. advise the government on measures required to secure internal production on the most economical cost basis;

e. recommend measures required for protection against dumping from abroad;

f. undertake studies on the effects of *ad valorem* and specific duties and tariff valuations on various articles and the effects of tariff concessions granted to other countries; and

g. report to the government as and when necessary on combinations, trusts, monopolies and other restrictions on trade which may tend to affect the industries enjoying protection by restricting production or maintaining or raising prices and to suggest ways and means of preventing such practices.

Most of these additional functions were not actually carried out. The main work of the Board consisted of investigating the claims of protection and inquiring into the cost of production of prices of articles such as steel. To anticipate slightly the developments which took place after 1946, the Tariff Board followed the methods of equating domestic cost with the landed cost of equivalent imports to determine the quantum of protection and also allowed a margin of up to 20 per cent (generally 10 per cent) for consumer prejudice against the domestic product. In a few cases, subsidies and import restrictions were also recommended. Apart from these, it also made other recommendations covering:

a. placing of government orders;
b. modification of capital structure of companies in applicant industries;
c. safeguards for companies registered in India competing with foreign companies manufacturing in India;
d. refund of duty on capital goods or raw materials required by the industry;
e. increased employment and training of Indian nationals and assistance for technical training and employment of foreign experts;
f. formation of manufacturers' associations and institution of joint sales organisations; and
g. prescription of suitable standard specifications.

During the five years 1945-50, the interim Tariff Board conducted 90 enquiries, including five price enquiries, against 51 carried out between 1923 and 1939, and the government announced its decisions in most cases within two months of the receipt of its recommendations. This was in striking contrast with the period of 3 to 24 months taken by the government to make its decisions between 1926 and 1937, after 5 to 18 months taken by the then Board to submit its report, quite apart from the delay in referring applications to the Board or outright rejections without reference to the Board.[16] The interim Board recommended protection for the first time to 38 industries and continuance of protection to 22 industries. Among the important industries which received protection during 1945-50 were aluminium, antimony, caustic soda, bleaching powder, soda ash, textile machinery, bicycles, electric motors, plastics, preserved fruits, sewing machines, sheet glass, starch and calcium chloride.

Industries in princely states

The leading progressive states planned and carried out a number of enterprises during and immediately after the war. In 1940, Mysore, in collaboration with industrialist Walchand Hirachand, established Hindustan Aircraft but, soon after, the Government of India bought out Walchand and took it over as an aircraft repair shop. The state also established an industrial and testing laboratory, and took up a large part of the equity of several companies established for the manufacture of matches, radio and electrical equipment, lac and paints, chrome tanning, and chemicals and fertilizers. Departmental enterprises entered into the manufacture of vegetable oils, glass, enamel, electric bulbs, porcelain and plywood. A survey in 1951 found that the state had invested a little more than Rs. 5 crores in departmental enterprises, Rs. 84 lakhs in joint ventures with private interests and advanced loans exceeding Rs. 30 lakhs to the latter. The Mysore Iron and Steel Works which had started in 1923 with a wood distillation plant and a 61-tonnes per day capacity charcoal blast furnace had changed over to the production of steel and cast iron pipe in 1936; two years later a cement unit was added and, in 1942, a ferro-silicon plant was added.

In Hyderabad, the mining areas under Singareni Collieries (established in 1920) were further developed. After the war, the state promoted and financed a large number of enterprises for the manufacture, among other things, of machine tools and forgings, cotton, sugar, heavy chemicals, sheet glass, glucose, starch, casein, plastics, and metal products. By 1949, there were 43 industrial concerns in which the government held large blocks of shares.

Travancore promoted and invested heavily in companies for the manufacture of fertilizers and chemicals, sugar, rubber, cement, rayon, electro-chemicals, titanium and timber. It also set up departmental enterprises for the production of soap, porcelain, bicycles and an assorted variety of other goods.

While many of these enterprises became the nuclei of growth and contributed to the industrialisation of the regions, the arrangements for their management, finance and marketing were not always satisfactory. Nearly all of them enjoyed guaranteed markets and various other concessions such as free or cheap land, power, and so on, but these in turn imposed obligations of a constricting nature. Departmental enterprises were stifled by administrative controls, while private managements were not always keen to give their best since their own equity was disproportionately small. There was no overall policy to regulate promotion, assistance and supervision; each project was taken up or aided on an *ad hoc* basis. Most of these enterprises had to be drastically reorganised in the fifties. These mistakes notwithstanding, there is no doubt that assistance and concessions from princely states played a key role in the promotion of industrial entrepreneurship in the South, and laid the foundation for the impressive and relatively broad-based progress witnessed later during the fifties and sixties in that region.

SUMMING UP

Early industrial policy wavered between a paternalistic urge which manifested itself, during peace-time, in sporadic and fitful essays in industrial demonstration, education and unviable small direct assistance and concessions, during the two war periods in hectic procurement and liberal promises of post-war generosity, and acceptance of orthodox non-interventionist economic dogmas. The influence of British manufacturers was strong, till 1914, in the determination of tariff policy and, later, in a more sophisticated direction of the course of discriminating protection and government and railway purchases. The feelings of the Indian entrepreneurial class were assuaged with protection to cotton, sugar and steel, in which the British hold over the Indian market was being severely eroded by imports from non-sterling countries. In so far as protection led to industrialisation during the twenties and thirties, a growing new market for industrial machinery was created for the benefit of British manufacturers who continued to enjoy a practical monopoly of supply of major engineering items to the railways. The engineering industry, largely British-controlled then, built itself up for repair and job functions, to which assembling of imported components was added during and after the war.

Curiously enough, both the periods—1870s to 1890s and the late 1920s to early 1930s—in which there were something like minor and limited investment booms, coincided with world-wide decline in machinery prices. This remarkable coincidence took away what little incentive there might have been to establish the manufacture of machinery. A representative of Tatas stated before the Tariff Board in 1932 that financial and technical conditions were such that private industrialists were not able or inclined to enter into heavy engineering and chemicals without the promise of substantial support from the government. For its part, the government was determined during the twenties and thirties to cut down expenditure and purchase commitments; guarantees of government purchases or inducement of domestic purchases of plant and machinery at higher than import prices were unthinkable. Government production of railway, cotton and jute equipment (which had a relatively large market) would have run foul of orthodox policies and British manufacturers; production of equipment for sugar, paper and cement was ruled out, among other reasons, by the small size of the market and the once-for-all nature of the investment in these import substitutive industries. While the policy of discriminating production and high revenue duties was partial and halting, the real failure was not just of what industrial policy there was but lay in the absence of an overall economic policy designed to arrest the decline of general purchasing power and employment opportunities and thereby to create an environment of growth. Protection could only give a shot in the arm for partial and fragmented import substitution in the short run; it could not expand aggregate demand for industrial products and create prospects of indefinite expansion.

The Indian entrepreneurial class exhausted its energies during the inter-war years in the expansion of cotton, sugar and cement. Its horizons did not stretch any wider due to lack of promoters' capital, technical skill and know-how of selling unfamiliar goods. Except for the princely states and rich zamindars, which constituted a rather narrow and unpredictable class of long-term investors, there were no institutions to provide long-term finance for projects requiring considerable capital and likely to take a long time to earn a return from goods with uncertain sales prospects. The twenties and thirties were decades of lost opportunities mainly because the government refused to take an active and direct part in industrial development, and the entrepreneurial class was distracted by the temporary—and in the long run costly—advantages of protection for selected goods.

The pace of industrial investment, as measured by imports of "machinery and millwork", was extremely slow even after allowing for decline in import prices. Such imports averaged Rs. 5 to Rs. 6 crores a year from 1904 to 1918, rose to nearly Rs. 22 crores (when prices were inflated) in the period 1919-20 to 1923-24 and fell to about Rs. 13 crores between 1929-30 and 1936-37 (Table 4). The index of all import prices declined by 37 per cent between 1927-28 and 1936-37; even on the outside but unrealistic assumption that machinery prices declined in the same proportion, the investment in industry during the inter-war years could hardly be described as substantial.

TABLE 4: **Annual imports of machinery and millwork, 1899-1939**

Period/year	Amount (Rs. lakhs)
1899-1900 to 1903-04 (av)	279
1904-05 to 1908-09 (av)	558
1909-10 to 1913-14 (av)	561
1914-15 to 1918-19 (av)	513
1919-20 to 1923-24 (av)	2164
1924-25 to 1928-29 (av)	1619
1929-30 to 1933-34 (av)	1336
1934-35	1264
1935-36	1368
1936-37*	1276
1937-38	1714
1938-39	1904

Source: Vera Anstey, *Economic Development of India* (4th ed.), p. 624.
*Excluding Burma.

The war squeezed out the last ounce of production from existing industrial capacity but gave little scope for expansion of capacity, particularly in areas crucial for future growth. Its main contribution lay in the building up of immense trading and industrial fortunes through price inflation and drastic curtailment of mass consumption, and in familiarising a key section of the population with new material aspirations and goods. Barring some import of steel and a little equipment on the recommendation of the Roger Mission, no concerted effort was made to import machinery under the U.S. Lend-Lease arrangements. The immediate problem for industry after the war was to make up the damage caused by excessive wear and tear and lack of maintenance. World-wide shortage of machinery and shipping, political disturbances and blocking of sterling balances made it difficult to launch any major industrial expansion soon after the war.

On the eve of Independence, India was one of the top dozen industrial countries of the world, measured by the size of its industrial output. Most of this output consisted of cotton piece-goods and yarn, jute, steel, paper, cigarettes, cement, coal and sugar. There was practically no production of capital goods in 1946, when India produced machine tools worth Rs. 91 lakhs, electric motors of 46,000 HP., power transformers of 39,000 kva and 473 diesel engines (Table 5). Non-ferrous metals, electrical engineering, automobiles, tractors, prime movers and heavy

TABLE 5: **Production of major industries, 1946**

Industry	Unit	Production
Consumer Goods		
Cotton cloth	m. metres	3,574
Woollens	th. kg.	122
Sugar	th. tonnes	9.05
Cigarettes	m. no.	18,879*
Drugs (tinctures and galenicals)	th. litres	2,273*
Paper and paper board	th. tonnes	107.7
Matches	50 gross	412,000
Electric lamps	th. no.	6,31
Storage batteries	th. no.	27
Electric fans	th. no.	1,10
Vanaspati	th. tonnes	88.4
Intermediate and Producer Goods		
Cotton yarn	m. kg.	520
Chrome tanned hides	th. no.	10,87**
Vegetable tanned hides	th. no.	19,53**
Cement	th. tonnes	1,567
Asbestos cement sheets	th. tonnes	77.2**
Conduit pipes	th. metres	520**
Steel ingots and castings	th. tonnes	1,314
Aluminium	tonnes	3,288
Antimony	tonnes	134
Copper	tonnes	6,311

TABLE 5: (*Contd.*)

Industry	Unit		Production
Sulphuric acid	th.	tonnes	61
Superphosphates	th.	tonnes	5.1
Caustic soda	th.	tonnes	3
Soda ash	th.	tonnes	12.1
Chlorine liquid	tonnes		1,524
Bleaching powder	tonnes		2,032
Bichromates	tonnes		2,114
Industrial alcohol	th.	litres	21,911*
Power alcohol	th.	litres	13,274*
Dry cells	lakh	no.	8,80
Belting	tonnes		625*
Refractories	th.	tonnes	159
H.T. Insulators	th	no.	74*
L.T. Insulators	th.	no.	14,30*
Sheet glass	th.	sq. m.	515
Abrasives	th.	reams	61
Jute mnf.	th.	tonnes	1,106
Plywood	lakh	sq. metres	30,87
Bare copper conductors	tonnes		5,974**
Winding wires	tonnes		335**
Rubber insulated cables	th.	metres	18,395**
Capital Goods			
Machine tools	th.	Rs.	91,25
Electric motors	th.	h.p.	46
Power transformers	th.	kva	39
Diesel engines	no.		473
Fuel and Power			
Coal	m.	tonnes	29.5
Electricity	m.	kwh.	4,935

Source: 1. *Report of the Second Fiscal Commission*, Appendix V.
2. C.N. Vakil, *Economic Consequences of Divided India.*

*1947
**1948

chemicals were either non-existent or still in their infancy. The output of chemicals was nominal: sulphuric acid 60,963 tonnes (against 19,305 tonnes in 1919), and a few thousand tonnes of caustic soda, soda ash, chlorine and bichromates.

The partition fortunately left India with nearly the entire industry of undivided India (Table 6). As compared with the country's resources and population, however, only the surface had

TABLE 6 : **Industrial establishments and employment in India, 1945**

Industry	India		Pakistan		Total	
	No. of factories	No. of workers ('000)	No. of factories	No. of workers ('000)	No. of factories	No. of workers ('000)
Textile	1656	1194	46	32	1702	1226
Engineering	1734	429	278	53	2012	482
Minerals and metals	347	130	51	4	398	134
Food, drink and tobacco	3749	360	467	30	4216	390
Chemicals	1009	115	56	5	1065	120
Paper and printing	616	72	57	5	673	77
Wood, stone and glass	1035	142	65	11	1100	153
Hides and skins	294	39	8	2	302	41
Ginning and pressing	2123	141	353	39	2476	180
Miscellaneous	600	312	33	26	633	338
Total:	13163	2936	1406	206	14569	3142

Source: C.N. Vakil, *Economic Consequences of Divided India*, pp. 286-87.

been scratched. Per capita income was Rs. 200 and per capita consumption of electrical energy 9.2 kwh. Total industrial employment was 15 million, of which 2.6 million or less than 2 per cent of the total working population was employed in large-scale factories. National income originating in factory establishments in 1948-49 (when national income was first officially estimated) was Rs. 550 crores, about 6 per cent of total national income, while small and cottage enterprises accounted for Rs. 870 crores, another 10 per cent of the national income.

INDUSTRIAL POLICY 1947-66

Contemporary industrial policy has aimed at rapid growth of industry as a spearhead of all-round economic development through a vigorous and strategic expansion of public sector enterprises, strong inducements for private investment and simultaneous efforts to bring about institutional changes and social reforms which would ultimately facilitate sustained industrial growth.

The broad outlines of industrial policy and the demarcation between public and private sectors are stated at length in the Industrial Policy Statements of 1948 and 1956 (the roots of both of which can be perceptibly traced back to the 1945 policy statement) but these provide no more than flexible guidelines for policy thinking and implementation. A comprehensive view of industrial policy has to include, besides the 1948 and 1956 statements, the programmes and priorities laid down in the Five-Year Plans, the considerable amount and variety of legislation enacted to create and strengthen the desired institutional structure for planned development, and the administrative interpretation and implementation of all these. The last is not the least important. The texts of policy statements and laws are the results of balancing of various conflicting ideas and interests; they do not provide a comprehensive logical framework readily applicable to individual situations and problems. The policy statements explicitly accept the need for exceptions and flexibility; the laws vest considerable discretion in executive agencies.

The major role of industry, especially heavy industry, in economic development, and active state participation in and direction of industrial growth were two common elements in all programmes of development, beginning with Visvesvaraya's pioneering essay in planning in the mid-thirties, through M.N. Roy's People's Plan, the Bombay Industrialists' Plan, the Gandhian Plan, the official post-war reconstruction schemes, the reports of the Congress National Planning Committee, and, finally, the report of the Advisory Planning Board under the chairmanship of K.C. Neogy in 1946. The government's immediate concern after Independence, however, was to deal with the steep fall in production levels since the termination of the war owing to shortage of raw materials and transport, backlog of equipment replacement and labour unrest. An Industries Conference attended by representatives of central and provincial governments, industrialists and labour was held in December 1947, and it considered ways and means of (i) utilising the existing capacity more fully, and (ii) harnessing industry to the growing requirements of the people. On the recommendation of this Conference, the government drew up an emergency plan for the provision of essential capital goods and raw materials to 30 industries, including steel, cotton textiles, cement, superphosphates, paper, drugs, machine tools, motor car batteries, and electrical motors. A Coal Transport Committee was established in Calcutta to expedite the movement of coal from coal-fields to industrial centres. A tripartite agreement, the forerunner of several to come, was reached on a three-year industrial truce between labour and employers. The industrial policy statement, which followed in April 1948, was based largely on the recommendations of this conference. A resolution on labour-capital relations, later accepted by the government, stated:

> The system of remuneration to capital as well as labour must be so devised that, while in the interests of the consumers and the primary producers, excessive profits should be prevented by suitable methods of taxation and otherwise, both will share the product of their common effort, after making provision for payment of fair wages to labour, a fair return on capital employed in the industry and reasonable reserves for the maintenance and expansion of the undertaking.

The number of mandays lost owing to industrial disputes, which had risen from 4 million in 1945 to 16.5 million in 1947, fell to 7.8 million the next year and further to 3.8 million in 1951. This achievement was greatly facilitated by the spate of arbitration awards raising wages and cost-of-living allowances and providing for profit-sharing bonuses. Thanks to the better industrial climate and some improvement in the transport and raw material position, production in various key industries tended to revive.

1948 statement

The Government Resolution on industrial policy of 6 April, 1948 (Appendix I) emphasised the need for the expansion of production as the pre-requisite for more equitable distribution. Within its limited resources and trained personnel, the government would expand its existing units and start new ones in other fields rather than acquire and run existing private units. In order to eliminate the uncertainties and fears engendered in the private sector by statements of various ministers, etc., the government declared that only atomic energy and railway transport would be state monopolies; in six industries, coal, iron and steel, aircraft manufacture, ship-building, communication equipment and mineral oils, all new undertakings would be under state auspices "except where, in the national interest, the State itself finds it necessary to secure the co-operation of private enterprise subject to such control and regulation as the Central Government may prescribe". Existing undertakings in these fields would be allowed "all facilities for efficient working and reasonable expansion" for 10 years, after which the whole matter would be reviewed. Fair and equitable compensation would be paid in the event of nationalisation. State enterprises will as a rule be managed through statutory corporations. "The rest of the industrial field will normally be open to private enterprise, individual as well as co-operative", but 18 specified industries of national importance or which require considerable investment or a high degree of technical skill will be subject to central regulation and control.

The resolution made no economic or technical distinction between cottage and small industries but promised all assistance, including protection against competition from large units, for their survival and expansion. Great stress was laid on co-operativisation of these industries. "The present inter-national situation is likely to lessen to a marked degree our chances of getting capital goods for large-scale industry, and the leeway must be made up by having recourse to small-size industrial co-operatives throughout the country".

The government indicated its readiness to extend assistance to private or co-operative enterprise, in particular by removing transport difficulties, facilitating the import of essential raw materials, imposing tariffs to prevent unfair foreign competition, and by reviewing the system of taxation to encourage saving and productive investment.

Looking back, after a lapse of many years, the 1948 statement appears to lack both vision and perspective. It was overly concerned with soothing the fears of industries reeling under threats of nationalisation and offering industrial labour a recognition of its rights as a partner in industry. The ten-year reprieve granted to existing private undertakings in basic industries led to more, not less, uncertainty and little was done by the state itself for some years to enter these industries. New state enterprises were confined to fertilizers, telephone cables, penicillin, machine tools, telephone instruments and steam locomotives. Private investment in steel was curbed till 1952 by prospective state entry and unremunerative prices, and in cotton mills by restrictions on modernisation of equipment in the name of protecting handlooms. A number of new private industries did, however, come up during the period: automatic looms, gramophone needles, aluminium powder, electric meters, miniature electric lamps, machine tools, piston rings, ball-bearings, electric motors up to 7 HP., electric transformers, scientific glassware, and machine-made glass ampoules.

State industrial enterprises, it was soon found (as the Damodar Valley Corporation got bogged down in organisational difficulties), could not work well as statutory corporations; they came to be registered as joint stock companies. Large joint ventures with private enterprise in basic industries, which were expected to proliferate after the floatation of Air India International in 1949 with Tata collaboration, went out of favour soon; Air-India (along with domestic aviation), Hindustan Shipbuilding and Eastern Shipping were taken over wholly by the government after a short partnership with private interests which (Tata in Air-India excepted) found the financial burdens onerous.[17]

The statement betrayed absence of a clear understanding of the distinctive problems and prospects of small and cottage industries, and perception of the specific fields in which co-operativisation could make headway. No plans were announced for long-term finance for setting up new industries or for modernisation. The setting up of the Industrial Finance Corporation did mark a step forward in this direction but, for a number of years, it financed mainly the traditional industries. In 1948, neither the government nor businessmen nor economic experts had any clear idea of the wide variety of basic engineering and chemical industries, other than basic iron and steel, required for industrial development.

Second Fiscal Commission 1949-50

The government appointed the Second Fiscal Commission in April 1949 to examine afresh the question of protection in the general setting of industrial development. The Commission looked upon the process of industrialisation as "basically a problem of the reorganisation of the occupational pattern". Whether and how far it should take the form of cottage, small-scale and large-scale industries depended, in its view, upon:

a. the nature of the industry;
b. the technological character of the industry;
c. the relative proportions of capital and labour needed for the industry;
d. the extent to which decentralisation in production in small units is economical on the basis of private and social costs; and
e. the rate at which it is desired to effect a change in the occupational pattern.

State initiative and assistance, it recommended, should play an important part in the promotion of cottage and small-scale industries. Where no conflict existed between these sectors, programmes of development should be framed in consultation with all the interests concerned. Where, however, there is competition between large-scale industries, on the one hand, and small and cottage industries, on the other, and it is established that the latter deserve support against competition from the former, the government should take the necessary steps to safeguard the position of the latter in consultation with the interests affected till such time as they are able to stand on their own legs.

The Commission recommended the following order of priorities for the public sector:

a. essential defence industries;
b. industries connected with the development of natural resources, for example, water power, and key minerals such as coal and petroleum;
c. public utility industries, for example, railways, power generation, etc.; and
d. heavy key and basic industries which, in the absence of private enterprise, the state may have to initiate and develop.

and for the private sector:

a. increase of production in existing undertakings up to the maximum of their installed capacity;
b. expansion of existing industries up to the limits of effective demand in their market with special reference wherever possible to export markets;
c. establishment and development of industries which are complementary to existing industries in the public or private sector, for example, industries which manufacture the components of other industries or which carry the processes of production a stage nearer final consumption;
d. establishment of such industries as are related to existing industries and may increase the external economies resulting from the establishment of a group of connected industries; and
e. establishment of industries catering for a large market, internal or external, rather than those satisfying a limited or specific demand.

For the location of relatively 'foot-loose' industries, the Commission recommended reliance in the first instance upon negative measures to prevent further concentration in areas already congested, together with simultaneous positive steps to improve the attractiveness of areas which were socially more desirable for migration of new or existing industries. The Commission ended its general remarks on what it considered a realistic note:

> Having regard to the available capital resources and technical ability, we do not think that it is possible to achieve a more intensive pattern of large-scale industrialisation than that visualised (by the Commission)...except through a measure of austerity or regimentation which, in the circumstances of this country, we consider it extremely difficult to enforce.

On tariff policy, the Commission was of the view that protection should be related to overall planning of economic development to avoid unequal distribution of the burdens of tariffs and unco-ordinated growth of industries. It divided industries into three categories: (a) defence and other strategic industries; (b) basic and key industries; and (c) other industries. It recommended that industries in category (a) should be protected regardless of cost on national considerations. Regarding basic and key industries in the plan, the Tariff Commission to be set up with enlarged powers should decide the form and quantum of protection and lay down the terms and conditions for grant of protection or assistance and review from time to time the extent to which these conditions have been or were being complied with by the protected industries. For the third category, it laid down the following criteria:

> Having regard to the economic advantages enjoyed by the industry or available to it and its actual or probable cost of production, it is likely within a reasonable time to develop sufficiently to be able to carry on successfully without protection or assistance and/or it is an industry to which it is desirable in the national interest to grant protection or assistance and, having regard to the direct and indirect advantages, the probable cost of such protection or assistance to the community is not excessive.

The Commission also gave liberal clarifications of certain specific issues:

1. Local availability of raw materials need not be a necessary condition for protection so long as there are other countervailing advantages.
2. The potential export market can be taken into account.
3. Ordinarily an industry should be able to satisfy the entire domestic demand but this need not be an overriding consideration in the short run.
4. Compensatory protection to industries using the products of protected industries should be considered on merits.
5. Protection to new and embryonic industries prior to their actual establishment should be considered in those industries which require heavy capital outlay or highly specialised personnel.
6. Excise duties on protected articles should be generally avoided.
7. Price fixation of raw materials for protected industries,

wherever necessary, should be done by the Centre and not by States.

A portion of the revenues collected from protective duties should be set aside in a Development Fund, out of which subsidies in lieu of protective tariffs could be given to selected industries. Quantitative restrictions should be used sparingly and temporarily. Subsidies should be preferred to tariffs where domestic supply meets only a small portion of the domestic demand and where the commodities are essential raw materials. The obligations of protected industries should mainly be with regard to prices, production, quality of production, adoption of technological improvements, research, training of apprentices and higher grades of labour and avoidance of anti-social activities.

As for stores purchases, the Commission suggested a reasonable margin or preference for domestic goods so long as they conformed to standard specifications, and a higher margin of preference to the products of cottage and small industries.

Industries Act, 1951

Licensing and regulation of important industries were the main instruments of the centralised social and economic control envisaged in the 1948 statement. Opposition from private industrial interests led to delay and changing of the title of the bill from 'Industries Control and Regulation' to 'Industries Development and Regulation'. The law finally enacted in 1951 applied initially to 37 industries listed in the First Schedule. Its important provisions are:

1. All existing industrial undertakings in the scheduled industries have to be registered with the government within a prescribed period.
2. No new industrial unit can be established or substantial extensions to existing plants made for a fixed investment exceeding Rs. 5 lakhs without a licence from the Central Government.
3. The government can order an investigation in respect of any scheduled industry or undertaking if, in its opinion, there has been or is likely to be an unjustifiable fall in the volume of production in the industry or undertaking

or if there is a marked deterioration in quality or an increase in price for which there is no justification; a similar investigation can also be ordered in respect of any industrial undertaking being managed in a manner likely to cause serious injury or damage to consumers.

4. In the event of an industry or undertaking not carrying out the direction issued after such an investigation, the government can take over its management.

These powers have to be exercised in consultation with a Central Advisory Council. Moreover, Development Councils are to be established for maintaining the necessary liaison between the public and private sectors, for ensuring that private industry conforms more and more to the planned pattern of development, and for building up a cadre of specialists in each industry. The more important of their functions are to:

a. recommend targets for production, co-ordinate production programmes and review progress;
b. suggest norms of efficiency and reduce costs;
c. recommend measures for full utilisation of capacity and improved working of less efficient units;
d. assist in distribution of controlled materials and obtaining local supplies;
e. promote scientific and industrial research and collect statistics;
f. investigate possibilities of decentralisation of processes and development of ancillary, small and cottage industries;
g. promote training and retraining of personnel; and
h. undertake enquiries for advising the government.

The Act was amended in 1953 to include more industries. By that year, ten Development Councils had been set up for various industries.

The glow of exhortations to private industry to place itself under social discipline or face the consequences progressively dimmed as the agricultural and price situation continued to grow worse from 1948 to 1951 and industrial production failed to increase sufficiently. As the First Plan was being drawn up in

1951, the overwhelming degree of attention required for agriculture, power, transport and utilisation of existing industrial capacity led to a gradual change in emphasis from control of private enterprise to its harmonious but regulated growth as an integral part of overall development. The most tangible evidence of this change of attitude was provided by the agreements signed in 1951-52, after prolonged negotiations, with the three foreign oil companies which controlled the distribution of oil products, Standard Vacuum, Burmah Shell and Caltex, for the setting up of petroleum refineries. The government promised to exempt them from certain provisions of the Industries Act, promised not to nationalise the refineries for 25 years, guaranteed availability of foreign exchange for annual remittance of profits in foreign exchange, permitted them to import crude from areas of their choice, exempted imports of crude oil from customs duty, authorised the companies to sell products at prices equivalent to imported prices and decided to assess their machinery imports at a specially low rate of 5.5 per cent *ad valorem*. Many features of these agreements were to cause difficulties and call for frequent readjustments as the international oil market became steadily more competitive but their conclusion in 1951-52 implied that the industrial policy was flexible enough to accommodate technically and economically useful exceptions.

First Five Year Plan

The philosophy of industrial policy in a mixed economy was elaborated in the First Plan:

> It is clear that in the transformation of the economy that is called for (under democratic planning) the state will have to play the crucial role. . .a rapid expansion of the economic and social responsibilities of the State will alone be capable of satisfying the legitimate expectations of the people. This need not involve complete nationalisation of the means of production or elimination of private agencies in agriculture or business and industry. It does mean, however, a progressive widening of the public sector and a re-orientation of the private sector to the needs of a planned economy.
>
> The distinction between the public and the private sectors is one of relative emphasis; private enterprise should have a

> public purpose and there is no such thing under present conditions as completely unregulated and free private enterprise. Private enterprise functions within the conditions created largely by the state . . . . The points of interaction between private and public enterprises are multiplying rapidly . . . the private and public sectors cannot be looked upon as anything like two separate entities: they are and must function as parts of a single organism.

For the duration of the First Five-Year Plan, the government admitted that it had no alternative but to give the topmost priority to agriculture, including irrigation and power, largely because of the projects in hand, but also because, without a substantial increase in the production of food and raw materials needed for industry, it would be impossible to sustain a higher tempo of industrial investment. The high priority given to agricultural investment in the state programme limited the investment which the state itself could undertake in industries. Progress in this field was, therefore, to depend to a great extent on effort in the private sector, though in key and basic industries which came in the state sphere, long-term demands had to be anticipated and "in fact, supply must come first for demand itself to develop at the required rate".

In view of the high priority for agriculture and the limitation of resources even for essential defence industries, the following general priorities were laid down in the First Plan:

a. fuller utilisation of capacity in producer goods industries such as jute and plywood, and consumer goods industries such as cotton textiles, sugar, soap, vanaspati, paints and varnishes;
b. expansion of capacity in capital and producer goods industries such as iron and steel, aluminium, cement, fertilizers, heavy chemicals, machine tools, etc.;
c. completion of industrial units on which a part of the capital expenditure had already been incurred;
d. establishment of new plants which would lend strength to the industrial structure by rectifying, as far as resources permit, the existing lacunae and drawbacks, for example, manufacture of sulphur from gypsum, chemical pulp for

rayon, etc.

Some of the policy questions that were later to assume greater importance were touched upon. Regarding the capital versus consumer goods controversy, it was stated that a larger supply of consumer goods had to come mainly from fuller utilisation of existing capacity which could be modernised and made more efficient. As for economies of scale in industrial projects (a rather premature issue at the time), the Plan recognised that some conflicts of considerations were bound to arise but licensing under the Industries Act "should ensure an impartial consideration of all the issues involved in a substantial expansion of existing units or establishment of new ones".

Public sector industrial investment during the First Plan was targeted at Rs. 101 crores, the bulk of it in projects directly under the Centre. The main components of the programme were an iron and steel project, completion and expansion of Sindri Fertilizers, Integral Railway Coach Factory, expansion of Chittaranjan Locomotive Works, machine tools and ship-building, besides relatively lighter projects like penicillin, D.D.T. and newsprint. Actual investment was Rs. 57 crores. The targets of production and actual achievement are given in Table 7.

TABLE 7: **First plan—Public sector production**

		Target	Actual 1955-56
Pig iron capacity	lakh tonnes	3.55	nil
Finished steel capacity	lakh tonnes	1.0	0.35
Locomotives	no.	92	125
Integral coaches	no.	50	20
Ships	th. GRT		13
D.D.T.	tonnes	7111	289
Penicillin	m. mega units	4.8	6.6
Ammonium sulphate	lakh tonnes	3.20	3.31
Superphosphate	th. tonnes	16.76	nil
Newsprint	th. tonnes	30.5	4.3
Cables	km.	756	845
Telephones	th. no.	50 (revised)	50
Exchange lines	th. no.	35 (revised)	35
Cement	lakh tonnes	2	1.80
Lathes	no.	1600 (revised 200)	77

It was recognised that in the formulation and assessment of the programme in the private sector, "it is necessary to keep in mind the fact that, in an economy which is not completely centralised, the government can influence but not determine the actual course of investment. Nevertheless, the programmes of development, as now presented, are in the nature of best judgements as to what is feasible and desirable". Against the targeted aggregate gross investment of Rs. 463 crores on new projects, replacement and modernisation in the private sector, actual investment came to Rs. 340 crores (Table 8). In cotton textiles and power, investment exceeded the targets. Much of the investment was in existing units, to which extent there was no question of a more balanced regional location of industry.

TABLE 8: **First plan—Private sector investment**

(*Rs. crores*)

	Target (net)	Actual (gross)
Cotton textiles	9	80
Petroleum refining	64	45
Iron and steel	43	49
Engineering	12	25
Chemicals and plastics	14	15
Cement and refractories	115	18
Paper	5	11
Sugar	neg.	15
Power	16	32
Jute	—	15
Rayon and staple fibre	15	8
Others	40	27
Total	233*	340

Note: Actual include' expenditure on modernisation and rehabilitation. Target figures are for net investment only.

*Excludes Rs 230 crores for replacement and modernisation.

Village and small industries

The village industry programme in the First Plan was imbued with a spirit of nationalist revivalism and village self-sufficiency. It was described as having a central place in the rural development programme and was based on the feeling that products of large-scale industry had increasingly limited the market for the products of several classes of rural artisans. In other words, these industries were considered as being the victims of competition from large industry. A Rs. 7 crore programme was drawn up for the development of such industries as oilseed crushing, soap-making, paddy husking, palm gur, gur and khandsari, leather, woollen blankets, hand-made paper, bee-keeping and cottage matches, besides the provision of facilities for organisation, finance, raw materials research, technical guidance, supply of equipment, and marketing assistance. Wherever a large-scale industry competed with a cottage industry (which was not clearly distinguished from a village industry as such), a common production programme was recommended to enable the latter to organise itself. While some criteria for such protection (for example, comparison of efficiency, scope for development through small-scale methods, employment potentials, social considerations, etc.) were laid down, and controls for this purpose over large industry were envisaged, no safeguards, time limits or enquiry procedures were laid down as prerequisites on the analogy of protection against external competition. No priorities *inter se* were recommended for various industries. One or more of the following elements could enter into the framing of common production programmes :

a. reservation of spheres of production;
b. non-expansion of the capacity of a large-scale industry;
c. imposition of a cess on a large-scale industry;
d. arrangement for the supply of raw materials; and
e. co-ordination of research, training, etc.

All India and State Boards were set up for handlooms, khadi and village industries, sericulture and coir during the First Plan period. The production of certain varieties of cloth (mainly for dhotis and saris) was reserved for handlooms and khadi, mill printing of cloth was limited to the best year's production in the period 1949-54, and the expansion of large units capacity for garment-making was restricted. All applications for a substantial expansion of existing units or for the establishment of new large units in leather footwear and tanning industries were examined from the point of view of their effect on cottage and small units; an excise duty was also levied on large-scale leather footwear production.

The excise rebate for cottage match units was enhanced. A differential excise was imposed on washing soap and a subsidy given for neem and non-edible oils used in making soap. In certain other industries, including some types of agricultural implements, furniture-making, sports goods, slates and pencils, bidis, writing inks, chalks, crayons and candles, further expansion was reserved for small units. The progress of co-operativisation was, however, extremely poor except in the case of handlooms.

The main targeted beneficiaries of this policy were handlooms and khadi. The production of handloom cloth was estimated to have increased from 678 million metres in 1950-51 to 1,325 million metres in 1955-56 (the latter was probably an over-estimate), while the value of khadi went up from Rs. 1.3 crores in 1950-51 to over Rs. 5 crores in 1955-56, when its production was 31 million metres.

As for small industries, that is, small-scale units using power and/or functioning as ancillaries to large units, it was recognised that considerable development had taken place in this field without much direction or assistance from the government but this growth lacked some of the elements that make for efficiency and stability. Apart from providing Rs. 15 crores for their development (including handicrafts and handlooms), and seeking to encourage the development of ancillaries, reliance was placed upon state purchases. It was agreed that, where basic considerations, such as quality, delivery date, etc., were comparable, the products of cottage and small industries would receive preferential treatment. In those items in which cottage industry had advantages over large-scale industry or had established itself as a supplier on competitive terms, orders would be placed with cottage and small units to the fullest extent before placing any orders with large units. For other products, a price preference and suitable relaxation of specifications would be allowed on merits.

The impact of these measures on actual purchases was, however, rather small. The total value of purchases made from cottage and small industries by the Directorate General of Supplies and Disposals rose from Rs. 66 lakhs in 1952-53 to Rs. 105 lakhs in 1954-55. A number of emporia and sales depots for handloom, handicrafts and village industries were established during the plan period. Total outlay on village and small industries during the four years 1951-55 amounted to Rs. 15 crores.

First plan—summing up

Industry was more of an appendage to rather than an important central part of the First Plan. Apart from this overriding consideration and a general recognition of the strategic role of industrialisation, the government was only groping its way towards an understanding of industrial problems and the industrial needs of the community, as distinct from the acceptance of the idea of social control over the management, expansion and profits of private industry. Many of the implications of a mixed economy were as acceptable to private industry as to the government but there was no consciousness of the instrument required to integrate plan priorities with the working of the price mechanism which continued to dominate the allocation of resources. This consciousness, though not the instrument in itself, was to come many years later. Meanwhile, the government relied on such broad measures as industrial licensing, uniform tax incentives and concessions for power, land, etc. Licensing under the Industries Act, it was soon found, belied the great expecta-

TABLE 9: **First Plan: Major industrial targets and achievements**

Item	Production 1950-51	Additional Production by Plan-end	
		Target	Achievement
Finished steel (lakh tonnes)	9.95	6.8	3.05
Pig iron (lakh tonnes)	15.95	12.8	2.23
Cement (lakh tonnes)	27.3	21.4	19.3
Aluminium (th. tonnes)	3.75	8.4	3.65
Ammonium sulphate (th. tonnes)	47.0	411.1	352.3
Superphosphate (th. tonnes)	55.9	127.1	16.25
Locomotives (no.)	3	17.0	176
Cotton yarn (m. kg.)	435	209	206
Mill cloth (m. metres)	3400	898	1165
Handloom cloth (m. metres)	741	814	584
Jute mnfactvres (th. tonnes)	837	382	234
Bicycles (th. no.)	97	433	416
Sewing machines (th. no.)	33	59	78
Power alcohol (m. litres)	22.7	59	22.7
Sugar (th. tonnes)	1118	406	772

tions that were set by it, except in so far as, together with import restrictions, it created safe and sheltered markets.

The stepping up of machinery imports and private investment during the latter half of the Plan was not wholly due to unblocking of sterling balances held in London and liberalisation of import policy. It represented in large measure the response of Indian capital and enterprise to larger government expenditure in the aggregate, larger government and railway purchases, together with faith in the continuity and growth of all these and of private investment and consumption. This faith proved to be amply justified.

1956 Statement

In December 1954, Parliament accepted a socialistc pattern of society as the objective of social and economic policy. In conformity with this objective, and the Directive Principles of State Policy embodied in the Constitution adopted in 1950, and the higher aspirations which were justified by the growth achieved during the First Plan, it was considered desirable to issue a new Industrial Policy Statement in April 1956 (Appendix III). The need to allay private sector fears of nationalisation was not altogether absent for (apart from the Reserve Bank which was nationalised in 1948), the Imperial Bank was taken over by the Reserve Bank in 1955 (seven years after the announcement of its proposed nationalisation), and air transport and life insurance were nationalised in 1953 and early 1956, respectively.

The new policy was aimed at accelerating the rate of economic growth and speeding up industrialisation, in particular, through the development of heavy industries and machine-making industries, expansion of the public sector in industry and trade, and building up of a large and growing co-operative sector. The lists of industries in the 1948 resolution were elaborated and re-categorised in three schedules:

A. Industries, the future development of which will be the exclusive responsibility of the state. These included, apart from armaments, atomic energy and transport, also iron and steel, heavy plant and machinery, coal and other mining, petroleum and power. All new units in these industries, except for approved cases and expansion of existing private units, will be under state auspices or where collaboration with private interests is considered necessary, the state will ensure that it can guide and control the operations.

B. Industries in which the state will increasingly establish new undertakings but in which private enterprises will also have the opportunity to operate on its own or with state participation, for example, aluminium, machine tools, ferro-alloys, basic and intermediate chemicals, essential drugs, fertilizers, synthetic rubber, road and sea transport.

C. All remaining industries will ordinarily be developed through private, including co-operative, initiative but state enterprise will not be altogether excluded from this list.

Unlike the 1948 Statement, which was concerned primarily with the imposition of social discipline over the private sector, this resolution set out in somewhat greater detail the positive role of the state in relation to the private sector. Besides ensuring the development of transport, power and other services, and providing appropriate fiscal and other concessions, the state also undertook to provide through institutions, as well as directly, financial aid to industries, especially to enterprises organised on co-operative lines for industrial and agricultural purposes. The idea of a ten-year reprieve before possible nationalisation was dropped altogether. After reiterating the need for social and economic controls, the resolution explicitly promised freedom to expand and non-discrimination between public and private units in the same industry:

> The Government of India recognise that, it would, in general, be desirable to allow such undertakings to develop with as much freedom as possible, consistent with the targets and objectives of the national plan. When there exist in the same industry both privately and publicly owned units, it would continue to be the policy of the state to give fair and non-discriminatory treatment to both of them.

The Resolution further reiterated the policy of supporting cottage and small-scale industries on the grounds stated in the First Plan but, after narrating various measures for their protection and assistance, it emphasised the need to make these industries self-supporting and to bring about a technological transformation in them:

> . . . the aim of the state policy will be to ensure that the decentralised sector acquires sufficient vitality to be self-supporting and its development is integrated with that of large-scale industry. The state will, therefore, concentrate on measures designed to improve the competitive strength of the small-scale producer. For this it is essential that the technique of production should be constantly improved and modernised, the pace of transformation being regulated so as to avoid, as far as possible, technological unemployment.

Industrial estates were conceived as one of the instruments for the development of cottage and small industries, preferably on a co-operative basis.

To anticipate some major developments which took place later during the Second and Third Plan periods, it may be stressed here that, notwithstanding the ups and downs of development after 1956 and varying interpretations of the Resolution in the framing and implementation of detailed policies, the broad framework and the spirit of the Resolution have been implemented faithfully. In Schedule A, existing large coal, steel, and power units were permitted and assisted to expand; the question of their nationalisation which was never seriously under consideration ceased to be a practicable proposition after World Bank loans were granted to private units in these industries, *inter alia*, on an undertaking from the government that they would not be nationalised. The government, at the same time, considerably stepped up its share in the output of these three industries. In copper and manganese, existing private units, many of them foreign controlled, continued undisturbed. In all other major industries except ship-building (from which the private interest concerned was eager to retire for financial reasons), where there were no private units to deal with, all new units were set up under state auspices. A joint Government-Stanvac oil exploration project in Bengal—which proved to be a failure—was the only exception and since then there has been no foreign equity participation in oil exploration. All new oil refineries are either fully government-owned or are under government majority control; in both cases, internal distribution of products is in the public sector.

As for Schedule B, with regard to which there has been some misunderstanding about alleged state withdrawal from certain industries, the Resolution clearly states that private enterprise will also have the opportunity to operate on its own. The private sector, in collaboration with foreign investors in several cases, has gone into aluminium, low grade machine tools, ferro-alloys, special steels, synthetic rubber, coal carbonisation, chemical pulp, and essential drugs. A modicum of private interest in fertilizers, which aroused ideological controversy for some time, almost petered out when the uncertainty of price regulation, profits and foreign collaboration cast its gloom. In the field of basic and intermediate chemicals and essential drugs, the government received a project report in or about 1958 from a Russian team, which also offered financial and technical assistance for the setting up of a comprehensive complex of plants. Western private influence had something to do with the emasculation of and considerable delay in this series of projects, but the issues were not so simple as made out in certain quarters. The offer of Russian assistance did not cover all material, technical and financial aspects of the project; some of the processes offered involved either a breach of patent rights or the adoption of a relatively inferior technology; rapid changes in chemical technology due to the use of petro-chemicals, etc., created doubts about the feasibility of some aspects of the project; in some cases either the equipment or basic materials or both had to be imported from Western sources which were not willing to oblige; finally the USSR itself accepted certain international patent obligations.

Second Plan

The principal objectives of the Second Plan were:

a. a sizeable increase in the national income so as to raise the level of living in the country;
b. rapid industrialisation with particular emphasis on the development of basic and heavy industries;
c. a large expansion of employment opportunities; and

d. reduction of inequalities in income and wealth and a more even distribution of economic power.

The basic strategy of the Second Plan was stated lucidly in the Mahalanobis Draft Plan-frame. The food and agricultural raw materials problem, it was believed, had approached towards a solution; the time was, therefore, ripe for a massive push to industrialisation. To achieve the fourfold objectives of a high rate of growth (defined more in terms of investment than output or consumption), high employment potential, minimum foreign exchange cost over a period of time, and price stability, the Mahalanobis draft proposed concentration on the building up of heavy industry. The extra demand for consumer goods resulting from this investment was to be met in full by the expansion of cottage industries, which were assumed to have low capital and high labour requirements in relation to output. Large-scale units in consumer goods industries should not expand except to the limit of their existing capacity because such expansion would (i) create a demand for foreign exchange for the import of the necessary equipment which would not be indigenously available (the new heavy industry would be building machines for making machines), and (ii) create excess demand for consumer goods. This strategy was spelt out in the plan itself as follows:

> . . . if industrialisation is to be rapid enough, the country must aim at developing basic industries and industries which make machines to make the machines needed for further development. This calls for a substantial expansion in iron and steel, non-ferrous metals, coal, cement, heavy chemicals, and other industries of basic importance. The limitation is, of course, the scarcity of resources and the many urgent claims on them. Nevertheless, the criterion is not merely immediate needs but the continuing and expanding needs in the coming years as development goes forward. India's natural resources are relatively large, and in many of these fields, as in steel, for instance, she is likely to have a comparative cost advantage. It is desirable to aim at proceeding farthest in the direction of developing heavy and capital goods industries which conform to this criterion . . . Investment in basic industries creates demands for consumer goods in the short run; but it does not

directly absorb any large quantities of labour. A balanced pattern of industrialisation, therefore, requires a well-organised effort to utilise labour for increasing the supplies of much needed consumer goods in a manner which economises the use of capital. A society in which labour is plentiful in relation to capital has to develop the art and technique of using labour-intensive modes of production effectively—and to much social advantage—in diverse fields. Indeed, in the context of prevailing unemployment, the absorption of labour becomes an important objective in itself. In using labour-intensive methods, it may well be that the cost of the product is somewhat higher. This entails a sacrifice which can be reduced through technical and organisational improvements. In any case, a measure of sacrifice in the matter of consumption is inevitable while the economy is being strengthened at the base. The sacrifice diminishes as more power, more transport, and better tools, machinery and equipment become available for increasing the productivity of consumer goods industries, and in the long run the community gets increasingly large returns. Meanwhile, the stress on utilisation of unutilised or under-utilised labour power alleviates the immediate problem of unemployment. Another point that may need stressing in this connection is that the use of labour intensive methods often implies that a smaller proportion of the incomes generated is available for saving and reinvestment. Steps must be taken to ensure that this does not happen on any significant scale.

. . . conditions have to be created in which modern techniques can be adopted and introduced more and more in (small and cottage industries) and the transition should be orderly . . . development along new lines has to be the keynote of policy. As national income increases, demands get diversified, and as power, transport and communications are developed, the scope for small enterprises of various kinds, which either cater for new consumer demands or function in a way complementary to large-scale industry, increases steadily. From the point of view of enlarging employment opportunities as well as of increasing production, these new lines of development have to be fostered energetically.

The sector of village and small-scale industry has to be

organised more and more on co-operative lines so as to enable the small producer to secure the advantages of buying raw materials and selling his products on a large scale, of getting access to institutional credit and of utilising improved methods and techniques. An integral programme of production may in some cases work on the basis of differential taxation; in others, buying over of the product at stated prices and a state-sponsored or co-operative marketing arrangement may be needed.

The programme for expansion of industrial capacity was conceived in terms of the following priorities:

1. increased production of iron and steel and of heavy chemicals, including nitrogenous fertilizers, and development of heavy engineering and machine building industries;
2. expansion of capacity in respect of other developmental commodities and producer goods, such as aluminium, cement, chemicals and pulp, dyestuffs, and phosphatic fertilizers and of essential drugs;
3. modernisation and re-equipment of important national industries which have already come into existence, such as jute, cotton and sugar;
4. fuller utilisation of existing installed capacity in industries where there are wide gaps between capacity and production; and
5. expansion of capacity for consumer goods keeping in view the requirements of common production programmes and the production targets for the decentralised sector of industry.

These priorities were justified at some length: (a) steel determines the tempo of progress as a whole and India has a comparative advantage in its production; (b) heavy engineering is a natural corollary to iron and steel and internal availability of machinery would remove the difficulties and uncertainties of dependence upon external aid; (c) fertilizers are essential for agricultural development; (d) cement ranks next only to iron and steel as a development commodity; (e) modernisation of equipment in cotton and jute is necessary for earning foreign exchange, but additional production in these industries should be achieved to the maximum extent possible through greater use of idle capacity to save capital resources; and (f) expansion of capacity in consumer goods industries would be permitted only for export purposes.

The proposed outlay on village and small industries was raised substantially to Rs. 200 crores, of which Rs. 55 crores was specifically for small as distinct from cottage and village industries. The amount was distributed as shown in Table 10.

TABLE 10: **Second Plan outlay on village and small industries**

(Rs. crores)

Handlooms	60
Khadi	17
Village industries	39
Handicrafts	9
Small industries	55
Sericulture and coir	6
General administration and research	15
Total (excluding working capital requirements)	200

This amount was exclusive of the provision made for these industries under rehabilitation of displaced persons (Rs. 11 crores) and community development blocks (Rs. 1.5 lakhs each). The role of the centre was restricted to all-India administrative, research and hire-purchase schemes costing in all Rs. 25 crores; the remaining amount of Rs. 175 crores was in the state sector. The problems of small industries, their urban or semi-urban location, use of machines, power and modern techniques, were viewed in a separate perspective for the first time. Their performance in training for entrepreneurship was strikingly demonstrated by the manufacture of bicycle and sewing machine parts in Ludhiana. A working definition of identifying small industrial units was laid down: all units or establishments having a total capital investment of less than Rs. 5 lakhs and employing less than 50 persons when using power or less than 100 persons when not using power. (Later, the employment and energy dimensions were dropped, and the limit for plant and equipment was set at less than Rs. 20 lakhs or, in the case of ancillaries, Rs. 25

lakhs). Facilities for their technical, financial and marketing assistance on a basis separate from village and cottage industries, service institutes and industrial extension centres in each state, National Small Industries Corporation for hire-purchase of equipment and marketing assistance, and industrial estates to discourage further concentration of population in large urban centres, were designed specifically for their development.

Planned regional diffusion of industrial activity had received little attention in the First Plan. Only marginal deviation could be made from the compulsions of economic and technical considerations in the case of the larger industries, but the claims of relatively backward areas were nevertheless kept in view in the location of public sector projects, including steel plants. Regional patterns of development could be and were fostered for a wide range of consumer goods and processing industries. These included cotton textiles (especially spinning), sugar, light engineering such as bicycles, sewing machines, electric motors and radio receivers, re-rolling of steel and non-ferrous metals from billets and semis, moulded plastics, and processing of drugs in bulk. Cotton mills were licensed in Rajasthan, Orissa, Assam and Punjab by fixing state quotas and persuading applicants to locate in these states. New sugar factories (especially co-operatives financed by state governments, Industrial Finance Corporation and State Bank) and distilleries were encouraged in Andhra Pradesh, Tamil Nadu, Karnataka and Maharashtra, steel re-rolling mills in Assam, Madhya Pradesh, Kerala and North Bihar, and factories for tyre and tubes, cables and electric lamps in Kerala. A synthetic rubber plant based on industrial alcohol was established in Uttar Pradesh. The decision to sell steel at a uniform price at all railheads was an important step forward in the wider dispersal of light engineering industries.

Industry claimed about 17 per cent of the total public outlay in the Second Plan, as compared to 8 per cent in the First. In absolute terms, the allocation for large-scale industry was raised from Rs. 94 crores in the public sector and Rs. 233 crores in the private sector in the First Plan to Rs. 620 crores and Rs. 575 crores (latter include mining), respectively. Almost the entire public sector outlay, which actually came to Rs. 870 crores or 56 per cent of the total investment in organised industry, was for development of basic industries such as iron and steel, coal, fertilizers, heavy engineering and heavy electrical equipment. This helped to strengthen the public sector and "also to create conditions conducive to a rapid growth of medium and light industries in the private sector". The net output of factory establishments was to increase by 64 per cent and of capital goods by 150 per cent. Measured by the Index of Industrial Production (1956-100) in Table 16 the actual increase was about 40 per cent in the aggregate, 118 per cent for capital goods, 60 per cent for intermediate and producer goods (including mining and electricity), and 19 per cent for consumer goods.

The main industrial targets of the Second Plan which were not achieved were those set for iron and steel, fertilizers, certain items of industrial machinery (for example, paper and cement plant machinery, heavy castings and forgings), aluminium, newsprint, raw films, chemical pulp, soda ash, caustic soda, dyestuffs and cement (Table 11) and for most cottage and village industries which were to supply the additional consumer goods.

TABLE 11: **Second Plan's major industrial targets and achievements**

Item	Unit	Production target	Actual production
Steel finished	m. tonnes	4.37	2.23
Fertilizers: N	th. tonnes	294.6	111.8
P	th. tonnes	121.9	55.9
Textile machinery	Rs. crores	17.0	9.0
Cement machinery	Rs. crores	2.0	0.6
Paper machinery	Rs. crores	4.0	—
Aluminium	th. tonnes	25.4	18.8
Newsprint	th. tonnes	16.0	25.4
Chemical pulp	th. tonnes	30.5	—
Soda ash	th. tonnes	233.7	147.3
Caustic soda	th. tonnes	137.2	101.6
Dyestuffs	m. kg.	10.0	5.2
Cement	m. tonnes	13.2	8.6

The shortfalls were concentrated in those very industries which were crucial for future growth and price stability. Investment in most cases exceeded the target (Table 12), largely due to price increases but partly also due to initial underestimation of

TABLE 12: **Second Plan—Investment in industry**

(*Rs. crores*)

	Plan estimate	Actual investment
Metallurgical industries	503	770
Engineering, light and heavy	150	175
Chemical	132	140
Cement, electric porcelain and refractories	93	60
Petroleum refining	10	30
Paper	54	40
Sugar	51	56
Textiles: (i) natural fibres	36	50
(ii) rayon	24	34
Others	42	115
Replacement and modernisation	150	150
Total	1,244	1,620

requirements, but production remained in arrears. There were specific reasons in each industry for underfulfilment of production targets, in addition to the shortage of foreign exchange that began to be felt acutely after 1957.

Principal deficiencies and defects

The private enthusiasm for industrial expansion that was aroused in the latter half of the First Plan received a fresh stimulus during the Second Plan from heavy deficit financing, relatively liberal import licensing, easier availability abroad of capital goods, and liberal distribution of industrial licences. The widespread urge for industrialisation and the material requisites of well-being was a favourable development but neither at the fiscal and specific level nor within the planning-cum-price mechanism were there any means in operation for the direction of private investment in accordance with Plan priorities. Barring the expansion of private steel and shipping brought about primarily by massive financial assistance and assurance of demand, rather than by price incentives, the official attitude in general was that, so long as a project was in the Plan, every industry and every industrial licence granted had an equal priority. Tax concessions such as development rebate, tax holiday, extra depreciation, etc., were available in an identical measure to nearly all industries, instead of being graded or differentiated according to priorities. There was, similarly, no grading or differentiation in the provision of finance, power, land, materials, water, etc. While it would be quite incorrect to say that the essential industries, being subject to price and other controls, lacked incentives to expand or could not mobilise capital—since they did in fact expand and raise large amounts of capital—there was no self-correcting or planning mechanism for restricting investment or production in relatively less or non-essential industries as resources, especially foreign exchange, became more scarce than anticipated. This became quite clear after the foreign exchange crisis in 1958: adequate foreign exchange could not be found for power and import of components, spare parts and materials for essential users but imports of equipment for less essential industries were deemed to have high priority just because they were capital goods.

In the course of licensing industrial projects and later, foreign collaboration, sufficient attention was not given to the economics of optimum location and scale of production. The underlying belief was that economic concentration would be avoided by licensing a relatively large number of units in each industry, dispersed over a number of regions, each having a separate foreign collaboration from a different country as far as possible. Consequently, uneconomically small units proliferated, and burdened the economy with high capital (especially foreign exchange) costs and low utilisation of capacity as the shortage of materials became more pronounced. Each collaborator tended to install a different kind of plant, spare parts of which had to be imported for a long time from the country of origin alone, and each made a separate charge for imparting his technology and skill, which could have been avoided with fewer but larger plants and a policy for the use and transfer of trained manpower. In the event, even an increase in the concentration of economic power was not avoided. In certain industries, such as cement, on the other hand, the policy of denying substantial expansion to large units tended to slow down the growth of output since those who received the licences were in many cases unable to utilize them.

The Mahalanobis strategy could not be accepted in full, among other things, owing to the pressing demands for higher consumption—and consequent import of equipment for consumer goods production. Agricultural failures and higher food prices, and transport bottlenecks led to price inflation which became, paradoxically, the only instrument, a crude and indiscriminate one, of restraining consumption, with almost no support from fiscal, monetary and direct policies. Even if these mishaps had been avoided, the strategy would not have worked so neatly as its author postulated for, some of its assumptions proved to be unrealistic or premature. One of the major premises of this strategy was that cottage industries were capital-saving. This proved incorrect for, it was found in the case of the *Ambar Charkha,* to take only one example, that it required more labour as well as more capital per unit of output as compared with mill spinning and the product was not entirely suitable for handloom weaving. In spite of rebates, subsidies, freight concessions, etc., the products of cottage industries (handlooms excepted) were not acceptable to consumers on grounds of both price and quality. Given the existing technology, there was a limit beyond which the total output of each cottage industry could increase. The organisational effort required for improved technology and marketing was also seriously underestimated. And, to top it all, the official predilections in favour of khadi tended to distract attention from the promotion of intrinsically more promising industries like footwear, coir, bidi, handicrafts, and small establishments using power.

The public sector was expected to and did play a crucial and strategic role in raising investment and filling gaps in the industrial structure: three steel plants, lignite, ship-building, fertilizers, heavy electricals, machine tools, antibiotics, cables, railway locomotives and coaches, besides large expansion in coal, railways and power, all these started the process of changing the face of the country. But the costs of nearly all of them by far exceeded the Plan estimates, and fulfilment of production targets was inordinately delayed, thereby upsetting the foreign exchange budget and the production programmes of inter-related industries. Equally serious was the failure of the public sector to develop in good time a large technical and managerial cadre and sufficient trained labour to supply its manpower requirements and, wherever necessary, to provide the necessary guidance to the private sector. The development of such a cadre was an important part of the Industrial Policy Resolution.

While the plan progressed—and more than 80 per cent of its physical targets were achieved—many of the fundamental questions of industrial planning in a mixed economy were not answered; they were, in fact, not raised at all in the context of planning as such. What level and structure of direct business taxation would ensure private investment in accordance with priorities and also offset the disincentive to efficiency and cost reduction brought about by a high statutory rate of income tax? Should a scarcity premium be attached (by means of notional or shadow pricing or through the actual price mechanism) to the use of foreign exchange, domestic capital and essential commodities and, if so, what should be the mechanism of charging this premium in accordance with changing situations and requirements? Granted the objectives, strategy and targets for individual industries, what are the non-market or quasi-market criteria for determining the priorities between them *inter se* ? Finally, how is the administration of policy to combine negative fiats with positive directions?

Third Five Year Plan

On the eve of the Third Plan, national income (at 1960-61 prices) had gone up over the decade of planning by 42 per cent to Rs. 14,500 crores and per capita income by 16 per cent to Rs. 330. Industrial production was 94 per cent higher than in 1950-51. The share of public sector industries in the net output of organised manufacturing industries had gone up from 1.5 per cent to 8.4 per cent and much of this increase had taken place in key industries like steel, coal-mining and heavy chemicals. Besides the building up of a metallurgical and chemical base for future industrialisation, considerable progress had been made in industries manufacturing consumer durables, in small industries and in the modernisation and re-equipment of older industries like cotton, jute and sugar, part of it from indigenously manufactured equipment.

Far-reaching gains had been secured in the industrial field but these were insufficient to make any great impact on the general condition of the mass of the population or to alter radically the structure of the economy. Over the decade, national income originating in industry at current prices rose from Rs. 1,460 crores to Rs. 2,440 crores, but as a proportion of the total, the increase was from 16 to 19 per cent only, and from 6 to 9 per cent, if factory establishments alone are taken into account. Employment in manufacturing industries rose only by 17 per cent but the crude index of productivity went up by 49 per cent.

The principal objective relating to industry in the Third Plan was "to expand basic industries like steel, chemicals, fuel, and power, and establish machine-building capacity, so that the requirements of further industrialisation can be met within a period of 10 years or so mainly from the country's own resources". Industrial production was to increase by 70 per cent over the five years (at a compound annual rate of 11 per cent) against 30 per cent for national income as a whole. About 29 per cent of total investment, public and private, against 27 per cent in the Second Plan, was allocated to industry and minerals. Total investment in industry of the public sector was targeted to increase from Rs. 960 crores (including Rs. 90 crores in village and small industries) to Rs. 1,245 crores (including Rs. 150 crores for village and small industries). In the private sector, the targeted increase was from Rs. 850 crores (village and small industries Rs. 175 crores) to Rs. 1,475 crores, of which Rs, 150 crores was for replacement and modernisation and Rs. 275 crores for village and small industries. Proposed aggregate investment in large-scale industry, thus, amounted to Rs. 2,720 crores and in village and small industries to Rs. 425 crores.

Of basic importance in the Third Plan was the programme for the expansion of capital and producer goods industries with special emphasis on machine building, and development of managerial skill, technical know-how and designing capacity. In this programme, the public sector was assigned a key role but the private sector was also expected to play an important part. The share of the public sector in the net output of organised manufacturing industries would rise from 8 per cent to 25 per cent and the bulk of this would comprise capital and producer goods in the fields of metallurgy, industrial machinery, machine tools, fertilizers, basic chemicals and intermediates, essential drugs and petroleum refining. The emphasis was on industries which would help to make the economy self-sustaining, and reduce as rapidly as possible the need for external assistance to purchase these goods, and also permit a broadening of the export base. The production of consumer goods was also to be expanded substantially, mainly in the private sector.

The industrial plan for the period 1961-66 was governed by the overriding need to lay the foundation for further rapid industrialisation over the next 15 years; at the same time, provision was made to the extent possible for meeting the demand for other manufactured goods over the next five years. Power and fuel, it was anticipated, were likely to be inhibiting factors in the first half of the Third Plan, which might entail forgoing the adoption of industrial processes which make a heavy demand on electric power, notwithstanding their attractiveness. (This fear proved misplaced largely because industrial production failed to achieve the projected growth rate).

Without departing from the 1956 Resolution, the Third Plan laid much greater emphasis than before on the "supplementary and complementary" nature of the public and private sectors. Specific attention was drawn to the entry of the private sector into nitrogenous fertilizers "in a bigger way than in the past". In pig iron, it was proposed to allow private plants with a maximum capacity of 1.016 lakh tonnes (raised to 3.048 lakh tonnes in 1964 on reconsideration of economies of scale and production requirements) as compared with 15,241 tonnes permitted till then. Programmes for the manufacture of dyestuffs, plastics and drugs in the private sector were envisaged to be largely complementary to the programme for manufacture of primary aromatic compounds as by-products at steel works and of organic intermediates to be undertaken in the public sector. Similarly, public manufacture of bulk drugs was to be complemented by subsequent processing in the private sector. Roughly identical policies were later adopted in respect of electric motors and switchgear, and petro-chemicals. This change in what may be described as interpretation or implementation of industrial policy resulted, in large measure, from the pace of industrial growth and diversification, both achieved and proposed, and acceptance in general terms by both the sectors of their relative places in integrated development.

Among the general considerations for fixing industrial priorities, the Plan emphasised: (i) greater and more intensive utilisation of existing capacity through multi-shift operation and/or installation of balancing equipment; (ii) expansion of existing plants in preference to establishment of new units in the interests of quicker completion and bringing down of the investment cost of output; and (iii) accent on those projects which would earn or save foreign exchange and discouragement of those heavily dependent upon import of raw materials. Subject to these, the following priorities were laid down for programmes and projects:

1. Completion of Second Plan projects which were under implementation or were deferred in 1957-58 due to foreign exchange difficulties.
2. Expansion and diversification of the capacity of heavy engineering and machine-building industries, castings and forgings, alloy tools and special steels, iron and steel and ferro-alloys and increasing the output of fertilizers and petroleum products.
3. Increased production of major basic raw materials and producer goods such as aluminium, mineral oils, dissolving pulp, basic organic and inorganic chemicals and intermediates, including petro-chemicals.
4. Increased production from domestic industries of commodities required to meet basic consumer needs like essential drugs, paper, cloth, sugar, vegetable oils and housing materials.

The Plan did not fail to take into account the growing concentration of economic power in the private sector as a result of the rapid growth of large business groups which had been able to make disproportionate use of the greater and wider opportunities for investment.[18] "Against the background of the goal of a socialistic pattern of society", it stated, "steps would be taken to safeguard against the concentration of development in the hands of a few entrepreneurs leading to complete or partial monopolies". Later, in April 1967, a Monopolies Commission was appointed to inquire "into certain matters connected with the concentration of economic power in private hands and the prevention of monopolistic practices".

In the Third as in the Second Plan, care was taken, subject to economic and technical considerations, to disperse the location of new major public projects as well as expansion of existing ones. The claims of underdeveloped regions were also kept in view in the licensing of private industrial projects. The progress, programmes and production targets of a number of industries were examined from time to time with a view to securing the location of new capacity on a zonal basis. Special attention was paid in the allocation not merely of cotton mills and light engineering industries but also of new industries like aluminium, cellulose acetate, artificial fibres, chemical processing, fertilizers and rubber tyres and tubes, to industrially backward states like Rajasthan, Uttar Pradesh, Assam and Kerala. It was accepted as a matter of policy that each major public project should act as a nucleus of growth through the establishment of industrial estates in its neighbourhood, and that fully developed industrial areas with necessary infrastructure should be provided in selected centres in each state.

There was, among other things, a steep increase in domestic purchases by the Director-General of Supplies and Disposals (Table 13).

TABLE 13: **DGSD purchases of equipment and stores**

	Indigenous Rs. crores (1)	Imported Rs. crores (2)	Total Rs. crores (3)	(1) as % of (3) (4)
1961-62	210	50	259	81
1962-63	353	52	405	87
1963-64	453	100	553	82
April-November 1964	227	64	291	78

Village and small industries

The main objectives laid down in the village and small industries programme of the Third Plan were:

a. to improve the productivity of the worker and reduce production costs by placing relatively greater emphasis on positive forms of assistance, such as improvement of skill, supply of technical advice, better equipment and credit, etc.;
b. to reduce progressively the role of subsidies, sales rebates and sheltered markets;
c. to promote the growth of industries in rural areas and

small towns;

d. to promote the development of small-scale industries as ancillaries to large industries; and

e. to organise artisans and craftsmen on co-operative lines.

There was, thus, a clear shift in policy away from the negative and protective attitudes of earlier years in favour of a positive, intrinsically economic programme for placing village and small industries on a sound productive basis. It was clearly recognised that small industries combine the advantages of modern technology and the use of power with those of increased employment and greater opportunity for small entrepreneurs as well as for co-operatives. Programmes have been drawn up for the extension of government guarantees for bank credit to small industries, enlargement of the hire-purchase scheme of the National Small Industries Corporation, large government purchases from small and cottage industries, and for the setting up of 300 new industrial estates against 120 sanctioned (and 60 commissioned) during the Second Plan. Regarding industrial estates, there was still an official belief that they could be the instrument for dispersion of industries away from congested areas. The record of industrial estates actually in operation, however, indicated clearly that most of the successful estates were those located close to large industrial centres.

This shift in policy was confirmed by the minor increase in the outlay allocated for traditional village and cottage industries and the greater concentration proposed on small industries and industrial estates (Table 14).

Government purchases of the products of small-scale industries have increased considerably since 1951 (Table 15). About 70 items are reserved for exclusive purchase from this sector.

Fiscal and allied developments

As foreign exchange difficulties became more serious, returns from investments in public enterprises were smaller and more delayed than expected, and it was realised that the planning and price mechanism were not inherently antithetical but could usefully supplement each other, a number of changes in policy and policy administration were effected from 1963 onwards. Some of these concerned licensing procedures, quicker utilisation of

TABLE 14: **Outlay on village and small industries—Second and Third Plans**

(Rs. crores)

	Second Plan actual	Third Plan
Handlooms	30	34
Powerlooms in handloom sector	2	4
Khadi and village industries	82	92
Sericulture	3	7
Coir	2	3
Handicrafts	5	9
Small industries	44	85
Industrial estates	12	30
Total	180	264

TABLE 15: **Government purchases of small industry products**

(Rs. crores)

	Total	Annual average
First Plan period 1951-56	7	1.4
Second Plan period 1956-61	21	4.2
Third Plan period (1961-Dec. 1964)	92	25.5

foreign aid, and removal of price and distribution controls on certain essential commodities such as steel and chemicals and which had, therefore, a direct bearing on industrial policy. Other changes related to tax concessions, export incentives, import duties, monetary policy and large-scale financial assistance and which had, at first sight, only an indirect relationship with industrial policy but were, in fact, of fundamental significance for directing private investment—and for that matter disciplining the managements of public enterprises, too—into consistency with Plan priorities and the realities of pricing of scarce inputs.

Much of the licensing, estimated at about 80 per cent of the total for the Third Plan period, was completed almost *en bloc* in or about 1960. Measures were taken from 1962 to start weeding out the dormant licences, and to list the industries in which no further licences would be given. At the same time on the recommendation of the Swaminathan Committee, a list of priority industries was drawn up for prompt clearance of licensing and foreign exchange formalities. There was, however, no laying down of priorities within this list or assurance of full and prompt satisfaction of exchange requirements for equipment and materials to the industrial units concerned. In some cases, for example, alloy steel, a high priority in licensing was not matched by expeditious approval of liberal terms of foreign collaboration which were in fact allowed to some low-priority industries. The period of validity of licences for maintenance imports was extended to facilitate continuity of supplies.

The report of the Raj Committee on steel prices and distribution marked a basic change in the attitudes towards controls on the prices and distribution of scarce essential commodities. The committee expressed itself firmly in favour of using the price mechanism for rationing and rationalising demand and as an incentive for regulating the pace of investment and pattern of production, and restricting distribution controls to the prior satisfaction of priority demands only. Price and distribution controls on structural steel were lifted in 1964 and on pig iron in August 1965, and were replaced by increased excise duties to keep down demand.

From January 1963, the raising of the bank rate and subsequent tightening up of credit policies ushered in a policy of dearer money—and higher price of capital, whether borrowed or equity. The setting up of the Industrial Development Bank of India with the promise that this institution would see high priority projects through to completion was expected to cushion high priority investments against the quantitative impact of restrictive monetary policies. The raising of import duties in 1964 and again twice in 1965 as an alternative to devaluation was expected to give a stimulus to import substitution in equipment and materials; their impact on profitability was sought to be cushioned by substantial raising of the rate of development rebate over the entire period of the Fourth Plan for the essential industries listed in the Finance Acts of 1964 and 1965. The absence of any deliberate link between this list of essential industries and that operative for licensing purposes, however, remained a lacuna.

Evaluation

Post-Independence industrial policy marks a clear break from pre-Independence days, though the conscious adoption of a mixed economy represents essentially a continuity of tradition. A public sector existed at the time of Independence. In British India it was practically confined to major public utilities and supply of a part of government requirements of defence and industrial goods. A few princely states like Mysore, Travancore, Hyderabad and some small states in the United Provinces, Saurashtra and Madhya Pradesh had ventured directly or indirectly into the production of a limited variety of consumer and producer goods. This species of public sector was not part of any overall programme of industrial development; it was largely the result of various ad hoc and vaguely strategic considerations. The Industrial Policy Statements of 1948 and 1956 demarcated the roles of the public and private sectors and also promised official blessings for co-operativisation and cottage and small industries. As of mid-sixties, industry, especially factory industry, had yet to acquire a dominant position in the economy, in terms of both output and employment, but it had climbed to a plateau from which further ascent was assured. At the same time, the rate of the growth of industrial production had been erratic in spite of planning (Table 16). True, it was less erratic than the increase in agricultural output, and fluctuations in the latter inevitably affected industry since industries with a weightage of about 55 per cent in the

TABLE 16: **Index of industrial production (1956-100)**

Year	Index	Increase over previous year (%)
1951	73.5	
1952	75.8	3.13
1953	77.7	2.51
1954	83.1	6.95
1955	91.9	10.59
1956	100.0	8.81
1957	104.2	4.20
1958	107.7	3.36
1959	116.9	8.54
1960	130.1	11.29
1961	139.2	6.54
1962	151.3	8.00
1963	163.8	8.26
1964	174.6	6.59

index of industrial production were directly based upon the supply of agricultural raw materials. On the other hand, there was no escaping the fact that plan targets had been under-fulfilled principally in the basic industries, not in the material-based industries.

Industrial licensing

An industrial licence is necessary under the Industries (Development and Regulation) Act, 1951 for setting up new or additional industrial capacity in scheduled industries covered by the Act. The exemption limit for fixed investment was Rs. 5 lakhs till the Third Plan when it was raised to Rs. 10 lakhs, and further to Rs. 25 lakhs in 1964. The ostensible purposes of industrial licensing were: (a) to limit industrial capacity within the target set by the Plans; and (b) to direct investment in industries according to Plan priorities. The policy of industrial licensing went through various phases.[19] From 1951 to 1958, licensing tended to be restricted within the Plan targets, mainly because the tempo of industrial development was not very rapid and the demand for licences was not overwhelming; imports were allowed reasonably freely and new industrial projects had to face competition from imported goods, unless they obtained tariff protection. The second phase lasted from 1958 to 1961, when the foreign exchange crisis had its first effect. Imports, especially of materials and components, were restricted and the government decided to liberalise the issue of licences, whenever a case for import substitution was made. Licences were issued far in excess (in some cases 25 per cent but normally 10 per cent) of capacity targets in several industries. For example, in paper, spun pipe, steel tube and many other industries, the licences issued by the end of 1960 were far in excess of the capacity targets set for 1965-66, on the ground that many licensees often failed to establish capacity. The effect of this policy was to make investment plans more akin to those in a free market economy but without being subjected to market discipline. In the third phase, beginning with 1962, industrial licensing again became strict, mainly owing to the growing stringency of foreign exchange, and revocation of licences was initiated. The number of licences issued was 1,363 per year during 1959-61, 1,104 in 1962, 976 in 1963 and 782 in 1964. There were 315 revocations in 1962, 204 in

1963 and 202 in 1964.

Generous and en bloc licensing during the period 1958-61 for Second and Third Plan capacity targets, together with restrictive import licensing which reduced statutory protection to insignificance (see Appendix IV for the list of protected industries as of March 1963), imposed great strains on foreign exchange resources and the order books of domestic machinery manufacturers. No explicit criteria were laid down to guide licensing policies, except for the banned, restricted and priority lists published after 1962. Some conclusions could, however, be deduced from the decisions made:

1. In some industries where economies of scale operate, certain minimum size was laid down, for example, paper in the First and Second Plan Industrial Programmes but, in most other industries where also economies of scale operate, there was no such insistence.
2. Since regional decentralisation was favoured, applications for location in backward areas received preferential treatment.
3. Licences were issued to new entrepreneurs in preference to existing business houses in order to broaden the entrepreneurial base.
4. To reduce monopoly power, licences were given to those applicants, including some from large business houses, who did not have any establishment in a particular industry, for example, Birla in cement and aluminium.
5. The government fostered consortia for the manufacture of complete industrial plants, for example, cement, sugar and paper but the licences were issued for specific plant manufacturing only, not for general fabrication, so that, even if their capacity was versatile and idle, they could not change over to the manufacture of other plant.
6. To reduce the strain on foreign exchange, licensees were required in some cases to manufacture the required components or intermediates, for example, pulp for paper, compressors for refrigerators and air-conditioners, intermediates for chemicals and pharmaceuticals, glass tubes for incandescent lamps, plastic materials for polystyrene, apart from the more generalised version of this applied to

automobiles, machine tools, etc. This led in many cases to uneconomical vertical integration and development of captive supplies at the expense of the final consumer.

7. Export obligations were imposed on certain licensees as a condition for the release of foreign exchange for the import of plant and raw materials, and to cover the liabilities arising out of foreign collaboration.

The impact of licensing on the pace and pattern of growth was uneven and quite often unrelated to priorities. Though investment opportunities were far larger than the internal and external resources available, no criteria were laid down for undertaking the manufacture of specified items according to their suitability for economic manufacture. Consequently, in many industries the cost of manufacture was avoidably higher than international levels. Quite often, when an item came to be domestically manufactured, users could continue to live off their imported stocks, as happened in the case of polystyrene in 1958, PVC in 1962, synthetic rubber and ball-bearings in 1964-65. Over-licensing and en bloc Plan licensing, instead of phased issues, have tended to slow down the actual utilisation of licences due to fears of over-production. Instead of the normally expected plan criteria of maximum value added or maximum net foreign exchange saved or maximum employment provided, there were, by and large, only *ad hoc* decisions taken "on the merits of each proposal", which inevitably led to delays.

GROWTH OF CORPORATE SECTOR

Joint stock companies came into existence in 1845 when an Act was passed to incorporate the Assam Company with an authorised capital of Rs. 50 lakhs. The Companies Act followed in 1850; but the principle of limited liability was introduced only in 1857. Banking and insurance companies received the privilege of limited liability three years later. The growth of the corporate sector was, however, very slow till the boom after the First World War. In 1900, there were only 1,340 companies with a paid-up capital of Rs. 34.70 crores (Table 17). Of these, 152 were cotton mills with a share capital of Rs. 11.67 crores and 129 were tea plantations with a share capital of Rs. 3.25

TABLE 17: **Companies registered and at work in India—1900-1964**

As on 31 March	Number of companies	Paid-up capital (Rs. crores)
1900	1340	34.7
1910	2216	61.4
1920	3668	123.2
1925	5204	275.5
1930	6919	286.3
1935	9842	304.0
1939	11114	290.4
1946	17343	424.2
1950	27558	723.9
1955	29625	969.6
1957	29357	1077.6
1960	26397	1618.7
1964	26457	2537.5

Source: Nigam and Chaudhuri: *The Corporate Sector in India.* *Company News and Notes*, 17 May, 1965, p. 66.

crores (there were, besides, a number of sterling tea companies but data for these are not available readily in comparable form). There were also 21 jute mill companies with a share capital of Rs. 2.68 crores.

By 1919, the total number of companies rose to 2,789 and their share capital crossed the Rs. 100 crores mark for the first time to reach the figure of Rs. 106.6 crores. The industrywise distribution remained broadly unchanged, except for the growth of coal mines and rice and flour mills. Thereafter, growth was rapid (by contemporary standards) up to 1925; the number of companies in that year reached 5,204 and their share capital amounted to Rs. 275.5 crores, in spite of the winding up (liquidation) of 1,836 companies with a share capital of Rs. 39 crores during the period, mainly in 1922-25. In the ensuing slump that lasted through 1938, the number of companies increased consistently (except for a decline between 1937 and 1938) but their share capital remained sluggish. There were 10,657 companies in 1938, more than twice the number in 1925 but their share capital was Rs. 279 crores only.[20] This sluggishness notwithstanding, there was some growth in banking and insurance, cotton, jute, coal and inland navigation; thanks to protection, the number of sugar companies increased from 20 in 1919 to 172 in 1939 and their share capital expanded from Rs. 82 lakhs to Rs. 11.18 crores; interest came to be evinced in paper and rubber plantation also.

The corporate sector has not looked back since then. By 1947, there were 21,853 companies with a share capital of Rs. 479 crores which, on the eve of the First Five-Year Plan in 1951, rose to 28,432 companies and Rs. 775 crores, respectively. At the end of March 1956, which marked the end of indifferent and decentralised administration of the Companies Act, the number of companies stood at 29,874 and their share capital aggregated Rs. 1,024 crores. Out of nearly 13,000 companies which "ceased to work" (as defined by the Company Law Administration) between April 1956 and March 1962 more than one-half were struck off by Registrars of Companies for non-fulfilment of various statutory obligations. While traditional industries like cotton, jute, sugar, etc., retained their importance, engineering and chemicals started assuming greater significance. Moreover, there was an increasing tendency towards diversification within the large companies.

Following British law and practice, companies in India are either public or private. The latter have a minimum of two shareholders and a maximum of fifty; their shares cannot be offered to the public nor are the shares freely transferable; under the Companies Act, 1956, they are exempt from restrictions regarding appointment and remuneration of managerial personnel, etc., applicable to public companies but they must insert "private" after their name. Public companies must have a minimum of seven shareholders; their shares can be offered to the public but there is no statutory obligation upon them to do so by prospectus or otherwise.

More than three-fourths of the companies registered in India are private (Table 19). Their relative importance in share capital is not equally impressive and would have been even less so but for the fortuitous registration of most government companies as private companies. Curiously enough, the predominance of private companies is a post-1946 phenomenon; till 1946, the majority of companies were public, though most of these were closely owned. In fact, during the first two decades of the present

TABLE 18: **Number and paid-up capital of companies in important industrial groups**

(As on 31 March, 1964)

Industrial groups	No.	Paid-up capital ('n *Rs. crores*)
Tea plantations	575	34.6
Sugar factories and refineries	193	50.0
Cotton spinning and weaving	763	165.1
Iron and steel (basic manufacture)	573	538.1
Transport and equipment manufacture	635	83.2
Manufacture of electrical machinery, etc.	706	81.4
Machinery other than transport and electric	1115	167.9
Basic industrial chemicals, fertilizers, etc.	425	104.1
Products of petroleum and coal	39	62 5
Manufacture of cement	40	46.4
Paper and paper products manufacture	199	48.4
Wholesale trade	4139	121.0
Banking, loan and other financial institutions	2132	107.9

TABLE 19: **Public and private companies—1917-64**

As on 31 March	Public companies		Private companies	
	No.	Paid-up capital (Rs. crores)	No.	Paid-up capital (Rs. crores)
1917	2306	85.0	207	5.8
1920	3000	104.6	668	18.5
1939	6859	213.2	4255	77.2
1946	10129	323.1	7214	101.1
1951	12568	566.5	15964	208.9
1956	9575	690.4	20299	333.8
1960	7188	840.5	19709	778.2
1964	5968	1164.9	20489	1372.9

century (data are available only from 1917 onwards) there were very few private companies. The preference for private companies that has been so much in evidence since 1946 is, perhaps, only partly attributable to the desire to avoid the greater statutory regulation of public companies; mainly the private ocmpany appears to have become the favourite vehicle of trading and urban financial activity and nascent industrial enterprise.

The number and relative importance of government companies have increased substantially since the beginning of planning. This category of companies was recognised for the first time in the Companies Act, 1956, section 617 of which defined a government company as one in which 51 per cent or more of the share capital is held by the government. Understood in this sense, there were 36 government companies with a share capital of Rs. 26 crores in 1951 and 61 with a share capital of Rs. 66 crores at the end of March 1956. They accounted for about 3 per cent of the share capital of all companies in 1951 and a little more than 6 per cent in 1956. Their growth since then has been impressive (Table 20).

TABLE 20 : **Government companies at work—1951-61**

As on 31 March	Public companies		Private companies		Total	
	No.	Share capital (Rs. crores)	No.	Share capital (Rs. crores)	No.	Share capital (Rs. crores)
1951	—	—	—	—	36	26
1956	—	—	—	—	61	66
1961	39	33	103	514	142	547

Finally, reference may be made to foreign companies. These are companies registered outside India but with a place of business in India. There should be clearly distinguished from foreign controlled companies registered in India. The number of foreign companies at work increased from 579 in 1913 to 901 in 1933, declined to 819 in 1955, and further to 583 in 1963 (Table 21). The decline is attributable entirely to the weeding out of non-reporting branches of foreign companies. Most of these companies were engaged in tea plantation, insurance, trade, business, services and transport; 390 of thém were of U.K. origin and 72 of U.S. origin.

INDUSTRIAL MANAGEMENT

Early history

The management of public industrial companies in India was,

TABLE 21: **Foreign companies working in India**

Year	Number
1913	579
1923	720
1933	901
1939	870
1943	827
1947	834
1950	845
1955	819
1960	565
1963	583

Source: Nigam and Chaudhuri: *The Corporate Sector in India. Company News and Notes*, 1 September, 1964.

in most cases, in the hands of managing agents since the beginning of industrialisation. As in Malaya, Hong Kong, the former Treaty Ports of pre-Communist China, and Indonesia, this institution was the product of gradual evolution. The managing agency developed on the ruins of the agency house system (founded by ex-servants of the East India Company) which failed in 1833. It grew out of the enterprise of European individuals who came to Calcutta as representatives of trading companies. They found the country lacking in industrial leaders, since imports from Britain had crippled the master craftsmen and traders; money-lenders and big landowners had neither the inclination nor the experience to go into modern industry. The prospects of local processing and rudimentary manufacture for export were attractive because of the availability of raw materials and cheap labour. With the opening of the Suez Canal and laying of railways, the Indian market also appeared on the business horizon. Exploitation of the prospects required capital, contacts with suppliers of equipment and buyers of produce, and skilled labour; these the European representatives were well-qualified to supply or procure. Their mercantile experience and connections proved invaluable; the deficiency of technical expertise was made up by hiring it from Britain. The field open to each entrepreneur was wide; mistakes could be made without burning of fingers. Entrepreneurs moved from jute into coal, from tea into steamers, from these into some kind of engineering, to find a market for one in the other. The Industrial Commission of 1916-18 noted:

> A characteristic feature of organised industry and commerce in all the chief Indian centres is the presence of the large agency firms, which, except in the case of Bombay, are mainly European. In addition to participating in the export and import trade, they finance and manage industrial ventures all over the country and often have several branches in the large towns. The importance of these agency houses may be gauged from the fact that they control the majority of the cotton, jute and other mills, as well as of the tea gardens and the coal mines. This system originated and has still continued owing to the ability of these houses to furnish financial help to industries; it also owes its existence to some extent to the difficulty, in the case of companies under European control, of finding among the relatively small class of leading men of business available in India, directors, especially managing directors, who will remain in the country long enough to guarantee continuous supervision. . . . An agency firm as a rule comprises several partners, some of whom are in India, while the others attend to the firm's affairs in London or elsewhere. There is no doubt that the system is in many ways well adapted to present conditions in India, and has a far greater list of successes to its credit than can be shown by ordinary company management under individual managing directors.

In Calcutta, the system, thus, combined ownership mainly by residents in Britain with management by partners and assistants in India. Although family influences predominated and the partnership was carried on from generation to generation, the more enterprising and ambitious of the junior assistants could look forward to becoming partners ultimately. Managing agents did the preliminary work of starting new concerns, promoted joint stock companies, employed their own funds or arranged for finance by acting as guarantors, and also managed the concerns. Besides these promotional, financing and managerial functions, they acted as agents for sales and purchases. The more important managing agencies also carried on export and import trade, insurance, banking and various kinds of agency business.

On the West Coast, the managing agents were, with some exceptions, Indian. The first written managing agency agreement was between the Bombay Spinning and Weaving Company and Cowasjee Nanabhoy Davar concluded on 7 July 1854; under the agreement he was appointed manager and broker for life, on a remuneration of 5 per cent of the sale proceeds of yarn.[22] It can be safely presumed that the managing agency arrangements in Calcutta were imitated in Bombay by Indian merchants, who made fortunes from the opium trade with China and later, during the American Civil War, from the export of raw cotton to Lancashire; the latter alone was said to have earned Rs. 51 crores worth of gold and silver. Cowasjee Davar and Manockjee Petit in Bombay and Ranchhoddas Chotalal in Ahmedabad, and those who followed them raised most of the capital from their own resources but also secured substantial monetary and other assistance from agents of British machinery suppliers and friends. Though the mill companies were public, they had very few shareholders. In Ahmedabad, where, unlike Bombay, most of the bigger managing agents were by tradition bankers, rather than traders, funds were raised in the form of deposits, too. The larger suppliers of capital got a share in the managing agency remuneration, contingent upon taking up a specified part of the share capital of the managed company—a rudimentary form of underwriting. In both these centres, capital was also raised from potential selling agents, etc., in consideration of future contracts. Commission to agents of machinery suppliers was often paid for in shares. The managers and technicians were generally British till the twenties. The privilege of sharing the fruits of managing agency was, however, normally restricted to members of the founding family with financiers as the only co-sharers, if any. From the thirties and forties onwards, some Indian managing agents in these centres and in Delhi, Kanpur, etc., began to give a share in the managing agency commission also to senior employees.

The common practice with managing agents (leaving aside the fly-by-night variety found in all countries) was to promote and set up a concern and, when it was reasonably well established, either to make it a public company and throw open its share capital to the public or otherwise dispose of their holdings. Care was taken at all times to retain permanent management rights: in most cases, adequate share capital was also retained in order to frustrate any move to oust them. What little evidence there is of shareholdings by managing agents in the first half of this century indicates that, whatever the position might have been in the nineteenth century, the well-known managing agents held only a small part of the share capital of the companies under their management, and the proportion tended to decline even before 1939.

The holdings of managing agents in managed companies were small and in many cases the holdings belonged to the partners/directors of the managing agent.[23] The Bombay Shareholders Association testified on the basis of shareholding data before the Tariff Board in 1932 that managing agents had ceased to be the principal shareholders in Bombay cotton mills. A representative of Martin & Co. stated that his firm did not hold even 20 per cent of the share capital of the companies under their managing agency but they prided themselves on the fact that they were successful agents. Managing agents were, therefore, not, in general, inclined to lock up their resources but took the earliest opportunity to free their funds for investment in other directions. The Tariff Board of 1932 observed:

> Where the managing agent represents a high standard of ability and sense of responsibility, it may make little difference to the company to what extent the managing agent is interested in the share capital of the company. The better class of managing agent works partly for the remuneration fixed for him under his agreement but partly also out of regard for his reputation and out of a sense of pride in the tradition of management associated with his concern.

Control and remuneration

Leaving aside their role as financiers, it is clear that, as their direct contribution to share capital tended to decline, they sought security in permanent and comprehensive rights of management. These rights were assured through agreements in which managing agents acted in a dual capacity as managers and as shareholders. Until 1913, the law did not require an elected board of directors. When the law made elections mandatory, the outside directors depended for their continuance upon the loyalty they showed to the managing agents. Thus, although the managed companies were joint stock concerns with boards of directors, they were more akin to partnerships with outside shareholders as sleeping partners. As the holders of considerable shares (either in their own names or through partners and associated companies), it was in the managing agents' interest that the companies be managed efficiently and fair dividends be paid. But managing agents were paid in a number of other ways, too: commissions on profits, purchases, sales and insurance, remuneration to relatives and associates, and so on.

Managing agency by itself secured a certain value because of its rights and privileges apart from its ability to show profit in the concerns managed; the dividend earnings of agents were subordinate to their earnings in other forms. As the managers-cum-key owners were not chiefly interested in returns on investment, the general inducement to invest and public confidence in investment were adversely affected. Managing agency rights became a negotiable asset. In every boom period, the rights in many companies were transferred at fabulous prices and capitalised at inflated values; during slumps, transfers took place because the managing agents as distinct from the managed companies were in trouble and could no more raise finances on their own. Even the Tatas handed over the majority control in the managing agency of their electric companies in the 1920s to an American syndicate without the prior sanction of the shareholders of the companies.

Originally, the common method of remuneration to managing agents was a commission on output. When ring spindles replaced mules in cotton mills, this system led to abuses. J. N. Tata was the first in 1886 to change over to a commission on profits. Till 1946, however, Ahmedabad cotton mills and Calcutta jute mills generally gave a commission on output, in addition to an office allowance. The tea industry paid 2.5 per cent on sales and a further 2.5 per cent on profits. Coal and cement companies paid on the basis of profits while, in sugar, both the systems existed side by side. In 1916, Tata Iron and Steel adopted a sliding scale of remuneration, rising from 5 per cent to 9 per cent of profits according to various slabs of dividends declared. With the notable exception of Tata companies, profits were defined for this purpose as profits before interest and depreciation.

Many reputable managing agents surrendered their commission when the managed companies were in difficulties, and even gave up the interest due on debenture holdings, besides providing or securing large finances. In 1928, managing agents of 73 cotton mills in Bombay surrendered Rs. 1.91 lakhs of managing agency commission and Rs. 7.40 lakhs of interest on loans and debentures. From 1922 to 1927, Ahmedabad mill agents surrendered Rs. 13.31 lakhs of managing agency commission. The surrender in Bombay was not exactly munificent.

TABLE 22: **Managing agency commission**

Year	No. of companies	Profit or loss (Rs. lakhs)		Total allowances and commission to managing agents (Rs. lakhs)
		Before depreciation	After depreciation	
1927	75	157.00	— 7.36	30.87
1928	73	—126.46	—298.78	18.32
1929	76	— 71.85	—230.67	20.26
1930	71	— 94.23	—236.99	13.45

Source: Lokanathan: *Industrial Organisation in India*, p. 345.

Mixed blessing

That the managing agency system was a mixed blessing was being realised even before 1920. The Industrial Commission was impressed by the high financial prestige of "the better-class agency firms and the readiness of the investing public to follow their lead" but was not altogether complacent about their performance:

> ... they (the better class agency firms) have not escaped criticism as being unduly conservative in their methods of business and as exhibiting undue reluctance to embark on new ventures. They have been charged with lack of enterprise and an unwillingness to follow up lines of development naturally proceeding from the expansion of operations in their own specialised industries. In other words they have been inclined to develop commerce rather than industries, and thus been at times less helpful than might have been the case, in clearing

the way for continuous industrial progress.

The Central Banking Enquiry Committee 1931 had the benefit of considerable evidence on the working of the system during the twenties, especially in the western region. Appraisal of this evidence induced the Committee to recommend lesser dependence on the managing agency system for industrial development:

> Although the Managing Agency system is reported to have done a great deal for the industrial development of Bombay, it is admitted that it is not by any means a perfect arrangement but has many serious drawbacks. There have been cases where the Managing Agents have, besides managing their own mills, traded and speculated and the resulting weakness in their position has reacted on the financial position of the mills themselves and led to banks withdrawing their cash credits even when the mills were intrinsically sound, merely because the Managing Agents had become weak. Further, although it is true that in times of crisis such as Bombay had been going through, Managing Agents have incurred extensive losses as a direct result of financing the mills under their control, there have been a few cases in which these Agents have turned their loans to the mills into debentures, with the result that the concerns have passed into their hands and the shareholders have lost all their capital. . . . This system works well when everything goes on smoothly and when the industries are prosperous. When conditions alter and the industry or the particular concern comes up against bad times and the Managing Agents find themselves compelled to find more money to support the industry, it is found that they are not able in all cases to cope with the requirements.
>
> We suggest, therefore, that attempts should be made to make industrial enterprise in India less dependent on this system for future development. The establishment of direct financial relations between industrial companies and commercial banks is desirable. . . .

With the passage of time more dissatisfaction was expressed with the working of the system in all its three main aspects.

Writing in 1935, P. S. Lokanathan said:

> There have been cases of waste (and) ill conceived and fraudulent promotion. They (the managing agents) have been unwilling to pioneer and risk in new enterprises, where the profits have been neither large nor certain. However successful the managing agency system of promotion might have been in the past, it cannot be concluded that it is so at present or will continue to be so in the future.
>
> Since most Indian concerns have been under-capitalised, with share capital barely sufficient for block expenditure, the balance has to be raised from various short-term or undependable or expensive sources. With debentures and preference capital unpopular, funds had to be raised by or through managing agents which had the result of further strengthening the managing agency system. Had the share and permanent capital raised at the start been sufficient to cover the needs of working expenses, there would not have been the same need for the continuance of an institution like the managing agent to finance industrial concerns.
>
> While its (the system's) power for doing injury may be great, its capacity to do good is limited. So far as the Indian section of the managing agency system is concerned, its continuance can be explained and justified only because of the concentration of ability, experience and capital in the hands of a few persons who have done great service to industrial development. If it became possible to persuade them to do for industry in an altered status what they have been doing as members of agency firms, the result would perhaps be wholly good. There are no benefits which would be lost by such a change, for those benefits are not the result of the system but of the ability and resources of the persons who run the system.

Companies Amendment Act

Statutory restrictions on the power of managing agents were imposed for the first time in 1936. The duration of the appointment of a managing agent in public companies was limited to 20 years at a time; but there was no restriction on reappointments long before the expiry of the initial appointment. Managing agents could be removed if they were convicted of a non-bailable offence punishable under the Penal Code in relation to the affairs of the company. They could transfer their office only with the approval of the company in a general meeting. Powers of management were vested in the board of directors but subject to the articles of association of the company, which proved a gaping loophole. In 1938, insurance companies were debarred from having managing agents. Banking companies were similarly excluded in 1949.

Multiple directorships

One of the minor reasons for the existence and continuance of the (British) managing agency houses was the difficulty of finding a sufficient number of Europeans to constitute boards of directors for industrial companies. Till 1913, and even for some years thereafter, the managing agents were the sole directors; later, the managing agents found a few friends, generally solicitors and business associates, later Indian aristocrats and brokers, to serve as directors to conform to legal requirements. In 1931 out of 52 jute mills for which information was available, 2 had no directors (being incorporated before 1913) and the remaining 50 mills had 92 directors between them. Seventy-two coal companies had 80 directors between them, with four having none. In Bombay, around the same time, directorial talent was even more scarce: one person, for instance, was a director of 65 industrial concerns, another of 42, a third of 35, two others of 29 each, and another of 26.

The Companies Act, 1956 limited the number of directorships held by an individual to 20 excluding those held in non-profit associations and those private companies which were neither holding companies nor subsidiaries of public companies. A study of the directors of 117 companies with a paid-up share capital of Rs. 50 lakhs and above registered in the western region in 1956-57 showed that these companies had 917 directorships held by 546 persons who, on an all-India basis, held 4,174 directorships in 1,905 companies, giving an average of about eight directorships per person. Of these 546 directors, 113 held one directorship each, 294 had between 2 and 10 directorships, 95 had between 11 and 20, and 44 had 21 or more; the last mentioned had 1,099 directorships between themselves.

The occupations of directors were defined rather vaguely in the relevant documents. The predominant majority, 441 out of 546, declared business as their occupation, and 33 were accountants or lawyers. Only 23 were specialists or technicians, and 49 were executives. Most of the directors were, in other words, businessmen-at-large.

Information regarding the age of directors was available for 505 out of 546. Of these, 36 were up to 30 years old, 142 were between 31 and 45, 172 were between 46 and 55, and 92 between 56 and 65. The remaining 63 were above 65 and their re-appointment in public companies required under the Companies Act, 1956 a special resolution by three-fourths majority of the share-holders.

Of the 117 companies studied, 43 had both Indian and foreign directors. The distribution of directors by nationality in these companies was as follows:

TABLE 23: **Distribution of directors by nationality in 1957**

	No. of companies	No. of Indian directors	No. of foreign directors	Ratio of Indian to foreign
Companies with mainly foreign directors	10	10	60	1:6
Companies with equal number of Indian and foreign directors	4	15	15	1:1
Companies with mainly Indian directors	29	201	58	3:1
Total	43	226	133	2:1

Companies Act, 1956

A large number of flagrant abuses in the promotion, management and financing of companies came to light in the late forties and early fifties. The abuses included cornering of shares of some leading companies listed at stock exchange with a view to dislodging their managements, fraudulent promotions, trafficking in managing agency rights, large-scale inter-company loans and investments to drain away the funds of widely owned prosperous companies into enterprises closely owned by controlling interests, widespread use of dummy shareholders and directors, oppression of minority shareholders and frauds upon creditors and tax authorities. The Company Law (Bhabha) Committee was appointed in 1951 to draft a new and consolidated Company Law. The Companies Act, 1956 was based largely upon the recommendations of the Bhabha Committee. A department was set up within the Central Government to administer the Companies Act which had been administered till then by part-time officials in states. The Act required public companies and their subsidiaries to obtain prior government approval of the appointment and remuneration of managerial personnel and their relatives and associates, inter-company investments, changes in the constitution of the managerial firms, etc. The government was given the power to abolish the system in notified industries or businesses and government companies were not to appoint managing agents after August 1960. Four categories of managerial personnel were recognised and defined for the first time: managing agents, secretaries and treasurers, managing director and manager.[25] All the four categories were specifically subject to the superintendence, control and direction of directors. The first two could be companies, firms or individuals but the latter two had to be individuals; all had to be appointed by the company in a general meeting or hold office by virtue of the company's memorandum and articles. A director having any powers of management was deemed a to be managing director. The maximum remuneration to managing agents was fixed at 10 per cent of profits after depreciation. The maximum for secretaries and treasurers was 7.5 per cent and for managing directors and managers 5 per cent. Managerial personnel (and their partners or members if any) was not permitted to hold any other office of profit under the company. The period of appointment was five years at a time for managing directors, but up to a maximum of 10 years for managing agents. No company could have more than one category of managerial personnel.

The Act tightened up the conditions of issue of prospectus, required greater disclosure of accounts and interests of managerial personnel (which term does not include other officers of the company), abolished the issue or continuance of shares with disproportionate voting power, and restrained fraudulent persons from managing companies. No person could be a director of more than 20 public companies; managing agents (including managing agents under the same control) could manage not more than 10 companies but there was no restriction on the employment of former managing agents as secretaries and treasurers who could manage any number of companies; managing directors and managers could manage not more than two companies each. Important decisions required shareholders' approval through special resolutions, which had to be passed by a three-fourths majority.

Amendments between 1960 and 1965 tightened up or introduced provisions relating to inter-company investments, private companies in which 25 per cent or more of share capital was held by public companies, audit and cost audit, powers of investigation by the government, appointment of sole selling agents, and preventing undesirable persons from exercising their voting power as shareholders. A Public Trustee was appointed to take over the voting power of large trusts. The government had the power to nominate two directors to protect minority interests and/or in the public interest.

A study carried out by the Company Law Administration in 1962-63 revealed that the nature of services rendered by managing agents to companies managed by them varied very widely. While some managing agents provided guidance on policy matters and the benefit of common expert services to their managed companies by employing whole-time paid directors and senior technical personnel, others gave only the benefit of their personal advice and guidance to the managed companies. In some cases the cost of the common expert services was borne by the managing agents, while in others the entire cost of the services was distributed over companies benefiting from them. The study also disclosed that it was difficult to find any reasonable common measure of service rendered by all or most of the managing agency houses in India. The Department also felt that it was not easy to distinguish between purely managerial and executive services. In the light of the results of the study, the Department came to the conclusion that, by and large, an illustrative list of services which could ordinarily be regarded as falling within the scope of the direct responsibility of the managing agents would include:

a. overall supervision and control of the various operations subject to the general policy laid down by the Board of the managed company;

b. co-ordination and integration of the departmental or divisional activities;
c. dissemination of useful information;
d. advice and guidance, regarding sale of the company's products;
e. undertaking of research;
f. purchase of raw materials; import of capital goods and replacement of personnel; and
g. planning and development, etc.

Apart from the services enumerated above, the managing agents were also expected to render promotional and financial services and to maintain a central organisation for providing legal, accounting, taxation, technical, secretarial and other such administrative and routine services. The expenditure incurred by them for rendering non-managerial services could be reimbursed to the extent permissible under the law.

In January 1965, the government, as required by Section 324 of the Companies Act, 1956, appointed a committee of five senior officials to enquire into and report on the continuance of the managing agency system in five established industries—cement, cotton, paper, sugar and jute—and in any other industry or business as may be deemed fit.

In the meantime, the government had been exercising its administrative discretion to weed out managing agents in several cases. Between 1 April, 1964, and 28 February, 1965, the government renewed the appointment of managing agents in 33 companies and refused permission to 40.

Statistical data on the significance of the managing agency system became available from the mid-fifties. In 1954-55, there were 3,944 managing agents, of which 2,522 were unincorporated firms, 1,238 private companies and 184 public companies. These managing agents, managed in all 5,055 companies, out of the total of 28,568 companies (excluding banking, insurance and government companies) in that year. The 5,055 managed companies accounted for 54 per cent of the total share capital of 28,568 companies. Out of 3,944 managing agents, 3,526 managed only one company each and 250 managed two companies each. About 93 per cent of the managing agents thus managed two companies or less. Only 17 managing agents managed 10 or more companies each.

In 1962-63, the number of managing agents came down to 1,044, of which 548 were unincorporated firms, 402 were private companies and 94 were public companies. The 1,044 managing agents managed 1,440 companies, out of a total of 24,598 companies (excluding banking, insurance and government companies) in that year. Out of 1,044 managing agents in 1962-63, 899 managed one company each and 67 two each. About 93 per cent of the managing agents thus managed two companies or less. Only 7 managing agents managed 10 companies each, which excludes others which they managed as secretaries and treasurers.

In 1954-55, the system was of predominant importance in plantations, coal, grains and pulses, vegetable oil, sugar, textiles, iron and steel, transport equipment, cement, clay and glass, paper, power and transport. Its importance was relatively nominal in services and in two industries, tobacco and rubber, which were mainly under the control of international combines. By 1960-61, when all old managing agreements expired, the importance of the system in the aggregate was greatly reduced by the formation of government companies, transmutation of erstwhile managing agents into secretaries and treasurers, greater frequency of subsidiaries, and flotation of new companies with other forms of management. In that year, managing agents continued nevertheless to be of predominant importance in plantations (in tea, subsidiaries and director-managed companies became more significant), vegetable oil and dairy products, sugar, textiles, cement, power and basic iron and steel.

The institution of secretaries and treasurers was recognised for the first time in the Companies Act, 1956. There was no reference to it in the report of the Bhabha Committee. The intention of the then Finance Minister, Shri C.D. Deshmukh, in encouraging the adoption of this system was, among other things, to smoothen the transition from managing agency to other forms of management and to enable those managing agents who managed more than 10 companies to retain the management of the excess number. Under the Act, secretaries and treasurers had practically the same powers as managing agents, except that they had no right to nominate directors and their maximum remuneration was 7.5 per cent of the profits.

TABLE 24: **Companies managed by managing agents—Industrywise**

(Paid-up capital in Rs. crores)

	1954-55					1960-61				
	Total no. of companies	Total paid-up capital	No. of companies managed by managing agents	Paid-up capital	(4) as % of (2)	Total no. of companies	Total paid-up capital	No. of companies managed by managing agents	Paid-up capital	(9) as % of (7)
	1	2	3	4	5	6	7	8	9	10
Industry										
1. Agriculture (excl. plantations)	854	4.43	190	1.29	29.1	290	2.49	7	0.23	9.2
2. Tea plantations	591	27.86	266	16.09	57.7	583	32.30	130	12.34	38.2
3. Other plantations	234	7.90	75	4.09	51.8	129	8.14	39	4.27	52.5
4. Coal mining	495	22.73	204	18.31	80.6	436	93.42	62	9.93	10.6
5. Other mining	421	14.55	90	5.86	40.3	338	14.95	16	5.21	34.8
6. Grains and pulses	263	5.11	52	3.04	59.4	230	6.09	15	1.21	19.9
7. Vegetable oil and dairy products	436	15.02	139	7.83	52.2	361	13.19	24	11.31	85.7
8. Sugar	216	30.23	108	22.84	75.5	203	44.08	62	28.21	64.0
9. Tobacco	68	19.24	12	1.77	9.2	58	19.73	2	1.41	7.1
10. Textiles	1678	184.52	724	147.00	79.7	1012	212.36	313	122.67	57.8
11. Beverages	328	9.01	84	2.85	31.6	128	4.79	7	0.79	16.5
12. Leather	178	3.61	45	1.12	32.0	148	3.96	11	9.87	22.0
13. Basic ferrous metal	318	34.22	85	29.97	87.6	505	379.15	23	57.91	15.3
14. Transport equipment	435	35.60	81	18.77	54.5	423	49.77	22	21.09	42.4

TABLE 24 (*Contd.*)

	1	2	3	4	5	6	7	8	9	10
15. Electrical engineering	400	18.18	93	6.30	34.6	61	2.25	4	1.03	45.8
16. Machinery and workshops	646	26.67	148	12.50	46.9	804	60.89	54	14.25	23.7
17. Metal products	507	16.25	91	5.71	35.1	585	31.20	30	6.25	20.0
18. Chemicals and pharma centicals	1858	70.44	495	21.49	35.6	1145	99.22	62	16.27	16.4
19. Perfumes and toiletry	—	—	—	—	—	76	0.74	4	0.29	39.2
20. Paint and varnish	—	—	—	—	—	137	3.65	—	0.62	17.0
21. Matches	—	—	—	—	—	31	3.38	3	0.33	9.8
22. Cement	30	23.98	13	21.23	88.6	33	41.52	12	34.01	81.9
23. Clay and glass	440	12.38	126	7.40	59.8	400	13.30	30	4.60	34.9
24. Rubber	90	4.37	22	1.07	24.4	113	10.48	10	3.56	34.0
25. Paper and stationery	201	15.98	60	30.53	79.6	247	33.99	30	15.89	46.7
26. Power	354	34.48	209	30.53	88.6	257	39.19	85	33.59	85.7
27. Other manufactures	2174	19.35	368	4.51	23.3	1478	46.02	35	2.14	4.7
28. Transport	1550	42.15	120	28.27	67.1	1464	59.90	30	8.43	15.9
29. Commerce, finance, storage and real estates	13564	291.94	799	51.32	17.6	8347	238.25	87	6.86	2.9
30. Other services	2457	18.79	443	5.75	30.6	1142	14.16	29	1.76	12.4
Total:	29625	970.82	5055	465.44	47.9	21194	1574.76	1234	420.37	26.7

Source: 1954-55: Nigam: *Managing Agencies in India (First Round)*, 1957.
1960-61: *Company News and Notes*, 16 December. 1964.

Before the expiry of all old managing agency agreements on the notified date, namely, 15 August, 1960, there were only 9 companies with a paid-up capital of Rs. 1.6 crores which were managed by secretaries and treasurers. As on 16 August, 1960, 179 companies were managed by 45 secretaries and treasurers.

After 1956, the number of new companies proposing the appointment of managing agents declined steeply. Between April 1956 and March 1963, 9,150 new companies were formed. Of these, 134 companies had managing agents, 15 had managers, 18 had secretaries and treasurers, and 2,681 had managing directors; the remaining 6,302 were managed by boards of directors without any statutory managerial personnel.

In 1964, nevertheless, the relative importance of the managing agency system in terms of the share capital of public non-government companies remained practically unassailed. More than one-half of the share capital of non-government public companies was in companies managed by managing agents and their close variant, secretaries and treasurers. If banks, insurance and other service companies, and subsidiaries of international combines, which by tradition did not or under the statute could not have managing agents were excluded, the proportion would have risen from one-half to about three-fourths or more. In spite of the decline in its popularity, the managing agency system was far from dead or dying. Managing directors and their variant, managers, were comparatively insignificant as a form of management.

It should be emphasised, at the same time, that remuneration to managing agents was tending to decline. It was 13.4 per cent of profits before tax (which is slightly different from the definition of profit for calculating the remuneration of managerial personnel in the Companies Act) in the aggregate Reserve Bank sample of public companies (including those not managed by managing agents) in 1950 and 4.9 per cent in 1962-63 (Table 25). The decline took place mostly in large-sized companies, that is, those having a paid-up capital of Rs. 50 lakhs and above (Table 26). Separate data for companies actually managed by managing agents are available only for 1955-59. The number of companies so managed declined during this period and remuneration as percentage of profits came down from 14.3 per cent in 1955 to 9.1 per cent in 1959 (Table 27). Shrinkage in remuneration was

TABLE 25: **Remuneration of managing agents—1950-63**

	No. of companies	Profits* (in Rs. crores)	Remuneration to managing agents (in Rs. crores)	(3) as % of (2)
1950	751	73.26	9.81	13.4
1951	751	96.93	12.42	12.8
1952	751	66.63	10.41	15.9
1953	751	76.05	10.36	13.6
1954	751	89.40	11.16	12.5
Total**		401.27	54.16	13.5
1955	749	98.60	14.13	14.3
	(30)	(2.36)	(57)	(24.2)
1956	736	102.17	11.49	11.2
	(27)	(3.35)	(.36)	(12.2)
1957	690	72.04	8.29	11.5
	(24)	(1.43)	(13)	(9.1)
1958	665	88.90	8.77	9.9
	(25)	(1.43)	(13)	(9.1)
1959	630	117.41	10.66	9.1
	(49)	(4.55)	(33)	(7.3)
Total***		479.12	53.34	11.1
		(13.12)	(1.52)	(11.6)
1960-61	1333	228.12	13.03	5.7
1961-62	1333	243.88	12.53	6.1
1962-63	1333	267.40	13.20	4.9
Total***		739.40	38.76	5.2

Source: Reserve Bank of India.

*Before managing agents' remuneration and taxation.

**Figures for 1950-54 and 1960-62 relate to all companies in the Reserve Bank sample, including those not managed by managing agents.

***Figures for 1955-59 relate exclusively to companies managed by managing agents.

Figures in parentheses are for companies managed by secretaries and treasurers. These data are not comparable with earlier and subsequent data.

most obvious in traditionally managing agency-managed industries like tea, coal, sugar and textiles.

TABLE 26: **Remuneration to managing agents by size of companies—1959-1963**

(As percentage of profits before tax and remuneration)

Paid-up capital (in Rs. lakhs)	1959 (1001)	1960 (1333)	1961-62 (1333)	1962-63 (1333)
5—10	7.4	7.5	7.5	7.5
10—25	8.2	7.2	7.4	7.7
25—50	7.0	7.7	6.8	6.5
50—100	8.3	6.9	6.5	6.1
Above 100	5.2	4.3	3.8	3.7
Total:	6.4	5.7	5.1	4.9

Source: Reserve Bank of India.
Note: Figures in parentheses give the number of companies.

Comparable data on remuneration to managing directors were not available. A sample study of 125 companies having this form of management in 1962 found (rather inconclusively since the sample was heterogeneous and included government and managing

TABLE 27 : **Remuneration to managing agents by industry—1955 and 1959**

Industry	1955		1959	
	No. of companies	% of profits	No. of companies	% of profits
1. Tea plantation	124	17.0	109	8.9
	(11)	(15.5)	(4)	(8.3)
2. Coal mining	46	20.2	36	11.4
			(5)	(10.3)
3. Sugar	61	14.6	47	10.2
	(1)	(4.7)	(4)	(29.2)
4. Cotton textiles	174	19.4	149	12.9
	(13)	(25.6)	(6)	(8.3)
5. Jute textiles	44	51.3	33	9.7
			(5)	(8.3)
6. Iron and steel	2	3.6	2	2.4
7. Transport equipment	8	11.7	5	10.5
			(1)	(—)
8. Electrical engineering	13	13.3	12	10.9
9. Other machinery	36	15.0	34	10.9
	(1)	(6.1)	(1)	(8.5)

TABLE 27 (*Contd.*)

10. Aluminium	2	9.7	2	10.2
11. Basic chemicals	8	12.3	7	11.5
	(1)	(–)	(1)	(–)
12. Pharmaceuticals	8	23.8	5	10.5
13. Matches	1	16.0	1	9.6
14. Other chemicals	12	12.8	11	9.8
			(1)	(–)
15. Cement	9	10.9	9	10.6
16. Pottery	10	17.7	2	10.5
17. Rubber	2	13.9	7	15.0
18. Paper	13	10.8	12	9.6
			(1)	(7.1)
19. Construction	4	13.6	4	9.6
20. Power	20	11.8	14	9.4
	(1)	(23.9)	(4)	(8.4)
21. Trading	10	14.1	6	10.3
22. Shipping	9	26.8	8	18.6
23. Hotels and restaurants	3	13.0	2	8.3
			(1)	(11.5)
Total (incl. others)	749	14.3	630	9.1
	(30)	(24.2)	(49)	(7.3)

Source: Reserve Bank of India.

Note : Data relate to only those companies, which were actually managed by managing agents. Profits are taken as before managing agency commission and taxation.
Figures in parentheses relate to secretaries and treasurers.

agency companies) that this system appeared somewhat expensive at lower levels of profits but quite economical at higher levels of profits.

REFERENCES

1. Sabyasachi Bhattacharya: "Laissez-faire in India", *Indian Economic and Social History Review*, January 1965.
2. Sunil Kumar Sen: *Studies in Industrial Policy and Development of India*. This work is the exclusive source used here for industrial policy on non-tariff matters till 1913.
3. Balakrishna: *Economic Development of Mysore*.
4. Sen: *op. cit.*, pp. 24-27.
5. For the text of the Rules, see Sen: *op. cit.*, Appendix A.

6. Clow: *The State and Industry*, 1928.
7. It is interesting that these deficiencies and the concerted measures required to overcome them were reiterated in the Planning Commission's Notes on Perspective of Development, 1960-61 to 1975-76, published in 1964.
8. Clow: *The State and Industry*. This is the main source for policy during the twenties.
9. *The Indian Tariff Problem*, p. 90.
10. *Op. cit.*, pp. 238-39.
11. Paish estimated total British investment in India and Ceylon in 1911 at £365 mn., of which £183 mn. was in government and municipal bonds, £141 mn. in railways and tramways, £24 mn. in plantations, £3 mn. each in mines, banks and oil, and £2.5 mn, in commerical and industrial enterprises. Quoted in Mitchell: *Industrialization of the Western Pacific*, p. 281.
12. K. Mukerji: *Levels o, Economic Activity and Public Expenditure in India*, pp. 89-90.
13. The capital at charge of Indian railways rose from Rs. 831 crores in 1928-29 to Rs. 880 crores in 1936-37 while working expenses were reduced during the period from Rs. 75 crores to Rs. 70 crores. (Indian Railways: *One Hundred Years*, 1853-1953).
14. *Report on Conditions and Prospects of United Kingdom Trade in India*, 1939. (Department of Overseas Trade, London.)
15. The principal sources of information for this period are: Prest: *War Economies of Primary Producing Countries*; Mitchell: *Industrialisation of the West Pacific*; *Report of the Second Fiscal Commission*, and Tyson: *India Arms for Victory*. Data on stores purchases from 1942 to 1945 appear to have been suppressed for security reasons.
16. *Report of the Second Fiscal Commission*, p. 1.
17. During the Third Plan, such joint ventures of the Centre with private interests were revived but almost wholly with foreign collaborations in oil refining and explosives.
18. In a statement laid before Parliament, it was implicitly admitted by the government that during the calendar years 1960 and 1961, at any rate, licensing policy had, in effect, operated to the advantage of large business groups. (*Company News and Notes*, 16 May 1963, p. 45.) This was inevitable to some extent because in the private sector these groups alone had the capacity to undertake large new projects, but such exclusive ability has been tending to get diluted of late.
19. Arthagnani's articles in *The Economic Times*, 10 July 1961, 27, 28 and 30 May 1965, are the principal source for this section.
20. Liquidations were a prominent feature from 1917-18 through 1930-31 during which period the paid-up capital of companies that went into liquidation exceeded in every year the paid-up capital of new companies registered. Lokanathan : *Industrial Organisation in*

India, p. 143.

21. For an account of the agency houses, see A. Tripathi: *Trade and Finance in the Bengal Presidency 1793-1833*.
22. S.D. Mehta: *The Indian Cotton Mill Industry, 1854-1954*, pp. 26-27.
23. Lokanathan: *Industrial Organisation in India*, pp. 41-43.
24. By Nigam and Joshi of Company Law Department.
25. The distinction between a statutory manager and other persons holding that designation or rank is that the former has powers of management as defined under the Companies Act and is or can be remunerated on the basis of a commission on profits.

GOVERNMENT OF INDIA RESOLUTION ON INDUSTRIAL POLICY, 6 APRIL, 1948

No. I (3)-44(13)/48.—The Government of India have given careful thought to the economic problems facing the country. The nation has now set itself to establish a social order where justice and equality of opportunity shall be secured to all the people. The immediate objective is to provide educational facilities and health services on a much wider scale, and to promote a rapid rise in the standard of living of the people by exploiting the latent resources of the country, increasing production and offering opportunities to all for employment in the service of the community. For this purpose, careful planning and integrated effort over the whole field of national activity are necessary; and the Government of India propose to establish a National Planning Commission to formulate programmes of development and to secure their execution. The present statement, however, confines itself to government's policy in the industrial field.

Any improvement in the economic conditions of the country postulates an increase in national wealth; a mere redistribution of existing wealth would make no essential difference to the people and would merely mean the distribution of poverty. A dynamic national policy must, therefore, be directed to a continuous increase in production by all possible means, side by side with measures to secure its equitable distribution. In the present state of the nation's economy, when the mass of the people are below the subsistence level, the emphasis should be on the expansion of production, both agricultural and industrial; and in particular on the production of capital equipment, of goods satisfying the basic needs of the people, and of commodities the export of which will increase earnings of foreign exchange.

The problem of state participation in Industry and the conditions in which private enterprise should be allowed to operate must be judged in this context. There can be no doubt that the state must play a progressively active role in the development of industries, but ability to achieve the main objectives should determine the immediate extent of state responsibility and the limits to private enterprise. Under present conditions, the mechanism and the resources of the state may not permit it to function forthwith in Industry as widely as may be desirable. The Government of India are taking steps to remedy the situation; in particular, they are considering steps to create a body of men trained in business methods and management. They feel, however, that for some time to come, the state could contribute more quickly to the increase of national wealth by expanding its present activities wherever it is already operating and by concentrating on new units of production in other fields, rather than on acquiring and running existing units. Meanwhile, private enterprise, properly directed and regulated, has a valuable role to play.

On these considerations the government have decided that the manufacture of arms and ammunition, the production and control of atomic energy, and the ownership and management of railway transport should be the exclusive monopoly of the Central Government. Further, in any emergency, the government would always have the power to take over any industry vital for national defence. In the case of the following industries, the State—which, in this context, includes Central, Provincial and State Governments and other Public Authorities like Municipal Corporations—will be exclusively responsible for the establishnent of new undertakings, except where, in the national interest, the state itself finds it necessary to secure the co-operation of private enterprise subject to such control and regulation as the Central Government may prescribe:

1. Coal (the Indian Coalfields Committee's proposals will be generally followed).
2. Iron and Steel.
3. Aircraft Manufacture.
4. Shipbuilding.
5. Manufacture of telephone, telegraph and wireless apparatus, excluding radio-receiving sets.
6. Mineral Oils.

While the inherent right of the State to acquire any existing industrial undertaking will always remain, and will be exercised whenever the public interest requires it, the government have decided to let existing undertakings in these fields develop for a period of 10 years, during which they will be allowed all facilities for efficient working and reasonable expansion. At the end of this period, the whole matter will be reviewed and a decision taken in the light of circumstances obtaining at the time. If it is decided that the state should acquire any unit, the fundamental rights guaranteed by the Constitution will be observed and compensation will be awarded on a fair and equitable basis.

Management of state enterprise will, as a rule, be through the medium of public corporations under the statutory control of the Central Government, who will assume such powers as may be necessary to ensure this.

The Government of India have recently promulgated a measure for the control by the state of the generation and distribution of electric power. This industry will continue to be regulated in terms of this measure.

The rest of the industrial field will normally be open to private enterprise, individual as well as co-operative. The state will also progressively participate in this field; nor will it hesitate to intervene whenever the progress of an industry under private enterprise is unsatisfactory. The Central Government have already embarked on enterprises like large river-valley developments, which are multi-purpose projects of great magnitude, involving extensive generation of hydro-electric power and irrigation on a vast scale, and are calculated in a comparatively short time to change the entire face of large areas in this country. Projects like the Damodar Valley Scheme, the Kosi Reservoir, the Hirakud Dam, etc., are in a class by themselves and can stand comparison with any of the major schemes in America or elsewhere. The Central Government have also undertaken the production of fertilizer on a very large scale and have in view other enterprises like the manufacture of essential drugs, and of synthetic oil from coal; many Provincial and State Governments are also proceeding on similar lines.

There are certain basic industries of importance, apart from those mentioned in paragraph 4, the planning and regulation of which by the Central Government is necessary in the national interest. The following industries whose location must be governed by economic factors of all-India import, or which require considerable investment or a high degree of technical skill, will be the subject of Central regulation and control:

1. Salt.
2. Automobiles and tractors.
3. Prime movers.
4. Electrical engineering.
5. Other heavy machinery.
6. Machine tools.
7. Heavy chemicals, fertilizers and pharmaceuticals and drugs.
8. Electro-chemical industries.
9. Non-ferrous metals.
10. Rubber manufactures.
11. Power and industrial alcohol.
12. Cotton and woollen textiles.
13. Cement.
14. Sugar.
15. Paper and newsprint.
16. Air and sea transport.
17. Minerals.
18. Industries related to defence.

The above list cannot obviously be of an exhaustive nature. The Government of India, while retaining the ultimate direction over this field of industry, will consult the Governments of the Provinces and States at all stages and fully associate them in the formulation and execution of plans. Besides these Governments, representatives of Industry and Labour will also be associated with the Central Government in the Industrial Advisory Council and other bodies which they propose to establish, as recommended by the Industries Conference.

Cottage and small-scale industries have a very important role in the national economy, offering as they do scope for individual, village or co-operative enterprise, and means for the rehabilitation of displaced persons. These industries are particularly suited for the better utilisation of local resources and for the achievement of local self-sufficiency in respect of certain types of essential consumer goods like food, cloth and agricultural implements.

The healthy expansion of cottage and small-scale industries depends upon a number of factors like the provision of raw materials, cheap power, technical advice, organised marketing of their produce, and, where necessary, safeguards against intensive competition by large-scale manufacture, as well as on the education of the worker in the use of the best available technique. Most of these fall in the Provincial sphere and are receiving the attention of the Governments of the Provinces and the States. The Resolution of the Industries Conference has requested the Central Government to investigate how far and in what manner these industries can be co-ordinated and integrated with large-scale industries. The Government of India accept this recommendation. It will be examined, for example, how the textile mill industry can be made complementary to, rather than competitive with the handloom industry, which is the country's largest and best organised cottage industry. In certain other lines of production, like agricultural implements, textile accessories, and parts of machine tools, it should be possible to produce components on a cottage industry scale and assemble these into their final product at a factory. It will also be investigated how far industries at present highly centralised could be decentralised with advantage.

The Resolution of the Industries Conference has recommended that the government should establish a Cottage Industries Board for the fostering of small-scale industries. The Government of India accept this recommendation and propose to create suitable machinery to implement it. A Cottage and Small-scale Industries Directorate will also be set up within the Directorate General of Industries and Supplies.

One of the main objectives will be to give a distinctly co-operative bias to this field of industry. During and before the last war, even a predominantly agricultural country like China showed what could be done in this respect, and her mobile industrial co-operative units were of outstanding assistance in her struggle against Japan. The present international situation is likely to lessen to a marked degree our chances of getting capital goods for large-scale industry, and the leeway must be made up by having recourse to small-size industrial co-operatives throughout the country.

The government, however, recognise that their objective, that is, securing the maximum increase in production, will not be realised merely by prescribing the respective spheres of the state and of private enterprise in Industry: it is equally essential to ensure the fullest co-operation between labour and management and the maintenance of stable and friendly relations between them. A Resolution on this subject was unanimously passed by the Industries Conference which was held in December last. Amongst other things, the Resolution states:

> . . .The system of remuneration to capital as well as labour must be so devised that, while in the interests of the consumer and the primary producers, excessive profits should be prevented by suitable methods of taxation and otherwise, both will share the product of their common effort, after making provision for payment of fair wages to labour, a fair return on capital employed in the industry and reasonable reserves for the maintenance and expansion of the undertaking.

The government accept this Resolution. They also consider that labour's share of the profits should be on a sliding scale normally varying with production. They propose, in addition to the overall regulation of industry by the state, to establish machinery for advising on fair wages, fair remuneration for capital, and conditions of labour. They will also take steps to associate labour in all matters concerning industrial production.

The machinery which the government propose to set up will function at different levels, central, regional and unit. At the Centre, there will be a Central Advisory Council, which will cover the entire field of industry, and will have under it Committees for each major industry. These Committees may be split up into sub-committees dealing with specific questions relating to the industry, for example, production, industrial relations, wage fixation, and distribution of profits. The regional machinery under the Provincial Governments will be Provincial Advisory Boards which, like the Central Advisory Council, will cover the entire field of industry within the province; they will have under them Provincial Committees for each major industry. The Provincial Committees may also be split up into various sub-committees dealing with specific questions relating to production, wage fixation and industrial relations. Below the Provincial Committees will come the Works Committees and the Production Committees attached to each major industrial establishment.

The Works Committees and the Production Committees will be bi-partite in character, consisting of representatives of employers and workers only, in equal numbers. All other committees will be tripartite, with representatives of the government, employers and workers.

The government hope that the machinery proposed will substantially reduce the volume of industrial disputes. In the case of unresolved conflicts, the government trust that management and labour will, in their own interests and in the larger interests of the country, agree to settle them through recognised channels of conciliation and arbitration, which will be provided by the government. The Industrial Relations machinery, both at the Centre and in the Provinces, is being strengthened, and permanent Industrial Tribunals are being established for dealing with major disputes.

The Government of India are also taking special steps to improve industrial housing as quickly as possible. A scheme for the construction of one million workers' houses in 10 years is under contemplation, and a Housing Board is being constituted for this purpose. The cost will be shared in suitable proportions between the government, employers and labour, the share of labour being recovered in the form of a reasonable rent.

In order to ensure quick decisions on the various matters arising out of the Industrial Truce Resolution, the government are appointing a special officer.

The Government of India agree with the view of the Industries Conference that, while it should be recognised that participation of foreign capital and enterprise, particularly as regards industrial technique and knowledge, will be of value to the rapid industrialisation of the country, it is necessary that the conditions under which they may participate in Indian industry should be carefully regulated in the national interest. Suitable legislation will be introduced for this purpose. Such legislation will provide for the scrutiny and approval by the Central Government of every individual case of participation of foreign capital and management in industry. It will provide that, as a rule, the major interest in ownership, and effective control, should always be in Indian hands; but power will be taken to deal with exceptional cases in a manner calculated to serve the national interest. In all cases, however, the training of suitable Indian personnel for the purpose of eventually replacing foreign experts will be insisted upon.

The Government of India are fully alive to their direct responsibility for the development of those industries which they have found necessary to reserve exclusively for state enterprise. They are equally ready to extend their assistance to private or co-operative enterprise in the rest of the industrial field and, in particular, by removing transport difficulties and by facilitating the import of essential raw materials to the maximum possible extent. The tariff policy of government will be designed to prevent unfair foreign competition and to promote the utilisation of India's resources without imposing unjustifiable burdens on the consumer. The system of taxation will be reviewed and readjusted where necessary to encourage saving and productive investment and to prevent undue concentration of wealth in a small section of the population.

The Government of India hope that this elucidation of their intentions on fundamental aspects of industrial policy will remove all misapprehensions, and they are confident that a joint and intensive effort will now be made by labour, capital and the general public, which will pave the way for the rapid industrialisation of the country.

STATEMENT MADE BY THE PRIME MINISTER IN THE CONSTITUENT ASSEMBLY OF INDIA (LEGISLATIVE) ON 6 APRIL, 1949

The policy as regards participation of foreign capital has already been announced in broad terms in the Government's resolution of the 6th April, 1948. The stress on the need to regulate, in the national interest, the scope and manner of foreign capital arose from past association of foreign capital and control with foreign domination of the economy of the country. But circumstances today are quite different. The object of our regulation should therefore be the utilisation of foreign capital in a manner most advantageous to the country. Indian capital needs to be supplemented by foreign capital not only because our national savings will not be enough for the rapid development of the country on the scale we wish, but also because in many cases scientific, technical and industrial knowledge and capital equipment can best be secured along with foreign capital.

In this context, foreign investors would no doubt wish to have some clear indication of our policy on certain matters, like the repatriation of capital, the remittance of profits, and the treatment of foreign enterprise vis-a-vis Indian enterprise. I propose to make the policy of the Government quite clear in this matter.

In the first place, I would like to state that the government would expect all undertakings, Indian or foreign, to conform to the general requirements of their industrial policy. As regards existing foreign interests, the government do not intend to place any restrictions or impose any conditions which are not applicable to similar Indian enterprise. The government would also so frame their policy as to enable further foreign capital to be invested in India on terms and conditions that are mutually advantageous.

Secondly, foreign interests would be permitted to earn profits, subject only to regulations common to all. We do not foresee any difficulty in continuing the existing facilities for remittance of profits, and, the Government have no intention to place any restriction on withdrawal of foreign capital investments, but remittance facilities would naturally depend on foreign exchange considerations. If, however, any foreign concerns come to be compulsorily acquired, the Government would provide reasonable facilities for the remittance of proceeds.

Thirdly, if and when foreign enterprises are compulsorily acquired, compensation will be paid on a fair and equitable basis as already announced in the Government's statement of policy.

The Government have stated before that, as a rule, the major interest in ownership and effective control of an undertaking should be in Indian hands. They have also stated that power will be taken to deal with exceptional cases in a manner calculated to serve the national interest. Obviously there can be no hard and fast rule in this matter. The Government will not object to foreign capital having control of a concern for a limited period, if it is found to be in the national interest and each individual case will be dealt with on its merits. In the matter of employment of personnel, the Government would not object to the employment of non-Indians in posts requiring technical skill and experience, when Indians of requisite qualifications are not available, but they attach vital importance to the training and employment of Indians even for such posts in the quickest possible manner.

I should like to add a few words about British interests in India which naturally form the largest part of foreign investments in India. Although it is the policy of the Government of India to encourage the growth of Indian industry and commerce (including such services like Banking, Shipping and Insurance to the best of their ability), there is and will still be considerable scope for the investment of British capital in India. These considerations will apply equally to other existing non-Indian interests. The Government of India have no desire to injure in any way British or other non-Indian interests in India and would gladly welcome their contribution in a constructive and co-operative role in the development of India's economy.

APPENDIX III

GOVERNMENT OF INDIA
INDUSTRIAL POLICY RESOLUTION
NEW DELHI, THE 30TH APRIL, 1956

No. 91/CF/48.—The Government of India set out in their Resolution dated the 6th April, 1948, the policy which they proposed to pursue in the industrial field. The Resolution emphasised the importance to the economy of securing a continuous increase in production and its equitable distribution, and pointed out that the state must play a progressively active role in the development of industries. It laid down that besides arms and ammunition, atomic energy and railway transport, which would be the monopoly of the Central Government, the state would be exclusively responsible for the establishment of new undertakings in six basic industries—except where, in the national interest, the state itself found it necessary to secure the co-operation of private enterprise. The rest of the industrial field was left open to private enterprise though it was made clear that the state would also progressively participate in this field.

2. Eight years have passed since this declaration on industrial policy. These eight years have witnessed many important changes and developments in India. The Constitution of India has been enacted, guaranteeing certain Fundamental Rights and enunciating Directive Principles of State Policy. Planning has proceeded on an organised basis, and the First Five Year Plan has recently been completed. Parliament has accepted the socialist pattern of society as the objective of social and economic policy. These important developments necessitate a fresh statement of industrial policy, more particularly as the Second Five Year Plan will soon be placed before the country. This policy must be governed by the principles laid down in the Constitution, the objective of socialism, and the experience gained during these years.

3. The Constitution of India, in its preamble, has declared that it aims at securing for all its citizens:

JUSTICE, social, economic and political;
LIBERTY of thought, expression, belief, faith and worship;
EQUALITY of status and of opportunity; and to promote among them all;
FRATERNITY assuring the dignity of the individual and the unity of the Nation.

In its Directive Principles of State Policy, it is stated that:

"The State shall strive to promote the welfare of the people by securing and protecting as effectively as it may a social order in which justice, social, economic and political, shall inform all the institutions of the national life."

Further that:

"The State shall, in particular, direct its policy towards securing:

a. that the citizens, men and women equally, have the right to an adequate means of livelihood;
b. that the ownership and control of the material resources of the community are so distributed as best to subserve the common good;
c. that the operation of the economic system does not result in the concentration of wealth and means of production to the common detriment;
d. that there is equal pay for equal work for both men and women;
e. that the health and strength of workers, men and women, and the tender age of children are not abused and that citizens are not forced by economic necessity to enter avocations unsuited to their age or strength;
f. that childhood and youth are protected against exploitation and against moral and material abandonment."

4. These basic and general principles were given a more precise direction when Parliament accepted in December 1954, the socialist pattern of society as the objective of social and economic policy. Industrial policy, as other policies, must therefore be governed by these principles and directions.

5. In order to realise this objective, it is essential to accelerate the rate of economic growth and to speed up industrialisation

and, in particular, to develop heavy industries and machine making industries, to expand the public sector, and to build up a large and growing co-operative sector. These provide the economic foundations for increasing opportunities for gainful employment and improving living standards and working conditions for the mass of the people. Equally, it is urgent, to reduce disparities in income and wealth which exist today, to prevent private monopolies and the concentration of economic power in different fields in the hands of small number of individuals. Accordingly, the state will progressively assume a predominant and direct responsibility for setting up new industrial undertakings and for developing transport facilities. It will also undertake state trading on an increasing scale. At the same time, as an agency for planned national development, in the context of the country's expanding economy, the private sector will have the opportunity to develop and expand. The principle of co-operation should be applied wherever possible and a steadily increasing proportion of the activities of the private sector developed along co-operative lines.

6. The adoption of the socialist pattern of society as the national objective, as well as the need for planned and rapid development, require that all industries of basic and strategic importance, or in the nature of public utility services, should be in the public sector. Other industries which are essential and require investment on a scale which only the state, in present circumstances, could provide, have also to be in the public sector. The State has therefore to assume direct responsibility for the future development of industries over a wider area. Nevertheless, there are limiting factors which make it necessary at this stage for the State to define the field in which it will undertake sole responsibility for further development, and to make a selection of industries in the development of which it will play a dominant role. After considering all aspects of the problem, in consultation with the Planning Commission, the Government of India have decided to classify industries into three categories, having regard to the part which the State would play in each of them. These categories will inevitably overlap to some extent and too great a rigidity might defeat the purpose in view. But the basic principles and objectives have always to be kept in view and the general directions hereafter referred to be followed. It should also be

remembered that it is always open to the State to undertake any type of industrial production.

7. In the first category will be industries the future development of which will be the exclusive responsibility of the state. The second category will consist of industries, which will be progressively State-owned and in which the State will therefore generally take the initiative in establishing new undertakings, but in which private enterprise will also be expected to supplement the effort of the State. The third category will include all the remaining industries, and their future development will, in general, be left to the initiative and enterprise of the private sector.

8. Industries in the first category have been listed in Schedule A of this Resolution. All new units in these industries, save where their establishment in the private sector has already been approved, will be set up only by the State. This does not preclude the expansion of the existing privately owned units, or the possibility of the State securing the co-operation of private enterprise in the establishment of new units when the national interests so require. Railways and air transport, arms and ammunition and atomic energy will, however, be developed as Central Government monopolies. Whenever co-operation with private enterprise is necessary, the State will ensure, either through majority participation in the capital or otherwise, that it has the requisite powers to guide the policy and control the operations of the undertaking.

9. Industries in the second category will be those listed in Schedule B. With a view to accelerating their future development, the State will increasingly establish new undertakings in these industries. At the same time private enterprise will also have the opportunity to develop in this field, either on its own or with State participation.

10. All the remaining industries will fall in the third category, and it is expected that their development will be undertaken ordinarily through the initiative and enterprise of the private sector, though it will be open to the State to start any industry even in this category. It will be the policy of the State to facilitate and encourage the development of these industries in the private sector, in accordance with the programmes formulated in successive Five Year Plans, by ensuring the development of transport, power and other services, and by appropriate fiscal and

other measures. The State will continue to foster institutions to provide financial aid to these industries, and special assistance will be given to enterprises organised on co-opertative lines for industrial and agricultural purposes. In suitable cases, the State may also grant financial assistance to the private sector. Such assistance, especially when the amount involved is substantial, will preferably be in the form of participation in equity capital, though it may also be in part in the form of debenture capital.

11. Industrial undertakings in the private sector have necessarily to fit into the framework of the social and economic policy of the State and will be subject to control and regulation in terms of the Industries (Development and Regulation) Act and other relevant legislation. The Government of India, however, recognise that it would, in general, be desirable to allow such undertakings to develop with as much freedom as possible, consistent with the targets and objectives of the national plan. When there exist in the same industry both privately and publicly owned units, it would continue to be the policy of the State to give fair and non-discriminatory treatment to both of them.

12. The division of industries into separate categories does not imply that they are being placed in watertight compartments. Inevitably, there will not only be an area of overlapping but also a great deal of dovetailing between industries in the private and public sectors. It will be open to the State to start any industry not included in Schedule A and Schedule B when the needs of planning so require or there are other important reasons for it. In appropriate cases, privately owned units may be permitted to produce an item falling within Schedule A for meeting their own requirements or as by-products. There will be ordinarily no bar to small privately owned units undertaking production, such as the making of launches and other light-craft, generation of power for local needs and small-scale mining. Further, heavy industries in the public sector may obtain some of their requirements of lighter components from the private sector, while the private sector in turn would rely for many of its needs on the public sector. The same principle would apply with even greater force to the relationship between large scale and small-scale industries.

13. The Government of India would, in this context, stress the role of cottage and village and small-scale industries in the

development of the national economy. In relation to some of the problems that need urgent solutions, they offer some distinct advantages. They provide immediate large-scale employment; they offer a method of ensuring a more equitable distribution of the national income and they facilitate an effective mobilisation of resources of capital and skill which might otherwise remain unutilised. Some of the problems that unplanned urbanisation tends to create will be avoided by the establishment of small centres of industrial production all over the country.

14. The state has been following a policy of supporting cottage and village and small-scale industries by restricting the volume of production in the large-scale sector, by differential taxation, or by direct subsidies. While such measures will continue to be taken, whenever necessary, the aim of the State policy will be to ensure that the decentralised sector acquires sufficient vitality to be self-supporting and its development is integrated with that of large-scale industry. The state will, therefore, concentrate on measures designed to improve the competitive strength of the small-scale producer. For this it is essential that the technique of production should be constantly improved and modernised, the pace of transformation being regulated so as to avoid, as far as possible, technological unemployment. Lack of technical and financial assistance, of suitable working accommodation and inadequacy of facilities for repair and maintenance are among the serious handicaps of small-scale producers. A start has been made with the establishment of industrial estates and rural community workshops to make good these deficiencies. The extension of rural electrification and the availability of power at prices which the workers can afford will also be of considerable help. Many of the activities relating to small-scale production will be greatly helped by the organisation of industrial co-operatives. Such co-operatives should be encouraged in every way and the State should give constant attention to the development of cottage and village and small-scale industry.

15. In order that industrialisation may benefit the economy of the country as a whole, it is important that disparities in levels of development between different regions should be progressively reduced. The lack of industries in different parts of the country is very often determined by factors such as the availability of the

necessary raw materials or other natural resources. A concentration of industries in certain areas has also been due to the ready availability of power, water supply and transport facilities which have been developed there. It is one of the aims of national planning to ensure that these facilities are steadily made available to areas which are at present lagging behind industrially or where there is greater need for providing opportunities for employment, provided the location is otherwise suitable. Only by securing a balanced and co-ordinated development of the industrial and the agricultural economy in each region, can the entire country attain higher standards of living.

16. This programme of industrial development will make large demands on the country's resources of technical and managerial personnel. To meet these rapidly growing needs for the expansion of the public sector and for the development of village and small-scale industries, proper managerial and technical cadres in the public services are being established. Steps are also being taken to meet shortages at supervisory levels, to organise apprenticeship schemes of training on a large scale both in public and in private enterprises, and to extend training facilities in business management in universities and other institutions.

17. It is necessary that proper amenities and incentives should be provided for all those engaged in industry. The living and working conditions of workers should be improved and their standard of efficiency raised. The maintenance of industrial peace is one of the prime requisites of industrial progress. In a socialist democracy labour is a partner in the common task of development and should participate in it with enthusiasm. Some laws governing industrial relations have been enacted and a broad common approach has developed with the growing recognition of the obligations of both management and labour. There should be joint consultation and workers and technicians should, wherever possible, be associated progressively in management. Enterprises in the public sector have to set an example in this respect.

18. With the growing participation of the State in industry and trade, the manner in which these activities should be conducted and managed assumes considerable importance. Speedy decisions and a willingness to assume responsibility are essential if these enterprises are to succeed. For this, wherever possible, there should be decentralisation of authority and their management

should be along business lines. It is to be expected that public enterprises will augment the revenues of the State and provide resources for further development in fresh fields. But such enterprises may sometimes incur losses. Public enterprises have to be judged by their total results and in their working they should have the largest possible measure of freedom.

19. The Industrial Policy Resolution of 1948 dealt with a number of other subjects which have since been covered by suitable legislation or by authoritative statements of policy. The division of responsibility between the Central Government and the State Governments in regard to industries has been set out in the Industries (Development and Regulation) Act. The Prime Minister, in his statement in Parliament on 6th April, 1949, has enunciated the policy of the state in regard to foreign capital. It is, therefore, not necessary to deal with these subjects in this resolution.

20. The Government of India trust that this restatement of their industrial policy will receive the support of all sections of the people and promote the rapid industrialisation of the country.

SCHEDULE A

1. Arms and ammunition and allied items of defence equipment.
2. Atomic energy.
3. Iron and steel.
4. Heavy castings and forgings of iron and steel.
5. Heavy plant and machinery required for iron and steel production, for mining, for machine tool manufacture and for such other basic industries as may be specified by the Central Government.
6. Heavy electrical plant including large hydraulic and steam turbines.
7. Coal and lignite.
8. Mineral oils.
9. Mining of iron ore, manganese ore, chrome ore, gypsum, sulphur, gold and diamond.
10. Mining and processing of copper, lead, zinc, tin, molybdenum and wolfram.
11. Minerals specified in the Schedule to the Atomic Energy (Control of Production and Use) Order, 1953.
12. Aircraft.
13. Air transport.
14. Railway transport.
15. Ship-building.
16. Telephones and telephone cables, telegraph and wireless apparatus (excluding radio receiving sets).
17. Generation and distribution of electricity.

SCHEDULE B

1. All other minerals except "minor minerals" as defined in Section 3 of the Minerals Concession Rules, 1949.
2. Aluminium and other non-ferrous metals not included in Schedule 'A'.
3. Machine tools.
4. Ferro-alloys and tool steels.

5. Basic and intermediate products required by chemical industries such as the manufacture of drugs, dyestuffs and plastics.
6. Antibiotics and other essential drugs.
7. Fertilizers.
8. Synthetic rubber.
9. Carbonisation of coal.
10. Chemical pulp.
11. Road transport.
12. Sea transport.

APPENDIX IV

LIST OF PROTECTED INDUSTRIES AS ON 31ST MARCH 1963

Sl. No.	Name of the industry	Date of grant of protection	Date of expiry of protection
1.	A.C.S.R. and A.C.C.	24-9-48	31-12-63
2.	Antimony	18-5-47	31-12-63
3.	Automobile spark plug	23-8-55	31-12-63
4.	Bicycles	18-4-47	31-12-63
5.	Cotton textile machinery	24-2-50	31-12-63
6.	Diesel fuel injection equipment	24-12-55	31-12-63
7.	Electric motors	24-9-48	31-12-63
8.	Engineers' steel files	24-12-55	31-12-63
9.	Piston assembly	24-12-55	31-12-63
10.	Power and distribution transformers	25-12-53	31-12-63
11.	Sericulture	1-5-34	31-12-63
12.	Aluminium	15-5-49	31-12-64
13.	Calcium carbide	30-11-56	31-12-64
14.	Caustic soda	23-8-55	31-12-64
15.	Dyestuffs	23-8-55	31-12-64
16.	Soda ash	24-4-50	31-12-54
17.	Titanium dioxide	26-12-53	31-12-64
18.	Ball bearings	16-3-53	31-12-65
19.	Non-ferrous metals	24-9-48	31-12-65
20.	Sheet glass	24-4-50	31-12-65
21.	Automobiles:		
	Items with revenue rates of duty	31-5-53	—
	Items with protective rates of duty	31-5-53	31-12-67
22.	Matches	1-9-28	Indefinitely

Source: *Eleventh Annual Report of the Tariff Commission for 1962-63*, p. 44.

APPENDIX V

MUKERJI'S INDEX OF INDUSTRIAL ACTIVITY 1900-01 to 1952-53

(1935=100)

Year	Index	Year	Index	Year	Index
1900-01	28	1918-19	76	1936-37	106
1901-02	32	1919-20	79	1937-38	112
1902-03	34	1920-21	90	1938-39	110
1903-04	36	1921-22	71	1939-40	125
1904-05	39	1922-23	72	1940-41	129
1905-06	36	1923-24	79	1941-42	139
1906-07	42	1924-25	86	1942-43	136
1907-08	45	1925-26	84	1943-44	151
1908-09	43	1926-27	84	1944-45	179
1909-10	38	1927-28	89	1945-46	166
1910-11	48	1928-29	91	1946-47	156
1911-12	53	1929-30	96	1947-48	155
1912-13	57	1930-31	87	1948-49	170
1913-14	59	1931-32	81	1949-50	175
1914-15	55	1932-33	81	1950-51	183
1915-16	59	1933-34	92	1951-52	198
1916-17	66	1934-35	94	1952-53	208
1917-18	69	1935-36	101		

Source: K. Mukerji: *Levels of Economic Activity and Public Expenditure in India*, p. 88. The compilation of the Index is explained by Mukerji on pp. 43-45.

BIBLIOGRAPHY

Anstey, Vera: *Economic Development of India* (4th ed.).

Arthagnani: *The Economic Times*, July 10, 1961; May 27, 28 and 30, 1965.

Balakrishna, R.: *Economic Development of Mysore.*

Bhattacharya, Sabyasachi: "Laissez-faire in India", *Indian Economic and Social History Review*, January 1965.

Clow, A.G.: *The State and Industry* (1928).

Companies Act 1956, Annual Reports on Working and Administration.

Company News and Notes (Government of India):

Dey, H.L.: *The Indian Tariff Problem.*

Five Year Plans: First, Second and Third.

Gopal, M.H.: *The Theory of Excess Profits Taxation.*

Government of India: Annual Reports of Various Ministries.

Hazari, R.K. (ed.): *Foreign Collaboration.*

Hazari, R.K.: "The Managing Agency System—A Case for its Abolition,": *The Economic Weekly* (Annual Number), February 1964.

Hazari, R.K.: *The Structure of the Corporate Private Sector.*

Hazari, R.K. and Mehta, S.D. : *Public International Development Financing in India* (Columbia University).

Indian Railways : *One Hundred Years—1853-1953.*

Kust, Matthew: *Foreign Enterprise in India.*

Lokanathan, P.S.: *Industrial Organisation in India.*

Mehta, S.D.: *The Indian Cotton Mill Industry 1854 to 1954.*

Mitchell, K.: *Industrialisation of the Western Pacific.*

Monthly Statistics of Production of Selected Industries.

Mukerji, K.: *Levels of Economic Activity and Public Expenditure in India.*

Nigam, Raj K.: *Managing Agencies in India* (*First Round*: *Basic Facts*).

Nigam, Raj K. and Chaudhuri, N.C.: *The Corporate Sector in India.*

Planning Commission (P.P. Division): *Notes on Perspective of Development* 1960-61 to 1975-76.

Prest, A.R.: *War Economies of Primary Producing Countries.*

Programmes of Industrial Development.: First, Second and Third Plans.

Report of the Central Banking Enquiry Committee (1931).

Report of the Company Law (Bhabha) Committee (1951).

Report of the Fiscal Commission, 1921-22.

Report of the Fiscal Commission, 1949-50.

Report of the Industrial Commission, 1916-17.

Report of the Powerloom Enquiry (Asoka Mehta) Committee, 1964.

Report of the (Raj) Committee on Steel Prices and Distribution.

Report of the (Swaminathan) Committee on Industrial Licensing.

Report of the (V.K.R.V. Rao) Committee on Utilisation of External Assistance (1964).

Report of the Taxation Enquiry Commission, 1953-1954.

Reserve Bank of India Bulletins.

Reserve Bank of India: *Survey of Foreign Liabilities and Assets* (1961).

"Resources for the Plan", *The Economic Weekly* (Special Number), July 1964.

Roy, Ajit: *Economic Planning in India.*

Sen, Sunil Kumar: *Studies in Industrial Policy and Development of India (1964).*

Tyson, G.: *India Arms for Victory.*

Vakil, C.N. and others: *Economic Consequences of Divided India.*

PART TWO

ECONOMIC POWER

Reproduced below (with some minor editorial changes) are chapters 1, 2, 8 and 9 from, *The Structure of the Corporate Private Sector—A Study of Concentration, Ownership and Control*, first published in 1966 (reprinted in 1967) by Asia Publishing House, Bombay.

The entire cost of this project, including the cost of publication of the first edition of this book, was borne by the Research Programmes Committee, Planning Commission, Government of India. The Director's services did not, however, carry any remuneration.

I am grateful to the Planning Commission for permission to reprint this work.

PREFACE

This work is based upon the proposition that the business group, not the individual joint stock company, is the unit of decision and, therefore, of economic power.

The study examines business groups individually and in the aggregate. It measures the proportion of corporate private assets controlled by twenty large and medium sized groups in 1951 and 1958. Each group is studied from the standpoint of its origin, composition, financial structure, pattern of ownership of share capital and investments by controlling interests. When aggregated, these data indicate the broad pattern of financing, ownership and control of the corporate private sector.

Data for the study were collected almost wholly from annual returns and other public documents which joint stock companies are required by statute to file with the Registrar of Companies. As compared with the general practice earlier, the Companies Act, 1956 requires greater disclosure of information by companies. Within its limited scope, this study has sought to make the maximum use of the information so disclosed.

Preliminary work on this project was begun in January 1958. The first results were published in an article "Inter-Corporate Investment: The Birla Group of Companies" in *The Economic Weekly*, November 8, 1958. Thereafter, the project received grants in aid up to January 1963 from the Research Programmes Committee of the Planning Commission. The first report, which dealt with five groups, was submitted to the Committee in October 1959. A summary of its findings and conclusions appeared in an article "Ownership and Control" in *The Economic Weekly*, November 26, December 3 and December 10, 1960. A second report, covering thirteen other groups, was completed in June 1961. At the request of the Mahalanobis Committee on Distribution of Income and Wealth, a third (interim) report, dealing with the change in concentration of economic power between 1951 and 1958, was made available at the end of December 1961. The research work was finally completed in January 1963 when an integrated report was submitted to the RPC, which approved it for publication in June 1963. The revised manuscript was sent to the press in early 1964.

Some of the findings and recommendations of this series of reports were found useful in amending the Companies Act and in framing policies for corporate regulation.

METHODS OF MEASUREMENT

Power is essentially a qualitative concept. It is not amenable to measurement in precise terms. Economic power can, however, be measured if it is interpreted to mean control over the disposition of the means of production. The power of control may be intangible but the area over which this control is exercised can be measured within certain limitations.

Various methods have been used in other studies to measure the concentration of economic power in the corporate private sector. These include (*a*) the share of the largest companies in industrial output; (*b*) the concentration of ownership of share capital; and (*c*) the concentration of management of companies. None of these methods really serves the purpose in view for reasons specified below.

(*a*) If one takes the largest companies in each industry (howsoever defined) and estimates their share in the assets and output of that industry, one is measuring concentration in particular industries, not the corporate private sector as a whole. This method does not give any idea of the total area of corporate activity which is controlled by the large business groups, which always have been and continue to be interested in many and diverse industries.

Alternatively, one could take, say, the 100 largest companies, the shares of which are listed at the stock exchanges, and measure their contribution to national industrial output. This procedure brings out the relative shares of the large and small units but it does not reveal the existence of common control and other link-ups between the largest companies *inter se* and between the largest and comparatively smaller companies.

(*b*) The concentration of the ownership of share capital can be measured either from income tax statistics or the distribution of shareholdings as recorded in the registers of shareholders. A study on these lines made by the Reserve Bank of India shows a high level of concentration.[1] This method is, nevertheless, unsatisfactory. Investment in shares constitutes a form of wealth. It does not, by itself, confer on the individual shareholder the power to control the disposition of resources. Joint stock enterprise is based on the separation of ownership and management. Most shareholders are interested only in dividends and capital gains. They are neither competent nor eager to participate in the management. At their annual meetings, the owners merely go through the ceremonial ritual of approving the decisions already made by the management on their behalf.

A study of the dispersion of shareholding cannot throw much light even on the distribution of wealth. Family affection and the universal desire to reduce tax burdens induce the prosperous shareholders to distribute the ownership of their shareholdings among the members of their families and/or to create various kinds of trusts for their benefit or for charitable purposes. This multiplication of owners brings about a statistically wider dispersion of wealth.[2]

(*c*) Management is a better measure of power than ownership but it does not constitute the source of power either. Management represents only delegation of authority or functions. The identification of managers does not uncover the persons who appoint and delegate authority or functions to them and to whom they remain responsible.

Top corporate management in India can be identified either with directors or managing agents or both. It is true that the formal power of management in each company is vested, under the Companies Act, in its board of directors. The board, however, is only a facade which masks the reality. The directors of a company are either nominated or invited to the board. They are not really elected. If they are nominees, one cannot treat them as independent persons; it is more pertinent to find out who has or could have nominated them.[3] If, on the other hand, the directors are invitees, it is obvious that they have no personal stake in the company, which may desire their presence on the board for reasons of prestige or for their individual competence and influence. A study of the concentration or interlocking of directorships can serve only a limited purpose, namely, of finding out the business influence of particular individuals or groups of individuals.

So far as the concentration of management by leading managing agents is concerned, the problem is discussed at some length in the following pages. Briefly, this method is unsatisfactory because (*i*) nearly every business group maintains a number of managing agencies, many of which are themselves owned by other corporate bodies, (*ii*) most companies are not managed by managing agents but have other forms of management, and (*iii*) managing agents are formally responsible to the board of directors and the shareholders, thereby leaving the source of power undefined again.

SHARE OF LEADING GROUPS

The unit of control and decision in the corporate private sector is the business group, not the individual joint stock company. The best way to measure the concentration of economic power in this sector, therefore, is to estimate the share of the leading groups and their minority interests in the physical assets of or the value added in the sector.

The choice between the two alternatives of measuring the physical assets in and value added by various groups of companies depends mainly upon convenience. In estimating the change in concentration between 1951 and 1958, the two reference years adopted in this study, both criteria would suffer from the limitation of the non-availability of data for private limited companies prior to 1956. The value added criterion is subject to the further limitation that trading and profit and loss accounts of private companies are not available even for 1958 nor, for that matter, are they available for any period since that year, except to government since 1961. This limitation is not very serious because most corporate assets and value added are in public limited companies.

This study uses the physical assets criterion. It is conceptually easier and subject to a lesser degree of error. Physical assets are the sum of fixed assets, net or gross of accumulated depreciation, and commodity inventory. These three items can be taken easily from company balance sheets. The computation of value added is a more involved process. It requires an analysis of the entire trading and profit and loss account, the detailed presentation of which varies widely and does not always give the necessary breakdown of items.

A study based upon balance sheets has a further advantage. It can supplement the physical asset criterion with other items like share capital, reserves and loans. Besides yielding many useful by-products, it permits an estimation of the concentration of physical assets in private companies also, and, therefore, in the entire corporate private sector, in years beginning with the fiscal year 1955-56.

This study also makes use of share capital data to measure concentration in the two reference years. Such data are available for public as well as private companies in both the reference years but they do not provide a satisfactory measure of concentration to the extent that asset formation during the period was financed from other sources like reserves, depreciation, loans and short-term liabilities, which acquired considerable significance between 1951 and 1958.

We turn now to the definition of the corporate group and its minority interests.

DEFINITION OF CORPORATE GROUP

A corporate group may be defined as consisting of units which are subject to the decision-making power of a common authority.

There may be a wide range of variation in the degree of control or influence which the decision-making authority exercises over the different units. This authority may delegate some functions to subordinates and specify their separate duties, but there should be no doubt about the source from which those who are placed in charge of the units or who are entrusted with various functions derive their authority.

The decisions made by this authority generally cover, besides prices and profits, investment, production, purchases and sales, employment and labour. The responses to particular economic and political developments are also derived from the same source and so are the measures to advance the interests of the group, and a host of other matters that crop up from time to time. The implementation of policies and the working out of their details may be delegated to subordinate authorities, but the extent of delegation and the allocation of functions at various levels are themselves matters of policy. The ultimate authority may make only the major investment decisions and rest content with periodical reports from units and functionaries. The group functions as a single organisation, nevertheless, though each of the corporate units under its control is a separate legal entity.

A company the decision making power of which is shared between two or more authorities can be said to be a 'majority', '50-50' or 'minority' company, as the case may be.

The above definition of the group explicitly provides for a frequent contingency in the business world: the need for or the expediency of entering into collaboration with other groups for the furtherence of common objectives, or a situation in which one group is burrowing its way into another. Collaboration may be needed in order to secure foreign exchange and know-how or to combine and face a market situation, or because one group may be in the process of acquiring another wholly or partially through acquisition of equity in its principal company or in one or more of its controlled companies. A group may also extend financial assistance to enterprises floated by other groups or independent businessmen.

These contingencies are illustrated in a number of joint enterprises. Tata joined the Associated Cement Companies in the 1930s, along with Killick, F. E. Dinshaw (now a Shapoorji company) and Khatau to face the depression in the cement market. After Independence, the Tata group gradually took over Forbes, Forbes & Campbell and acquired the minority interest in MacNeil & Barry. The need for foreign collaboration in the manufacture of a new product induced the group to form Indian Tube and Tata Fison in partnership with Stewart Lloyd and Fison, respectively. The Tata-controlled Investment Corporation of India has acquired a minority interest in a number of companies in the course of its investment banking operations.

The Mafatlal group has a large financial interest in several Ahmedabad mills, which are not under its management, as well as in Scindia Steam. Walchand has the largest single equity block in Scindia Steam, which is under the management of the Narottam Morarjee family. In the mid-forties, Walchand invited Kilachand and Khatau to join as partners in setting up and managing Premier Automobiles. Bangur recently took over Bengal Paper with the help of Dhanuka. Shapoorji has a minority interest in Associated Cement and the Nowrosjee Wadia group. Thapar's Greaves Cotton is a partner with foreign interests in several ventures.

The fanning out of group interests may (and actually does) take a variety of forms ranging from mere management or a sleeping partner's financial interest, on the one hand, to full participation in financial as well as managerial control, on the other. Martin Burn and Seshasayee manage several companies in which their equity interest is practically *nil*. Andrew Yule manages Bengal Nagpur Coal though the majority of the share capital of this company is held by Thapar. For some time, Andrew Yule continued to manage the three jute mill companies which were cornered by Dalmia Sahu Jain in the late forties, till it was voted out of the managing agency. On the other hand, Bangur, Mafatlal and Walchand have substantial financial interests in several concerns which are not under their management. Tata Steel holds the minority block in Bird Heilger's Bisra Stone Lime and Kumardhubi Fireclay without, it is believed, taking an active part in their management.

A partner is a partner, nevertheless, whether he is an active or a sleeping partner, and whether he is liked by the other partners or not.

Some groups, moreover, have clusters of companies which

function as *sub-groups* in the sense that the management of the clusters is more or less autonomous and the ownership of shares is not always closely inter-connected with the rest of the group, but their operations generally appear to form part of the group's activities. Somani, for instance, constitutes a sub-group within Bangur. The Birla group includes within its fold the Kanorias, Thiranis, Kotharis, Mantris, Newars, Kejriwals, Himatsingkas, Nevatias, Rajgarhias, Somanys, etc. (All persons with these surnames do not belong to the Birla group.) The phenomenon of sub-groups is akin to the former native states which enjoyed a kind of internal autonomy but their subjects were British protected subjects and, except in the technical sense, no different from British subjects.

The groups which contain sub-groups also generally include some companies owned and superficially controlled by nominees. Such persons are connected with these groups either as relatives or executives in some capacity, or others who may, among other things, derive some social security benefits as *quid pro quo* for lending their names to the property of the beneficial owners.

INNER AND OUTER CIRCLES

The group is, therefore, not always a closed circle. Rather, it may be compared to a series of concentric circles.

The innermost circle may be said to consist of the decision-making authority (whether it can be detected straightaway or not) which exercises control and influence in varying degrees, through investments made by it or on its behalf over the series of circles. More tangibly, it is made up of a hard core of bodies which are in general but not always, largely or wholly owned by, and are under the sole control of, the decision-making authority.

Also within the inner circle are other bodies (including companies in sub-groups and those superficially controlled by nominees) which are under the sole control of this authority but have varying degrees of public participation, which brings in share capital from external sources but leaves the power of control essentially intact in the hands of the decision-making authority.

There is, next, a circle formed by the majority companies in which one or more interests outside the group have a share in the control, but the majority vote is retained with the group.

Defined in terms of controlling power, the group proper ends at this stage. For the sake of convenience, sole control and majority companies may be collectively called the Inner Circle.

The influence of the group extends also to the outer circles, in which the group has 50-50 or minority participation or, merely looks after the management with only a nominal participation in share capital. These companies may be referred to in general as the Outer Circle, in which the group (or rather its decision-making authority) has a voice and a material influence, but not *the* controlling voice. The group's financial interest in them may range from 49 per cent to a negligible proportion. The two Circles together can be referred to as the Complex.

CONTROLLING INTEREST

Since the group has been defined as the area over which a decision-making authority holds sway, it is necessary to complement it with a definition of the controlling interest.

In the abstract, the controlling interest may be defined as that interest which has sufficient voting power, exercised directly or indirectly, to get formal sanction or approval from shareholders for decisions which it has always made for and on behalf of the company concerned. The controlling interest need not hold the majority of equity capital except, when the ownership of shares is very narrowly distributed or, when the group has entered into partnership with other groups and desires to retain the majority block of shares or, as a matter of deliberate policy.

In fact, if the shareholding is widely dispersed, even a fractional holding of equity can suffice to ensure control over the company. For instance, the Tatas seem to hold only about 5 per cent of the equity of Tata Steel, while the total controlling block (most of it held by a trust) in Indian Iron equity is only 17 per cent. The actual proportion of controlling blocks in these two leading companies might be larger, owing to the registration of some part of the controlling blocks in the names of banks.[5] Even if allowance is made for under-estimation, the fact, nevertheless, remains that the control of Tata and Martin Burn over Tata Steel and Indian Iron, respectively, is unquestioned though Birla has acquired substantial equity interest in Tata Steel, the

Life Insurance Corporation owns about 6 per cent of the equity of Tata Steel and more than 7 per cent of Indian Iron; Bangur also holds a substantial part of Indian Iron equity.

One need not, however, generalise too far on the basis of Tata Steel and Indian Iron since their controlling interests can, in the event of a contingency, count upon the support of the large body of uncommitted shareholders, as well as government backing.[6] Other groups are, in general, not so well placed, nor is the size of their companies so large that they must, of necessity, rely upon wide public participation for their requirements of share capital. Barring Seshasayee, whose holding in its companies is extremely small and whose group is kept together more by means of common management than control of equity, most controlling interests tend to have fairly substantial equity holdings in their companies. The fear that speculators might corner the equity of their companies has also led some groups, for example, Andrew Yule and Bird Heilger, to hold in recent years a larger equity than they might, perhaps, have held otherwise. Some controlling interests, moreover, do not like to dilute their holdings. In most Mafatlal, Shri Ram and Walchand companies, for example, the controlling interests generally have a very substantial equity holding though the shares of these companies are quite popular with investors.

A controlling interest must have sufficient voting power (it need not be any fixed percentage in the company, whether controlled singly or jointly) to get formal approval and/or sanction for its decisions, *and* must also have control, explicit or implied, over the management of the company.

The possession of voting power alone is not always sufficient to enable an interest to control a company or bring it within the Complex, unless more than 50 per cent (like, for example, the Birla holding in Hukumchand Jute, which is managed by Goenka) or a comparable proportion of its equity is held by or on behalf of a particular interest. In the case of companies like Bisra Stone Lime and Kumardhubi Fireclay of the Bird Heilger group, it can, for example, be safely assumed that no major investment and price decisions can be taken without the express consent of the minority partner, namely, Tata Steel, which absorbs a large part of their production, but does not interfere in their routine management.

CLASSIFICATION OF JOINT VENTURES

The distinction of sole control, majority, 50-50, minority and 'under management' companies from one another has to rely essentially on the application of arithmetic, tempered with an element of discrimination, to the list of shareholders. This distinction cannot be made mechanically in all cases on the basis of fixed percentages.

Generally, one can classify a *narrowly owned* company, whether public or private, as under sole control if the relevant controlling interest holds roughly about 80 per cent or more of its equity. In some cases, however, the remaining 20 per cent or an even smaller proportion may be held by a major group (for example, Tata, Birla, Bangur, or J.K.), the significance of whose participation cannot be ignored, in which case it is justifiable to label the company as 'majority' rather than 'sole control' for the first group and as a 'minority' company for the second group. Otherwise, it is generally not difficult to distinguish majority, 50-50 and minority companies on the basis of arithmetical ratios.

'Under management' companies form the fringe of the Outer Circle. These are companies in which the group concerned has no or practically no equity interest but retains the power of management through a managing agency agreement. For instance, in 1958, Seshasayee held the managing agency of three government companies in Kerala but had practically no equity interest in them. In the same year, Forbes Forbes & Campbell remained as the managing agent of Simplex Mills without holding any significant part of its equity, most of which was held by Damani who, later, took over the management as well. Among other companies, attention may be drawn to West Bokaro which is wholly owned by Tata Steel but was managed by Anderson Wright (a Kedia firm) till 1960, and Tinplate of India, which is jointly owned by Burmah Oil and Tata Steel but is managed by Shaw Wallace. West Bokaro and Tinplate would be 'under management' companies for Kedia and Shaw Wallace, respectively.

The real difficulty arises in the case of *widely owned* public companies. The large number of small investors in these companies can be safely ignored but how does one treat the holdings of the large investors? Among the large investors are banks, L.I.C., state governments and some private financiers.

A significant part of the share capital of many big public companies is registered in the names of banks, mainly in their capacity as pledgees, trustees, nominees and executors, not as beneficial owners. It is seldom possible in such cases to discern the identity of the actual shareholders. The holdings of banks, even if substantial, have, therefore, to be generally ignored.

The Life Insurance Corporation has acquired a dominant position in the private capital market and holds a significant part of the share capital of large companies. Much of this holding, however, is in the form of preference shares which do not, in general, carry voting rights. Besides, the L.I.C. explicitly refrains from intervention in the management of companies in which it is a large shareholder—though there have been a few exceptions to this rule in certain extraordinary cases. The L.I.C. holding can also, therefore, be ignored.

Several state governments have inherited large blocks of equity in certain companies from the former princely states. In addition, the central as well as the state governments have made fresh investments also. Such investments give the government an 'interest' in the companies concerned when they are quantitatively significant in relation to those of the controlling interest. Correspondingly, such investments can be treated as mere investments without conferring an 'interest' if they are insignificant in terms of total share capital or the investment by the controlling interest.

This brings us to the rather intricate and broader question of distinguishing, in general, a minority interest from a mere investment. Basically, the distinction rests upon the motives of the large investors and the formal or informal understanding between the controlling interest, on the one hand, and the large outside investors, on the other. Since these motives and understandings are a closed book to the disinterested observer, he has to fall back upon the facts, documented and other, available to him.

In general, the classification of a widely owned public company can be based upon the relative size of the total holdings of large investors alone, by applying roughly the same ratios in the case of narrowly owned companies. This method does not work always, as is evident from the examples of Tata Steel, Indian Iron and some Seshasayee and Kirloskar companies. The varying nature and degree of foreign collaboration also cause complications in some companies. In a few companies (for example, some companies under the management of Andrew Yule), a further difficulty is introduced by the retention of the managing agency by one group and acquisition of substantial equity by another. Such difficulties have to be resolved by deductive judgement.

To add another twist to the complications, how does one treat the fairly common case in which a company, that has been classified as a minority company in relation to a particular group, in turn, holds an interest in other companies?

What is, for instance, the position of the subsidiaries of Scindia Steam in relation to Walchand? Obviously, since Walchand has a minority interest in Scindia Steam, it can be deemed to have a minority interest in the subsidiaries of Scindia Steam as well. The problem becomes more complicated in the case of Scindia Steam's minority interests, for example, Hindustan Shipyard. Because of the well-known close association of the Walchand group with the shipyard, this company can also be classified as a Walchand minority company, though the minority interest is indirect, that is, of a second order.

On a comparable basis, the minority interest of A.C.C. in Asbestos Cement gives Shapoorji, Tata and Khatau also a joint minority interest in Asbestos Cement.

Similarly, Tata has a minority interest in all companies in the MacNeil & Barry-Kilburn group, except those companies in which these two managing agencies are mere managing agents and hold no equity. Jenson and Nicholson (a subsidiary of a British company) is, for example, treated in this study as a Tata minority company, since MacNeil & Barry is not only its managing agent but also holds nearly one-third of its equity. In 1951, MacNeil & Barry held 50 per cent of the equity of Kettlewell Bullen (later wholly acquired by Bangur); the companies controlled by Kettlewell Bullen are included in the Tata Outer Circle in 1951. On the other hand, the Tata Outer Circle in 1951 excludes Rameshwara Jute, which was merely managed by MacNeil & Barry without the latter having any stake in Rameshwara Jute equity. On the same ground, the Tata Outer Circle in 1951 excludes some companies which were merely managed by Forbes & Campbell, then a Tata minority company; such companies, for example, Goodlass Nerolac Paints, became 'under management' companies in 1958, by which year Forbes came fully under Tata control.

This chain-of-holdings-carrying-interest has to end somewhere for, beyond a point, the indirect investments cease to be meaningful in terms of some degree of control over the management of companies in which these investments are made. The final line of demarcation of the Complex in this study is drawn at minority companies of the second order, i.e., if A has a minority interest in B, which in turn has a minority interest in C, which in turn has an interest, majority or minority in D, etc. the Complex is terminated at C, and the subsequent links, if any, in the chain are disregarded.

For the sake of convenience, however, the Outer Circle data are presented as a whole without further distinctions of the extent and form of interest.[7] This does not affect the conclusions significantly, first, because the concentration of economic power is measured primarily from the size of the Inner Circles, and, second, because this problem of indirect minority interests is practically confined to the Tata, Walchand, Shapoorji and Khatau Complexes.

POSSIBILITY OF ERROR

The identification of groups and their ramified interests cannot, in other words, be carried out with the help only of mechanical formulae, and has to depend in part upon the analyst's assessment of deductive and qualitative information. The judgement of an outsider who cannot have access to inside facts is not infallible but the difficulty is inherent in the problem itself. The possibility of error does not justify the giving up of the attempt. The errors, if any, in this study would mainly relate to some small obscure companies, the assets of which are insignificant.

MANAGING AGENTS—A POLEMICAL DIGRESSION

It should be clear from the above that the definition of the corporate group adopted in this study is much wider than that in current use, which generally refers to a managing agency and the companies under its management. Whatever validity this definition of a group might have had in the past, it has ceased to be valid due to a number of reasons:

(a) Nearly every group maintains a number of managing agencies. Tata, for instance, has five companies which act as managing agents; it has, in addition, a minority interest in four other managing agencies. Birla has nine corporate managing agencies, two unincorporated managing agencies, and holds the minority block in two more. Mafatlal has four active managing agencies, one of which is an unincorporated firm, and has a 50-50 or minority interest in three more. Bangur has seven managing agency companies while J.K. has six. Khatau has a minority interest in four managing agencies, in addition to the one under sole control.

Besides, till 1956, when the new Companies Act put an end to this practice, some managing agents, for example, Scindia Steam, Premier Construction and Jiyajeerao Cotton were in turn managed by managing agents.

(b) Barring some notable exceptions, like Andrew Yule, Martin Burn, W. H. Brady, MacNeil & Barry, and Forbes Forbes & Campbell, the managing agency companies are no longer significant investors in the companies under their management. The analysis of shareholders' registers indicates that, except in some cases, the managing agent only manages the company under its management, and leaves investment for purposes of control and finance to other companies, trusts and individuals belonging to the same group.

Tata Industries and Tata Hydro-Electric Agencies, for instance, have no investments in the companies under their management. The incorporated managing agencies in the Mafatlal Complex have no investments whatever. The two leading Birla managing agencies, Birla Brothers and Cotton Agents, do have such investments but these are insignificant as a proportion both of the share capital of managed companies as well as of the total controlling block. This phenomenon is prominent in the Bangur, J.K., Shri Ram and Thapar groups also.

(c) In fact, a large proportion of managing agency companies are themselves owned by other corporate bodies and/or trusts. This is so in the case of all the managing agencies in the Tata and Andrew Yule Complexes, and most of those in the Birla,

Mafatlal, Bangur, J.K. and Thapar groups. It logically follows, therefore, the control over a group does not originate in the managing agency as such.

(d) In some cases, moreover, the managing agents are mere managers of companies which are owned and/or controlled by other interests.

For instance, many leading managing agencies in Calcutta manage foreign-owned or foreign-incorporated companies. Seshasayee managed three government companies till 1960. Birla managed one government company, Hyderabad Allwyn, before it ceased to be a government company. Thapar became managing agent of Ballarpur Paper, when it was still a government company.

Some managing agents have been appointed by the government under the Industries Development and Regulation Act in place of former managements, for example, J. K. Commercial for Muir Mills and for some time (after 1958) Karamchand Thapar & Brothers for Ajudhia Textiles.

There is also the example of the two subsidiaries of Tata Steel, which have managing agents outside the Tata Complex. West Bokaro is wholly owned by Tata Steel but had Anderson Wright (a Kedia firm) as its managing agent till 1960. Another subsidiary, Eagle Rolling Mills, still remains under the managing agency of Bird.

Tinplate of India, in which the bulk of equity is held by Burmah Oil and the rest of it by Tata Steel, is under the managing agency of Shaw Wallace, which does not hold any shares in the company.

Though Ramdutt Ramkissendas, a Goenka firm, is the managing agent of Hukumchand Jute, more than 50 per cent of the equity capital of the latter is held by or on behalf of the Birlas.

Andrew Yule continues as managing agent of several companies in which other groups have a majority or minority interest.

Andhra Cement, a Ramakrishna company, is nominally under the managing agency of Andhra Engineering, in which Ramakrishna has practically no interest.

(e) The predominance of the managing agency system has always been and is still practically confined to public industrial companies.[8] Most private and non-industrial companies never had managing agents, and do not have them now. Banking and insurance companies are not allowed under the law to have managing agents. It does not follow, however, that such companies do not or cannot form part of a group.

(f) The general criticism and statutory restrictions which the managing agency system has been subjected to in the last three decades has led in some cases to the resignation of managing agents and to floatation of new companies without managing agents. That certainly does not mean that the managing agency houses have stopped growing.

(g) Finally, there are the heterogeneous companies which are created and managed through nominees to avoid the burdens of taxation or restrictions imposed by the Companies Act or for providing gainful employment to relatives, friends and dependants. The legal ties may be tenuous or non-existent, but it is not impossible to find out the controlling interest behind them and, generally, there is no mistaking the hand of the group which uses these, often fictitious, companies as instruments for its own purposes.

FACADE AND REALITY

For the identification of a group and for tracing its wide ramifications, one has to go behind the managing agencies and/ or boards of directors, probe into the group's participation in share capital and trace its nominees and, thus, pierce through the elaborate facade which obscures the location of the decision-making powers which control corporate activity.

REFERENCES

1. *Reserve Bank of India, Bulletin,* May 1962, pp. 677-92.
2. A contrary trend is witnessed when shares belonging to a considerable number of persons are registered in the names of a few banks and executor and trustee companies.
3. This is all the more necessary because the Companies Act, 1956 restricts the number of directorships that an individual can hold in public companies, and because directorships can be easily distributed among family members, executives and professional consultants.

4. The problem of finding out who is a nominee and when is extremely difficult. It is further complicated by the fact that some nominees have their own trading interests, of which they are the beneficial owners. It is justifiable to presume, nevertheless, that, by and large, all the activities of nominees are subject to the *control* of their principals, whether the latter are benefical owners or not in the sense of getting dividends, etc.

   The status of a nominee, in other words, has a much wider connotation in this study as compared with common and legal usage. It includes individuals and what have been described above as sub-groups who may be the beneficial owners of their properties but who are under the protective umbrella of some higher authority. The treatment of certain individuals and sub-groups as nominees in this sense is not meant to cast aspersions or to attribute ulterior motives to them or their principals.
5. The actual proportion in Tata Steel is said to be about 11 per cent, a little more than one-half of which is registered in the names of banks.
6. Since 1951, a change in the managing agency of a company requires prior government approval.
7. Except in III where minority interests of the second order are distinguished from the first order.
8. See Raj K. Nigam: *Managing Agencies in India* (First Round : Basic Facts), Government of India, Department of Company Law Administration, 1958.
9. Most of the leading managing agents which managed more than 10 companies in 1960 have, after resigning the managing agency of the 'excess' companies (under Section 332 of the Companies Act, 1956), become their secretaries and treasurers. The latter system of management hardly differs from the managing agency system. The two are treated as identical in this study.

CHANGE IN CONCENTRATION

We now proceed to measure the change in the concentration of economic power between 1951 and 1958.

CHOICE OF AGGREGATES

Only two sets of aggregate data for the corporate private sector as a whole are available. One, published by the Company Law Administration,[1] gives the figures of paid up share capital of public and private companies registered in India at the end of fiscal years. The other is K.A. Antony's estimate of physical assets in non-financial private sector companies at the end of the fiscal years 1958-59 and 1951-52.[2]

According to the Company Law Administration, the share capital of non-government companies increased from Rs. 810 crores in 1951-52 to Rs. 1086 crores in 1958-59. In public companies, the share capital expanded from Rs. 219 crores to Rs. 321 crores (Table 1).

There are no official data on the aggregate physical assets of the corporate sector. One can, nevertheless, make an approximate estimate of these assets by boosting the data in the Reserve Bank studies of company finances.[3] Antony's estimate is derived from the Reserve Bank data for 750 public companies in 1951-52 and 1001 public companies in 1958-59, which accounted for two-thirds and three-fourths, respectively, of the share capital of all non-government non-financial public companies in those years.

The estimation of the assets of private limited companies is somewhat more difficult since the first Reserve Bank study of such companies relates to 1955-56. Antony assumes that the rate of growth of private limited companies during the period 1951 to 1956 was the same as that for public limited companies, and applies this growth rate backwards to find out the physical assets of private companies in 1951-52. His estimate for 1958-59 alone,

TABLE 1: **Share capital of companies registered in India**

(*Rs. crores*)

		1951-52	1958-59
A.	(*i*) All public companies	607	784
	(*ii*) Government public companies	16	19
	(*iii*) (i)–(*ii*)	591	765
B.	(*i*) All private companies	249	726
	(*ii*) Government private companies	30	405
	(*iii*) (*i*)–(*ii*)	219	321
C.	All non-government companies [A(*iii*)+B(*iii*)]	810	1086

Note: Official data on government companies (which were not distinguished from other companies till 1956) are not available for 1951-52. Dr. Nigam of the Company Law Department estimates the share capital of about 40 government companies in that year at Rs. 46 crores. Its breakdown into public and private companies has been computed on an approximate basis by finding out the share capital of government companies registered before 31 March, 1952, from the All-India Index of Companies.

however, is relevant for our purpose since we do not have any balance sheet data for private companies in 1951. This is derived from the Reserve Bank study of 333 private companies which account for 30 per cent of the share capital of this sector.

For both public and private companies, Antony has boosted the Reserve Bank data on the basis of share capital ratios. The use of such ratios may be questioned on the ground that it does not explicitly allow for variations in the structure of liabilities and assets during the period. Intensive work on the data in the Reserve Bank, however, has shown that there is a fairly close relationship between share capital and physical assets throughout the Reserve Bank sample of public companies.[4]

Antony's estimate of the capital stock of non-government companies (Table 2) excludes banking, insurance and purely financial companies. The data collected in this study indicate that the categories excluded by him account for only a little more than 2 per cent of the gross capital stock of all companies.

Both the sets of aggregate data relate to fiscal years, that is, April to March, while the data for this study were collected on a calendar year basis. This difference hardly affects comparability.

TABLE 2: **Physical assets of non-government companies**

(*Rs. crores*)

	Public		Private		All companies	
	1951-52	1958-59	1951-52	1958-59	1951-52	1958-56
(*a*) Net fixed assets	464	1200	91	153	555	1353
(*b*) Inventory	512	756	186	240	698	996
(*c*) Net capital stock ($a+b$)	976	1956	277	393	1253	2349
(*d*) Depreciation	420	719	63	136	483	855
(*e*) Gross capital stock ($c+d$)	1396	2675	340	529	1736	3204

On the whole, it would tend to under-estimate rather than magnify the level of concentration in the two calendar years, 1951 and 1958, since the calendar year lags behind the fiscal year.

CHOICE OF UNITS

We now come to the selection of units for the measurement of concentration of economic power. Since this study identifies groups as the realms of economic power in the corporate private sector, the selection of units boils down to the question of identifying the leading groups.

The 20 groups studied here have been selected on the basis of various criteria to yield a cross-section of the corporate private sector. Collectively, they are not the 20 largest in India, though even the smallest among them had a gross capital stock of more than Rs. 5 crores in 1958. The four top groups, Tata, Birla, Martin Burn and Dalmia Sahu Jain, are, nevertheless, certainly the four largest.

It is possible that a few groups of companies registered in India not included in this study might be larger than one or more of the other *nine fairly large* groups covered, namely, Andrew Yule, Bird Heilger, Bangur, J.K., Shri Ram, Thapar, Walchand, Mafatlal and Kasturbhai. This possibility does not affect the measurement of concentration on the basis of the four largest groups.

The power f control over the disposition of resources, in

terms of which economic power has been defined, ends at the boundaries of the group, that is, the Inner Circle, but it ramifications extend to the Outer Circle of 50-50 and minority interests as well. The measurement of concentration here, therefore, is based primarily upon the size of each Inner Circle, but the Complex is also brought in to give a more comprehensive idea of the importance of the group in th corporate private sector as a whole.

VALUATION OF PHYSICAL ASSETS

The period under reference covers only eight years but has recorded a phenomenal increase in corporate assets. T e book value of the gross capital stock of non-government public companies nearly doubled between 1951 and 1958. The increase remains substantial even if allowance is made for the fact that the prices of capital equipment, as indicated roughly by the U.K. index of export prices for capital goods, rose by about 30 per cent during the period.

The rise in the prices of capital equipment does affect the comparability of the *absolute* amounts of book values at the two points of time. It does not, however, affect the validity of the es imates of concentration expressed in the form of *ratios*, which indicate the share of the leading groups in aggregate asset , identically defined (that is, at book values) at these two point of time. The concentration ratios given below are, therefore, practically independent of price changes between 1951 and 1958.

The method followed here is the best under the circumstances, even though it may not satisfy the purist. Any adjustment of book values to allow for price changes would run into a number of conceptual and practical difficulties.

There are no comprehensive and detailed data on the age distribution of fixed assets. Even if these data were available, the variety of fixed assets, almost each portion of which possesses unique qualities, would defy scientific treatment.

There is, similarly, no national index of prices of capital equipment. Even if such a general index were made, it would not be of much use in adjusting the value of different kinds of equipment in various industries and various groups of companies.

In any event, no price adjustment is called for in the case of inventory valuation. Inventory, it may be emphasised, accounted for nearly one-third of aggregate gross capital stock in 1958, and more than two-fifths of it in 1951.

RANKING OF GROUPS

The 20 groups studied had an interest of one kind or other in 983 companies with a share capital of Rs. 236 crores in 1951 and 1073 companies with a share capital of Rs. 352 crores in 1958.[5] These companies accounted for 29.16 per cent and 32.44 per cent of the share capital of non-government companies in 1951 and 1958, respectively.

Since balance-sheet data are not available for private companies in 1951, the comparison of the size of physical assets in 1951 and 1958 has to be restricted to *public* companies.

The share capital, net fixed assets, net capital stock and gross capital stock of public companies are given in Table 3. On the basis of these data, the ranking of the 20 groups, that is, Inner Circles, in 1951 and 1958 was as in Table 4.

It is clear from the ranking that, regardless of the criterion adopted, Tata, Birla, Martin Burn and Dalmia Sahu Jain were the four largest groups in both the reference years. Leaving aside the slight freak of Ramakrishna net fixed assets in 1958, the next nine groups were Bird Heilger, Bangur, Andrew Yule, Shri Ram, Thapar, J.K., Kasturbhai, Mafatlal, and Walchand.

These rankings and the data are hardly affected by the stray cases of conversion of private companies into public companies, and *vice versa*, during the period. The only significant change of this nature took place in Mahindra, in which the principal company was converted from private to public in 1955, but this group was not among the 13 largest groups in either of the two years.

In Birla and Dalmia Sahu Jain, some companies were converted from public to private. In quantitative terms, these changes were significant only in the share capital of Dalmia Sahu Jain, but were insignificant in both in terms of physical assets.

The conversion of three J.K. companies from public to private between 1951 and 1958 was of little quantitative significance for the group, as well as in the aggregate.

TABLE 3: **Share capital and physical assets of 20 groups**

(Public companies only)

(*Rs. crores*)

Group	Circle	Share capital		Net fixed assets		Net capital stock		Gross capital stock	
		1951	1958	1951	1958	1951	1958	1951	1958
1. Andrew Yule	(a) Inner	10.38@	9.96	8.81	10.29	15.45	15.97	24.13	28.53
	(b) Outer	1.15	1.45	1.22	0.51	3.91	1.97	6.21	2.46
	(c) Complex	11.53	11.41	10.03	10.80	19.36	17.94	30.34	30.99
2. Bangur	(a) Inner	6.46	13.82	2.94	14.08	6.64	25.75	8.24	33.66
	(b) Outer	0.34	3.73	0.59	5.56	0.68	9.13	0.82	18.14
	(c) Complex	6.80	17.55	3.53	19.64	7.32	34.88	9.06	51.80
3. Bird Heilger	(a) Inner	10.36@	10.38	7.91	13.47	15.82	21.91	29.42	35.95
	(b) Outer	0.15	0.29	0.05	0.45	0.14	0.72	0.19	1.30
	(c) Complex	10.51	10.67	7.96	13.92	15.96	22.63	29.61	37.25
4. Birla	(a) Inner	36.75	61.26	23.28	61.15	49.34	107.41	62.55	143.44
	(b) Outer	0.99	3.01[1]	0.95	2.64[1]	2.07	5.51[1]	2.70	7.63
	(c) Complex	37.74	64.27	24.23	63.79	51.41	112.92	65.25	151.07
5. Dalmia Sahu Jain	(a) Inner	20.14	24.58	13.77	38.13	22.21	54.11	29.70	71.58
	(b) Outer	1.51	0.63	0.55	1.00	0.89	1.58	1.48	1.78
	(c) Complex	21.65	25.21	14.32	39.13	23.10	55.69	31.18	73.36
6. Indra Singh	(a) Inner	1.55	1.39	1.38	2.21	2.22	4.13	3.66	7.30
	(b) Outer	—	0.17	—	0.15	—	0.29	—	0.39
	(c) Complex	1.55	1.56	1.38	2.36	2.22	4.42	3.66	7.69
7. J.K.	(a) Inner	6.28	8.98	3.88	7.43	7.46	14.04	9.55	20.05
	(b) Outer	0.77	1.35	0.45	1.32	0.53	3.33	0.59	5.11
	(c) Complex	7.05	10.33	4.33	8.75	7.99	17.37	10.14	25.16

8. Kasturbhai	(a) Inner	2.73	4.97	2.95	7.43	7.41	13.05	10.04	19.79
	(b) Outer	0.05	0.03	—	0.02	—	0.02	—	0.02
	(c) Complex	2.78	5.00	2.95	7.45	7.41	13.07	10.04	19.81
9. Khatau	(a) Inner	0.70	0.90	0.43	0.93	2.31	2.65	3.69	5.05
	(b) Outer	13.87	21.96	11.01	25.80	18.85	48.24	26.05	63.33
	(c) Complex	14.57	22.86	11.44	26.73	21.16	50.89	29.74	68.38
10. Kirloskar	(a) Inner	0.81	1.30	0.64	1.38	1.62	3.86	2.26	5.35
	(b) Outer	0.01	0.01	neg.	0.01	0.01	0.01	0.01	0.01
	(c) Complex	0.82	1.31	0.64	1.39	1.63	3.87	2.27	5.36
11. Mafatlal	(a) Inner	3.07	3.89	2.75	4.92	6.93	9.35	11.02	16.68
	(b) Outer	1.95	14.27	1.23	26.54	4.06	32.15	5.75	43.88
	(c) Complex	5.02	18.16	3.98	31.46	10.99	41.50	16.77	60.01
12. Mahindra	(a) Inner	0.57	2.68	0.86	2.06	0.97	6.54	1.05	7.19
	(b) Outer	—	0.13	—	0.06	—	0.17	—	0.17
	(c) Complex	0.57	2.81	0.86	2.12	0.97	6.71	1.05	7.36
13. Martin Burn	(a) Inner	14.09	19.42	17.22	48.29	26.97	72.95	39.25	89.90
	(b) Outer	0.38	0.52	0.65	0.50	0.67	0.91	0.92	1.38
	(c) Complex	14.47	19.94	17.87	48.79	27.64	73.86	40.17	91.28
14. Ramakrishna	(a) Inner	0.98	1.69	0.97	5.19	2.01	7.92	2.34	9.27
	(b) Outer	0.10	0.30	0.02	0.60	0.11	0.93	0.11	1.17
	(c) Complex	1.08	1.99	0.99	5.79	2.12	8.85	2.45	10.44
15. Seshasayee	(a) Inner	1.42	2.41	1.79	2.48	2.32	4.01	2.83	6.36
	(b) Outer[1]	0.52	—	0.42	—	1.14	—	1.85	—
	(c) Complex	1.94	2.41	2.21	2.48	3.46	4.01	4.68	6.36
16. Shapoorji	(a) Inner	0.28	2.01	0.03	1.09	0.03	3.38	0.03	5.49
	(b) Outer	11.81	22.14	9.88	28.72	15.97	47.22	22.56	64.81
	(c) Complex	12.09	24.15	9.91	29.81	16.00	50.60	22.59	70.30

TABLE 3 (*Contd.*)

17. Shri Ram	(a) Inner	3.79	5.63	4.02	8.29	9.85	19.02	13.02	27.98
	(b) Outer	0.39	0.24	0.96	0.26	1.13	0.66	1.24	0.90
	(c) Complex	4.18	5.87	4.98	8.55	10.98	19.68	14.26	28.88
18. Tata	(a) Inner	34.88	65.60	39.24	161.60	64.95	220.47	105.23	287.22
	(b) Outer	20.38[1]	28.42	15.07	34.56	28.77[1]	58.86	46.37[1]	83.50
	(c) Complex	55.26	94.02	54.31	196.16	93.72	279.33	151.60	370.72
19. Thapar	(a) Inner	5.32	9.06	3.50	9.94	6.68	17.68	8.60	25.15
	(b) Outer	0.02[1]	—	0.02[1]	—	0.03[1]	—	0.03[1]	—
	(c) Complex	5.34	9.06	3.52	9.94	6.71	17.68	8.63	25.15
20. Walchand	(a) Inner	4.63	4.67	2.59	3.70	6.87	12.60	9.14	16.32
	(b) Outer	10.65[1]	13.78	15.42[1]	25.21	19.02[1]	32.71	25.45[1]	41.68
	(c) Complex	15.28	18.45	18.01	28.91	25.89	45.31	33.59	58.00
Total	(a) Inner	165.19	254.60	138.96	404.06	258.06	636.80	375.75	862.21
	(b) Outer	65.04	112.43	58.49	153.91	97.98	244.41	141.33	337.16
	(c) Complexes (gross)	230.23	367.03	197.45	557.97	356.04	881.21	517.08	1199.37
	Less Overlap	27.54	56.74	21.99	97.15	38.58	121.76	54.51	165.55
	(d) Complexes (net)	202.69	310.29	175.46	478.82	317.46	759.45	462.57	1033.82

1. Excluding government companies.

Note: Figures differ *slightly* from those in later chapters owing to (i) the exclusion of government companies, and (ii) the inclusion of the share capital of a few companies for which balance sheets were not available.

TABLE 4: **Ranking of 20 groups**
(Inner Circle public companies only)

Group	Share capital		Net fixed assets		Net capital stock		Gross capital stock	
	1951	1958	1951	1958	1951	1958	1951	1958
Tata	2	1	1	1	1	1	1	1
Birla	1	2	2	2	2	2	2	2
Martin Burn	4	4	4	3	3	3	3	3
Dalmia Sahu Jain	3	3	3	4	4	4	4	4
Bird Heilger	6	6	6	6	5	6	5	5
Bangur	7	5	10	5	13	5	13	6
Andrew Yule	5	7	5	7	6	9	6	7
Shri Ram	11	10	7	9	7	7	7	8
Thapar	9	9	9	8	12	8	12	9
J.K.	8	8	8	10	8	10	10	10
Kasturbhai	13	11	13	11	9	11	9	11
Mafatlal	12	13	11	13	10	13	8	12
Walchand	10	12	12	14	11	12	11	13
Ramakrishna	16	17	16	12	17	14	17	14
Indra Singh	14	18	15	16	16	16	15	15
Mahindra	19	14	17	17	19	15	19	16
Seshasayee	15	15	14	15	14	17	16	17
Shapoorji	20	16	20	19	20	19	20	18
Kirloskar	17	19	18	18	18	18	18	19
Khatau	18	20	19	20	15	20	14	20

INCREASE IN CONCENTRATION

There was a clear and significant increase in concentration of economic power in the corporate private sector between 1951 and 1958.

The change in concentration can be measured by estimating the share of the four top Inner Circles and Complexes in the share capital and gross capital stock of non-government companies at the beginning and the end of the period. The scope of this measurement can be enlarged by taking the 13 largest Inner Circles and Complexes in the sample.

Owing to the non-availability of balance-sheet data for private companies in 1951, the estimates below are given separately for public companies, and then to the extent possible, for public and private companies together.

The four top Inner Circles had 17.91 per cent of the *total share capital* of non-government ublic companies in 1951. This proportion rose to 22.34 per cent in 1958. The comparable ratio for their Complexes went up from 21.85 per cent to 26.60 per cent (Table 5).

The share of the four top Inner Circles in the *total gross capital stock* of non-government public companies went up from 16.95 to 22.14 per cent,[6] and of their Complexes from 20.44 to 25.66 per cent.

In 1958, the public companies in the two largest Complexes Tata and Birla, had nearly one-fifth of the gross capital stock of all non-government public companies.

If on takes public and private companies together, the share of the four top Inner Circles increased, as a proportion of the total share capital of all non-government companies, from 14.84 to 17.24 per cent. The comparable proportion for the four top Complexes rose from 18.16 to 20.76 per cent. The increase took place in spite of the reduction in the proportionate share o Dalmia Sahu Jain, caused by the liquidation of a large number of companies, and practically no change in the proportionate share of Martin Burn (Table 6)

The conclusion is not affected by the inclusion of another nine large groups in the measurement of concentration

The public companies in the thirteen largest groups accounted for 26.78 per cent of the share capital, and 25.78 per cent of the gross capital stock of all non-government public companies in 1951. The ratios increased to 31.67 per cent and 30 52 per cent, respectively, in 1958. Th. comparable proportions for the 13 Complexes[7] rose from 33.09 per cent and 31.69 per cent to 38.41 per cent and 36.35 per cent, respectively. This rise took place in spite of a contraction in the shares of Andrew Yule and Bird Heilger.

POLICY LIMITATION OF STUDY

A study of this nature cannot determine whether the increase in concentration that took place between 1951 and 1958,[8] and the absolute level of concentration attained in 1958, subserve the common good or are to the common detriment Nor can it determine whether the increase in concentration is attributable to

TABLE 5: Share of 20 groups in corporate private capital
(Public companies only)

(Percentages)

Group	Circle	Share capital		Net fixed assets		Net capital stock		Gross capital stock	
		1951	1958	1951	1958	1951	1958	1951	1958
All non-government public companies	(Rs. crores)	591	765	464	1200	976	1956	1396	2675
	%	(100.0)	(100.0)	(100.0)	(100.0)	(100.0)	(100.0)	(100.0)	(100.0)
1. Andrew Yule	Inner	1.76	1.30	1.90	0.86	1.58	0.82	1.73	1.07
	Complex	1.95	1.49	2.16	0.90	1.98	0.92	2.17	1.16
2. Bangur	Inner	1.09	1.81	0.63	1.17	0.68	1.32	0.60	1.26
	Complex	1.15	2.29	0.76	1.64	0.75	1.78	0.65	1.94
3. Bird Heilger	Inner	1.75	1.36	1.70	1.12	1.62	1.12	2.11	1.34
	Complex	1.78	1.39	1.72	1.16	1.64	1.16	2.12	1.39
4. Birla	Inner	6.22	8.01	5.02	5.10	5.06	5.49	4.48	5.36
	Complex	6.39	8.40	5.22	5.32	5.27	5.77	4.67	5.65
5. Dalmia Sahu Jain	Inner	3.41	3.21	2.97	3.18	2.28	2.77	2.12	2.68
	Complex	3.66	3.30	3.09	3.26	2.37	2.85	2.23	2.74
6. Indra Singh	Inner	0.26	0.18	0.30	0.18	0.23	0.21	0.26	0.27
	Complex	0.26	0.20	0.30	0.20	0.23	0.23	0.26	0.29
7. J.K.	Inner	1.06	1.17	0.84	0.62	0.76	0.72	0.68	0.75
	Complex	1.19	1.35	0.93	0.73	0.82	0.89	0.73	0.94

TABLE 5 (*Contd.*)

8. Kasturbhai	Inner	0.46	0.65	0.64	0.62	0.76	0.67	0.72	0.74
	Complex	0.47	0.65	0.64	0.62	0.76	0.67	0.72	0.74
9. Khatau	Inner	0.12	0.12	0.09	0.08	0.23	0.14	0.26	0.19
	Complex	2.47	2.99	2.47	2.23	2.17	2.60	2.13	2.56
10. Kirloskar	Inner	0.14	0.17	0.14	0.12	0.17	0.20	0.16	0.20
	Complex	0.14	0.17	0.14	0.12	0.17	0.20	0.16	0.20
11. Mafatlal	Inner	0.52	0.51	0.59	0.41	0.71	0.48	0.79	0.62
	Complex	0.85	2.37	0.86	2.62	1.13	2.12	1.20	2.24
12. Mahindra	Inner	0.10	0.35	0.18	0.17	0.10	0.33	0.08	0.27
	Complex	0.10	0.37	0.18	0.18	0.10	0.34	0.08	0.28
13. Martin Burn	Inner	2.38	2.54	3.71	4.02	2.76	3.72	2.81	3.36
	Complex	2.45	2.61	3.85	4.07	2.83	3.78	2.88	3.41
14. Ramakrishna	Inner	0.17	0.22	0.21	0.43	0.21	0.40	0.17	0.35
	Complex	0.18	0.26	0.21	0.48	0.22	0.45	0.18	0.39
15. Seshasayee	Inner	0.24	0.31	0.39	0.21	0.23	0.21	0.20	0.24
	Complex	0.33	0.31	0.48	0.21	0.35	0.21	0.34	0.24
16. Shapoorji	Inner	0.05	0.26	neg.	0.09	neg.	0.17	neg.	0.21
	Complex	2.05	3.16	2.14	2.48	1.64	2.59	1.62	2.63
17. Shri Ram	Inner	0.64	0.74	0.87	0.69	1.01	0.97	0.93	1.05
	Complex	0.71	0.77	1.07	0.71	1.12	1.01	1.02	1.08
18. Tata	Inner	5.90	8.58	8.46	13.47	6.65	11.27	7.54	10.74
	Complex	9.35	12.29	11.70	16.35	9.60	14.28	10.86	13.86
19. Thapar	Inner	0.90	1.18	0.75	0.83	0.68	0.90	0.62	0.94
	Complex	0.90	1.18	0.76	0.83	0.69	0.90	0.62	0.94

20. Walchand		**Inner Complex**	**0.78**	**0.61**	**0.56**	**0.31**	**0.70**	**0.64**	**0.65**	**0.61**
			2.59	**2.41**	**3.88**	**2.41**	**2.65**	**2.32**	**2.41**	**2.17**
Total:										
20 Groups		Inner Complexes (gross)	27.95	33.28	29.95	33.67	26.44	32.56	26.92	32.23
			38.97	47.96	42.56	46.50	36.48	45.05	37.05	44.85
	Less	Overlap	4.67	7.40	4.75	6.60	3.95	6.22	3.91	6.20
		Complexes (net)	34.30	40.56	37.81	39.90	32.53	38.83	33.14	38.65
13 Largest groups		Inner Complexes (gross)	26.78	31.67	28.64	32.40	25.25	30.89	25.78	30.52
			33.44	40.50	36.64	40.62	31.61	38.45	32.28	38.26
	Less	Overlap	0.35	2.09	0.33	2.49	0.44	1.79	0.59	1.91
		Complexes (net)	33.09	38.41	36.31	38.13	31.17	36.66	31.69	36.35

TABLE 6: **Share of 20 groups in corporate private capital**
(Public and private companies)

(*Rs. crores and percentages*)

Group	Circle	Share capital		Net fixed assets	Net capital stock	Gross capital stock
		1951	1958	1958	1958	1958
All non-government companies		810.00	1086.00	1353.00	2349.00	3204.00
%		(100.00)	(100.00)	(100.00)	(100.00)	(100.00)
1. Andrew Yule	Inner	13.34	10.92	10.71	16.60	29.21
	%	(1.65)	(1.00)	(0.79)	(0.71)	(0.91)
	Complex	14.64	12.37	11.22	18.57	31.67
	%	(1.81)	(1.14)	(0.83)	(0.79)	(0.99)
2. Bangur	Inner	7.91	15.57	14.48	26.54	34.53
	%	(0.98)	(1.43)	(1.07)	(1.13)	(1.08)
	Complex	8.67	19.69	20.50	36.13	53.13
	%	(1.07)	(1.81)	(1.52)	(1.54)	(1.66)
3. Bird Heilger	Inner	11.85	12.07	13.59	22.53	36.81
	%	(1.46)	(1.11)	(1.00)	(0.96)	(1.15)
	Complex	12.23	12.96	14.25	23.50	38.38
	%	(1.51)	(1.19)	(1.05)	(1.00)	(1.20)
4. Birla	Inner	39.07	65.45	63.76	112.87	149.91
	%	(4.82)	(6.03)	(4.71)	(4.81)	(4.68)
	Complex	40.10	68.53*	66.41*	118.49*	157.63*
	%	(4.95)	(6.31)	(4.91)	(5.04)	(4.92)

5. Dalmia Sahu Jain	Inner	23.71	27.67	38.63	55.11	72.84
	%	(2.93)	(2.55)	(2.86)	(2.35)	(2.27)
	Complex	25.29	28.51	39.81	57.48	75.67
	%	(3.12)	(2.63)	(2.94)	(2.45)	(2.36)
6. Indra Singh	Inner	1.94	1.80	2.39	4.41	7.77
	%	(0.24)	(0.17)	(0.18)	(0.19)	(0.24)
	Complex	1.94	1.97	2.54	4.70	8.16
	%	(0.24)	(0.18)	(0.19)	(0.20)	(0.25)
7. J.K.	Inner	7.76	10.05	9.06	16.80	23.93
	%	(0.96)	(0.93)	(0.67)	(0.72)	(0.75)
	Complex	9.13	11.80	10.90	21.32	30.71
	%	(1.13)	(1.09)	(0.81)	(0.91)	(0.96)
8. Kasturbhai	Inner	2.75	4.99	7.43	13.06	19.81
	%	(0.34)	(0.46)	(0.55)	(0.56)	(0.62)
	Complex	2.80	7.03	9.05	14.98	21.91
	%	(0.35)	(0.65)	(0.67)	(0.64)	(0.68)
9. Khatau	Inner	1.07	1.41	1.02	2.82	5.25
	%	(0.13)	(0.13)	(0.08)	(0.12)	(0.16)
	Complex	16.50	26.10	28.20	57.79	76.45
	%	(2.04)	(2.40)	(2.08)	(2.46)	(2.39)
10. Kirloskar	Inner	0.84	1.36	1.41	3.93	5.46
	%	(0.10)	(0.13)	(0.10)	(0.17)	(0.17)
	Complex	0.85	1.67	1.67	6.56	8.11
	%	(0.10)	(0.15)	(0.12)	(0.28)	(0.25)
11. Mafatlal	Inner	4.55	6.05	6.20	11.46	19.85
	%	(0.56)	(0.56)	(0.46)	(0.49)	(0.62)
	Complex	6.55	21.54	34.90	46.23	66.38
	%	(0.81)	(1.98)	(2.58)	(1.97)	(2.07)

TABLE 6 (*Contd.*)

12. Mahindra	Inner	0.80	2.83	2.13	6.74	7.44
	%	(0.10)	(0.26)	(0.16)	(0.29)	(0.23)
	Complex	0.80	3.17	2.20	7.72	8.43
	%	(0.10)	(0.29)	(0.16)	(0.33)	(0.26)
13. Martin Burn	Inner	14.50	19.42	48.29	72.95	89.90
	%	(1.79)	(1.79)	(3.57)	(3.11)	(2.81)
	Complex	14.88	20.05	48.81	74.38	91.87
	%	(1.84)	(1.85)	(3.61)	(3.17)	(2.87)
14. Ramakrishna	Inner	1.05	1.86	5.39	8.19	9.55
	%	(0.13)	(0.17)	(0.40)	(0.35)	(0.30)
	Complex	1.20	2.18	6.00	9.13	10.74
	%	(0.15)	(0.20)	(0.44)	(0.39)	(0.34)
15. Seshasayee	Inner	1.65	2.67	2.67	4.25	6.63
	%	(0.20)	(0.25)	(0.20)	(0.18)	(0.21)
	Complex*	2.49	2.67	2.67	4.25	6.63
	%	(0.31)	(0.25)	(0.20)	(0.18)	(0.21)
16. Shapoorji	Inner	1.17	2.91	2.50	11.18	13.51
	%	(0.14)	(0.27)	(0.18)	(0.48)	(0.42)
	Complex	13.60	27.60	32.47	62.19	83.06
	%	(1.68)	(2.54)	(2.40)	(2.65)	(2.59)
17. Shri Ram	Inner	4.29	6.21	8.50	19.82	28.79
	%	(0.53)	(0.57)	(0.63)	(0.84)	(0.90)
	Complex	4.68	6.45	8.76	20.49	29.69
	%	(0.58)	(0.59)	(0.65)	(0.87)	(0.93)
18. Tata	Inner	42.90	74.56	163.81	223.41	290.81
	%	(5.30)	(6.87)	(12.11)	(9.51)	(9.08)
	Complex	66.83*	108.23	201.13	292.93	388.72
	%	(8.25)	(9.97)	(14.87)	(12.47)	(12.13)

19. Thapar	Inner	6.04	10.81	10.47	19.60	27.25
	%	(0.75)	(1.00)	(0.77)	(0.83)	(0.85)
	Complex	6.63	12.08	11.67	22.37	30.74
	%	(0.82)	(1.11)	(0.86)	(0.95)	(0.96)
20. Walchand	Inner	4.82	4.93	3.73	12.63	16.37
	%	(0.60)	(0.45)	(0.28)	(0.54)	(0.51)
	Complex	15.76	19.89*	31.14*	48.39*	61.66*
	%	(1.95)	(1.83)	(2.30)	(2.06)	(1.90)
Total: 20 groups	Inner	192.01	283.54	416.17	664.90	895.62
	%	(23.70)	(26.11)	(30 76)	(28.31)	(27.95)
	Complexes (gross)	265.57	414.48	584.30	947.60	1279.74
	%	(32.79)	(38.17)	(43.19)	(40.34)	(39 94)
	Less overlap	29.38	62.21	83.26	133.74	179.68
	%	(3.63)	(5.73)	(6.15)	(5.69)	(5.52)
	Complexes (net)	236.19	352.27	501.04	813.86	1102.06
	%	(29.16)	(32.44)	(37.03)	(34.65)	(34.33)

TABLE 6 (*Contd.*)

13 Largest groups	Inner	183.49	268.70	398.66	623.38	840.01
	%	(22.65)	(24.74)	(29.46)	(26.54)	(26.22)
	Complexes (gross)	228.19	349.12	508.55	795.26	1078.16
	%	(28.17)	(32.15)	(37.59)	(33.86)	(33.65)
	Less overlap	2.30	17.17	32.02	38.02	54.71
	%	(0.28)	(1.58)	(2.37)	(1.62)	(1.71)
	Complexes (net)	225.89	331.95	476.53	757.24	1023.45
	%	(27.89)	(30.57)	(35.22)	(32.24)	(31.94)

*Excluding government companies.

planned development or has occurred in spite of the declared objectives of Plan policy.

The fact that concentration in the corporate private sector has increased during a period of planned development implies nevertheless, that government policies and their implementation had not till the end of 1958, at any rate, succeeded in bringing about a wider diffusion of economic power.

REFERENCES

1. *Vide* Annual Report on the Working and Administration of the Companies Act.
2. Antony's estimates for 1958-59 are given in 'Industrial Capital in India', included in Rao and others (eds.): *Papers on National Income*, Vol. II, Asia Publishing House, 1962.
3. Published occasionally in the *Reserve Bank of India Bulletin.*
4. See Sastry and Antony: 'Capital Formation in the Corporate Business Sector in India', in Rao and others (eds.): *Papers on National Income*, Vol I, Asia Publishing House, 1960, p. 163.
5. Figures exclude government companies in which some groups had an interest.
6. From 15.76 to 21.03 per cent, if the Birla group is reduced to its minimum and Sahu Jain alone is taken in place of Dalmia Sahu Jain. See *Appendix.*
7. Companies classified under more than one Complex are counted only once in the aggregate.
8. This study cannot throw any light on developments after 1958.

APPENDIX

Birla and Dalmia Sahu Jain Companies[1]

The purpose of this Appendix is to show that

(i) the conclusions above would stand even if only the companies acknowledged as 'their own' by the Birla and Sahu Jain groups are taken into account, and

(ii) to demonstrate, by working forward and backward from the shareholding data of acknowledged companies, that the number of Birla companies is larger than what the group acknowledges.

Birla Inner Circle

A list of acknowledged Birla companies was published in the Birla Centenary Souvenir brought out in early 1962. These companies are specified in List A. Excluding private companies, and companies in which the Birlas had no interest in either of the two relevant years, and companies registered or acquired after 1958, the data for these acknowledged companies and the comparable data in this study are as follows:

Birla Inner Circle public companies

	Share capital		Gross capital stock	
	1951	1958	1951	1958
(1) Acknowledged companies in List A (Rs. crores)	24.64	46.11	51.35	120.23
(2) Acknowledged companies as per cent of total non-government companies	(4.16)	(6.04)	(3.68)	(4.49)
(3) Birla companies as in Tables 3, 4 (Rs. crores)	36.75	61.26	62.55	143.44
(4) Birla companies as per cent of total non-government companies	(6.22)	(8.01)	(4.48)	(5.36)
(5) Difference between (3) and (1) (Rs. crores)	12.11	15.15	11.20	23.21
(6) Difference between (4) and (2) (per cent)	(2.06)	(1.97)	(0.80)	(0.87)

Even by its own reckoning, the relative importance of the Birla group in the corporate private sector has gone up significantly. The absolute differences between the ratios in lines 2 and 4 are not substantial under gross capital stock, and are narrowed down further below.

Dalmia Sahu Jain

It is claimed that the Dalmia Jain group was partitioned in 1948 between the three main partners, Ramakrishna Dalmia, Jaidayal Dalmia and Shanti Prasad Jain. Assuming that the data collected in this study are deceptive owing to holdings on blank transfers and/or because my interpretation of the data is wrong or uninformed, one can take instead what is commonly described as the Sahu Jain group.

The acknowledged companies in this group, controlled by Shanti Prasad Jain and his family, are specified in List K. The relevant data for public companies in this context are as follows:

Dalmia Sahu Jain Inner Circle public companies

	Share capital		Gross capital stock	
	1951	1958	1951	1958
(1) Acknowledged Sahu Jain companies in List K (Rs. crores)	7.78	15.77	16.69	51.95
(2) Acknowledged companies as % of non-government companies	(1.32)	(2.06)	(1.20)	(1.94)
(3) Dalmia Sahu Jain companies as in Table 3 (Rs. crores)	20.14	24.58	29.70	71.58
(4) Dalmia Sahu Jain companies as % of non-government companies	(3.41)	(3.21)	(2.12)	(2.68)
(5) Difference between (3) and (1) (Rs. crores)	12.36	8.81	13.01	19.63
(6) Difference between (4) and (2) (%)	(2.09)	(1.15)	(0.92)	(0.74)

It will be seen that the proportionate share of acknowledged Sahu Jain companies went up substantially during the period. Sahu Jain would be the fourth largest group in 1958 in terms of gross capital stock, even if the other sub-groups within the Dalmia Sahu Jain group were excluded.

Enlargement of list of Birla Inner Circle public companies

The difference between the amounts of gross capital stock for acknowledged Birla public companies and the figures given in Table 4 can be narrowed down considerably. The relevant difference comes to Rs. 11.20 crores in 1951 and Rs. 23.21 crores in 1958. Of these amounts, a difference of Rs. 7.37 crores and Rs. 13.48 crores, respectively, is made up below.

The 'make-up', excluding private companies altogether, and exclusive of multiple counting, is as follows:

	Gross capital stock (Rs. lakhs)	
	1951	1958
1. Unacknowledged holding and joint holding companies of acknowledged companies (List B)	110.31	141.93
2. Unacknowledged subsidiaries of acknowledged companies (List C)	15.69	37.65
3. Unacknowledged joint subsidiaries of acknowledged companies (List D)	39.64	77.94
4. Unacknowledged banking and insurance companies (List E)	105.86	107.23
5. Unacknowledged companies apparently wholly owned by United Commercial Bank (List F)	—	1.66
6. Unacknowledged companies holding substantial interest (less than 50%) in banking and insurance companies (List G)	49.79	118.38
7. Birla public managing agency companies (List H)	3.28	—
8. Unacknowledged companies in which Birla trusts hold more than 50% of equity (List I)	4.31	5.47
9. Unacknowledged companies in which acknowledged and unacknowledged companies listed above have substantial interest (List J)	408.54	857.50
Total 1 to 9	737.42	1347.76

Note: Holding and subsidiary companies have the same meaning as in the Companies Act. Joint holding companies are those companies under the same control which jointly hold more than 50 per cent of the equity of another company. Joint subsidiaries are those in which more than 50 per cent of the equity is jointly held by more than one company under the same control.

When the above figures are added to those of acknowledged companies, the position is :

Birla public companies

	Gross capital stock (Rs. crores)	
	1951	1958
(1) Acknowledged companies	51.35 (3.68)	120.23 (4.49)
(2) Unacknowledged companies from above Table	7.37 (0.53)	13.48 (0.50)
(3) (1)+(2)	58.72 (4.21)	133.71 (4.99)
(4) Birla Inner Circle Public Cos. as in Table 3	62.55 (4.48)	143.44 (5.36)
(5) Difference between (4) and (3)	3.83 (0.27)	10.78 (0.40)

Note : Figures in parentheses are percentages of non-government public companies.

The divergence between the figures presented in this study and the minimum estimate of Birla gross capital stock is, thus, limited to only about 0.3 to 0.4 per cent of the total gross capital stock of non-government companies, and does not affect the conclusions drawn earlier.

If one takes the Birla gross capital stock and the Sahu Jain data the change in concentration of economic power so far as the four top Inner Circles are concerned would be as follows:

Gross capital stock of public companies in four top Inner Circles

(Rs. crores)

	As in Tables 3 and 5		As in this Appendix	
	1951	1958	1951	1958
1. Tata (no change)	105.23 (7.54)	287.22 (10.74)	105.23 (7.54)	287.22 (10.74)
2. Birla	62.55 (4.48)	143.44 (5.36)	58.72 (4.21)	133.71 (4.99)
3. Martin Burn (no change)	39.25 (2.81)	89.90 (3.36)	39.25 (2.81)	89.90 (3.36)
4. D.S.J./Sahu Jain	29.70 (2.12)	71.58 (2.68)	16.69 (1.20)	51.95 (1.94)
Total	236.73 (16.95)	591.14 (22.14)	219.89 (15.76)	562.78 (21.03)

Note: Figures in parentheses are percentages of non-government public companies.

List A: Acknowledged Birla companies

1. Aditya Investments (Private in 1958)
2. Assam Jute Supply
3. Bally Jute (No in 1951)
4. Bharat Commerce & Industries
5. Bharat Kala Bhandar
6. Bharat Sugar
7. Birla Cotton
8. Birla Jute
9. C & E Morton
10. Central Distributors
11. Central India Coalfields
12. Century Spinning & Weaving
13. Cimmco (Texmaco Gwalior)
14. Electric Construction
15. Express Dairy
16. Gobind Sugar (No in 1951)
17. Gwalior Rayon
18. Hind Cycles
19. Hindustan Gas
20. Hindustan Motors
21. Hindustan Woollen
22. Hyderabad Allwyn & Metal (A government company) (No. in 1951, excluded in 1958)
23. Hyderabad Asbestos (No in 1951)
24. Indian Linoleums
25. Indian Plastics
26. Indian Shipping
27. Indian Smelting & Refining
28. Indian Tool Manufacturing
29. Jayashree Tea Gardens
30. Jayashree Textiles
31. Jiyajeerao Cotton
32. Kesoram Cotton Mills
33. Narkatiaganj Farms
34. National Engineering Industries
35. New India Sugar
36. New Swadeshi Mills of Ahmedabad
37. New Swadeshi Sugar
38. Nilgiri Plantations (No. in 1951)
39. Orient General Industries
40. Orient Paper Mills
41. Oudh Sugar
42. Padmavati Raje
43. Premier Stores Supply

44. Rajpur Farms
45. Rameshwara Jute (No. in 1951)
46. Shree Digvijaya Woollen (No. in 1951)
47. Sirpur Paper (No. in 1951)
48. Sirsilk (No. in 1951)
49. Soorah Jute
50. Sutlej Cotton Mills
51. Texmaco
52. Tims Products
53. Tungabhadra Industries
54. Upper Ganges Sugar
55. Western Bengal Coalfields
56. Woodcrafts Assam
57. Woodcraft Products

List B: *Unacknowledged holding and joint holding companies of acknowledged companies*

1. Bengal Rubber
2. Bharat Trading
3. Bikaner Commercial
4. Central India Industries
5. Commercial House (Private in 1958)
6. G. Das (Jute & Gunny)
7. Gwalior Commercial
8. Gwalior Finance
9. Gwalior Webbing
10. Hindustan Cellulose & Paper
11. Hindustan Investment Corporation
12. Indore Exporting & Importing
13. Industrial Trust
14. Kamal Trading (Private in 1958)
15. Kingsley Golaghat Assam Tea
16. Kothari (Private in 1958)
17. Mahabir Commercial
18. Merchandise & Stores
19. New Asiatic Insurance
20. Paper Distributors (Private in 1958)
21. Pilani Investment Corporation
22. Premier Tea
23. Punjab Ginning & Pressing
24. Punjab Produce & Trading
25. Rajasthan Industries
26. Rajputana General Dealers
27. Rajputana Investment
28. Shekhavati General Traders

29. Sutlej Cotton Mills Supply Agency
30. United Commercial Bank
31. Ujjain General Trading (Private in 1958)
32. Vijay Paper Corporation

List C: Unacknowledged subsidiaries of acknowledged companies

1. Bihar Journals
2. Champaran Marketing
3. Darbhanga Marketing
4. Hindustan Cellulose & Paper
5. Hindustan Motor Corporation
6. Motolite
7. National Bearing (Jaipur)
8. Saran Trading
9. Uttar Pradesh Trading
10. Usha Development

List D: Unacknowledged joint subsidiaries of acknowledged companies

1. Birla Buildings
2. Eastern Economist
3. Eastern Equipment & Sales
4. Ghillidhary Tea
5. Gwalior Webbing
6. Indian Air Travels
7. Industry House
8. Mundulpore Coal
9. Newspapers

List E: Unacknowledged banking and insurance companies

1. New Asiatic Insurance
2. Ruby General Insurance
3. United Commercial Bank

List F: Unacknowledged companies apparently wholly owned by United Commercial Bank

1. Hindustan Discounting
2. National Playing Card

List G: Unacknowledged companies holding substantial interest in List E companies

1. Bengal Jute Baling
2. Central India Industries
3. General Fibre Dealers
4. Industrial Trust
5. Indian Starch Products
6. Jute and Stores
7. Kingsley Golaghat Assam Tea
8. Pilani Investment Corporation
9. Punjab Produce & Trading

List H: Public managing agency companies

1. Birla Gwalior (Private in 1958)
2. Hindustan Investment Corporation

List I: Unacknowledged companies in which Birla trusts hold more than 50 per cent of equity

1. Central India General Agents (Private in 1958)
2. Eastern India Marketing
3. Himalayan Products (in liquidation in 1958)
4. Indian Press Exchange
5. Mahabir Commercial
6. Pilani Industrial Corporation
7. Shekhavati General Traders

List J: Unacknowledged companies in which Lists A to I companies have substantial interest

1. General Industrial Society (No in 1951)
2. Hind Construction
3. Hindustan Times
4. Hukumchand Jute
5. Jaipur Development
6. Kusum Products
7. New Gujarat Cotton (No in 1951)
8. Shree Bhawani Cotton

List K: Acknowledged Sahu Jain companies

1. Albion Jute (1951 only)

2. Albion Plywood
3. Ashoka Agencies (Ashoka Viniyoga)
4. Ashoka Cement
5. Ashoka Marketing
6. Bennett Coleman (Private in 1951)
7. Bharat Bank (Bharat Nidhi)
8. Bharat Collieries
9. Dehri Rohtas Light Railways
10. Dhrangadhra Chemicals
11. Hindustan Vehicles
12. Jaipur Udyog (Private in 1951)
13. Lothian Jute (1951 only)
14. National Safe Deposit & Cold Storage (Sahu Properties)
15. New Central Jute
16. Punjab National Bank
17. Rohtas Industries
18. Sahu Jain
19. Sahu Rubber (Private in 1958)
20. Shree Rishabh Investment (No in 1951)
21. S.K.G. Sugar
22. Sone Valley Portland Cement (No in 1951)
23. Universal Bank of India

NOTE ON SELECTION OF GROUPS

The 20 selected groups represent a purposive cross-section of the corporate private sector. The size of physical assets is only one of the diverse criteria used in selecting groups. Among others are caste, provincial origin,[2] age, occupation, corporate structure and pattern of financing, distribution of ownership, relative size of controlling blocks and techniques of control. It may be useful to give a brief account of this diversity here.

Size

Ten groups, namely, Tata, Birla, Martin Burn, Dalmia Sahu Jain, Andrew Yule, Bird Heilger, Bangur, J.K., Shri Ram and Thapar, have probably the largest amount of physical assets among groups of companies incorporated in India. Another two, Mafatlal and Walchand, are not far behind them.

Of the remaining eight, two, Khatau and Shapoorji, have substantial minority interests. The other six, Indra Singh,

Kasturbhai, Kirloskar, Mahindra, Ramakrishna and Seshasayee, are fairly representative of medium-sized groups in various parts of the country.

Caste and provincial origin

Two of the groups, Tata and hapoorji, are controlled by Parsis, who were the first Indian community to go into large scale manufacturing.

Ten groups, Birla, Dalmia Sahu Jain, Bangur, J.K., Shri Ram, Thapar, Khatau, Walchand, Kasturbhai and Mahindra, come from the Bania community. Of these, three, Birla, Dalmia Sahu Jain and Bangur are acknowledged Marwaris, and another two, J.K. and Shri Ram, trace their original 'native places' to areas that may be sociologically described as Marwari[8] homelands. Three, Dalmia Sahu Jain, Walchand and Kasturbhai, are Jains, of whom the latter two are Gujaratis, but Walchand's activities are concentrated in Maharashtra, while those of Kasturbhai are in Gujarat. Two, Thapar and Mahindra, are from the Doab area in Punjab, Khatau represents the enterprising Bhatias from Kutch in Gujarat.

Two groups, Andrew Yule and Bird Heilger, are European-controlled and another, Martin Burn, is partly European.

Two groups, Kirloskar and Seshasayee, are Brahmin. The Indian majority interest in Martin Burn is also Brahmin. Kirloskar is from the Maharashtra-Mysore border, Seshasayee comes from Madras, while the Mookherjees and Banerjis in Martin Burn are Bengalis.

The remaining three groups, Mafatlal, Ramakrishna and Indra Singh, are originally of farmer castes. Mafatlals are Patels from Gujarat, Ramakrishna is a Kamma from Andhra while Indra Singh is a Sikh Jat from Punjab. These three castes are the most powerful agricultural caste groups in the country.

Age

Andrew Yule, Bird Heilger and Martin Burn are among the oldest surviving groups in India. Their origin can be traced back 100 years or longer.

Tata, Shri Ram and Khatau established themelves as industrial groups in the last quarter of the nineteenth century.

Birla, J.K., Walchand, Mafatlal, Kasturbhai, Kirloskar and Seshasayee came up in the 1920s.
The thirties witnessed the emergence of Dalmia Sahu Jain, Thapar, Shapoorji and Indra Singh.
Bangur, Mahindra and Ramakrishna came into industry only after the second world war.

Of all the groups studied, only Andrew Yule and, to a lesser extent, Bird Heilger, have tended to stagnate during the reference period.

Occupation

Almost every group has a variety of occupations, especially if the minority interests are also taken into account. A list of the occupations of all of them would read like a catalogue. Only a few highlights are, therefore, mentioned here.

All groups with the exception of Martin Burn, Walchand, Kirloskar, Seshasayee, Mahindra and Ramakrishna, are interested in textiles (cotton or jute or both).

Tata and Martin Burn are interested mainly in steel, engineering and power, but Tata has a much wider variety of interests, including cement, cotton, chemicals, vegetable oils, etc., besides insurance, investment and trade.

Birla has a stake in almost every major industry, except steel, power and transport. In addition, it controls one of the largest banks and has considerable interest in investment, trade and insurance.

Dalmia Sahu Jain is in jute, cement, paper, chemicals, etc., besides banking, insurance, investment and trade.

Andrew Yule and Bird Heilger are mainly in jute and coal. The former has also a large interest in tea, and the latter in paper.

Bangur is enaged in jute, cotton, cement, paper, tea, real estate, investment and trade. J.K. is in cotton, aluminium, woollen, jute, engineering, chemicals, mining, besides banking, insurance and investment. Shri Ram combines cotton, rayon, chemicals, sugar, engineering, vegetable oil and ceramics. Thapar covers coal, cotton, sugar, engineering and trade.

Khatau is mainly in cotton but has a large minority interest in cement and automobile engineering. Shapoorji includes construction and cotton, besides a substantial interest in cement. Walchand is in sugar and construction with substantial minority interests in shipping and automobile engineering. Mafatlal is in cotton, jute and dyestuffs, with minority interests in sugar and shipping.

Kasturbhai is almost wholly in cotton and dyestuffs, and Kirloskar is in engineering. Ramakrishna combines sugar and cement, Seshasayee power, chemicals and engineering, Mahindra engineering and trade, while Indra Singh is in engineering, cement, cotton and non-ferrous metals.

Corporate structure

Some groups concentrate most of their assets in a few companies while others disperse them over a large number of companies.

Among the large groups, Tata, Martin Burn and Shri Ram have most of their assets in a handful of companies, though Tata has a fairly large number of small companies too. Between them, only Tata and Martin Burn are compelled by the capital-intensive nature of their major industrial interests to have very large companies. Shri Ram's choice in favour of a few but individually large companies appears to be deliberate, particularly since it combines a number of occupations in one diversified company. Seven other large groups disperse their assets over a large number of companies, obviously, as a matter of policy. Among the medium-sized groups, Khatau and Indra Singh seem to favour very small companies for some of their activities but others, on the whole, have companies of reasonable size without an excessive profusion of the number of companies.

Only Mafatlal, Kasturbhai and Indra Singh have a very strong net worth position. Others rely, though in varying degrees, rather heavily on loan finance. Tata, Martin Burn and Ramakrishna, particularly, have depended mainly on loans for their expansion.

At least four groups, Mafatlal, Walchand, Khatau and Shapoorji, have minority interests that far exceed the size of their inner circles. Of these, Shapoorji's minority interests are mainly of a financial nature, and the same can be said to some extent of Mafatlal. Walchand and Khatau, on the other hand, appear to take a keen interest in the management of their respective outer circles.

Another group, Seshasayee, is primarily a managerial rather than a financial group. It had a large stake in the management of some government companies in Kerala till 1960.

Of the remaining groups, Tata, Mahindra and Indra Singh alone seem to have a strong propensity for joint ventures. Bangur's joint ventures are the result of investment operations. The other groups rarely favour such enterprises.

Ownership and control

The pattern of ownership varies widely between the groups.

Andrew Yule, Bird Heilger, Tata, Martin Burn, Kirloskar and Mahindra have a significant amount of foreign shareholding.

The dispersion of ownership (that is, shareholding by persons other than those constituting the controlling interests) is fairly wide in Tata, Martin Burn, Andrew Yule, Kasturbhai, Ramakrishna and Seshasayee, and in the minority companies of Khatau, Shapoorji, Walchand and Mafatlal.

The techniques of control also differ to a considerable extent. Tata, Andrew Yule, Bird Heilger, J.K., Thapar and Ramakrishna use inter-corporate investment to a much greater extent as compared with other groups.

Tata, Martin Burn, Shri Ram and Birla appear to make considerable use of trust investments for purposes of control.

Kasturbhai and Kirloskar depend mainly upon investments by family members and, perhaps, partnership firms.

On the whole, inter-corporate investment as an instrument of control plays the key role in all groups, except Kasturbhai, Kirloskar and Seshasayee.

The managing agency system of management predominates in practically all groups, so far as public industrial companies are concerned. Private and non-industrial companies are, however, managed by directors.

REFERENCES

1. This is a modified version of an explanatory note submitted to a sub-committee of the Mahalanobis Committee on Distribution of National Income and Wealth, which met on 29 September, 1962, to

examine an earlier version of this study.

2. The selection is not, perhaps, as representative of the Southern groups as one might wish.
3. The term 'Marwari' should, strictly speaking, apply only to a person from Marwar, that is, Jodhpur, but commonly denotes origin also from Bania castes in Ajmer, Jaipur and Bikaner in Rajasthan, Rohtak and Hissar in Haryana, and Meerut in U.P.

TECHNICAL NOTE

This te hnical not explains the definitions and terms used in Part II. The description of the concepts nd methods adopted would, it is hoped, facilitate further work in this and related fi lds of research.

Sources

This study did not make any use of the questio naire method. It relied almost wholly on data collected fro shareholders' lists, balance sheets and other documents available with the Company Law Offices of the Government of India.

These data were supplemented by personal oral inquiries. *The groups studied were not requested to supply any data.*

Industrial classification

Companies have been classified under 28 industrial heads according to the actual business as reveal d in their annual reports and accounts. Private com anies are classified in 1951 mainly on the basis of their occupation in 1958 and, faili g that, the principal object clause in their memorandum.

The 28 heads are as follows:

1. Coal mining
2. Other mining
3. Power supply and generation
4. Cotton
5. Rayon fibre and yarn
6. Woollen
7. Jute and linoleum
8. Iron and steel (basic)
9. Non-ferrous metals
10. Other engineering
11. Sugar and farms
12. Tea, coffee and other plantations

13. Food, vegetable oil and soap
14. Chemical and paints
15. Paper
16. Printing and publishing
17. Real estate
18. Construction
19. Glass, plastics and ceramics
20. Cement, firebrick and asbestos
21. Transport
22. Hotels and services
23. Banking
24. Insurance
25. Finance and investment
26. Managing agency
27. Other industry, including diversified units
28. Trade.

These 28 heads have been lumped under 4 major occupational categories: Banking and Insurance (23 and 24), Finance (25 and 26), and Service (16, 17, 22 and 28). All others are treated as Industrial.

Many companies have more than one business in the sense of having assets or income which straddle more than one occupation :

(a) Managing agency companies generally combine a number of occupations. Of late, many of them have come to depend increasingly upon sources of income other than commission from managed companies. In view o the traditional importance of managing agencies, a company has been classified in 1958 almost without exception as a managing agent, regardless of its principal source of income, if it acts as managing agent or as secretaries and treasurers. This definition could not be applied consistently in 1951 because managing agency was rather loosely defined till 1956 and some industrial companies also acted as managing agents.

(b) Diversification is becoming increasingly significant in industrial companies, especially among cotton and jute companies. Where an industrial company has more than one major activity, it has been classified under Other Industry, which inevitably leads to some distortion in the industrywise distribution of physical assets and financial liabilities.

The data for the two reference years are not fully comparable because the balance sheet data for 1951 relate only to public companies, while the 1958 data cover private companies as well. Moreover, some companies changed their occupation between 1951 and 1958 due to diversification or other reasons.

The purpose of presenting the industrywise data in this study is only to give a broad picture of the industrial interests of a complex and, among other things to show that measurement of concentration in each industry is hardly meaningful in the Indian context. The data might be of some use to those who want to study the extent of each group's participation in an industry, if they keep in mind the severe limitations of the definition of 'industry', the diversified activities of almost every major company, and the differences in the valuation of assets between companies *inter se* and within each company, according to the period of acquisition and depreciation of assets.

The above industrial classification differs from that of the Company Law Department, which is based mainly, if not exclusively, on the principal objects clause in the Memoranda of companies. A departure from the official classification was necessary because a large number of companies were found doing a business different from that stated in the principal objects clause of their Memoranda. A number of companies officially classified as industrial or trading, for example, were actually found doing the business of finance and investment.

Composition of complex

The number of companies in each complex has changed between 1951 and 1958 due to liquidation, sales or acquisitions and setting up of new companies. In some cases, the location of companies within the concentric circles of the complex has also changed.

Since the unit of comparison at the two points of time is the group or complex, and not the individual company, the changes in the composition of the units during the period call merely for an appropriate qualification of the conclusions. The changes do not render the conclusions invalid.

Lists of companies

Companies registered outside India are excluded altogether, but companies registered in India are included even if all or part of their assets are outside India.

The 1951 lists exclude those companies which were (a) liquidated before the end of 1951, or (b) registered towards the end of 1951 and filed their first annual returns late in 1952 or later.

The 1958 lists exclude those companies which were (a) liquidated between 1951 and the end of 1958, (b) registered towards the end of 1958 and filed their first annual returns late in 1959 or later, and (c) those companies in which the groups concerned ceased to have an interest between 1951 and 1958.

Some companies changed their names between 1951 and 1958. The names given in the lists are as in the particular years.

The classification of small companies under public and private is subject to minor errors.

Accounting years

With minor exceptions, the calendar years 1951 and 1958 cover company accounting periods ending in any month of the respective calendar years.

As far as possible, the complementary shareholders' lists are also taken for the same year so that the share capital as taken from the shareholders' lists is the same as in the balance sheets. In a few cases, the two figures do not coincide due to the issue of fresh capital between the end of the accounting year and the date of the shareholders' meeting or the date of the nearest complete shareholders' list.

Combined balance sheet

Balance sheets have been combined, *not consolidated*. That is to say, balance sheet items have been added up without making any adjustments for inter-corporate investments and loans. Consequently, the combined balance sheet involves some multiple counting of financial items, as in the case of Reserve Bank studies.

Physical assets, i.e., fixed assets and inventory, however, can be counted only once and that is the reason for the emphasis on physical assets throughout the study.

The values of items have been taken straight from balance

sheets, without making any adjustments for changes in price levels, allowance for which would have involved almost an actuarial revaluation.

The Companies Act of 1956 altered the content, and standardised the presentation of balance sheet items. Accordingly, the balance sheets for 1958 are drawn up, with some minor exceptions, in conformity with Part I of Schedule VI to the Act. The balance sheets for 1951 were not required to be presented in the same manner. The data for 1951 have, therefore, been re-cast as far as possible to make them comparable with 1958 data, but a small element of non-comparability is bound to remain.

Balance sheet items

Share capital is taken at the value of actual subscribed capital excluding share premium and forfeited shares, but including bonus and other shares issued for consideration other than cash.

Reserves are total reserves and surplus, *plus* share premium and forfeited shares, *minus* intangibles and specific reserves for taxation, gratuity and bad debts, etc. Realised capital reserve, development rebate reserve, special depreciation and repair and maintenance reserves are included in reserves as far as possible.

Net worth is share capital *plus* reserves.

Loans, on the liabilities side, include debentures, and other secured, as well as unsecured, loans, except in the case of banking and insurance companies where they are all included under other liabilities.

Other liabilities are total liabilities *minus* share capital, reserves and loans. In general, this item is equal to current liabilities and provisions *plus* specific reserves. In banking and insurance companies, however, this item corresponds to total liabilities *minus* share capital and reserves.

Total liabilities or assets (net) coincide with the balance sheet total exclusive of depreciation.

Net fixed assets include land, buildings, plant and machinery, furniture, motor vehicles and capital works in progress, but exclude such intangible items as goodwill, trade marks, mining rights and revaluation of assets.

Investments are as stated in balance sheets *minus* interest and dividends accrued, immovable properties, and fixed deposit receipts. The item includes investments declared as stock-in-trade.

Inventory is the sum of stores, raw materials, goods in process, finished stock, spares and tools. Shares under stock-in-trade are excluded as far as possible.

Receivables and cash is the sum of book debts, deposits, loans and advances (including income tax advances), cash in hand, and deposits with banks.

Other assets are found by deducting the sum of the above assets from total assets (net), that is, the balance sheet total.

Net capital stock is the sum of net fixed assets and inventory. Gross capital stock is net capital stock *plus* accumulated depreciation.

Sources and uses of finance

It is impossible to make out from a balance sheet the precise use of funds from each distinct source. The total funds that accrue over a period can be measured from the increase in gross total liabilities, that is, total liabilities *plus* depreciation.

Of this amount, the internal resources correspond to reserves and depreciation, while external resources consist of share capital, loans and other liabilities.

The analysis of the sources and uses of finance is restricted to Inner circle companies, since the group's control over the disposition of funds is logically confined to the inner circle. The analysis covers only public companies since 1951 data are not available for private companies. Banking and insurance companies are excluded because their data distort the overall pattern.

The results of this analysis should be treated with caution for a number of reasons.

First, there is often a change in the composition of the inner circle during the period owing to the going out of some companies and the entry of others. Consequently, the absolute figures are less meaningful than the broad structural pattern of sources and uses of funds.

Second, some part at least of the loans and other liabilities, not to speak of share capital, is raised within the group and is, therefore, not really external to the group, though the items may be external to the constituent companies.

Third, the capitalisation of reserves over a period of time is, in fact, only a book transfer from reserves to share capital but it affects the pattern of sources of finance.

Fourth, the appropriations to tax reserves are often in excess of foreseeable tax liabilities. The excess should form part of free reserves, but is treated as specific reserve and, hence, included in other liabilities instead of reserves.

Fifth, the write-off of capital revaluation on the uses side (for example, in Bird Heilger) distorts the overall pattern of use of funds.

Sixth, the significance of this analysis can be grasped only if it is taken in conjunction with the structure of liabilities and assets at the beginning and the end of the period.

Seventh, while making inter-group comparisons, especially in regard to the relative importance of inter-corporate investments, it should be remembered that the structure of the assets of a group depends, partly, upon whether the group's principal investing companies are organised as public or private companies. This distinction is significant because the analysis here covers public companies only.

Pattern of ownership

The shareholders' lists taken up for analysis pertain generally to the date of the annual general meeting convened to adopt the respective balance sheets for 1951 and 1958. If the lists pertaining to those dates happened to be only lists of transfers, the last available complete lists of shareholders were taken.

In about 10 companies, nearly all of them registered in West Bengal, the pattern of ownership had to be computed because their complete shareholders' lists were not available.

Share capital is valued at par, throughout.

The figures of share capital as taken from shareholders' lists sometimes differ slightly from those in balance sheets, owing to the issue of rights or bonus shares between their dates. The difference is not significant in proportional terms, except in a few companies.

Only two types of share capital, ordinary and preference, are distinguished. The term equity is used inter-changeably with ordinary shares. These include deferred or promoters' shares, which are valued at par regardless of their voting power under the articles of association.

The analysis of ownership is generally done in the aggregate for the complex as a whole. The ownership of inner circles is analysed in detail where it serves a useful purpose.

For the universe as a whole, the breakdown covers the ownership of public and private companies, each of the 28 industrial heads under which the occupations of companies are classified, the distribution of ownership by size of companies, as well as the pattern of inter-industrial corporate holdings.

The size ranges are based not on share capital but on net worth plus loans. The latter was found to be a more satisfactory indicator of financial size. Moreover, it bears the closest approximation on the liabilities side to net capital stock on the assets side. The adoption of this criterion meant the exclusion of private companies in 1951 (due to the non-availability of their data in that year) and the lumping together of public and private companies in 1958. The consequent element of incomparability in size analysis between 1951 and 1958 is not very great because such an element would remain in any event due to the shift of some companies from one size range to another, and the entry and exit of some others.

The size ranges are as follows: (net worth plus loans)

A—under Rs. 10 lakhs
B—Rs. 10 lakhs to Rs 25 lakhs
C—Rs. 25 lakhs to Rs. 50 lakhs
D—Rs. 50 lakhs to Rs. 1 crore
E—Rs. 1 crore to Rs. 10 crores
F—Rs. 10 crores and above

The owners of shares are classified under seven different heads:

(*a*) *Indian companies* are those registered under the Companies Act in India. They also include, for the sake of convenience, exchange banks incorporated elsewhere but doing business in India, the State Bank of India and a few co-operative banks.

(*b*) *Foreign companies* are bodies corporate registered outside India. They exclude exchange banks, but include foreign insurance companies doing business in India, and foreign trustee and nominee companies.

(*c*) The holdings of the *Life Insurance Corporation* in 1958 also include those registered in the names of nationalised private life insurers, as well as the holdings of L.I.C. subsidiaries doing general insurance business. This category was non-existent in 1951, since life insurance was nationalised only in 1956.

(*d*) The head *Government* covers all holdings in the names of Government and Government personnel (including the Industrial Investment Fund of Andhra Government, where specifically mentioned) and Universities, but excludes the holdings of Government companies (for example, Provident Investment).

(*e*) *Individuals in India* covers the holdings of individuals and unincorporated firms with Indian addresses. If there is evidence to show that some of these are trust holdings, they are classified under trusts.

(*f*) *Trusts*[1] includes the shareholdings of unincorporated charity and family trusts of all kinds, where specifically and otherwise mentioned, and of individuals who are known to be trustees and hold shares in that capacity.

It has not been possible to identify most of the trust holdings due to the statutory and other restrictions on the registration of trusts as shareholders.

(*g*) *Individuals Abroad* covers all unincorporated firms and individuals with addresses outside India. Specific mention may be made of the large holdings of the Rana family of Nepal. These are uniformly included in 'Individuals Abroad', even if the shareholder's address is given as in India.

In the summary tables, *individuals* means individuals and firms in India. Foreign companies and individuals abroad are lumped together as *foreign investors*.

The occupational breakdown of shareholding of Indian companies has been done under five heads: (*i*) banking and executor and trustee, (*ii*) insurance, (*iii*) finance, (*iv*) industrial, and (*v*) service.

The holdings of banking and executor and trustee companies include their holdings as trustees, nominees and pledgees, and so on.

Controlling blocks

The controlling block is used as a generic expression to indicate the *total* investment of the controlling interest in the share capital, both equity and preference, of the controlled companies.

The various holders of the controlling blocks are classified as under:

1. Managing agents (including secretaries and treasurers)
2. Investment companies
3. Banking companies
4. Insurance companies
5. Industrial companies
6. Service companies
7. Trusts
8. Individuals
9. Companies outside India
10. Individuals outside India

A holder of controlling block in a company is classified as managing agent only if it is the managing agent of that particular company.

Individuals include members of the controlling families, executives and nominees.

Banks as holders of controlling blocks are relevant only in the few complexes which include banks. It is true that banks need not, and do not always, hold shares on behalf of their own controlling interests. In the case of the banks included in this study, however, the presumption is, perhaps, justifiable that the large blocks of shares registered in their names actually belong to their controlling interests.

In some Birla and Dalmia Sahu Jain companies, the holdings of certain banks which are outside the respective groups have been treated as the holdings of investment companies, on the basis of a cross-check.

The inter-corporate controlling investments consist, for the most part, of investments made and held by sole control and majority, that is, inner circle, companies. Some of the controlling investments, particularly by certain groups in their outer circles, are held by and through 50-50, minority ond 'under management' companies. As indicated in the text, even these indirect investments have to be treated as part of the controlling blocks, in so far as the group in question is concerned. It may be stated specifically that this group block in the outer circle excludes the holdings of other groups which participate in the control, unless the block in question is held by and through a company under the joint control of the participating groups.

The holdings under sole control, and through majority, 50-50, and minority (including 'under management' companies in a few cases) companies are clearly distinguished, where necessary, before proceeding to the analysis of the breakdown of various holders of the controlling block.

The data on control through inter-corporate investments have been used, among other things, to bring out the importance of joint subsidiaries. A *joint subsidiary* is a company in which more than 50 per cent of the voting power is held by two or more companies (excluding banks and executor and trustee companies) representing the same controlling interest or more than one joint controlling interest.

For the sake of convenience, it is assumed (i) that preference shares have no voting power, and (ii) that different types of equity shares have voting power in proportion to their paid up value. These assumptions are not always valid, particularly before 1956, till which year the Companies Act then in force permitted the holders of certain types of equity to have disproportionate voting power.

Where a part of the controlling block is registered in the names of banks which cannot be identified straightaway with the controlling interest, the proportion of the controlling block to total share capital is inevitably reduced below the actual figure.

The computation of the contribution of the controlling interest to the increase in the share capital of the companies in the group between 1951 and 1958 includes the receipt of bonus shares issued during the period. It is extremely difficult to eliminate the value of bonus shares, because the statutory documents of companies mention only the total value of shares issued for consideration other than cash since inception, and not during a particular period. Moreover, once they are issued, bonus shares rank on par with other shares and are, therefore, equally transferable.

Techniques of control

The analysis of technique of control is confined to 1958, mainly for the sake of convenience. This is essentially in the nature of a bird's eye view, concerned with the pattern and direction of controlling investments in so far as they can be discerned from the shareholders' lists. It does not and cannot within the purview of this study, deal with the *mechanics* of the actual exercise of control.

The depth in which the technique is studied in each group is determined primarily by the simplicity or complexity of the techniques used by the controlling interest concerned. Among other things, the study endeavours to find out the range of variation of controlling blocks in various companies and groups, and the extent to which some controlling interests resort to direct interlocking or circular-chain-holdings of equity, and use the funds of industrial companies to control other companies which have an altogether different business.

Types of management

Only two types of management are distinguished in the chapters that follow. These are managements by (i) managing agents, and (ii) boards of directors. The former also includes management by secretaries and treasurers.

The identification of secretaries and treasurers with managing agents is justified because there is, in fact, practically no difference between the two. The Companies Act, 1956, made a distinction between the two, mainly, in order to enable the leading managing agency houses to avoid the application of Section 332 (which limits the number of companies managed by a managing agency to 10) and to cut down the total remuneration received by such managing agencies from the companies under their management.

All other types of management, for example, managers, managing directors, secretaries, committees of directors, and so on, are taken to be management by boards of directors. This simplification is motivated purely by convenience—and the frequent difficulty of identifying the precise form of management of a company when it is not managed by managing agents.

REFERENCES

1. These correspond roughly to the American 'foundations'.

STATISTICAL SUMMARY

THE amount and variety of data uncovered in this study indicate that a study of the corporate sector in India is not greatly hindered by lack of information or inaccessibility of sources.

REPRESENTATIVE SAMPLE

Before summing up the findings, it would be useful to indicate how representative this study is. It covers approximately 1,00 public and private companies in which 20 selected corporate groups had an interest of one kind or the other in 1951 and 1958. These companies (excluding a few government companies) accounted for about 29 per cent and 32 per cent of the share capital of non-government companies in 1951 and 1958, respectively.

The 20 groups were selected so as to secure a purposive cross-section of different groups by size, age, occupation, caste and regional origin, pattern of ownership of share capital and technique of making controlling investments. More than 10 of them are among the largest in India and the remaining are fairly representative of medium-sized groups. The distribution of their companies and assets by industries (see Tables 7 and 8) also indicates a fairly satisfactory cross-section of the corporate private sector.

The question may well be asked that, if this cross-section is satisfactory, why is its coverage much smaller than that of the Reserve Bank samples which cover 78 per cent and 33 per cent of the share capital of (non-government, non-financial) public and private companies, respectively?

The 'representativeness' of a sample depends primarily upon its purpose. The purpose of the Reserve Bank sample is to evaluate the trends in the finances of the largest companies so as to get an idea of the sources and uses of funds in the corporate sector as well in certain industrial categories. The purpose of the sample in the

TABLE 7: Twenty groups: Physical assets by industry

(*Rs. lakhs*)

Industry	Inner circle or complex	Public companies 1951: No. of coys.	Net fixed assets	Net capital stock	Gross capital stock	Public and private companies 1958: No. of coys.	Net fixed assets	Net capital stock	Gross capital stock
1	2	3	4	5	6	7	8	9	10
Coal	A	22	7,45	9,65	17,24	36	10,10	13,44	25,73
	B	30	8,82	12,24	23,82	48	12,54	17,07	34,18
Other mining	A	6	18	35	84	13	1,39	2,40	3,70
	B	6	18	35	84	16	2,19	3,40	5,10
Power	A	16	17,94	19,53	28,07	16	34,07	36,77	49,19
	B	19	18,53	20,20	28,86	18	35,31	38,07	51,07
Cotton[1]	A	42	13,27	44,83	63,80	54	29,93	62,04	93,53
	B	51	15,30	51,31	74,06	64	39,14	80,65	1,22,01
Rayon[1]	A	1	38	56	56	4	10,22	13,41	15,17
	B	1	38	56	56	5	10,25	13,47	15,24
Woollen[1]	A	1	57	1,97	2,48	2	45	1,00	1,28
	B	1	57	1,97	2,48	2	45	1,00	1,28
Jute	A	28	8,61	22,52	36,33	28	12,96	24,17	40,22
	B	31	10,69	27,25	45,47	31	15,22	28,12	47,13
Iron and steel	A	3	26,25	42,42	76,48	2	1,43,46	1,76,51	2,28,78
	B	3	26,25	42,42	76,48	2	1,43,46	1,76,51	2,28,78
Non-ferrous engg.	A	5	1,41	2,71	3,48	4	3,98	5,97	8,36
	B	5	1,41	2,71	3,48	5	4,12	6,28	8,79

TABLE 7: (*Contd.*)

Other engg.	A	31	31,34	27,12	33,60	62	38,10	89,44	1,13,09
	B	37	15,53	31,87	39,60	86	49,93	1,23,20	1,55,01
Sugar[1]	A	22	4,45	12,06	15,63	26	7,62	20,03	28,95
	B	24	5,34	13,69	17,76	30	9,34	23,74	34,14
Plantations	A	22	1,56	3,00	3,79	25	3,94	6,24	8,24
	B	45	2,78	5,90	7,39	47	5,74	9,88	13,19
Food and veg. oil	A	12	2,76	5,52	6,81	14	2,46	6,11	8,44
	B	14	3,04	5,93	7,23	18	3,06	6,88	9,38
Chemicals	A	14	5,02	7,43	8,60	19	9,15	14,24	19,37
	B	16	8,36	11,39	13,51	29	16,07	24,15	32,97
Paper	A	6	4,25	7,19	11,79	9	22,92	31,11	42,14
	B	7	5,05	8,01	12,61	11	23,63	32,54	45,20
Printing and publishing	A	8	61	70	79	16	2,97	4,12	5,74
	B	10	67	78	99	21	3,11	4,33	6,16
Real estate	A	14	2,25	2,63	2,69	26	2,94	4,40	4,70
	B	15	2,26	2,64	2,70	31	3,07	4,53	4,87
Construction	A	2	20	1,44	1,52	7	82	12,00	12,66
	B	3	58	1,83	2,16	9	1,03	13,00	14,13
Glass, plastics and pottery	A	7	1,10	1,67	1,97	7	2,03	3,16	4,28
	B	8	1,88	2,52	2,89	8	2,05	3,17	4,30
Cement, asbestos and	A	9	4,70	6,96	10,56	13	20.07	28,12	37,95
fireclay[1]	B	11	14,13	22,39	32,55	15	44,44	69,73	93,11
Transport	A	13	6,40	8,50	10,59	10	3,72	3,98	4,48
	B	21	21,27	25,54	33,04	15	28,92	29,52	37,32
Hotels and services	A	3	26	28	79	6	30	36	1,00
	B	4	28	29	84	7	32	38	1,02

Banking	A	7	1,58	1,58	2,08	7	2,61	2,61	3,34
	B	8	1,68	1,68	2,22	7	2,61	2,61	3,34
Insurance	A	15	3,80	3,80	4,21	13	49	49	66
	B	18	4,02	4,02	4,52	14	49	49	66
Investment and finance	A	131	1,39	2,19	2,99	253	3,27	5,92	7,43
	B	134	1,42	2,47	3,29	266	3,66	6,53	8,09
Managing agency	A	22	24	1,38	1,47	61	2,23	10,03	11,01
	B	26	40	1,55	1,66	77	2,70	11,27	12,49
Other industry	A	13	8,51	17,46	23,81	24	42,05	72,49	1,01,03
	B	17	8,79	18,30	24,90	39	43,73	76,43	1,06,66
Trade	A	49	47	2,64	2,78	127	1,92	14,37	15,10
	B	53	50	3,05	3,24	157	2,94	24,10	25,31
Total	A	524	1,38,96	2,58,06	3,75,74	884	4,16,18	6,64,92	8,95,60
	B	618	1,80,11	3,22,87	4,69,15	1,078	5,09,51	18,31,03	11,20,96

A: Inner circle.
B: Complexes adjusted for companies counted more than once.
Slight differences in totals are due to rounding.
Figures include a few government companies falling under certain complexes.
1. Excluding diversified companies which go under other industry.

TABLE 8: **Twenty groups: Financial liabilities by industry**

(*Rs. lakhs*)

Industry	Inner circle or complex	Public companies 1951					Public and private companies 1958				
		No. of coys.	Share capital	Net worth	Net worth plus loans	Total liabilities (net)	No. of coys.	Share capital	Net worth	Net worth plus loans	Total liabilities (net)
1	2	3	4	5	6	7	8	9	10	11	12
Coal	A	22	6,03	9,45	11,42	16,26	36	8,70	12,16	14,64	22,74
	B	30	6,97	11,51	14,19	21,42	48	9,10	14,31	18,85	29,03
Other mining	A	6	32	46	48	1,03	13	1,22	1,96	2,90	4,47
	B	6	32	46	48	1,03	16	1,77	2,66	3,72	5,85
Power	A	16	12,93	15,99	21,19	25,27	16	16,34	22,49	36,37	43,15
	B	19	13,26	16,33	21,87	25,99	18	16,89	23,31	37,65	44,62
Cotton[1]	A	42	20,91	50,55	59,50	76,78	54	19,60	41,12	70,16	89,27
	B	51	23,24	55,48	65,74	85,46	64	25,27	53,39	90,08	1,15,03
Rayon[1]	A	1	1,17	1,17	1,17	1,21	4	7,76	8,94	13,18	15,12
	B	1	1,17	1,17	1,17	1,21	5	7,79	8,96	13,26	15,21
Woollen	A	1	97	1,20	2,13	2,49	2	47	48	1,27	1,38
	B	1	97	1,20	2,13	2,49	2	47	48	1,27	1,38
Jute[1]	A	28	9,61	17,78	23,86	35,39	28	11,26	16,19	26,02	33,48
	B	31	11,60	20,97	29,19	41,40	31	12,83	18,66	29,87	38,35
Iron and steel	A	3	19,00	33,98	40,69	64,89	2	39,91	77,35	1,65,51	2,24,40
	B	3	19,00	33,98	40,69	64,89	2	39,91	77,35	1,65,51	2,24,40

Non-ferrous engg.	A	5	1,27	1,48	2,90	3,34	4	2,23	4,94	6,11	8,03
	B	5	1,27	1,48	2,90	3,34	5	2,28	5,20	6,58	8,65
Other engg.	A	31	15,68	19,82	29,34	36,87	62	32,73	43,07	76,17	1,15,95
	B	37	18,88	23,63	34,35	42,91	86	47,92	62,41	1,09,43	1,60,82
Sugar[1]	A	22	4,33	7,14	11,43	16,27	26	6,31	11,51	21,13	27,44
	B	24	5,05	8.33	13,05	18,16	30	7,55	13,66	24,38	32,66
Plantations	A	22	1,36	2,63	2,94	4,28	25	2,24	5,06	5,92	8,51
	B	45	2,64	5,00	5,51	8,27	47	3,62	8,04	9,25	13,38
Food and veg. oil	A	12	2,31	2,82	5,52	6,93	14	2,57	3,78	7,07	9,08
	B	14	2,58	3,10	6,03	7,49	18	2,90	4,11	7,88	10,32
Chemicals	A	14	4,24	5,26	8,43	9,31	19	8,09	9,56	16,04	19,18
	B	16	7,82	8,93	12,87	13,96	29	15,83	18,24	26,43	33,25
Paper	A	6	3,68	7,48	9,08	13,01	9	12,07	49,43	27,90	40,59
	B	7	4,27	8,07	10,43	14,37	11	12,78	20,58	29,12	42,47
Printing and	A	8	77	85	1,11	1,35	16	1,68	3,70	4,99	6,56
publishing	B	10	85	95	1,22	1,49	21	1,82	3,87	5,23	6,95
Real estate	A	14	2,99	3,20	3,64	4,49	26	3,79	4,19	5,81	6,63
	B	15	3,01	3,22	3,66	4,51	31	3,91	4,32	5,99	6,83
Construction	A	2	82	1,12	1,65	3,53	7	1,11	1,84	3,81	15,68
	B	3	89	1,37	1,98	4,13	9	1,34	2,27	4,24	17,14
Glass, plastics and	A	7	1,16	1,26	1,70	1,94	7	1,74	1,98	3,10	4,17
pottery	B	8	1,46	1,56	2,60	2,94	8	1,76	2,00	3,12	4,22
Cement, asbestos	A	9	5,70	6,96	9,66	11,48	13	13,11	15,88	29,47	38,33
and fireclay[1]	B	11	17,28	23,89	26,59	33,35	15	33,98	45,07	63,40	86,85
Transport	A	13	5,76	8,35	10,02	12,64	10	1,56	3,38	4,23	5,42
	B	21	17,71	27,00	38,10	44,82	15	14,01	22,97	39,16	53,76
Hotels and services	A	3	31	49	66	77	6	38	57	66	98
	B	4	34	52	70	82	7	41	60	69	1,01

TABLE 8: (*Contd.*)

Banking	A	7	6,84	9,39	9,39	1,30,81	7	5,16	8,91	8,91	2,97,68
	B	8	7,34	9,92	9,92	1,32,24	7	5,16	8,91	8,91	2,97,68
Insurance	A	15	3,13	5,37	5,37	58,15	13	2,89	6,22	6,22	24,28
	B	18	3,41	6,17	6,17	66,11	14	2,99	6,41	6,41	24,68
Investment and	A	131	18,18	34,45	48,85	54,83	253	30,34	60,16	80,53	96,07
finance	B	134	18,51	34,95	49,62	55,93	266	31,34	61,39	82,03	97,95
Managing agency	A	22	6,42	10,64	15,52	20,33	61	17,18	24,34	39,81	56,14
	B	26	9,68	14,38	20,09	25,54	77	20,48	28,85	46,43	65,06
Other industry	A	13	7,75	10,32	16,99	20,92	24	25,91	44,96	74,24	94,79
	B	17	8,26	11,21	18,24	22,70	39	27,88	47,98	78,59	1,00,97
Trade	A	49	1,38	2,45	6,74	10,95	127	6,54	8,44	20,02	39,50
	B	53	1,63	2,89	7,29	11,72	157	8,85	11,29	27,00	60,91
Total	A	524	1,65,03	2,72,04	3,61,38	6,45,51	884	2,82,22	4,62,61	7,72,20	13,49,00
	B	618	2,09,40	3,37,66	4,46,76	7,58,69	1,078	3,60,84	5,77,31	9,44,47	15,99,40
Add Private	A	293	26,78								
	B	370	33,45								

A: Inner circles.
B: Complexes adjusted for companies counted more than once.
Slight differences in totals are due to rounding.
Figures included a few government companies falling under certain complexes.
1. Excluding diversified companies which go under 'other industry'.

present study is different. This study takes the group, not the individual company, as the unit of corporate activity. Instead of selecting just the largest companies, it takes a cross-section of groups on the basis of a variety of criteria.

The structure of the combined balance sheet of public companies in the 20 complexes, nevertheless, bears a striking similarity to that of the Reserve Bank sample. The combined pattern of ownership of share capital in 1958 also closely resembles the results of the Reserve Bank survey of ownership of shares in 1959 (Tables 9 and 10).

TABLE 9: **Structure of combined balance sheet of public companies**

(Percentages)

	1951		1958	
	20 Complexes*	R.B.I. sample@	20 Complexes*	R.B.I. sample@
Liabilities				
1. Share capital	35	35	28	29
2. Reserves	22	19	16	18
3. Loans	20	21	30	28
4. Other liabilities	23	25	26	25
Total	100	100	100	100
Assets				
1. Net fixed	31	31	43	44
2. Investments	14	6	9	6
3. Inventory	26	35	26	29
4. Receivables and cash	26 }	29	20 }	21
5. Other assets	3 }		2 }	
Total	100	100	100	100

*Excluding banking and insurance but including finance companies.
@Excluding government, banking, insurance and finance companies.

In short, though the sample of companies in this study has a smaller coverage as compared with the Reserve Bank samples, it can be used on par with the latter for generalisations regarding the corporate private sector. Besides, it has the

TABLE 10: **Ownership of public companies**

(Percentages)

	Owners	20 Complexes 1958 (643)	R.B.I. 1959 (70)
1.	Individuals	51.6	52.0
2.	Joint stock companies	36.7	39.6
3.	Trusts	2.6*	1.3
4.	Other institutions (incl. L.I.C.)	5.6@	5.8
5.	Others	3.5	1.3
	Total	100.0	100.0

Note: Figures in parentheses indicate the number of companies.
*Including holdings registered in the names of trustees.
@L.I.C. only.

additional merit of giving a groupwise and group-cum-industry-wise picture, which the Reserve Bank samples do not provide.

CONCENTRATION OF ECONOMIC POWER

The study discloses a clear and significant increase in the concentration of economic power in the corporate private sector between 1951 and 1958.

The four largest groups—Tata, Birla, Martin Burn and Dalmia Sahu Jain—had nearly 18 per cent of the *share capital* of non-government public companies in 1951. This proportion rose to more than 22 per cent in 1958 (Table 11). If their outer circles, that is, 50-50 and minority interests, are also taken into account, the ratio went up from 22 per cent to 27 per cent.

The share of the four largest groups in the *gross capital stock*, that is, net fixed assets plus accumulated depreciation plus inventory, of non-government public companies expanded during the same period from 17 per cent to 22 per cent. Including the outer circles, their share rose from 20 to 26 per cent.

In 1958, the public companies in the Tata and Birla complexes had nearly one-fifth of the gross capital stock of all non-government public companies.

These conclusions are not affected by the possibility of over-estimation of the size of the Birla group and the alleged partition of the Dalmia Jain group.

TABLE 11: **Public companies in four top inner circles**

(Gross capital stock in Rs. crores)

	As in Tables 3 and 5		As in Appendix	
	1951	1958	1951	1958
1. Tata	105.23	287.22	105.23	287.22
	(7.54)	(10.74)	(7.54)	(10.74)
2. Birla	62.55	143.44	58.72	133.71
	(4.48)	(5.36)	(4.21)	(4.99)
3. Martin Burn	39.25	89.90	39.25	89.90
	(2.81)	(3.36)	(2.81)	(3.36)
4. D.S.J./Sahu Jain	29.70	71.58	16.69	51.95
	(2.12)	(2.68)	(1.20)	(1.94)
	236.73	592.14	219.89	562.78
	(16.95)	(22.14)	(15.76)	(21.03)

Note: Figures in parentheses are percentages of all non-government public companies.

OCCUPATIONAL DIVERSIFICATION

Each one of the 20 complexes is occupationally diversified. The larger the complex, the more diversified it generally tends to be. This is clear from the industrywise distribution of the assets of all complexes. Consequently, *concentration in India is far from synonymous with monopoly in a particular industry.*

Tata is interested mainly in steel, engineering and power, and has a variety of other interests including cement, cotton, chemicals, soap and vegetable oil, etc., besides, insurance, investment and trade.

Birla has a stake in almost every industry except steel, power and transport. Its industrial interests are spread over cotton, rayon, engineering, paper, sugar, jute, tea, chemicals, vegetable oil, construction, non-ferrous metals, glass and plastics, woollen and coal. Other interests include banking, insurance, investment, trade, real estate and newspapers.

The interests of *Martin Burn* are rather limited by contrast. They cover only steel, engineering, power and transport.

Dalmia Sahu Jain is in jute, cement, paper, chemicals, newspapers, banking, insurance, investment and trade.

Andrew Yule and *Bird Heilger* are mainly in jute and coal. The former has also a large interest in tea, and the latter in paper.

Bangur is engaged in jute, cotton, cement, paper, tea, real estate, investment and trade. *J.K.* is in cotton, aluminium, woollen, jute, engineering, chemicals, and mining, besides banking, insurance and investment. *Shri Ram* combines cotton, rayon, chemicals, sugar, engineering, vegetable oil and pottery. *Thapar* covers coal, cotton, sugar, engineering and trade.

Khatau is mainly in cotton, but has a significant minority interest in cement and automobile engineering. *Shapoorji* includes construction and cotton, besides a substantial minority interest in cement. *Walchand* is in sugar and construction, with unusual minority interests in shipping and automobile engineering. *Mafatlal* is in cotton, jute and dyestuffs, with minority interests in sugar and shipping.

Among the medium-sized groups, three are hardly diversified: *Kasturbhai* is almost wholly in cotton and dyestuffs, *Kirloskar* is in engineering and *Mahindra* is in engineering and trade. Another two have only a little variety: *Ramakrishna* combines sugar and cement, *Seshasayee* power, chemicals and engineering. *Indra Singh*, on the other hand, has spread its interests over engineering, cement, cotton and non-ferrous metals.

PROLIFERATION OF COMPANIES

Tata, Martin Burn and Shri Ram alone among the larger groups prefer to concentrate most of their assets in a few large companies. In Tata and Martin Burn, this is a necessity in view of their preponderant interest in such capital-intensive industries as steel, power and engineering. Shri Ram's choice is obviously deliberate, as is indicated by the highly diversified occupations of Delhi Cloth & General Mills.

In Birla, Dalmia Sahu Jain, Bird Heilger, Bangur, and J.K., on the other hand, there is a tendency to disperse industrial, trading and financial activity over a large number of companies. This tendency is attributable only in part to the nature and variety of their occupational interests for, all of them (except Bird Heilger) have diversified many of their leading companies, for example, Century, Kesoram, Birla Jute and Jiyajeerao in Birla, Rohtas and New Central in Dalmia Sahu Jain, Fort Gloster in Bangur, and Raymond in J.K.

Among the relatively smaller groups, some degree of proliferation of the number of companies is necessitated by the variety of occupations and joint ventures with other interests. Even among them, Ramakrishna has diversified two companies, K.C.P. and Jeypore Sugar.

These differences notwithstanding, almost every group (the exceptions are Martin Burn, Andrew Yule, Shri Ram, Kasturbhai and Kirloskar) appears to maintain a number of dormant companies, that is, companies the accounts of which show hardly any activity. This phenomenon is especially prominent in Birla, Dalmia Sahu Jain, Bird Heilger and Khatau. Besides, Birla and Dalmia Sahu Jain, particularly the latter, had a high level of corporate mortality, too, during the reference period.

JOINT VENTURES

Joint ventures, that is, companies having more than one controlling interest, are a frequent and important phenomenon in the corporate sector. The phenomenon is fully reflected in this study.

Table 12 gives a synoptic view of joint ventures including those with foreign partners. The overall significance of joint ventures is indicated by the fact that, in 1958, out of 1078 companies having a share capital of Rs. 361 crores and gross capital stock of Rs. 1121 crores, 274 companies with a share capital of Rs. 119 crores and gross capital stock of Rs. 328 crores, were joint ventures. Of these joint venture companies, 96 companies with share capital of Rs. 40 crores and gross capital stock of Rs. 127 crores, had foreign partners, that is, either companies registered abroad or companies under foreign control registered in India.

Of the 274 joint venture companies, 82 companies with a share capital of Rs. 41 crores and gross capital stock of Rs. 106 crores, were in the inner circles of the twenty complexes, that is to say, the groups concerned had the majority interest in them. Foreign minority partners played a significant role in these ventures, accounting for 25 companies which had share capital of Rs. 20

TABLE 12: **Joint ventures 1958**

(*Rs. lakhs*)

Complex	Circle	All companies: No. of companies	All companies: Share capital	All companies: Gross capital stock	All joint ventures: No. of companies	All joint ventures: Share capital	All joint ventures: Gross capital stock	Of which with foreign partners: No. of companies	Of which with foreign partners: Share capital	Of which with foreign partners: Gross capital stock
1. Andrew Yule	I	37	10,92	29,21	5	1,90	11,47	1	14	5
	01	5	1,45	2,46	5	1,45	2,46	1	6	33
2. Bangur	I	100	15,57	34,53	9	1,55	2,09	5	1,22	1,14
	01	14	4,12	18,60	13	4,05	18,51	5	2,48	14,45
	02				1	7	9	1	7	9
3. Bird Heilger	I	67	12,07	36,81	6	71	2,94	—	—	—
	01	9	89	1,57	8	88	1,57	2	5	1
	02				1	1	neg.	1	1	neg.
4. Birla	I	280	65,45	1,49,91	8	2,25	9,27	1	16	67
	01	18	3,19	8,80	16	3,17	8,65	2	1,94	3,63
	02				2	2	15	—	—	—
5. D.S.J.	I	94	26,36	72,84	5	1,14	1,96	—	—	—
	01	6	84	2,83	6	84	2,83	—	—	—
6. Indra Singh	I	13	1,80	7,77	7	60	1,71	—	—	—
	01	1	17	39	1	17	39	1	17	39
7. J.K.	I	52	10,05	23,93	2	93	3,46	—	—	—
	01	11	1,75	6,78	10	1,71	6,67	1	40	95
	02				1	4	11	—	—	—
8. Kasturbhai	I	15	4,99	19,81	2	2,02	4,52	2	2,02	4,52
	01	2	2,03	2,11	2	2,03	2,11	1	2,00	2,09

9. Khatau	I	14	1,41	5,25	—	—	—	—	—	—
	01 }	31	24,69	71,19	20	22,41	66,28	2	60	2,64
	02 }				11	2,28	4,91	1	1,85	3,64
10. Kirloskar	I	7	1,36	5,46	3	65	2,35	2	62	2,32
	01	2	31	2,66	2	31	2,66	1	30	2,64
11. Mafatlal	I	17	6,05	19,85	3	61	1,70	—	—	—
	01 }	21	15,49	46,53	13	13,97	41,23	—	—	—
	02 }				8	1,52	5,30	—	—	—
12. Mahindra	I	7	2,83	7,44	3	12	22	2	4	3
	01	3	34	99	3	34	99	3	34	99
13. Martin Burn	I	19	19,42	89,90	—	—	—	—	—	—
	01 }	4	63	1,97	3	61	1,60	2	30	1,31
	02 }				1	2	37	1	2	38
14. Ramakrishna	I	11	1,86	9,55	—	—	—	—	—	—
	01	2	32	1,19	2	32	1,19	—	—	—
15. Seshasayee	I	14	2,67	6,63	3	95	2,21	—	—	—
	01	4	4,46	8,56	4	4,46	8,56	—	—	—
16. Shapoorji	I	18	2,91	13,51	2	72	2,65	—	—	—
	01 }	15	24,69	69,55	10	19,94	53,23	2	9	5
	02 }				5	4,75	16,32	1	1,85	3,64
17. Shri Ram	I	9	6,21	28,79	1	55	1,99	—	—	—
	01	2	24	90	2	24	90	—	—	—
18. Tata	I	52	74,56	2,90,81	13	24,55	52,75	8	14,81	51,97
	01 }	68	33,68	97,91	30	26,74	71,29	14	5,72	12,28
	02 }				38	6,93	26,62	37	6,93	26,62
19. Thapar	I	42	10,80	27,25	8	1,45	3,73	4	79	1,50
	01	3	1,27	3,49	3	1,27	3,49	2	1,12	2,33

TABLE 12: (*Contd.*)

20. Walchand	I	15	4,93	16,37	2	36	76	—	—	—
	01 }	15	19,98	53,91	6	13,74	42,00	1	2	38
	02 }				9	6,24	11,91	—	—	—
Total	I	884	2,82,22	8,95,60	82	41,06	1,05,78	25	19,80	62,20
	01*	236	1,40,54	4,02,39	159	1,18,65	3,36,61	60	15,59	44,47
	02				77	21,88	65,78	42	10,73	34,37
All companies	I+0**	1,078	3,60,84	11,20,96	274	1,19,38	3,28,49	96	40,13	1,26,86

Notes: 1. All outer circle companies are joint ventures by definition. Joint ventures in the inner circles, and minority companies of the second order in outer circles are appropriately marked in the List of Companies by Complexes 1958.

2. Foreign partners include companies registered abroad as well as companies under foreign control registered in India

3. Martin Burn is a joint venture at its very source but is not treated as such here.

*Gross of multiple counting.

**Adjusted for multiple counting.

I: Inner Circle 01: Outer Circle, first order 02: Outer Circle, second order.

crores and gross capital stock of Rs. 62 crores. This role is all the more significant because foreign participation in share capital became a necessity only after 1958 due to the foreign exchange crisis. Such inner circle joint ventures with foreign partners were prominent in Tata, Kasturbhai and Thapar.

On the whole, however, only a few groups had majority ventures. Besides Tata, Kasturbhai and Thapar, the others were Andrew Yule (owing to the Bangur incursion), Indra Singh, Kirloskar, Seshasayee and Shapoorji. In Khatau, Martin Burn and Ramakrishna, on the other hand, there were no majority joint ventures at all.

Most of the joint ventures took the form of minority participation by the groups concerned. Such participation was especially prominent in Tata, Bangur and Seshasayee, in addition to the four complexes, Shapoorji, Khatau, Walchand and Mafatlal, which owe most of their importance to their outer circles. In several cases, minority participation is indirect or of the second order, that is, a minority venture in turn holds a controlling interest in another venture, For example, Tata has a minority interest in A.C.C. which has a minority interest in Asbestos Cement. This second order minority participation is particularly noticeable in Khatau, Mafatlal, Shapoorji, Tata and Walchand.

As a broad generalisation, it would be true to say that deliberately formed joint ventures are, relatively speaking, not significant in Birla, Dalmia Sahu Jain, Andrew Yule, J.K., and Ramakrishna. They are rather common and significant in Tata, Bangur, Thapar, Shapoorji, Khatau, Mafatlal, Walchand, Seshasayee, Indra Singh, Mahindra and Kirloskar, but with marked differences *inter se*:

Most Thapar, Mahindra and Kirloskar joint ventures appear to owe their origin to the shortage of liquid resources within the group, and the need for foreign technical know-how.

Bangur and Shapoorji minority interests, on the other hand, represent an outflow of liquid resources available within the groups.

Seshasayee joint ventures seem to follow logically from the group's specialisation in management and its practice of raising almost all resources from outside interests.

The major joint ventures of Tata, Khatau and Walchand are, mostly, the products of adverse circumstances or were probably intended as safeguards against adversity, for example, the Tata and Khatau interest in A.C.C., the Tata entry into MacNiel & Barry in order, *inter alia*, to provide against possible nationalisation of steel and power, Walchand joining with Narottam Morarjee and Kilachand in Scindia Steam, and again with Kilachand and Khatau in Premier Automobiles. The Tata minority interest in relatively small companies is the result of either investment banking or vertical industrial integration.

Khatau and Mafatlal joint ventures represent a projection of their interests outside their traditional specialised field, that is, cotton textiles, a projection which they might not have risked on their own. Besides, Mafatlal needs an outlet for its surplus liquid funds.

Indra Singh's collaboration with other interests is attributable mainly to the partial takeover of enterprises from other interests.

FINANCIAL STRUCTURE

We turn now to the financial structure of the companies studied.

The 20 complexes included 592 and 622 *public* companies (excluding banks and insurance) in 1951 and 1958, respectively. The slight change in the number and identity of companies takes away the precise significance of the magnitude of changes under various balance sheet heads. It does not, however, affect the analytical value of the proportions in terms of balance sheet totals.

The companies financed the greater part of their substantial expansion during the period from external sources (Table 13). About 32 per cent of the gross total funds raised came from loans, and 24 per cent from short-term liabilities, making a total of 56 per cent for borrowings. Share capital (including capitalised reserves) provided nearly 16 per cent. About 9 per cent came from free reserves and 19 per cent from depreciation.

On the uses side, gross fixed assets absorbed more than 64 per cent of the gross total funds raised, and nearly 21 per cent went into inventory, making a total of 85 per cent for the formation of gross physical assets. Only 3 per cent was absorbed in investments, while more than 11 per cent went into receivables and cash.

TABLE 13: **Combined balance sheet of public companies***

(*Rs. lakhs*)

		Inner Circles		Complexes@	
		1951	1958	1951	1958
	No. of companies	502	523	592	624
	Liabilities				
1.	Share capital	1,55,06	2,46,52	1,98,65	3,07,00
		(33.9)	(26.8)	(35.5)	(27.6)
2.	Reserves	1,02,22	1,52,64	1,22,92	1,83,22
		(22.4)	(16.6)	(21.9)	(16.4)
3.	Loans	89,35	2,83,14	1,09,10	3,28,74
		(19.6)	(30.6)	(19.5)	(29.5)
4.	Other	1,09,92	2,39,23	1,29,66	2,95,11
		(24.1)	(26.0)	(23.1)	(26.5)
	Total (1+2+3+4)	4,56,55	9,21,53	5,60,33	11,14,07
		(100.0)	(100.0)	(100.0)	(100.0)
	Assets				
1.	(a) Gross fixed assets	2,50,35	6,25,44	3,19,65	7,57,45
	Less				
	(b) Depreciation	1,16,77	2,24,49	1,45,26	2,76,42
	(c) Net fixed assets (a—b)	1,33,58	4,00,95	1,74,39	4,81,03
		(29.3)	(43.5)	(31.2)	(43.2)
2.	Investments	64,05	82,36	76,32	97,06
		(14.0)	(8.9)	(13.6)	(8.7)
3.	Inventory	1,19,10	2,32,75	1,42,77	2,84,65
		(26.1)	(25.3)	(25.5)	(25.5)
4.	Receivables and cash	1,25,53	1,86,09	1,48,71	2,27,09
		(27.5)	(20.2)	(26.5)	(20.4)
5.	Other	14,29	19,38	18,14	24,24
		(3.1)	(2.1)	(3.2)	(2.2)
	Total (1+2+3+4+5)	4,56,55	9,21,53	5,60,33	11,14,07
		(100.0)	(100.0)	(100.0)	(100.0)

*Excluding banking and insurance companies.
@Adjusted for companies counted more than once.

This pattern of raising and utilisation of funds led to significant changes in the structure of liabilities and assets. In terms of total (net) liabilities or assets, that is, the balance sheet total, net worth declined from 57 per cent in 1951 to 44 per cent in 1958, while loan liabilities went up from 20 to 30 per cent. On the assets side, the ratio of net fixed assets moved up from 31 to 43 per cent but inventory remained constant at about 26 per cent; investments declined from 14 to 9 per cent, and receivables and cash from 27 to 20 per cent.

The period, thus, witnessed a substantial increase in the ratio of debt to equity, and of fixed to working capital. These changes brought about a degree of deviation from orthodox financial standards. In 1951, the share capital of public companies was more than adequate to cover net fixed assets, while reserves almost covered inventory requirements. In 1958, net worth was barely adequate even for net fixed assets.

This overall picture does not fully bring out the increasing dependence upon borrowings for, the aggregate ratio of borrowings for the 20 complexes was kept down in 1958 by the fairly strong net worth position of groups like Mafatlal, Kasturbhai, Indra Singh and Andrew Yule. It is interesting to note that these groups, which continued to maintain a strong net worth position, expanded at a much slower pace as compared with other groups, like Tata, Dalmia Sahu Jain, Bangur and Ramakrishna, which relied mostly upon borrowings to finance their expansion.

The decline in investments as a proportion of total (net) assets came about, principally, due to two reasons: (*a*) other assets, mainly fixed assets, expanded at a much faster pace, and (*b*) the amount of government securities held in investment portfolios declined substantially. The decline in this proportion should not be confused with the role of inter-corporate investment in the ownership and control of companies: the ratio of investments to the balance sheet total is not comparable with the ratio of inter-corporate share holdings to total share capital, particularly in a period in which share capital provided only a small part of the total funds raised for expansion.

Even in 1958, investments as a proportion of the total net assets of public companies were substantial in Birla, Dalmia Sahu Jain, Bangur, J.K., Thapar and Kasturbhai inner circles. There was, however, a marked trend towards a reduction of this proportion during the period in Birla and Dalmia Sahu Jain.

Balance sheet data for *private* companies are not available for 1951. The 1958 data indicate that their assets are mostly financial, not physical (Table 14). Investments constitute nearly 29

TABLE 14: **Combined balance sheet of private companies—1958**

(*Rs. lakhs*)

	Inner circles	Complexes*		Inner circles	Complexes*
No. of companies	341	433		341	433
Liabilities			*Assets*		
1. Share capital	27,66	45,69	1. (a) Gross fixed assets	17,43	37,99
	(26.2)	(28.0)	*Less*		
2. Reserves	20,66	26,08	(b) Depreciation	5,28	12,61
	(19.6)	(16.0)			
3. Loans	26,44	38,42	(c) Net fixed assets	12,15	25,38
	(25.1)	(23.6)			
4. Other	30,73	52,78		(11.5)	(15.6)
	(29.1)	(32.4)	2. Investments	30,44	32,04
				(28.9)	(19.7)
			3. Inventory	15,98	36,87
				(15.1)	(22.6)
			4. Receivables and cash	39,44	60,13
				(37.4)	(36.9)
			5. Other	7,49	8,55
				(7.1)	(5.2)
Total	1,05,50	1,62,97	Total	1,05,50	1,62,97
	(100.0)	(100.0)		(100.0)	(100.0)

*Adjusted for companies counted more than once.

per cent of the total net assets of inner circle private companies, against less than 14 per cent in inner circle public companies. The small proportion of physical assets is made up mostly of inventory, not fixed assets.

Most private companies are quite small, in terms of financial as well as physical assets, except in Tata and Dalmia Sahu Jain.

There were no significant cases of conversion of private into public companies during the period: J.K. Iron and Steel, J.K. Jute, D.S.J.'s Jaipur Udyog, and Mahindra & Mahindra were the only significant conversions of this kind. Several large D.S.J. and a few Birla investment companies were, on the other hand, converted from public to private companies.

PREFERENCE CAPITAL

Taking public and private companies together, the ratio of preference to total share capital declined slightly from 20 to 18 per cent during the period.

The Shapoorji, Indra Singh and Kirloskar complexes had no or practically no preference capital in both the reference years. In Mahindra and Seshasayee, it was 10 per cent or less of total share capital. The ratio was highest in the Walchand inner circle at 41 per cent in both the reference years.

During the period, the ratio declined in all complexes except Birla, Bangur, Thapar, J.K., Shri Ram and Ramakrishna.

OWNERSHIP OF SHARE CAPITAL

The data on shareholding cover 988 companies in 1951 and 1079 companies in 1958. The various types of owners are classified under seven major heads:

(a) Individuals in India
(b) Indian companies
(c) Life Insurance Corporation
(d) Government
(e) Trusts
(f) Foreign individuals
(g) Foreign companies.

The holdings of Indian companies are further sub-classified by occupation: (i) banking, (ii) executor and trustee, (iii) insurance, (iv) finance, (v) industrial, and (vi) service, and by type, that is, public and private.

It may be clearly stated at the outset that the holdings of trusts and foreign investors are probably underestimated, the former due to section 153 of the Companies Act which prohibits the registration of trusts as shareholders and the latter due to the registration of some of their holdings in the names of banks and trustee companies in India. On the other hand, the holdings of banks are certainly over-estimated because most of them are actually held in various capacities on behalf of different categories of clients, including individuals, companies and trusts.

In the aggregate, out of 988 and 1079 companies, only 258 and 214 in 1951 and 1958, respectively, were owned wholly by individuals and trusts.

In both years, individuals in India owned about one-half of the total share capital, Indian companies 37 per cent, foreign investors about 4 per cent, and trusts 3 per cent (Table 15). There was, thus, no *striking* change in the broad pattern of ownership of companies between 1951 and 1958.

More specifically, the proportion of total share capital owned by individuals, both Indian and foreign, and by government declined slightly during the period, in the case of individuals from 53 per cent to 48 per cent, and of government from 5 to 4 per cent. The proportion owned by Indian companies remained practically constant at 37 per cent. The Life Insurance Corporation, which was set up only in 1956, came to acquire about 5 per cent of total share capital (including 13 per cent of preference) by 1958.

If the holdings of Indian companies, foreign companies and L.I.C. are lumped together, the proportion held by them rose from 39 per cent to 45 per cent. *The ownership of share capital is, thus, evolving gradually in favour of corporate and away from individual owners.*

Finance and industrial companies were the major owners among Indian companies. These two categories held a little more than 20 per cent and 7 per cent, respectively, of total share capital in both the reference years. Industrial companies, it may be observed, effected a moderate increase in their equity holdings and a rather substantial reduction in their preference investments.

The proportion of total share capital held in the names of banks rose from 4 to 6 per cent, indicating a more frequent and wider use of this method of holding shares by individual, trustee and corporate investors. The small proportion held by executor and trustee companies was halved from 1.0 to 0.5 per cent, and involved even an absolute reduction—probably on account of individuals abroad.

The decline in the role of Indian insurance companies as shareholders was more significant. The actual disinvestment recorded exceeded Rs. 3.5 crores (mainly under preference) and brought down the percentage of total share capital held by them from

TABLE 15: **Ownership of companies* in 1951 and 1958**

(*Rs. lakhs*)

	1951			1958			Change between 1951 & 1958		
	Total	Ord.	Pref.	Total	Ord.	Pref.	Total	Ord.	Pref.
No. of companies	988			1,079			91		
Total share capital	2,44,05	1,94,36	49,69	3,63,38	2,98,89	64,49	1,19,33	1,04,53	14,80
	(100.0)	(100.0)	(100.0)	(100.0)	(100.0)	(100.0)	(100.0)	(100.0)	(100.0)
Owners:									
1. Individuals in India	1,21,95	97,29	24,66	1,70,80	1,42,29	28,51	48,85	45,00	3,85
	(50.0)	(50.1)	(49.6)	(47.0)	(47.6)	(44.2)	(40.9)	(43.0)	(25.9)
2. Indian companies	90,26	73,84	16,42	1,35,12	1,16,65	18,47	44,86	42,81	2,05
	(37.0)	(38.0)	(33.0)	(37.2)	(39.0)	(28.6)	(37.6)	(41.0)	(13.8)
a. Banking	10,15	7,53	2,62	21,52	15,46	6,06	11,37	7,93	3,44
	(4.2)	(3.9)	(5.3)	(5.9)	(5.2)	(9.5)	(9.5)	(7.6)	(23.2)
b. Executor and trustee	2,53	2,08	45	1,97	1,63	34	—56	—45	—11
	(1.0)	(1.1)	(0.9)	(0.5)	(0.5)	(0.5)	(—0.4)	(—0.4)	(—0.6)
c. Insurance	8,32	3,61	4,71	4,79	3,18	1,61	—3,53	—43	—3,10
	(3.4)	(1.9)	(9.5)	(1.3)	(1.1)	(2.4)	(—3.0)	(—0.4)	(—21.0)
d. Finance	49,92	44,56	5,36	73,90	66,21	7,69	23,98	21,65	2,33
	(20.5)	(22.9)	(10.8)	(20.3)	(22.1)	(11.9)	(20.1)	(20.7)	(15.6)
e. Industrial	18,00	14,93	3,07	28,54	26,30	2,24	10,54	11,37	—83
	(7.4)	(7.6)	(6.2)	(7.9)	(8.8)	(3.5)	(8.8)	(10.9)	(—5.6)
f. Service	1,34	1,13	21	4.40	3.87	53	3,06	2,74	32
	(0.5)	(0.6)	(0.4)	(1.3)	(1.3)	(0.8)	(2.6)	(2.6)	(2.2)
(i) Public	64,34	51,91	12,43	98,98	84,53	14,45	34,64	32,62	2,02
	(26.4)	(26.7)	(25.0)	(27.2)	(28.3)	(22.4)	(29.0)	(31.2)	(13.7)

(ii) Private	25,92	21,93	3,99	36,14	32,12	4,02	10,22	10,19	3
	(10.6)	(11.3)	(8.0)	(10.0)	(10.7)	(6.2)	(8.6)	(9.8)	(0.1)
3. Life Insurance Corporation	—	—	—	17,57	9,09	8,48	17,57	9,09	8,48
	(—)	(—)	(—)	(4.8)	(3.0)	(13.2)	(14.7)	(8.7)	(57.3)
4. Government	13,28	9,21	4,07	15,58	10,18	5,40	2,30	97	1,33
	(5.4)	(4.7)	(8.2)	(4.3)	(3.4)	(8.4)	(1.9)	(0.9)	(9.1)
5. Trusts	7,74	5,38	2,36	10,81	8,28	2,53	3,07	2,90	17
	(3.2)	(2.8)	(4.7)	(3.0)	(2.8)	(3.9)	(2.6)	(2.8)	(1.2)
6. Foreign individuals	6,19	4,88	1,31	3,91	3,24	67	—2,28	—1,64	—64
	(2.5)	(2.5)	(2.6)	(1.1)	(1.1)	(1.0)	(—1.9)	(—1.6)	(—4.2)
7. Foreign companies	4,63	3,76	87	9,59	9,16	43	4,96	5,40	—44
	(1.9)	(1.9)	(1.8)	(2.6)	(3.1)	(0.7)	(4.2)	(5.2)	(—3.0)

*All companies.

3.4 to 1.3.

There was an interesting change in the composition of foreign shareholders. Individuals disinvested heavily but this was over-compensated by the investments of foreign companies, some of which took over the holdings of individuals. In 1958, foreign companies owned nearly 3 per cent and foreign individuals about 1 per cent of total share capital.

GOVERNMENT AND L.I.C. HOLDINGS

The total investment of government in the sample companies amounted to Rs. 13.28 crores in 1951 and Rs. 15.58 crores in 1958. Of these amounts, Rs. 5.02 crores and Rs. 7.58 crores, respectively, was in government companies[1] as defined under section 617 of the Companies Act. The remaining Rs. 8.26 crores and Rs. 8.000 crores, respectively, was invested in other companies.

The Life Insurance Corporation had a total investment (*net* of multiple counting) of Rs. 17.57 crores in the sample companies in 1958. Of this amount, Rs. 6.38 crores was in Tata, Rs. 2.84 crores in Martin Burn and Rs. 1.66 crores in Birla.

The distribution of government and L.I.C. investments by complexes is given in Table 16. It will be observed that most of their investments are in the larger complexes. This pattern of distribution is largely the result of historical circumstances and market conditions at various times.

The government inherited large blocks of investments by the former princely states in several large companies in the Tata Complex, for example, Tata Loco and A.C.C. In Dalmia Sahu Jain, the Punjab Government disposed of its inherited investment in Dalmia Dadri Cement but this was replaced by a fresh Orissa Government investment in Orissa Cement. Most of the government holding in Birla was confined to certain companies in Hyderabad which were formerly state government companies. The government holding in Thapar represented a continuation of its interest in Ballarpur Paper, which was a government company in 1951.

Similarly, L.I.C. also inherited large holdings in various leading companies from the former private insurers. These were augmented when L.I.C. absorbed a large part of the 'floating stock' of the shares of the companies during the 1956-58 slump on the

TABLE 16: **Government and L.I.C. holdings in twenty complexes**

(*Rs. lakhs*)

Complex	Government				L.I.C.
	1951		1958		1958
1. Tata	6,65	(44)	3,93		6,38*
2. Birla	6		1,58	(6)	1,66
3. Martin Burn	9		10		2,84
4. D.S J.	1,32		1,33		73
5. Bird Heilger	7		12		90
6. Andrew Yule	5		2		1,11
7. Bangur	21		14		1,52
8. Thapar	47	(40)	39		18
9. J.K.	1		Neg.		69
10. Shri Ram	—		—		49
11. Shapoorji	40		38		2,06*
12. Khatau	32		30		2,13*
13. Walchand	1,48	(1,48)	4,39	(4,37)	61**
14. Mafatlal	—		1		57**
15. Kasturbhai	—		—		1
16. Seshasayee	2,73	(2,70)	3,20	(3,16)	13
17. Ramakrishna	1		1		5
18. Indra Singh	3		3		4
19. Mahindra	—		25		4
20. Kirloskar	1		1		3
Total (gross)	13,91	(5,02)	16,19	(7,58)	22,17
Less overlap	63		61		4,60
Total (*net*)	13,28	(5,02)	15,58	(7,58)	17,57

Note: Figures in parentheses relate to government companies. The investments of government companies are not included under government.

*Includes Rs. 184 lakhs in A.C.C.

**Includes Rs. 45 lakhs in Scindia Steam.

stock exchange. It also had to subscribe heavily to the new issues of these companies, particularly of preference capital, during the period.

OWNERSHIP OF PUBLIC AND PRIVATE COMPANIES

The belief that private companies are largely owned by family members is a myth, so far as the sample companies are concerned at any rate. As compared with public companies, private companies are owned to a much greater extent by other companies (Tables 17 and 18).

The proportion of the total share capital of private companies owned by Indian and foreign companies increased from about 54 per cent in 1951 to 60 per cent in 1958. The proportion owned by Indian and foreign individuals fell from 35 per cent to 25 per cent, and that owned by trusts from more than 7 per cent to less than 6 per cent.

In public companies, individuals owned more than one-half of the total share capital in both years (see Table 17) but the proportion clearly tended to decline.

Of the additional share capital raised by public companies during the period, individuals provided 44 per cent (net of some disinvestment by foreigners), while trusts contributed less than 3 per cent.

The remaining amount was raised from Indian (mainly finance) companies (34 per cent), L.I.C. (16 per cent) and foreign companies (3 per cent).

L.I.C. alone provided one-half of the additional preference capital. Two-thirds of this contribution was L.I.C.'s own and the remaining one-third appears to have been taken over from insurance companies.

Nearly 7 per cent of the total share capital of public companies in 1958, against less than 5 per cent in 1951, was registered in the names of banks. The true pattern of ownership of companies is obscured to that extent.

The analysis of the ownership of companies by size ranges (measured by net worth plus loans, Tables 19 and 20) indicates that giant companies raise most of their share capital from individuals, while the smaller companies depend relatively more upon other, mainly finance, companies. Government, L.I.C., and bank holdings are mostly in the large companies.

OWNERSHIP PATTERN BY INDUSTRIES

The data on the ownership of companies by industry in 1951 and 1958 are given in Tables 21 and 22. (The diversification of some cotton, jute and sugar companies and the consequent change in their classification during the period affects the comparability of the 1951 and 1958 data only to a nominal extent). The

TABLE 17: **Ownership of public companies in 1951 and 1958**

(*Rs. lakhs*)

	1951			1958			Change between 1951 and 1958		
	Total	Ord.	Pref.	Total	Ord.	Pref.	Total	Ord.	Pref.
No. of companies	618			644			25		
Total share capital	2,10,60	1,66,74	43,86	3,16,18	2,55,66	60,52	1,05,58	88,92	16,66
	(100.0)	(100.0)	(100.0)	(100.0)	(100.0)	(100.0)	(100.0)	(100.0)	(100.0)
Owners:									
1. Individuals in India	1,11,34	88,55	22,79	1,59,59	1,32,24	27.35	48,25	43,69	4,56
	(52.9)	(53.1)	(52.0)	(50.5)	(51.7)	(45.2)	(45.7)	(49.1)	(27.3)
2. Indian companies	74,48	59,67	14,81	1,10,65	93,68	16,97	36,17	34,01	2,16
	(35.4)	(35.8)	(33.8)	(35.0)	(36.6)	(28.1)	(34.2)	(38.3)	(12.8)
a. Banking	9,88	7,38	2,50	21,12	15,09	6,03	11,24	7,71	3,53
	(4.7)	(4.4)	(5.7)	(6.7)	(5.9)	(10.0)	(10.6)	(8.7)	(21.3)
b. Executor and trustee	1,58	1,20	38	1,80	1,46	34	22	26	—4
	(0.8)	(0.7)	(0.9)	(0.6)	(0.6)	(0.6)	(0.2)	(0.3)	(—0.2)
c. Insurance	8,00	3,59	4,41	4,62	3,10	1,52	—3,38	—49	—2,89
	(3.8)	(2.2)	(10.1)	(1.5)	(1.2)	(2.5)	(—3.2)	(—0.5)	(—17.5)
d. Finance	38,70	34,38	4,32	58,85	52,46	6,39	20,15	18,08	2,07
	(18.4)	(20.6)	(9.8)	(18.5)	(20.5)	(10.6)	(19.1)	(20.3)	(12.4)
e. Industrial	15,09	12,09	3,00	20,55	18,39	2,16	5,46	6,30	—84
	(7.2)	(7.3)	(6.8)	(6.5)	(7.2)	(3.6)	(5.2)	(7.1)	(—5.2)
f. Service	1,23	1,03	20	3,71	3,18	53	2,48	2,15	33
	(0.6)	(0.6)	(0.5)	(1.2)	(1.2)	(0.8)	(2.3)	(2.4)	(2.0)
(i) Public	56,48	44,83	11,65	86,16	72,14	14,02	29,68	27,31	2,37
	(26.9)	(26.9)	(26.6)	(27.3)	(28.2)	(23.2)	(28.1)	(30.7)	(14.1)

TABLE 17: (*Contd.*)

(ii) Private	18,00	·14,84	3,6	24,49	21,55	2.95	6,49	6,71	(—21)
	(8.5)	(8.9)	(7.2)	(7.7)	(8.4)	(4.9)	(6.1)	(7.6)	(—1.3)
3. Life Insurance	—	—	—	17,57	9,09	8,48	17,57	9,09	8,48
Corporation	(—)	(—)	(—)	(5.6)	(3.6)	(14.0)	(16.7)	(10.2)	(50.9)
4. Government	12,10	9.05	3,05	11,06	5,66	5,40	—1,04	—3,39	2,35
	(5.7)	(5.4)	(7.0)	(3.5)	(2.2)	(8.9)	(—1.0)	(—3.8)	(14.2)
5. Trusts	5,31	3,99	1,32	8,19	6,91	1,28	2,88	2,92	—4
	(2.5)	(2.4)	(3.0)	(2.6)	(2.7)	(2.1)	(2.7)	(3.3)	(—0.2)
6. Foreign individuals	5.11	4,08	1,03	3,41	2,79	62	—1,70	—1,29	—41
	(2.4)	(2.4)	(2.3)	(1,1)	(1.1)	(1.0)	(—1.6)	(—1.5)	(—2.4)
7. Foreign companies	2,26	1,40	86	5,71	5,28	43	3,45	3,88	—43
	(1.1)	(0.8)	(2.0)	(1.8)	(2.1)	(0.7)	(3.3)	(4.4)	(—6.2)

Note: Slight differences in totals are due to rounding.

ownership of share capital by companies is significant under every single industrial head.

Indian companies owned more share capital than Indian individuals in both 1951 and 1958 in 10 out of the 28 industrial heads: coal, other mining, cotton (allowing for transfer of some companies to 'other industry' by 1958), woollen, plantations, printing and publishing, construction, investment and finance, managing agency, and trade.

Moreover, between 1951 and 1958, Indian companies came to hold a larger proportion of share capital than Indian individuals in another six industrial heads: rayon, jute, engineering, food and vegetable oil, real estate and 'other industry'.

The industries in which the major part of share capital is owned by Indian individuals are power, basic iron and steel, non-ferrous engineering, sugar, glass and plastics and pottery, cement, transport, banking and insurance. In chemicals and paper, too, individuals hold slightly more share capital than companies.

Government's investment in both years was concentrated mainly in engineering, chemicals, and cement.

L.I.C.'s investments in 1958 were distributed fairly widely but tended to concentrate in basic iron and steel, cement, engineering, power, chemicals, transport, managing agency and other industry.

Trusts were significant shareholders in cotton and steel (in 1958), engineering, paper (1958), hotels, investment and finance, managing agency, and other industry (1958).

During the period, foreign investment increased only in iron and steel, engineering, chemicals, cement, other industry and trade. It remained constant in rayon, non-ferrous engineering, sugar, paper, real estate, glass and plastics and pottery, and insurance. It declined substantially in coal, other mining, power, cotton, jute, plantations, food and vegetable oil, transport, banking, investment and finance, and managing agency. It was nil or negligible in both years in woollen, printing and publishing, construction and hotels.

INTER-INDUSTRIAL CORPORATE HOLDINGS

The data on the pattern of inter-industrial corporate holdings in the two years are given in Tables 23, 24 and 25. The two main

TABLE 18: **Ownership of private companies in 1951 and 1958**

(*Rs. lakhs*)

	1951			1958		
	Total	Ord.	Pref.	Total	Ord.	Pref.
No. of companies	370			435		
Total share capital	33,45	27,62	5,83	47,20	43,23	3,97
	(100.0)	(100.0)	(100.0)	(100.0)	(100.0)	(100.0)
Owners:						
1. Individuals in India	10,61	8,73	1,88	11,21	10,04	1,17
	(31.7)	(31.6)	(32.2)	(23.8)	(22.2)	(29.5)
2. Indian companies	15,79	14.18	1,61	24.47	22,97	1,50
	(47.2)	(51.3)	(27.6)	(51.8)	(53.1)	(37.8)
a. Banking	26	14	12	40	37	3
	(0.8)	(0.5)	(2.1)	(0.8)	(0.9)	(0.8)
b. Executor and trustee	95	89	6	17	17	—
	(2.8)	(3.2)	(1.0)	(0.4)	(0.4)	(—)
c. Insurance	32	1	31	17	8	9
	(1.0)	(neg.)	(5.3)	(0.4)	(0.2)	(2.3)
d. Finance	11,23	10,19	1,04	15,05	13,75	1,30
	(33.6)	(36.9)	(17.8)	(31.9)	(31.7)	(32.7)
e. Industrial	2,92	2,84	8	7,99	7,91	8
	(8.7)	(10.3)	(1.4)	(16.9)	(18.3)	(2.0)
f. Service	11	11	—	69	69	—
	(0.3)	(0.4)	(—)	(1.4)	(1.6)	(—)

(i) Public	7,86	7,08	78	12,82	12,39	43
	(23.5)	(25.6)	(13.4)	(27.2)	(28.7)	(10.8)
(ii) Private	7,93	7,10	83	11,65	10,58	1,07
	(23.7)	(25.7)	(14.2)	(24.6)	(24.4)	(27.0)
3. Government	1,17	15	1,02	4,52	4,52	—
	(3.5)	(0.5)	(17.5)	(9.6)	(10.5)	(—)
4. Trusts	2,43	1,40	1,03	2,62	1,37	1,25
	(7.3)	(5.1)	(17.7)	(5.6)	(3.2)	(31.5)
5. Foreign individuals	1,08	80	28	50	45	5
	(3.2)	(2.9)	(4.8)	(1.1)	(1.0)	(1.3)
6. Foreign companies	2,37	2,36	1	3,88	3,88	—
	(7.1)	(8.5)	(0.2)	(8.1)	(9.0)	(—)

TABLE 19: **Ownership of public companies**

Net worth plus loans	Up to 10		10 to 25	
	Ord.	Pref.	Ord.	Pref.
No. of companies	201		122	
Total share capital	4,37	16	8,68	98
	(100.0)	(100.0)	(100.0)	(100.0)
Owners:				
1. Individuals in India	2,51	4	3,94	51
	(57.4)	(25.0)	(45.4)	(52.0)
2. Indian companies	1,61	9	4,06	43
	(36.8)	(56.3)	(46.8)	(43.9)
a. Banking	10	—	20	3
	(2.3)	(—)	(2.3)	(3.1)
b. Executor and trustee	1	—	2	—
	(0.2)	(—)	(0.2)	(—)
c. Insurance	5	1	22	9
	(1.1)	(6.3)	(2.5)	(9.2)
d. Finance	1,08	6	2,57	16
	(24.7)	(37.5)	(29.6)	(16.3)
e. Industrial	34	2	93	14
	(7.8)	(12.5)	(10.7)	(14.3)
f. Service	3	—	12	1
	(0.7)	(—)	(1.4)	(1.0)
(i) Public	1,31	8	3,13	30
	(30.0)	(50.0)	(36.1)	(30.6)
(ii) Private	30	1	93	13
	(6.8)	(6.3)	(10.7)	(13.3)
3. Government	4	—	8	2
	(0.9)	(—)	(0.9)	(2.0)
4. Trusts	10	2	18	1
	(2.3)	(12.5)	(2.1)	(1.0)
5. Foreign individuals	10	1	24	1
	(2.3)	(6.3)	(2.8)	(1.0)
6. Foreign companies	1	—	18	—
	(0.2)	(—)	(2.1)	(—)

Note: Slight differences in totals are due to rounding.

by size ranges—1951

(Rs. lakhs)

25 to 50		50 to 100		100 to 1000		1000 and above	
Ord.	Pref.	Ord.	Pref.	Ord.	Pref.	Ord.	Pref.
79		97		116		3	
12,03	1,65	24,71	5,62	97,03	27,77	19,93	7,69
(100.0)	(100.0)	(100.0)	(100.0)	(100.0)	(100.0)	(100.0)	(100.0)
7,27	81	13,23	3,09	46,04	12,89	15,56	5,46
(60.4)	(49.1)	(53.5)	(55.0)	(47.5)	(46.4)	(78.1)	(71.0)
3,88	72	9,62	2,17	37,01	9,69	3,48	1,71
(32.3)	(43.6)	(38.9)	(38.6)	(38.1)	(34.9)	(17.5)	(22.2)
25	7	91	54	3,81	1,32	2,11	54
(2.1)	(4.2)	(3.7)	(9.6)	(3.9)	(4.8)	(10.6)	(7.0)
7	3	15	4	80	20	14	11
(0.6)	(1.8)	(0.6)	(0.7)	(0.8)	(0.7)	(0.7)	(1.4)
43	17	64	82	1,92	2,85	34	46
(3.6)	(10.3)	(2.6)	(14.6)	(2.0)	(10.3)	(1.7)	(6.0)
2,08	36	5,37	49	22,65	2,74	62	52
(17.3)	(21.8)	(21.7)	(8.7)	(23.3)	(9.9)	(3.1)	(6.8)
94	9	2,45	27	7,21	2,44	22	3
(7.8)	(5.4)	(9.9)	(4.8)	(7.4)	(8.8)	(1.1)	(0.4)
11	—	10	1	62	14	5	5
(0.9)	(—)	(0.4)	(0.2)	(0.6)	(0.5)	(0.3)	(0.7)
3,03	50	7,22	1,92	27,22	7,74	2,92	1,11
(25.2)	(30.3)	(29.2)	(34.2)	(28.1)	(27.9)	(14.7)	(14.4)
85	22	2,40	25	9,79	1,95	56	60
(7.1)	(13.3)	(9.7)	(4.4)	(10.0)	(7.0)	(2.8)	(7.8)
30	2	75	6	7,48	2,80	41	14
(2.5)	(1.2)	(3.0)	(1.1)	(7.7)	(10.1)	(2.1)	(1.8)
23	3	64	15	2,73	89	11	23
(1.9)	(1.8)	(2.6)	(2.7)	(2.8)	(3.2)	(0.5)	(3.0)
28	7	37	8	2,74	75	36	11
(2.3)	(4.2)	(1.5)	(1.4)	(2.8)	(2.7)	(1.8)	(1.4)
7	—	10	7	1,03	75	1	4
(0.6)	(–)	(0.4)	(1.2)	(1.1)	(2.7)	(neg.)	(0.5)

TABLE 20: **Ownership of companies***

Net worth plus loans	Up to 10		10 to 25	
	Ord.	Pref.	Ord.	Pref.
No. of companies	441		201	
Total share capital	8,16	23	14.20	1,06
	(100.0)	(100.0)	(100.0)	(100.0)
Owners:				
1. Individuals in India	4,04	10	6,17	30
	(49.6)	(43.5)	(43.5)	(28.3)
2. Indian companies	3,73	11	7,00	66
	(45.7)	(47.8)	(49.3)	(62.3)
a. Banking	6	neg.	27	5
	(0.7)	(neg.)	(1.9)	(4.7)
b. Executor and trustee	1	—	4	neg.
	(0.1)	(—)	(0.3)	(—)
c. Insurance	2	1	28	18
	(0.2)	(4.3)	(2.0)	(17.0)
d. Finance	2,52	6	4,54	32
	(30.9)	(26.1)	(32.0)	(30.2)
e. Industrial	89	2	1,43	10
	(10.9)	(8.7)	(10.0)	(9.4)
f. Service	23	2	44	1
	(2.9)	(8.7)	(3.1)	(1.0)
(i) Public	2,15	6	4,99	51
	(26.3)	(26.1)	(35.1)	(48.1)
(ii) Private	1,58	5	2,01	15
	(19.4)	(21.7)	(14.2)	(14.2)
3. Life Insurance Corporation	1	neg.	8	5
	(0.1)	(neg.)	(0.6)	(4.7)
4. Government	5	neg.	12	2
	(0.6)	(neg.)	(0.8)	(1.9)
5. Trusts	14	2	27	3
	(1.7)	(8.7)	(1.9)	(2.8)
6. Foreign individuals	4	—	11	neg.
	(0.5)	(—)	(0.8)	(—)
7. Foreign companies	15	—	45	neg.
	(1.8)	(—)	(3.1)	(—)

*Both public and private.

Note: Slight differences in totals are due to rounding.

by size ranges—1958

(Rs. lakhs)

25 to 50		50 to 100		100 to 1000		1000 and above	
Ord.	Pref.	Ord.	Pref.	Ord.	Pref.	Ord.	Pref.
128		123		178		8	
17,47	3,50	28,95	4,76	1,52,47	39,94	77,64	15,00
(100.0)	(100.0)	(100.0)	(100.0)	(100.0)	(100.0)	(100.0)	(100.0)
6,53	1,18	12,62	1,84	63,21	16,70	49,72	8,39
(37.4)	(33.7)	(43.6)	(38.7)	(41.5)	(41.8)	(64.0)	(55.9)
9,22	1,72	13,05	2,04	65,52	12,13	18,13	1,81
(52.8)	(49.1)	(45.1)	(42.9)	(43.0)	(30.4)	(23.4)	(12.2)
52	39	1,01	41	5,44	4,43	8,16	78
(3.0)	(11.1)	(3.5)	(8.6)	(3.6)	(11.1)	(10.5)	(5.2)
13	3	13	6	71	18	61	7
(0.7)	(0.9)	(0.4)	(1.3)	(0.5)	(0.4)	(0.8)	(0.5)
25	9	36	22	1,40	1,07	87	4
(1.4)	(2.6)	(1.2)	(4.6)	(0.9)	(2.7)	(1.1)	(0.3)
5,54	82	7,41	71	40,32	4,93	5,88	85
(31.7)	(23.4)	(25.6)	(14.9)	(26.4)	(12.3)	(7.6)	(5.7)
2,28	31	3,04	49	16,33	1,29	2,33	3
(13.1)	(8.9)	(10.5)	(10.3)	(10.7)	(3.2)	(3.0)	(0.2)
50	8	1,10	15	1,32	23	28	4
(2.9)	(2.2)	(3.8)	(3.2)	(0.9)	(0.6)	(0.4)	(0.3)
6,63	1,39	9,48	1,80	46,40	9,79	14,88	90
(38.0)	(39.7)	(32.7)	(37.8)	(30.4)	(24.5)	(19.2)	(6.00)
2,59	33	3,57	24	19,12	2,34	3,25	91
(14.8)	(9.4)	(12.3)	(5.1)	(12.6)	(5.9)	(4.2)	(6.2)
22	22	62	64	3,44	5,44	4,72	2,13
(1.3)	(6.3)	(2.1)	(13.4)	(2.3)	(13.6)	(6.1)	(14.2)
34	5	64	3	8,07	3,13	96	2,17
(1.9)	(1.4)	(2.2)	(0.6)	(5.3)	(7.8)	(1.2)	(14.5)
25	19	52	13	4,81	1,85	2,29	31
(1.4)	(5.4)	(1.8)	(2.7)	(3.2)	(4.6)	(2.9)	(2.0)
32	14	26	3	1,73	31	78	19
(1.8)	(4.0)	(0.9)	(0.6)	(1.1)	(0.8)	(1.0)	(1.2)
59	—	1,24	5	5,69	38	1,04	neg.
(3.4)	(—)	(4.3)	(1.1)	(3.7)	(1.0)	(1.3)	(—)

TABLE 21: Ownership of companies by industry—1951

(Rs. lakhs)

Industry	No. of coys.	Type of shares	Total share capital	Owners				
				Individuals in India	Indian coys.	Govt.	Trusts	Foreign investors
1	2	3	4	5	6	7	8	9
1. Coal	47	Ord.	7,58	3,71	3,56	3	5	23
		Pref.	1,17	62	48	—	1	6
2. Other mining	14	Ord.	74	17	50	3	neg.	4
3. Power	20	Ord.	10,71	7,07	2,84	41	9	30
		Pref.	2,68	1,68	89	4	4	3
4. Cotton*	61	Ord.	20,76	8,07	11,19	2	1,13	35
		Pref.	3,91	2,77	96	7	5	6
5. Rayon*	3	Ord.	78	3	75	—	—	—
6. Woollen*	2	Ord.	75	26	49	—	—	—
		Pref.	22	2	20	—	—	—
7. Jute*	34	Ord.	8,80	4,68	3,43	1	16	52
		Pref.	3,72	2,05	1,42	neg.	10	15
8. Iron and steel	3	Ord.	8,61	4,89	3,16	9	10	37
		Pref.	10,39	7,17	2,46	14	31	31
9. Non-ferrous engineering	6	Ord.	99	66	27	2	—	4
		Pref.	40	25	13	—	neg.	2
10. Engineering	52	Ord.	18,30	9,34	5,73	1,63	54	1,06
		Pref.	4,33	1,12	90	2,02	11	18
11. Sugar*	25	Ord.	4,18	2,60	1,31	7	18	2
		Pref.	1,05	60	32	—	10	3

12.	Plantations	46	Ord.	2,63	92	1,39	—	2	30
			Pref.	9	8	1	—	neg.	neg.
13.	Food	16	Ord.	2,27	1,28	91	1	3	4
			Pref.	63	28	30	2	1	2
14.	Chemicals and paints	22	Ord.	7,27	3,48	70	2,62	1	46
			Pref.	98	57	34	6	neg	1
15.	Paper	7	Ord.	2,95	1,49	97	26	13	10
			Pref.	1,32	73	33	15	7	4
16.	Printing and publishing	15	Ord.	1,23	25	93	neg.	5	—
			Pref.	65	49	16	—	—	—
17.	Real estate	27	Ord.	3,30	1,65	1,54	—	4	7
			Pref.	69	29	39	—	—	1
18.	Construction	7	Ord.	62	11	51	—	—	—
			Pref.	31	23	7	—	1	neg.
19.	Glass, plastics and pottery	8	Ord.	1,04	69	32	—	1	2
			Pref.	41	22	18	—	1	neg.
20.	Cement, asbestos and fireclay	13	Ord.	17,82	10,39	6,18	36	7	82
			Pref.	2,31	84	20	1,25	neg.	2
21.	Transport	21	Ord.	17,06	9,56	3,73	3,09	22	46
			Pref.	64	15	49	neg.	neg.	neg.
22.	Hotels and services	5	Ord.	34	3	6	neg.	25	neg
23.	Banks	8	Ord.	6,80	4,36	2,23	—	9	12
			Pref.	54	36	8	—	6	4
24.	Insurance	18	Ord.	2,89	2,06	73	neg.	3	7
			Pref.	17	13	4	—	—	—
25.	Investment and finance	231	Ord.	23,12	9,14	11,21	15	1,12	1,50
			Pref.	6,33	1,49	3,41	28	98	17
26.	Managing agency	85	Ord.	13,19	4,84	5,95	23	60	1,57
			Pref.	4,44	1,30	1,66	4	44	1,00

TABLE 21: (*Contd.*)

27. Other industry	23	Ord.	6,33	4,05	1,77	18	28	5
		Pref.	2,06	1,13	87	neg.	4	2
28. Trade	169	Ord.	3,28	1,49	1,48	—	17	14
		Pref.	24	9	13	—	2	—
Total	988	Ord.	1,94,36	97,29	73,84	9,21	5,38	8,64
		Pref.	49,69	24,66	16,42	4,07	2,36	2,18

*Excluding diversified companies classified under other industry.

Note: Slight differences in totals are due to rounding.

TABLE 22: Ownership of companies by industry—1958

(*Rs. lakhs*)

Industry	No. of coys.	Type of shares	Total share capital	Owners					
				Individuals in India	Indian coys.	L.I.C.	Govt.	Trusts	Foreign investors
1	2	3	4	5	6	7	8	9	10
1. Coal	48	Ord.	7,84	3,01	4,28	38	neg.	7	10
		Pref.	1,25	67	45	9	neg.	2	2
2. Other mining	15	Ord.	1,37	56	65	neg.	14	neg.	2
		Pref.	12	8	3	1	—	neg.	—
3. Power	18	Ord.	14,05	9,25	3,46	83	18	26	7
		Pref.	2,84	1,63	38	72	2	7	2
4. Cotton*	63	Ord.	20,55	11,50	8,06	26	2	61	10
		Pref.	3,97	2,40	96	49	2	10	neg.
5. Rayon*	5	Ord.	3,99	1,46	2,28	1	18	2	4
		Pref.	3,80	1	3,17	—	62	—	neg.
6. Woollen*	2	Ord.	27	8	9	—	10	—	—
		Pref.	20	5	5	—	10	neg.	—
7. Jute*	31	Ord.	9,20	3,94	4,51	14	neg.	26	35
		Pref.	3,63	1,95	90	62	neg.	12	4
8. Iron and steel	2	Ord.	31,63	19,58	7,44	2,03	13	1,86	59
		Pref.	10,39	6,88	1,33	1,64	17	21	16
9. Non-ferrous engineering	5	Ord.	1,87	1,17	50	4	4	9	3
		Pref.	41	26	9	4	—	neg.	2
10. Engineering	86	Ord.	41,03	14,12	15,71	59	4,96	68	4,97
		Pref.	8,14	2,17	2,73	64	2,38	13	9

TABLE 22 (*Contd.*)

11. Sugar*	30	Ord.	6,29	3,48	2,15	26	15	16	9
		Pref.	1,29	78	41	4	2	4	neg.
12. Plantations	47	Ord.	3,44	1,29	1,86	3	3	2	21
		Pref.	18	8	9	neg.	neg.	neg.	neg.
13. Food	18	Ord.	2,35	1,09	1,17	4	1	3	1
		Pref.	56	30	15	7	2	2	neg.
14. Chemicals*	29	Ord.	13,87	5,71	4,18	10	3,16	4	68
		Pref.	2,03	89	34	46	27	2	5
15. Paper	11	Ord.	8,93	3,85	3,84	50	36	31	7
		Pref.	3,85	1,64	1,17	65	27	6	7
16. Printing and publishing	21	Ord.	1,32	11	1,20	neg.	neg.	neg.	1
		Pref.	47	12	35	—	—	—	—
17. Real estate	31	Ord.	3,35	1,49	1,78	3	—	neg.	5
		Pref.	57	14	38	—	—	1	4
18. Construction	10	Ord.	1,15	31	84	—	—	—	—
		Pref.	34	21	10	1	neg.	2	—
19. Glass, plastics and pottery	8	Ord.	1,30	73	55	1	—	neg.	1
		Pref.	47	14	30	neg.	—	2	1
20. Cement, asbestos and fireclay	15	Ord.	31,65	19,82	7,87	1,97	31	10	1,58
		Pref.	2,73	76	24	53	1,15	neg	5
21. Transport	15	Ord.	13,85	8,13	4,55	67	10	4	36
		Pref.	13	6	1	7	—	1	neg
22. Hotels and services	7	Ord.	42	7	10	neg.	neg.	25	—
23. Banks	7	Ord.	5,16	3,12	1,70	23	1	4	6
24. Insurance	15	Ord.	3,29	2,01	1,10	4	neg.	6	8
		Pref.	8	5	—	—	—	3	—

25.	Investments and finance	266	Ord.	26,73	10,14	14,59	5	24	1,55	16
			Pref.	5,70	2,41	1,57	19	33	1,06	14
26.	Managing agency	77	Ord.	15,65	5,98	7,73	17	1	31	1,45
			Pref.	4,22	87	1,79	78	3	41	34
27.	Other industry	39	Ord.	20,10	7,34	10,76	42	5	1,37	16
			Pref.	6,49	3,79	1,08	1,41	neg.	17	4
28.	Trade	158	Ord.	8,24	2,95	3,70	29	—	15	1,15
			Pref.	8,61	18	39	2	—	1	1
	Total	1079	Ord.	2,98,89	1,42,29	1,16,65	9,09	10,18	8,28	12,40
			Pref.	64,49	28,51	18,47	8,48	5,40	2,53	1,10

*Excluding diversified companies classified under other industry.

Note: Slight differences in totals are due to rounding.

TABLE 25: **Change in inter-industrial corporate holdings—1951 to 1958**

(*Rs. lakhs*)

	1951	1958	Change
No. of coys. with holdings by Indian companies	730	865	135
(a) Total share capital	2,32,31	3,53,37	1,21,06
(b) of (a) owned by Indian companies.	90,26	1,35,12	44,86
(b) as % of (a)	(38.8)	(38.2)	(37.1)
of (b) owned by			
1. Coal	75	1,08	33
2. Other mining	5	17	12
3. Power	71	72	1
4. Cotton*	5,94	3,13	—2,81
5. Rayon	1	2	1
6. Woollen	17	1	—16
7. Jute*	79	1,11	32
8. Iron and steel	3,87	5,41	1,54
9. Non-ferrous engineering	2	neg.	—2
10. Engineering	63	2,45	1,82
11. Sugar*	86	1,24	38
12. Plantations	11	39	28
13. Food and veg. oil	16	23	7
14. Chemicals	7	2,55	2,48
15. Paper	23	87	64
16. Printing and publishing	13	3	—10
17. Real estate	3	33	30
18. Construction	9	59	50
19. Glass, plastics and pottery	1	1	—
20. Cement, asbestos and fireclay	1,69	2,90	1,21
21. Transport	1,80	1,11	—69
22. Hotels and services	7	8	1
23. Banking	12,67	23,49	10,82
24. Insurance	8,32	4,79	—3,53
25. Investment and finance	44,37	65,86	21,49
26. Managing agency	5,56	8,04	2,49
27. Other industry	5	4,54	4,49
28. Trade	1,11	3,96	2,85

* Some large investing companies passed into 'Other Industry' between 1951 and 1958.

Note: Slight differences in totals are due to rounding.

and jute in 1951, cotton, paper and 'other industry' in 1958.

(xvii) *Cement, asbestos and fireclay* had investments from coal, cotton, sugar, transport and hotels in 1951, and were joined by plantations, real estate and 'other industry' in 1958.

(xviii) *Transport* (which included airlines in 1951) had some investments from cotton in 1961, and construction in 1958.

In addition, banking, insurance, investment and managing agency companies also had substantial holdings by industrial companies in both the reference years (Table 26). In the 1951 sample, industrial companies (that is, companies classified under heads other than publishing, real estate, hotels and services, banking, insurance, finance and investment, managing agency and trade) were found to have total inter-corporate investments of Rs. 18 crores. Of this amount, Rs. 2.42 crores was invested in banking, insurance, finance and investment, and managing agency companies. The corresponding amounts in 1958 were Rs. 28.63 crores and Rs. 3.99 crores, respectively. The increase in such investments by industrial companies, however, was directed wholly to finance and investment companies; a clear decline took place in respect of the other three categories.

TABLE 26: **Investment by industrial companies in financial companies**

(*Rs. thousand*)

Investment in	1951	1958
Banking	68,35	63,10
Insurance	22,63	15,54
Finance and Investment	1,07,02	3,01,93
Managing Agency	43,77	18,18
Total	2,41,93	3,98,75

CONTROLLING BLOCKS

We now proceed to analyse the investments by the controlling interests in the share capital of the companies under their control. This analysis is meaningful in the aggregate only for Inner circles.

The data on the holdings of the groups in their outer circles give an incomplete picture of total controlling blocks in outer circle companies and, at the same time, involve some multiple counting of large blocks of share capital held through jointly controlled and/or minority companies. Companies in the outer circles have two or more controlling interests, one or more of which may not be concerned with the groups studied. This problem occurs in the case of majority companies in the inner circles, too, but in their case, first, the number is not very large, and second, the majority control is in any event with one of the groups studied. It is the difficulty in eliminating multiple counting, however, which is mainly responsible for the author's hesitation in presenting aggregate group block data on outer circle companies. Some leading outer circle companies like A.C.C. and Scindia Steam enjoy the participation of more than one of the groups studied and have, in turn, several affiliated companies. The multiple counting of their investments in these affiliated companies can be eliminated easily in the aggregation of ownership data but such elimination is conceptually difficult in the case of controlling block data.

In the aggregate, the proportion of controlling block to the total share capital of inner circle companies tended to decline between 1951 and 1958 (Table 27). The controlling interests held nearly 49 per cent of the total share capital of their inner circles in 1951. The proportion came down to 43 per cent in 1958. These exact percentages might be under-estimates to the extent that some parts of the controlling blocks were registered in the names of banks in both years but the fact of the decline, as distinct from its precise magnitude, can hardly be contested.[3]

The respective percentages under equity in the two years were 55 and 49, and under preference 28 and 22. The voting power of the controlling interests must have declined to a greater extent than is indicated by the proportions of equity holding for, prior to the Companies Act, 1956, many public companies had deferred or promoters' shares which enjoyed disproportionate voting power and which were held almost wholly by the controlling interests.

The controlling interests contributed about 32 per cent of the additional total share capital raised by inner circle companies during the period. This comprised 37 per cent of additional equity but only 3 per cent of additional preference capital.

TABLE 27: **Controlling blocks in inner circles**

(*Rs. lakhs*)

	1951			1958			Change between 1951 and 1958		
No. of companies*	Total 817	Ord.	Pref.	Total 888*	Ord.	Pref.	Total 71	Ord.	Pref.
1. Total share capital	1,93,04	1,46,99	46,05	2,85,65	2,24,64	61,01	92,61	77,65	14,96
2. Controlling blocks	93,77	80,79	12,98	1,23,25	1,09,80	13,45	29,48	29,01	47
(2) as % of (1)	(48.6)	(55.0)	(28.2)	(43.1)	(48.9)	(22.0)	(31.8)	(37.3)	(3.1)
*Holders of blocks:***									
(a) Managing agents	4,65	4,24	41	6,49	6,02	47	1,84	1,78	6
	(5.0)	(5.2)	(3.2)	(5.3)	(5.5)	(3.5)	(6.2)	(6.1)	(12.7)
(b) Investment companies	35,09	32,11	2,98	51,04	45,98	5,06	15,95	13,87	2,08
	(37.4)	(39.7)	(23.0)	(41.4)	(41.8)	(37.7)	(54.1)	(47.8)	(442.6)
(c) Banking companies	1,68	1,38	30	1,82	1,31	51	14	—7	21
	(1.8)	(1.7)	(2.3)	(1.5)	(1.2)	(3.8)	(0.5)	(0.2)	(44.7)
(d) Insurance companies	3,28	1,76	1,52	2.37	1,60	77	—91	—16	—75
	(3.5)	(2.2)	(11.7)	(1.9)	(1.5)	(5.7)	(—3.1)	(—0.5)	(—159.6)
(e) Industrial companies	13,01	10,41	2,60	19,12	17,30	1,82	6,11	6,89	—78
	(13.9)	(13.0)	(20.0)	(15.5)	(15.8)	(13.5)	(20.7)	(23.7)	(—166.0)
(f) Service companies	58	51	7	2,52	2,28	24	1,94	1,77	17
	(0.6)	(0.6)	(0.5)	(2.0)	(2.1)	(1.8)	(6.6)	(6.1)	(36.2)
(g) Trusts	6,12	4,51	1,61	9,74	7,88	1,86	3,62	3,37	25
	(6.5)	(5.6)	(12.4)	(7.9)	(7.2)	(13.8)	(12.3)	(11.6)	(53.2)
(h) Individuals in India	27,25	24,08	3,17	28,93	26,27	2,66	1,68	2,19	—51
	(29.1)	(29.8)	(24.4)	(23.5)	(23.8)	(19.8)	(5.7)	(7.5)	(—108.5)

TABLE 27 (*Contd.*)

(i) Companies abroad	1,17	1,07	10	50	50	neg.	—67	—57	—10
	(1.2)	(1.3)	(0.8)	(0.4)	(0.5)	(—)	(—2.3)	(—2.0)	(—21.3)
(j) Individuals abroad	94	72	22	72	66	6	—22	—6	—16
	(1.0)	(0.9)	(1.7)	(0.6)	(0.6)	(0.4)	(—0.7)	(—0.2)	(—34.0)

*The number of companies differ from that in Table 11 owing to (i) non-availability of the shareholders' list of Muir Mills, and (ii) availability of shareholders' list of 5 companies (all in D.S.J. group) for which balance sheets are not available.

**The percentages under (a) to (j) in this and subsequent Tables are in terms of the total controlling block.

This decline in the proportion of controlling block to share capital came about mainly due to a diminution in the importance of individuals, insurance companies and foreign investors as holders of controlling blocks. Disinvestment by foreign holders was fairly substantial in the two wholly foreign controlled groups, Bird Heilger and Andrew Yule (in which it is estimated at a minimum of Rs. 31 lakhs and Rs. 1.31 crores, respectively) while insurance companies lost their entire life fund portfolios owing to nationalisation. Individuals in India and foreign investors held about 31 per cent of the total controlling block in 1951; this ratio came down to about 24 per cent in 1958. The comparable proportion for insurance companies declined from more than 3 to less than 2 per cent.

Inter-corporate investment is the main instrument, and an increasingly important one, for the control of companies. In both the years, more than two-thirds of the controlling block was held by companies. Their importance as holders of controlling blocks increased significantly during the period.

About 83 per cent of the additional contribution by the controlling interests came from companies, 12 per cent from trusts, and only 5 per cent from individuals.

The total share capital of the inner circles expanded during the period by Rs. 93 crores, from Rs. 193 crores to Rs. 286 crores. Individuals in India and abroad, taken together, contributed a little more than Rs. 38 crores towards this expansion. Out of this Rs. 38 crores, the individuals who constitute the ultimate controlling interests of the groups studied provided Rs. 1 crore only.

INTER-GROUP VARIATIONS

In public companies, the controlling interests held 49 per cent of equity and 23 per cent of preference in 1951, and 43 per cent and 17 per cent, respectively, in 1958 (Table 28). These aggregate proportions cover up fairly wide differences in the proportions held by the 20 controlling interests, which are given in Table 29.

The proportions have little to do with the relative size of the groups. If Tata and Martin Burn have relatively small controlling blocks, so have Kasturbhai, Ramakrishna, Mahindra and Kirloskar, while Seshasayee has the smallest among them all. If

TABLE 28: Controlling blocks in inner circle public companies

(*Rs. lakhs*)

	1951			1958		
	Total	Ord.	Pref.	Total	Ord.	Pref.
No. of companies	524			545		
1. Total share capital	1,66,26	1,25,63	40,63	1,56,70	1,99,42	57,28
2. Controlling blocks	69,54	60,30	9,24	95,77	85,88	8,89
(2) as % of (1)	(41.8)	(48.0)	(22.7)	(37.3)	(43.1)	(17.3)
Holders of blocks:						
(a) Managing agents	3,83	3,47	36	5,69	5,23	46
	(5.5)	(5.8)	(3.9)	(5.9)	(6.1)	(4.7)
(b) Investment companies	27,13	24,73	2,40	39,51	35,60	3,91
	(39.0)	(41.0)	(26.0)	(41.3)	(41.5)	(39.5)
(c) Banking companies	88	58	30	1,64	1,15	49
	(1.3)	(1.0)	(3.2)	(1.7)	(1.3)	(5.0)
(d) Insurance companies	3,01	1,75	1,26	2,22	1,54	68
	(4.3)	(2.9)	(13.6)	(2.3)	(1.8)	(6.9)
(e) Industrial companies	10,75	8,15	2,60	16,63	14,83	1,80
	(15.5)	(13.5)	(28.1)	(17.4)	(17.3)	(18.2)
(f) Service companies	53	46	7	2,36	2,12	24
	(0.8)	(0.8)	(0.8)	(2.5)	(2.5)	(2.4)
(g) Trusts	3,75	3,17	58	7,13	6,52	61
	(5.4)	(5.3)	(6.3)	(7.4)	(7.6)	(6.2)

(h) Individuals in India	18,63	17.13	1,50	19,78	18,12	1,66
	(26.7)	(28.3)	(16.2)	(20.7)	(21.1)	(16.8)
(i) Companies abroad	62	52	10	50	50	—
	(0.9)	(0.8)	(1.1)	(0.5)	(0.6)	(—)
(j) Individuals abroad	41	34	7	31	27	4
	(0.6)	(0.6)	(0.8)	(0.3)	(0.3)	(0.4)

TABLE 29: **Controlling blocks in public companies of twenty inner circles**

(Percentages of share capital)

Group	1951		1958	
	Ord.	Pref.	Ord.	Pref.
1. Tata	19.5	4.5	18.0	2.2
2. Birla	61.0	55.4	61.1	28.0
3. Martin Burn	25.9	7.4	23.7	3.1
4. Dalmia Sahu Jain	65.2	36.3	54.8	24.2
5. Bird Heilger	34.7	10.6	40.5	8.2
6. Andrew Yule	43.3	43.0	45.7	43.1
7. Bangur	79.8	46.5	68.8	25.4
8. Thapar	57.6	11.8	61.1	23.7
9. J.K.	72.8	46.0	74.7	36.4
10. Shri Ram	46.3	58.2	43.9	26.9
11. Shapoorji	72.3	—	35.5*	—
12. Khatau	67.2	16.4	68.6	17.7
13. Walchand	69.8	17.1	67.0	6.3
14. Mafatlal	68.5	2.7	69.5	7.4
15 Kasturbhai	23.4	36.2	20.1	34.3
16. Seshasayee	8.7	4.9	6.1	2.7
17. Ramakrishna	26.5	18.3	24.4	11.9
18. Indra Singh	62.6	—	40.6	41.0
19. Mahindra	8.0	22.5	37.8**	5.3
20. Kirloskar	27.9	—	27.9	1.7
Total	48.0	22.7	43.1	17.3

*The decline occurred owing to the acquisition of the Brady group in 1958.

**The increase is mainly due to the conversion of the principal company from private to public.

the smaller groups like Khatau, Shapoorji, and Indra Singh hold substantial blocks, larger groups like Birla, Dalmia Sahu Jain, Bangur, Thapar, J.K., Walchand and Mafatlal also hold very substantial blocks. Obviously, therefore, the proportion of controlling block to the total share capital of public companies is a matter of group policy and/or the need and ability of the group to attract outside capital, and is not determined by the size of the group alone.

The proportion is, nevertheless, closely related to the size of individual companies (see Table 30, which shows that the controlling block declines as the size of companies increases) and the nature of their occupation. Steel, power, heavy engineering, and heavy chemicals require so much capital that it has to be raised from outside. In Tata, Martin Burn and Shri Ram, moreover, most of the assets are concentrated in a few companies. Outside participation in the share capital of such companies is probably necessary to protect the controlling investments against excessive risks, as well as to provide the large magnitude of funds required.

In other large groups, the relatively larger number of companies generally tend to solve their problem of raising share capital by investing in one another. Seshasayee, Ramakrishna, Mahindra and Kirloskar, on the other hand, can afford to have large and lumpy outside participation, thanks to their reputation for good management, and the inability or unwillingness of their financiers to venture into industrial management.

It appears that, during the period, most controlling interests preferred to dilute their investment in preference, rather than in equity. The overall reduction in the proportion of controlling blocks to share capital was brought about mainly by a significant decline in Tata, Martin Burn, Dalmia Sahu Jain, Bangur, and Shri Ram.

In all groups, with the notable exception of Kasturbhai, nevertheless, controlling investments tended to pass from the hands of individuals to companies and trusts, during the period.

In *private* companies, the controlling interests, as may be expected, hold nearly all the share capital (Table 31). More significant than that, however, is the fact that even in private companies as a whole, the greater part of the controlling block is held by companies, mainly investment and industrial, though individuals and trusts hold a relatively larger proportion of it than in public companies. In 10 groups (Birla, Bangur, Shri Ram, Shapoorji, Khatau, Walchand, Mafatlal, Seshasayee, Indra Singh and Kirloskar), the greater part of the block in private companies is held by individuals and trusts (Table 29).

Tables 32, 33, 34 and 35 give the analysis of controlling blocks in inner circle banks, insurance, finance, industrial and service companies.

In banks and insurance and industrial companies, taken as a whole, controlling blocks are less than 50 per cent of share capital.

TABLE 30: **Controlling blocks in inner circles by size of companies**

(Rs. lakhs)

Net worth plus loans (Rs. lakhs)		1951: Public companies			1958: Public and private companies		
		No. of coys.	Ord.	Pref.	No. of coys.	Ord.	Pref.
Under 10	A	174	3,69	13	365	6,60	18
	B		3,02	6		5,92	13
	%		(81.8)	(46.2)		(89.7)	(72.2)
10 to 25	A	98	6,49	84	164	10,92	89
	B		4,59	34		9,08	53
	%		(70.7)	(40.5)		(83.2)	(59.6)
25 to 50	A	68	10,39	1,42	96	12,94	3,01
	B		5,62	52		8,60	1,24
	%		(54.1)	(36.6)		(66.5)	(41.2)
50 to 1,00	A	81	19,20	4,65	107	24,32	4,32
	B		9,44	1,13		14,34	1,51
	%		(49.2)	(24.3)		(59.0)	(34.9)
1,00 to 10,00	A	102	83,09	25,90	150	1,22,41	37,61
	B		37,48	6,92		64,35	9,53
	%		(45.1)	(26.7)		(52.6)	(25.3)
10,00 and above	A	1	2,77	7,69	6	47,45	15,00
	B		15	27		7,51	51
	%		(5.4)	(3.5)		(15.8)	(3.4)
Total	A	524	1,25,63	40.63	888	2,24,64	61,01
	B		60,30	9,24		1,09,80	13,45
	%		(48.0)	(22.7)		(48.9)	(22.0)

A: Total share capital. B: Total controlling block.

TABLE 31: Controlling blocks in inner circle private companies

(*Rs. lakhs*)

	1951			1958		
	Total	Ord.	Pref.	Total	Ord.	Pref.
No. of companies	293			343		
1. Total share capital	26,78	21,36	5,42	28,95	25,22	3,73
2. Controlling blocks	24,23	20,49	3,74	27,48	23,92	3,56
(2) as % of (1)	(90.5)	(95.9)	(69.0)	(94.9)	(94.8)	(95.4)
Holders of blocks:						
(a) Managing agents	82	77	5	80	79	1
	(3.4)	(3.8)	(1.3)	(2.9)	(3.3)	(0.3)
(b) Investment companies	7,96	7,38	58	11,53	10,38	1,15
	(32.9)	(36.0)	(15.5)	(41.9)	(43.3)	(32.3)
(c) Banking companies	80	80	—	18	16	2
	(3.3)	(3.9)	(—)	(0.7)	(0.7)	(0.6)
(d) Insurance companies	29	1	26	15	6	9
	(neg.)	(neg.)	(7.0)	(0.5)	(0.3)	(2.5)
(e) Industrial companies	2.26	2,26	—	2,49	2,47	2
	(9.3)	(19.0)	(—)	(9.1)	(10.3)	(0.6)

TABLE 31: (*Contd.*)

(f) Service companies	5	5	—	16	16	neg.
	(0.2)	(0.2)	(—)	(0.6)	(0.7)	(neg.)
(g) Trusts	2.37	1,34	1,03	2,61	1,36	1,25
	(9.8)	(6.5)	(27.5)	(9.5)	(5.7)	(35.0)
(h) Individuals in India	8,62	6,95	1,67	9,15	8,15	1,00
	(35.5)	(33.9)	(44.7)	(33.3)	(34.1)	(28.1)
(i) Companies abroad	35	55	—	neg.	neg.	—
	(2.3)	(2.7)	(—)	(neg.)	(neg.)	(—)
(j) Individuals abroad	53	38	15	41	39	2
	(2.2)	(1.9)	(4.0)	(1.5)	(1.6)	(0.6)

TABLE 32: **Controlling blocks in inner circle banks and insurance companies**

(*Rs. lakhs*)

	1951			1958		
	Total	Ord.	Pref.	Total	Ord.	Pref.
No. of companies	22			21		
1. Total share capital	9,62	8,91	71	8,23	8,35	8
2. Controlling blocks	3,71	3,60	11	3,14	3,09	5
(2) as % of (1)	(38.6)	(40.4)	(15.5)	(37.2)	(37.0)	(62.5)
Holders of blocks:						
(a) Investment companies	89	89	—	88	88	—
	(24.0)	(24.7)	(—)	(28.0)	(28.4)	(—)
(b) Banking companies	6	2	4	13	13	—
	(1.6)	(0.6)	(36.4)	(4.1)	(4.2)	(—)
(c) Insurance companies	45	38	7	36	36	—
	(12.1)	(10.6)	(63.6)	(11.5)	(11.7)	(—)
(d) Industrial companies	66	66	—	72	72	—
	(17.8)	(18.2)	(—)	(22.9)	(23.3)	(—)
(e) Service companies	2	2	—	11	11	—
	(0.5)	(0.6)	(—)	(3.5)	(3.6)	(—)
(f) Trusts	11	11	—	8	6	2
	(3.0)	(3.1)	(—)	(2.5)	(1.9)	(40.0)
(g) Individuals in India	1,52	1,52	—	86	83	3
	(41.0)	(42.2)	(—)	(27.5)	(26.9)	(60.0)

TABLE 33: Controlling blocks in inner circle finance* companies

(*Rs. lakhs*)

	1951			1958		
	Total	Ord.	Pref.	Total	Ord.	Pref.
No. of companies	285			315		
1. Total share capital	41,31	32,15	9,16	48,01	39,24	8,77
2. Controlling blocks	35,56	28,92	6,64	37,87	33,49	4,38
(2) as % of (1)	(86.1)	(90.0)	(72.5)	(78.9)	(85.3)	(49.9)
Holders of blocks:						
(a) Managing agents	33	22	11	91	91	—
	(0.9)	(0.8)	(1.7)	(2.4)	(2.7)	(—)
(b) Investment companies	12,42	11,20	1,22	17,30	15,63	1,67
	(34.9)	(38.7)	(18.4)	(45.7)	(46.7)	(38.0)
(c) Banking companies	1.04	96	8	53	36	17
	(2.9)	(3.3)	(1.2)	(1.4)	(1.2)	(3.9)
(d) Insurance companies	72	29	43	25	14	11
	(2.0)	(1.0)	(6.5)	(0.7)	(0.4)	(2.5)
(e) Industrial companies	2,98	1,01	1,97	1,32	1,23	9
	(8.4)	(3.5)	(29.6)	(3.5)	(3.7)	(2.1)

(f) Service companies	10	10	—	49	49	neg.
	(0.3)	(0.3)	(—)	(1.3)	(1.3)	(neg.)
(g) Trusts	2,45	1,38	1,07	3,07	1,85	1,22
	(6.9)	(4.8)	(16.1)	(8.1)	(5.5)	(27.9)
(h) Individuals in India	13,71	12,27	1,44	13,00	11,94	1,06
	(38.6)	(42.4)	(21.7)	(34.3)	(35.7)	(24.2)
(i) Companies abroad	1,16	1,06	10	50	50	—
	(3.3)	(3.7)	(1.5)	(1.3)	(1.5)	(—)
(j) Individuals abroad	65	43	22	50	44	6
	(1.8)	(1.5)	(3.3)	(1.3)	(1.3)	(1.4)

TABLE 34: Controling blocks in inner circle industrial* companies

(*Rs. lakhs*)

	1951			1958		
	Total	Ord.	Pref.	Total	Ord.	Pref.
No. of companies	330			375		
1. Total share capital	1,33,51	98,86	34,65	2,16,60	1,65,84	50,76
2. Controlling blocks	47,79	42,72	5,07	73,02	65,27	7,75
(2) as % of (1)	(35.8)	(43.2)	(14.6)	(33.7)	(39.4)	(15.3)
Holders of blocks:						
(a) Managing agents	4,01	3,71	30	5,41	4,94	47
	(8.4)	(8.7)	(5.9)	(7.4)	(7.6)	(6.1)
(b) Investment companies	19,58	18,05	1,53	28,65	26,04	2,61
	(41.0)	(42.3)	(30,2)	(39.2)	(40.0)	(33.7)
(c) Banking companies	51	40	11	1.12	81	31
	(1.1)	(0.9)	(2.2)	(1.5)	(1.2)	(4.0)
(d) Insurance companies	2,09	1,09	1,00	1,66	1,05	61
	(4.4)	(2.6)	(19.7)	(2.3)	(1.6)	(7.9)
(e) Industrial companies	8,45	7,86	59	15,56	13,93	1,63
	(17.7)	(18.4)	(11.6)	(21.3)	(21.3)	(21.0)

(f) Service companies	40	33	7	1,63	1,40	23
	(0.8)	(0.8)	(1.4)	(2.2)	(2.1)	(3.0)
(g) Trusts	3,07	2,55	52	6,17	5,58	59
	(6.4)	(6.0)	(10.3)	(8.4)	(8.5)	(7.6)
(h) Individuals in India	19,38	8,43	95	12,60	11,30	1,30
	(19.6)	(19.7)	(18.7)	(17.3)	(17.3)	(16.8)
(i) Companies abroad	1	1	—	—	—	—
	(neg.)	(neg.)	(—)	(—)	(—)	(—)
(j) Individuals abroad	29	29	—	22	22	neg.
	(0.6)	(0.7)	(—)	(0.3)	(0.3)	(—)

*Comprising all companies other than banks, insurance, finance and service companies.

TABLE 35: **Controlling blocks in inner circle service* companies**

(Rs. lakhs)

	1951			1958		
	Total	Ord.	Pref.	Total	Ord.	Pref
No. of companies	180			177		
1. Total share capital	8,61	7,07	1,54	12,61	11,21	1,40
2. Controlling blocks	6,71	5,56	1,15	9,22	7,95	1,27
(2) as % of (1)	(77.9)	(78.6)	(74.7)	(73.1)	(70.9)	(90.7)
Holders of blocks:						
(a) Managing agents	31	31	—	17	17	—
	(4.6)	(5.6)	(—)	(1.8)	(2.1)	(—)
(b) Investment companies	2,20	1,97	23	4,22	3,43	79
	(32.8)	(35.4)	(20.0)	(45.8)	(43.1)	(62.2)
(c) Banking companies	9	1	8	4	1	3
	(1.3)	(0.2)	(7.0)	(0.4)	(0.1)	(2.4)
(d) Insurance companies	3	1	2	10	5	5
	(0.4)	(0.2)	(1.7)	(1.1)	(0.6)	(3.9)
(e) Industrial companies	93	89	4	1,52	1,42	10
	(13.9)	(16.0)	(3.5)	(16.5)	(17.9)	(7.9)
(f) Service companies	5	5	—	30	28	2
	(0.7)	(0.9)	(—)	(3.3)	(3.5)	(1.6)
(g) Trusts	51	47	4	41	39	2
	(7.6)	(8.5)	(3.5)	(4.4)	(4.9)	(1.6)
(h) Individuals in India	2,59	1,85	74	2,46	2,20	26
	(38.6)	(33.3)	(64.3)	(26.7)	(27.8)	(20.4)

*Comprising printing and publishing, real estate, hotels and services, and trade.

In finance and service companies, however, the controlling interests hold an absolute majority of voting power.

In general, investment companies are the largest single corporate holders of controlling blocks in all the four occupational categories. The significance of industrial companies as holders, nevertheless, increased substantially during the period in all categories, except in finance companies.

The controlling block in *banks and insurance companies* taken together declined slightly from 40 per cent of equity in 1951 to 37 per cent in 1958 (see Table 32). Of the total controlling equity block, individuals and trusts held 45 per cent in 1951; this proportion came down to 29 per cent in 1958. The major part of the block was, thus, held by companies in both years. Among the corporate owners, investment, industrial and insurance companies, in that order, were the principal holders. Industrial companies, in fact, raised their holding from 18 per cent of total controlling equity in 1951 to 23 per cent in 1958.

To give some specific examples of leading companies in 1958, the Dalmia Sahu Jain block in *Punjab National Bank* was 31 per cent of its share capital; the block was held in the names of various individuals and companies. The Birla block in *United Commercial Bank* was about 20 per cent; it was held by various industrial, finance and insurance companies and individuals. In *Hindustan Commercial Bank*, the J.K. block of 56 per cent was distributed between nearly all the leading industrial, finance and insurance companies in the group. Karamchand Thapar trading and finance companies and individuals held about 90 per cent of the share capital of *Oriental Bank of Commerce*.

The Andrew Yule block of 31 per cent in *Concord of India Insurance* was held almost exclusively by investment companies. The Birla holding of a little more than 20 per cent in *New Asiatic Insurance* was held mainly by individuals and investment companies. In *Ruby General Insurance*, the Birla block was 45 per cent, held mainly by individuals, investment companies and trusts. In *Bharat Fire and General Insurance*, the D.S.J. group held 63 per cent of equity and 66 per cent of preference; these blocks were held largely by individuals, trusts and trading companies. The J.K. block of 80 per cent in *National Insurance* was held mostly by industrial companies, investment companies and individuals. The Tata block in *New India Assurance* was 8 per cent only; it was held mainly by investment companies, individuals and trusts. In *Indian Trade and General Insurance*, the Thapar block was 48 per cent, distributed between investment, industrial and trading companies.

The controlling block in inner circle *finance* companies was 86 per cent of total share capital in 1951 and 79 per cent in 1958 (see Table 33). Individuals and trusts in India and individuals abroad together held 47 per cent of the controlling block in 1951 and 44 per cent in 1958. The major part of the block was, thus, held by companies in both years, and, among them, investment and industrial companies were the principal holders.

Industrial companies have, relatively, the lowest controlling block, 36 per cent in 1951 and 34 per cent in 1958, but the block includes a rather significant amount of preference holding by the controlling interests (see Table 34). Their controlling blocks have, also, the lowest proportion held by individuals and trusts, 25 per cent altogether in both years. *The remaining three-fourths of the controlling block in both years was held by companies*, mainly investment and industrial companies. Managing agents should have been rather significant holders of controlling block in industrial companies but they held only 8 per cent of it in 1951 and 7 per cent in 1958.

Service companies tend to have large controlling blocks; they came to 78 per cent in 1951 and 73 per cent in 1958 (see Table 35). Even in their case, the proportion of controlling block held by individuals and trusts declined from 46 per cent to 31 per cent. At the same time, the proportion held by investment and industrial companies was stepped up substantially.

TECHNIQUE OF CONTROL

The techniques of holding controlling investments, as distinct from their size in relation to share capital, can be studied under two broad heads:

(i) how are the controlling blocks built up?
(ii) how do the controlling interests retain control over their companies?

This study cannot answer the second question in so far as it relates to the mechanics of the actual exercise of control. One can, nevertheless, infer from the data that the managing agency system[4] which still predominates in the management of public industrial companies, gives the controlling interests sufficient control over routine management as well as most policy decisions in companies. In most groups, this form of management is backed up by the predominant voting power of the controlling interest in the managed companies.

Where the controlling interest does not have the absolute majority of voting power, either the wide dispersion of ownership (as in Tata, Martin Burn, Kasturbhai and Birla's Hindusthan Motors) or the reluctance of large outside investors (as in Seshasayee, Kirloskar, Ramakrishna and Mahindra's Machinery Manufacturers' Corporation) to participate in management, enable the controlling interests to retain control. In giant companies like Tata Steel and Indian Iron, the large holdings of L.I.C. and the implicit support of government and uncommitted shareholders in the event of a contingency, also help to keep potential cornerers at bay.

A more interesting aspect of the technique concerns the building up of the controlling blocks. Except in Kasturbhai (and, to a lesser extent, in Seshasayee), inter-corporate and trust investments play the key role in providing the links between companies under the same control. Since this aspect has to be studied qualitatively, it would be useful to recapitulate briefly the techniques adopted by the various controlling interests.

In *Tata*, trusts own more than 80 per cent of the share capital of Tata Sons, which is the fountainhead of all controlling investments in the group. Tata Sons, together with its subsidiaries and joint subsidiaries, holds strategic investments in a number of large companies, most of which are managed by the subsidiaries and joint subsidiaries of Tata Sons. Some of the leading industrial companies, in turn, hold investments in vertically related companies. In the outer circle, the interest in A.C.C. and MacNeil & Barry is held jointly by a few investment and insurance companies. MacNeil & Barry, in turn, has large direct and indirect investments in the companies under its control.

The *Birla* technique of control involves (besides the use of managing agency agreements, trusts and nominees) predominant voting power built up through the creation of a large number of subsidiaries and joint subsidiaries, several circular chains of investments which return to their starting points, investments by industrial companies in other companies which have an altogether different business, and dispersion of controlling blocks among a large number and wide variety of holders. There is no single company which can be described as the nucleus of the group.

The three families which control *Martin Burn* hold about two-thirds of the equity of the principal company, while the remaining one-third is held by the public. This company acts as managing agent of almost every other company in the complex. The principal company, together with the Mookerjee and Banerjee families, hold almost the entire controlling block in all companies, except Indian Iron, in which a trust holds most of it.

Dalmia Sahu Jain, like Birla, has no single principal company to which the ultimate holding of controlling blocks can be traced. Each of the sub-groups has a number of investment and industrial companies which, helped by insurance companies and individuals including nominees, hold the group together with their investments.

In *Bird Heilger*, the Benthall family has invested, directly, in two managing agencies and, indirectly, through trustee companies registered in India, in other companies as well. Some associated families, for example, Ironside, Kinnison, etc. also have fairly large investments in some controlled companies. The large number of small subsidiaries and joint subsidiaries of the managing agencies, some large investment companies, and a few large industrial companies together hold most of the block in other companies.

In *Bangur*, *Thapar*, *J.K.* and *Shri Ram*, the controlling interests hold predominant voting power, built up mainly of inter-corporate investments, in almost every company. Besides, trusts are significant holders of controlling blocks in J.K. and Shri Ram. Thapar alone resorts to frequent direct interlocking of equity. Bangur and J.K. prefer a circular chain of investments which in J.K. often provides a mutual link between the equity of industrial and finance companies. Thapar and J.K. industrial companies also invest large amounts in other industrial companies which have altogether different business, as well as in banking and insurance companies. The handful of companies in Shri Ram, on the other hand, are controlled through a simple distribution of controlling blocks between a few finance companies, trusts and individuals.

Of the four groups, *Shapoorji*, *Khatau*, *Walchand* and *Mafatlal*, which have substantial minority interests, Shapoorji and Khatau depend mainly upon a few strategic investments on their own account and leave the remaining investments to minority companies. Walchand and Mafatlal, on the other hand, have a large number of subsidiaries and joint subsidiaries and also have substantial direct sole control investments in their outer circle companies. All the four rely predominantly upon the managing agency system for the management of their public companies but, with a few exceptions, the substantial equity blocks held by the controlling interests are mainly with investment and industrial companies, and individuals, not with managing agents.

Of the remaining six groups, *Kasturbhai*, *Seshasayee* and *Kirloskar* hardly use inter-corporate investments for purposes of control. Since their controlling blocks are relatively small, the continuance of their control over public companies depends to a considerable extent upon managing agency agreements but, in Kasturbhai, the wide dispersion of ownership also facilitates control.

Ramakrishna uses family investments to own and control two managing agencies but a diversified industrial company holds most of the controlling block in other companies. In *Indra Singh*, the sheer proportion of voting power held by the controlling interests simplifies the problem of control. The family wholly owns a managing agency which, in turn, holds most of the controlling block in other companies, with the help of an industrial subsidiary. The *Mahindra* technique is comparable to some extent with Martin Burn, though it differs in detail. The principal company in this group enjoys some public participation in share capital and combines trade, managing agency, automobile engineering and investment. This company is controlled through substantial family investments and, in turn, holds the controlling blocks and/or the managing agency of other companies. A trading subsidiary, in which Tata has a minority interest, also helps in the holding of controlling blocks.

In general, therefore, the technique of holding controlling

investments is comparable to a chain breeding process. The controlling families, in most cases, make an initial investment to own wholly or almost wholly a principal company or companies. These companies initiate a breeding process—in some groups an inbreeding process—that takes care of nearly all subsequent controlling investments of significance, without calling forth further substantial investments from the controlling families.

SUBSIDIARIES AND JOINT SUBSIDIARIES

The above is substantiated by the fact that nearly all complexes (the exceptions are Martin Burn, Shri Ram, Kasturbhai, Seshasayee and Kirloskar) have a large number of subsidiaries and joint subsidiaries.

In 1958, the Tata Complex had 73 subsidiaries and joint subsidiaries, Birla had 106, Dalmia Sahu Jain 30, Bird Heilger 44, Andrew Yule 20, Bangur 47, Thapar 31, J.K. 27, Shapoorji 15, Khatau 14, Walchand 16, and Mafatlal 13. Among the smaller groups, Ramakrishna had 3, Indra Singh 4 and Mahindra 5.

Out of the 1079 sample companies in 1958, 163 were subsidiaries and 26 were joint subsidiaries.

MANAGING AGENCIES

Notwithstanding the public pre-occupation with the managing agency system, and the availability of a considerable amount of primary data in the offices of Registrars of Companies, little has been known so far about the corporate structure of managing agency companies. The following is an attempt to throw some light on select aspects of this problem, namely, the number and resources of managing agents in the complexes studied, the number of companies managed by each managing agent, the pattern of ownership of these managing agents, the importance of the managing agency system as a form of management, and the investments made by managing agents in the companies under their management.

The number of joint stock managing agency companies covered in this study was 85 in 1951 and 77 in 1958. They were distributed between public and private companies as follows:

	1951	1958
Public companies	26	19
Private companies	59	58
Total	85	77

These companies had a total share capital of Rs. 17.63 crores in 1951 and Rs. 19.87 crores in 1958. The majority of the companies were very small, judged by both share capital and net worth plus loans.

Out of 85 managing agencies in 1951, 62 had a share capital of less than Rs. 10 lakhs each. In 1958, 52 out of 77 were in a similar position. In fact, 12 companies in both years had a share capital of less than Rs. 5,000 each (Table 36). One Indra Singh managing agency had a share capital of Rs. 255 only. Nearly all those companies which had a share capital of Rs. 50 lakhs and above, for example, Martin Burn, Andrew Yule, Mahindra and Mahindra, MacNeil Barry, and Greaves Cotton, had other business besides managing agency. Tata Industries, which has no business other than managing agency and which manages several of the largest public companies in India, had a share capital of Rs. 2.25 crores, issued wholly for consideration other than cash as compensation for the transfer of managing agency rights from Tata Sons; it had no investments in the companies under its management, barring a minor investment of Rs. 3,000 in Tata Oil Mills.

TABLE 36: **Distribution of managing agencies by share capital**

Share capital (Rs. thousand)	1951		1958	
	Public	Private	Public	Private
	Number of companies			
Up to 5	4	8	3	9
5 to 1,00	1	22	—	13
1,00 to 10,00	12	15	6	21
10,00 to 25,00	3	4	3	3
25,00 to 50,00	—	6	1	8
50,00 to 100,00	2	3	2	3
100,00 and above	4	1	4	1
Total	26	59	19	58

The smallness of their share capital was hardly compensated by reserves and loans: 36 managing agencies in 1958 had net worth plus loans of less than Rs. 10 lakhs each (Table 37).

TABLE 37: **Distribution of managing agencies by size**

Net worth plus loans (Rs. lakhs)	1951	1958	
	Public	Public	Private
	Number of companies		
Up to 10	8	6	30
10 to 25	5	1	8
25 to 50	3	3	7
50 to 100	5	3	6
100 and above	5	6	7
Total	26	19	58

The balance sheets of pure managing agenc es, actually, indicate very little resources for the performance of their traditional functions. Out of the 77 managing agencies in 1958, 61 could be described as pure, because they had practically no other business. The total assets of the 77 managing agencies amounted to Rs. 65.06 crores, of which the 61 pure managing agencies accounted for Rs. 27.31 crores. The net worth and loans of the pure managing agencies came to Rs. 21.66 crores, while their investments amounted to Rs. 7.73 crores, and receivables and cash aggregated Rs. 14.95 crores (Table 38).

In 1958, the 20 complexes had 89 active managing agents, including 16 unincorporated firms. Every complex, except Martin Burn, Andrew Yule and Mahindra, had more than one managing agency each. Birla had 13, Tata 9, and Bangur, Mafatlal, and Kasturbhai 7 each, to mention only the leading examples (Table 39).

Between them, these 89 managing agencies managed 353 companies (another 22 were managed by managing agents outside the 20 complexes). As many as 48 managing agents managed only 1 company each, and 15 only two each. At the other end of the scale, Andrew Yule managed 39, Bird 34, MacNeil & Barry 24, Karamchand Thapar & Brothers 22, Birla Brothers 20, Martin Burn 19, and Tata Industries 10. The general validity of this

TABLE 38: **Combined balance sheet of managing agency companies**

(*Rs. lakhs*)

	1951 Public companies	1958 Public and private companies	
		Total	Pure managing agencies
Number of companies	26	77*	61**
Liabilities			
1. Share capital	968	2048@	852
2. Reserves	470	837	429
3. Loans	571	1758	885
4. Other liabilities	545	1863	565
Total	2554	6506	2731
Assets			
1. Net fixed assets	40	270	65
2. Inventory	115	857	63
3. Investments }		1787	773
4. Receivables and cash }	2399	3137	1495
5. Other assets }		455	335
Total	2554	6506	2731

*Including 5 inactive managing agencies, that is those companies which had ceased to manage any company by the end of 1958, but excluding Tata's Investment Corporation of India which is classified as an investment company though it acted as managing agent of two companies in 1958.

**Excluding 5 inactive managing agencies, and 11 active managing agencies which had a significant interest in business other than managing agency.

@Amount differs slightly from figure given earlier, which is taken from shareholders' lists.

pattern in the corporate private sector as a whole is confirmed by the data published by the Company Law Division. (*Company News and Notes*, Vol. 1, No. 23, September 2, 1963, pp. 31-40).

The pattern of ownership of the incorporated managing agency companies in 1951 and 1958 is given in Tables 21 and 22. A detailed industrywise breakdown of the holdings by Indian com-

TABLE 39: **Distribution of managing agencies by complexes—1958**

Complex	No. of managing agents@	No. of companies managed by managing agents*	No. of companies managed by each managing agent
1. Tata	9	72 (11)	24+10+10+8+3+2+2+1+1
2. Birla	13	50 (4)	20+8+4+4+2+1+1+1+1+1+1+1
3. Martin Burn	1	19	19
4. Dalmia Sahu Jain	5	13 (1)	6+2+2+1+1
5. Bird Heilger	3	43 (2)	34+6+1
6. Andrew Yule	1	39	39
7. Bangur	7	28 (8)	9+5+2+1+1+1+1
8. Thapar	2	26 (1)	22+3
9. J.K.	6	12	4+3+2+1+1+1
10. Shri Ram	3	5 (2)	1+1+1
11. Shapoorji	5	11	5+3+1+1+1
12. Khatau	5	11	6+2+1+1+1
13. Walchand	3	12	9+2+1
14. Mafatlal	7	10 (2)	2+1+1+1+1+1+1
15. Kasturbhai	7	9	3+1+1+1+1+1+1
16. Seshasayee	4	9	4+3+1+1
17. Ramakrishna	2	6 (2)	2+2
18. Indra Singh	4	6 (1)	2+1+1+1
19. Mahindra	1	5	5
20. Kirloskar	4	7 (1)	2+2+1+1
Total (gross)	92	393 (35)	
Less counted more than once	3	18 (13)	
Total (net)	89**	375 (22)	

@Including unincorporated firms, but excluding managing agents outside the complex which manage companies within the complex.

*Including companies within the complex which are managed by managing agents outside the complex. The number of these companies is indicated in parentheses.

**Including 16 unincorporated firms and Tata's Investment Corporation of India, but excluding 5 inactive managing agency companies.

panies is given in Tables 23, 24 and 25. A compact analysis of the pattern is given in Table 40.

Most of the share capital of managing agency companies is not

TABLE 40 : **Ownership of managing agency companies**

(*Rs. lakhs*)

	1951				1958			
	Ord.	%	Pref.	%	Ord.	%	Pref.	%
Total share capital	13,19	(100.0)	4,44	(100.0)	15,65	(100.0)	4,22	(100.0)
Owners:								
Individuals in India	4,84	(36.7)	1,30	(29.3)	5,98	(38.2)	87	(20.6)
Indian companies	5,95	(45.2)	1,66	(37.4)	7,73	(49.4)	1,79	(42.4)
Government	23	(1.7)	4	(0.9)	1	(0.1)	3	(0.7)
Trusts	60	(4.5)	44	(9.9)	31	(2.0)	41	(9.7)
Foreign investors	1,57	(11.9)	1,00	(22.5)	1,45	(9.2)	34	(8.1)
L.I.C.	—	(—)	—	(—)	17	(1.1)	78	(18.5)

owned by individuals. Only 36 out of 85 managing agency companies in 1951, and 30 out of 77 in 1958, were owned wholly by individuals and trusts. In the aggregate, individuals owned a little more than one-third of total share capital in both the years, while trusts also held a significant proportion. The principal owners were Indian companies and the proportion of share capital owned by them recorded a significant increase between 1951 and 1958.

Seventeen managing agencies in 1951 and 22 in 1958 were subsidiaries or joint subsidiaries, that is, more than 50 per cent of their share capital was owned by one or more companies. These included, in 1958, such well-known and leading managing agencies as Tata Industries, Tata Hydro-Electric Agencies, Forbes Forbes and Campbell, Cement Agencies, MacNeil & Barry, Kilburn, Birla Gwalior, Cotton Agents, Andrew Yule, Kettlewell Bullen, J.K. Industries, Greaves Cotton and W.H. Brady (Table 41).

TABLE 41: **Managing agencies classified by ownership**

	1951		1958	
	Public	Private	Public	Private
Subsidiaries	—	2	—	3
Joint subsidiaries	4	11	7	12
Owned 50 : 50 by companies and individuals	1	—	1	—
Owned mainly by individuals and trusts	21	44	11	41
Owned mainly by foreign individuals	1	2	—	2
Total	26	59	19	58

In both 1951 and 1958, most of the holdings of Indian companies in managing agencies were on account of investment companies, but a significant part came from cotton mills, plantations, banks, insurance, trade, and, in 1958, also engineering, real estate, and other industries (see Tables 23 and 24). As stated earlier, industrial companies had an investment of Rs. 44 lakhs and Rs. 18 lakhs in 1951 and 1958, respectively, in managing agency companies.

Foreign investors, both individuals and companies, have a

substantial direct stake in managing agency companies. The proportion of share capital owned by them, however, clearly declined during the period mainly due, it appears, to a transfer of holdings to companies under the same control registered in India. Within this category of owners, there was a significant transfer of holdings from individuals to companies.

The shareholding by government in managing agency companies was nominal in both years. But L.I.C. came to own nearly 19 per cent of the preference share capital and one per cent of equity by 1958.

Several managing agencies are joint ventures of more than one controlling interest. Martin Burn is under the joint control of Martin, Mookherjee, and Banerjee. The control of MacNeil & Barry and its wholly owned subsidiary, Kilburn, is shared between Inchcape Mackay, and Tata. Cement Agencies (which manages ACC) is a combine of Killick, Shapoorji, Tata and Khatau. Tata Hydro-Electric Agencies is under the joint control of Tata (50.1%) and a foreign company (49.9%). Aero-Auto (which manages Premier Automobiles) is a combine of Walchand, Kilachand and Khatau. In 1951, Forbes Forbes & Campbell was under joint Tata and foreign control, and Kettlewell Bullen was owned to the extent of 50 per cent by MacNeil & Barry (that is, Inchcape Mackay and Tata). In 1958, Nowrosjee Wadia & Sons was jointly owned by Wadia and Shapoorji.

In all, there was more than one controlling family or interest in 29 out of 85 managing agency companies in 1951, and in 24 out of 77 in 1958.

We turn now to the significance of the managing agency system as a form of management. The majority of companies in India have always been under other systems of management, mainly because private companies, which constitute two-thirds of the number of companies, and small public companies did not, in general, have managing agents (Table 42). Moreover, banking and insurance companies and, since 1956, managing agency companies are debarred from having managing agents. The significance of the managing agency system lies, therefore, in its predominance in the management of large public, mainly industrial, companies.

This study covered 980 companies in 1958, excluding banking, insurance and managing agency companies. Of these, 375 or 38 per cent were managed by managing agents but they had nearly

TABLE 42: **Companies managed by managing agents**

	1954-55			1962-63		
	Public	Private	Total	Public	Private	Total
1. Total number of companies at work*	9,126	19,442	28,568	5,380	19,218	24,598
2. Companies managed by managing agents	4,091	964	5,055	1,217	223	1,440
3. (2) as % of (1)	44.8	5.0	17.7	22.6	1.2	5.9

Source: Government of India, Company Law Division.
*Excluding banking, insurance and government companies.

72 per cent of the share capital and 83 per cent of the gross capital stock. If public companies alone are taken into account, 54 per cent of the number were managed by managing agents and they had 79 per cent of the share capital and about 88 per cent of the gross capital stock. In private companies, however, the proportions were relatively very small (Table 43).

So far as industrial companies are concerned, that is, companies engaged in activities other than printing and publishing, real estate, hotels and services, investment and finance, and trade, there is no doubt about the predominance of the managing agency system. Out of 497 industrial companies in 1958, 317 were managed by managing agents and these had 81 per cent of the share capital and 86 per cent of the gross capital stock. This form of management predominated in every industrial category, except construction and transport, and it would have predominated in transport, too, but for the resignation of the managing agency of Scindia Steam by Narottam Morarjee shortly before 1958.

Given this predominance and the traditional financing role of managing agents emphasised in text-books, one would expect that the managing agents hold a significant part of the share capital of the companies under their management. This expectation has no foundation.

In 1958,[5] only 3.5 per cent of the share capital of the 375 managed companies was held by corporate managing agents (see Table 44). Their total investment amounted to Rs. 8.53 crores out of the share capital of Rs. 241.36 crores of the

TABLE 43: **Public and private companies managed by managing agents 1958**

	All Companies*	Companies managed by managing agents	(2) as % of (1)
	1	2	3
1. Public companies:			
(a) Number	605	327	54.0
(b) Share capital (Rs. cr.)	295	233	78.6
(c) Gross capital stock (Rs. cr.)	1032	905	87.7
2. Private companies:			
(a) Number	375	48	12.8
(b) Share capital (Rs. cr.)	37	6	16.2
(c) Gross capital stock (Rs. cr.)	72	11	15.3
3. All companies:			
(a) Number (1a+2a)	980	375	38.3
(b) Share capital (Rs. cr.) (1b+2b)	332	239	71.7
(c) Gross capital stock (Rs. cr.) (1c+2c)	1104	916	83.0

Note: Data are taken exclusively from balance sheets. The figures of share capital differ slightly from those taken from shareholders' lists.

*Excluding banking, insurance and managing agency companies.

managed companies. In as many as 153 managed companies, there was no holding whatever by managing agents, and in 33 companies the holding by managing agents was substantial only because they were subsidiaries of the managing agency companies.

In industrial companies, in fact, the proportion was slightly lower at 3.2 per cent. The investment by managing agents was substantial only in plantations, where they held 24 per cent of the share capital of managed companies.

Further, in both 1951 and 1958, managing agents held less than 6 per cent of the total controlling blocks in the inner circle public companies (see Table 28). Managing agents do not themselves hold an important part even of the investments by their controlling interests in the companies under their control. Most investments of this nature are held by investment companies, industrial companies, individuals and trusts within the groups.

The data do under-estimate slightly the investments by managing agents in the companies under their management because of:

TABLE 44: **Industrywise classification of companies managed by managing agents—1958**

(*Rs. lakhs*)

Industry	All companies			Companies managed by managing agents			Of (6) held by managing agents[aa]	Percentages		
	No.	Share capital	Gross capital stock	No.	Share capital	Gross capital stock		(6) as % of (3)	(7) as % of (4)	(8) as % of (6)
1	2	3	4	5	6	7	8	9	10	11
Coal	48	910	3418	35	888	3316	60	97.6	97.0	6.7
Other mining	15	149	510*	10	130	373	4	87.2	73.1	3.4
Power	18	1689	5107	17	1684	5101	19	99.7	99.9	1.2
Cotton	63	2452	12201**	39	1993	10042	72	81.3	82.3	3.6
Rayon	5	779	1524	2	694	1454	4	89.1	95.4	0.6
Wollen	2	47	128	1	47	127	—	99.7	99.2	—
Jute	31	1383	4713	24	1041	3848	50	75.3	81.6	4.8
Steel	2	4201	22878	2	4201	22878	29	100.0	100.0	0.7
Non-ferrous	5	228	879	2	182	657	2	79.8	74.7	0.9
Engineering	86	4918	15501	46	3059	11564	219	62.2	74.6	7.2
Sugar	30	759	3414	21	642	2822	33	84.6	82.7	5.1
Plantations	47	362	1319	38	317	1094	77	87.6	82.9	24.3
Food and veg. oil	18	290	938	7	208	756	3	71.7	80.6	1.5
Chemicals and paints	29	1590	3297	18	1298	2966	31	81.6	90.0	2.4
Paper	11	1278	4520	9	1113	4122	65	87.1	91.2	5.9
Printing and publishing	21	179	616	6	19	75	11	10.6	12.2	59.2

Real estate	31	391	487	2	101	93	3	25.8	91.1	3.3
Construction	10	149	1413†	1	61	440	neg.	40.9	31.1	0.3
Glass, plastics and pottery	8	176	430	3	84	242	—	47.7	56.3	—
Cement, asbestos and fireclay	15	3438	9311	10	3090	8280	30	89.9	88.9	1.0
Transport	15	1400	3732	10	184	460	11	13.1	12.3	6.1
Hotels and services	7	42	102	4	34	98	neg.	81.0	96.1	0.8
Investment and finance	266	3243	809	26	457	358	79	14.1	44.3	17.3
Other industry[a]	39	2659	10666	22	2501	10257	38	94.1	96.2	1.5
Trade	158	886	2531††	20	107	175	12	12.1	6.9	10.9
Total	930	33499	110447	375	24136	91616	853	72.0	83.0	3.5
Industrial companies	497	28758	105992	317	23418	90817	748	81.4	85.8	3.2

Notes:

(1) Slight differences in totals are due to rounding.

(2) The data on the number of companies and share capital are taken from shareholders' lists, on gross capital stock from balance sheets.

(3) Industrial companies exclude printing and publishing, real estate, hotels and services, investment and finance, and trade.

*16 companies **64 companies †9 companies ††157 companies.

[c]Includes diversified companies.

[ac]Excludes the holdings by un-incorporated managing agents but includes the holdings by managing agents outside the complexes studied.

(i) the exclusion of investments by un-incorporated managing agents, and

(ii) the registration of some part of the investments by corporate managing agents in the names of banks and other nominees.

So far as (i) is concerned, the under-estimation is negligible. As for (ii), a rough check is readily available. The data taken from shareholders' lists indicate an investment of Rs. 8.53 crores at par by managing agents in managed companies in 1958. The combined balance sheet of 77 managing agencies in the same year shows total investments at book value of Rs. 17.87 crores. All these investments are not in managed companies; they include some investments in government securities and debentures, and some of the investments in the shares of managed companies are valued at a substantial premium over their par values. On the outside assumption that the actual investment in managed companies is, say, half-way between Rs. 8.53 crores and Rs. 17.87 crores, it would come to only about 5.5 per cent of the total share capital of managed companies.

REFERENCES

1. Deccan Airways, Ballarpur Paper, Eastern Shipping, FACT and Forest Industries (Travancore) in 1951. Hyderabad Allwyn, FACT, Forest Industries (Travancore), Travancore Cochin Chemicals and Hindustan Shipyard in 1958.
2. Most of the investing 'other industry' companies are companies that have diversified from cotton or jute or sugar.
3. The aggregate holdings of banks and executor and trustee companies were 5.0 and 6.3 per cent of total Inner Circle share capital in 1951 and 1958, respectively. Unless all such holdings belonged to outsiders in 1951 and to the controlling interests in 1958, which is unlikely, the conclusion above cannot be contested.
4. The reader is reminded that, in this study, 'managing agent' includes 'secretaries and treasurers' and that Section 332 of the Companies Act, 1956, which restricts the number of public companies managed by a managing agent to 10, came into effect only in August 1960.
5. A comparison with 1951 is difficult because managing agency was rather loosely defined till 1956. An industrywise estimate of the holdings by corporate managing agents in companies which had

some corporate holding indicates that managing agents held 2.5 per cent of the share capital of such companies in both 1951 and 1958. See *The Economic Weekly*, Annual Number, February 1964, p. 319.

POLICY CONCLUSIONS

This study was concerned primarily with the collection and analysis of factual material. The statistical results have been summed up in the preceding pages but that does not exhaust the objectives of the study. No amount of detailed inductive analysis can yield ready-made policy conclusions. The lines of action recommended below are statements of opinion and are, therefore, debatable. They should be distinguished from the analysis of facts which the study has essayed so far.

The policy conclusions can be grouped under four main heads. These relate to:

(1) concentration of economic power;
(2) the managing agency system;
(3) inter-corporate investment; and
(4) other matters like diversification of industrial companies, nominee holdings, and so on.

CONCENTRATION OF ECONOMIC POWER

This study conclusively establishes that there was an increase in the concentration of economic power in the corporate private sector between 1951 and 1958. Whether this development was for the better or the worse from the standpoint of the rate of industrial growth, efficiency and utilisation of resources, etc., cannot be established. It is quite clear, nevertheless, that, by itself, the increase in concentration was inconsistent with the Directive Principles of State Policy laid down under the Constitution and the objectives of planned development stated in the Second and Third Five Year Plans.

If directives and value judgements are set aside and attention is focussed on the urgent needs of the economic situation, there is room for honest difference of opinion on whether the increase in concentration that took place between 1951 and 1958 was undesirable and excessive. An increase in concentration has its economic and technical advantages and can do some good.

The share of Tata and Martin Burn in corporate private activity increased during the reference period, largely because these two groups were interested mainly in steel, heavy engineering and power, the three industries which play a key role in industrial development and which require large capital investment per unit of output. Since they were well-established in these lines, prudence required that they should be actively associated with the expansion programmes. Tata and Martin Burn could deliver additional output at a lower unit cost as compared with the new plants to be set up by government or possible new private entrants. That is not all. They could do it in a shorter period of time for, expanding a plant is in many ways easier than putting up a new one. Their performance was subject to fewer uncertainties for they had the organisation, experience and skill to deal with contingencies. And, above all, they had some spare capacity in labour, equipment and top management which, as subsequent developments have shown, could be turned to national, and not just private, advantage. Experience has justified the expansion permitted to—or imposed upon—Tata and Martin Burn. They have delivered the goods at reasonable cost to the public and less than reasonable return to themselves. If concentration has increased in the process, the price has been worthwhile.

What should cause concern is the fact that the two largest complexes, Tata and Birla, accounted for approximately one-fifth of the physical assets of the corporate private sector in 1958. This absolute level of concentration is, in my opinion, certainly excessive. It reflects the continuance of a low level of development of resources and entrepreneurship in the economy. That is the basic problem which requires attention.

The measures to combat and reduce the excessive concentration of economic power can be negative or positive. The negative measures would include a break-up of the existing large groups or the placing of an embargo on their further growth. The positive measures have to be less spectacular, more diffused and essentially long-term. I am emphatically in favour of positive measures.

A break-up of the large groups is, legally, impossible and, on economic grounds, unwise.

The law can never provide an adequate definition of corporate groups and their ramified interests. The Companies Act does not define a group, except for the purpose of regulating inter-company loans and investments (Section 370) and restricting the number of public companies managed by a managing agent (Section 332). This study shows clearly that the statutory definition is inadequate and that a wider definition would also be inadequate in view of the variety of ways in which companies can be controlled.

Assuming that government draftsmen and legislation win the race against private legal ingenuity, and that the effort and cost are worthwhile, at what level would a group qualify for break-up? If size is the only criterion, would it be judged by share capital, networth or total capital employed? And how would the break-up be carried out and supervised?

An alternative is to nationalise the large groups. This lacks a precedent[1] since nationalisation in other countries has been confined to industries (for example, U.K.) or individual companies (for example, France), but that is not the main argument against such a course. The large groups have highly diversified occupations, and, in most cases, include a large number of companies of various sizes. Their legal position as groups is indefinite: the Tata and Martin Burn groups can be identified fairly easily, but many Birla and Dalmia Sahu Jain companies would escape the net. The act of nationalisation would, therefore, be highly discriminatory and wou'd involve the assumption of direct managerial and financial responsibility by government in diverse economic activities. Besides, it would be a violation of the spirit and letter of the Industrial Policy Statement of 1956.

The economic case against the break-up of groups is even stronger. The country lacks organisation even more than it lacks capital. The break-up of the few existing large organisations would entail the loss of the useful experience and skill that have been built up in and by these organisations. This experience and skill is not, as is believed in some circles, confined to financial manipulations. It embraces a much wider field which covers, besides financial management, marketing, technical expertise and managerial cohesion. A group is not just a collection of money and equipment. A group is an organisation larger than the sum total of its components and represents much more than an accumulation of physical and financial assets. It is a body of trained personnel, who have been accustomed to perform their functions in unison and to pool their experience and skill for the advancement of a common purpose. Such organisations can be divided only at the risk of impairing efficiency.

A complete embargo on the growth of the large groups would be suicidal in the present context. Their investment programmes are integral to the overall development effort, and are complementary to the public sector programme. Their existing undertakings can expand at a cost lower than that of new undertakings, without requiring a proportionate expansion in overheads and without involving all the difficulties of starting from scratch. There is no justification for allowing the managerial, financial and output capacity of the large groups to go waste. Moreover, the public sector programme itself would be endangered if the units which are part of large groups are not allowed to expand. If Tata Steel, Indian Iron, A.C.C. and Tata Loco, for instance, are not allowed to expand, there would be a shortage of steel, cement and engineering goods required for the public sector.

Risks are inherent in growth but there is a point beyond which it is unwise to take risks. One could think in terms of imposing severe restrictions on the growth of the large groups if one were reasonably confident that others, that is, small groups, independent and new industrialists, and the state, could set up and expand a wide variety of large scale industries with a speed and efficiency comparable with that expected of the large groups. There are no grounds for such confidence.

The anti-trust policy of the U.S.A. has often been cited in this connection. In the U.S.A., combinations which restrain or eliminate competition, as well as unfair trade practices, are illegal and are abhorred by the general public, which regards competition as one of the basic values of the American way of life. The U.S.A. anti-trust policy is, thus, clearly aimed at the promotion of competition.

There is no such well-defined objective in India. Competition is not one of the basic values of the Indian way of life. Official policy on industrial and import licensing, in fact, aims at the minimisation or elimination of competition to conserve economic resources. The promotion of competition cannot, in any event, be an effective remedy against the concentration of economic power in India. Concentration is not synonymous with monopoly in this country because, as stressed earlier, every large group has diversified industrial interests. There is practically no industry which can be said to be the monopoly of a particular group.

We are not suffering from the evils of monopoly in the conventional sense of the term. The common text-book evils of combinations in restraint of trade, like collusion in fixing prices, allocation of markets and restriction of output, are of little relevance in a sellers' market which is expanding rapidly and many features of which have official sanction. What would be called unfair and discriminatory trade practices in the U.S.A. are known to be quite common here. They are bound to flourish in a country in which a sellers' market has endured for more than twenty years and is expected to last another 10 years at least.

In one sense, there is, nevertheless, an underlying similarity between the American and Indian attitudes towards concentration. Much of the U.S.A. antipathy to combinations is based upon the fear that New York financiers, many of whom happen to be Jews, might dominate the entire economy if they are allowed to become more powerful. In India, industrial enterprise is still the practical monopoly of a few castes. Certain regions, moreover, feel that they are industrially backward and that what industries they have are controlled by 'outsiders'. Much of the latent public feeling against concentration in India has, thus, a caste-cum-regional basis. Part of this feeling is also no doubt attributable to the widely held belief that some people have become so powerful, thanks to their resources and contacts, that they can do practically anything and get away with it.

Two long-term remedies can be suggested to reduce the concentration of economic power. One is to encourage the growth of medium and small groups and new industrialists, the other to further expand the public sector.

The rapid expansion of the public sector, whatever its merits on other grounds, does not really dilute concentration. It only opposes the massive economic power of the state against the economic power of the large groups. Those who abhor excessive concentration of power, regardless of who enjoys it, might find it no remedy at all. Realism, nevertheless, demands a compromise. Till such time as the medium and small groups can achieve their 'take-off' only the state can countervail the economic power of the large groups. In the meanwhile, there need be little fear that the large groups will eat up the smaller fry for the opportunities of expansion are still almost unlimited.[2] This study establishes not merely that concentration of economic power has increased but also that the increase has taken place almost wholly through actual growth, not by means of mergers and other forms of corporate cannibalism. The medium-sized groups, too, have participated vigorously in the general expansion.

The task of public policy is, therefore, to see that, in future, the larger groups do not take away a disproportionate part of the available opportunities. Little reliance can be placed, for the specific purpose of reducing concentration, on the co-operative sector or the small corporate groups, which, their merits on other grounds notwithstanding, have neither the finances nor the organisational capacity to take up and implement large industrial projects. Attention must, therefore, be focussed on the medium-sized groups.

The medium groups, of which a fairly representative cross-section has been studied here, have demonstrated their ability to mobilise financial and organisational resources for fairly large industrial enterprises. The financial and technical performance of some of them has been even better than that of large groups. The record of Kasturbhai and Mafatlal in cotton, Seshasayee in chemicals, Kirloskar in engineering, and Ramakrishna in sugar and cement, for instance, has been far better in many ways than that of most large groups in the specific industries.

A rational and positive policy for the building up of countervailing economic power within the private sector has to be a continuing process, not a once-for-all operation. It must be based on the greatest possible exploitation of the organisational potential in medium-sized groups. This can be done by discriminating in their favour in such matters as licensing of projects, disbursement of foreign exchange and approval of foreign collaboration, supply of power and essential materials, investments of L.I.C. and State Governments, and loans from special financial institutions. Good care would have to be taken, of course, to see that the assistance does not go to large groups masquerading as medium groups, and that the genuine medium groups make proper use of the assistance extended to them.

Government spokesmen claimed at one time that the policy of licensing a large number of new units in each industry was meant to disperse economic power. This policy was based upon a complete misunderstanding of the concept and origin of economic power. It might have been appropriate in dealing with a monopolistic situation, but not for curbing the growth of the kind of concentration which exists in India. It is hardly surprising, therefore, that the policy has failed to achieve its stated objective.

The implementation of this policy has actually left a legacy of uneconomical, small-sized plants, to say nothing of the high foreign exchange cost it has entailed. To avoid repetition of this experience, government must insist upon economic size of plants and the attainment of certain minimum levels of efficiency while giving licences and assistance to medium groups. If monopoly or near-monopoly, in the traditional sense of the term, is thereby promoted or tolerated, it should be clearly recognised that this is the necessary price which has to be paid for modern technology, till such time as the size of market for individual products expands sufficiently to permit the economic working of a large number of producers of each product.

Towards the end of 1963, the Companies Act was amended to provide, among other things, for the taking over by the Public Trustee of the voting rights of trusts in companies (Section 187B read with Section 153A), without taking over the shareholdings and paying compensation for them. The Finance Minister explained that the intention behind this measure was to reduce the concentration of economic power, and to prevent the misuse of trust funds for purposes not intended by the donors. This is a vital and far-reaching change.

In 1958, trusts held a *minimum* of 3 per cent of the total share capital of the 1,079 companies covered in this study and 8 per cent of the total controlling block in 888 inner circle companies. Their actual holdings must have been larger for, technically, a trust could not be registered as a shareholder (Section 153) and the classification adopted for this study was based upon inference. In the Tata, Birla, J.K., Shri Ram and Mafatlal groups, particularly, trusts play a key role in the holding of controlling blocks. In most of the other groups, too, trusts appear to play a rather important role.

There is no doubt that the creation and maintenance of trusts is a common and quantitatively significant technique of keeping personal fortunes free of taxes on income and property and, thereby, preventing a dilution of the controlling investments in key companies. The income from the trust investments may be given away in charity (as the Tata and Birla trusts do on a large scale) but the voting power which is conferred by the investments remains intact in the hands of the trustees.

The amendment will definitely discourage the holding of *key* controlling blocks in the names of trusts. This will happen even if the government, as stated by the Finance Minister, does not actually take over the voting power of trusts or, having taken it over, and entrusted it to the Public Trustee, instructs him not to exercise it. Inter-corporate investments will grow further as a consequence. The dividends and capital gains on these investments will, however, be subject to tax. That is not the only merit of the amendment. In the long run, it will tend to reduce the magnitude of large blocks of tax-free wealth and income available for the purpose of controlling companies and will, to that extent, also tend to curb the concentration of economic power.

MANAGING AGENCY SYSTEM

The principal features of the managing agency system which emerge from this study can be summed as follows:

(a) The managing agency system is still the predominant form of management in large public industrial companies, but most other companies are under the direct management of boards of directors.[3]

(b) Almost every complex has a large number of managing agencies, most of which manage only one company each, while a few manage a very large number of companies with diverse occupations.

c. Barring a few, which have other business besides managing agency, nearly all managing agencies have very little resources. They provide only a fraction of the share capital of the companies under their management.

d. A large part of the share capital of managing agencies is owned by other companies. In fact, many leading managing agency companies are subsidiaries or joint subsidiaries of other companies. This goes to show that they are merely the management departments of the groups concerned, and do not constitute the fountainheads of control.

e. A fairly large number of managing agencies are under the joint control of more than one controlling interest.

The principal advantages claimed for this system, as distinguished from other methods of managing companies *under the same control*, are that

i. it provides firm and stable control over management;

ii. it secures the economies of large-scale operations, for example, in marketing, finance and management, to companies under the same management;

iii. it provides a flexible system of remuneration to top management.

Managing agency agreements do not, however, appear to be generally necessary for the purpose of exercising control over the management of public companies. The total controlling blocks in the public industrial companies of most groups are sufficiently large to enable the controlling interests to control the management of these companies without the additional power of control conferred by managing agency agreements. There are some exceptions, however, for example, Tata Steel, Indian Iron, Associated Cement, and some Seshasayee and Kirloskar companies, in which the controlling blocks are relatively small. In such cases, the loss of managing agency rights may make the controlling interests feel insecure. But even in these exceptional cases, large L.I.C. holdings, the power of the government to prevent the exercise of voting power by cornerers for up to three years under Section 250 of the Companies Act, and the support of uncommitted shareholders who have confidence in them, would help to keep the management in office.

It is remarkable indeed that no group has lost control over its banking and insurance companies, which cannot have managing agents, and in which the shareholding of the controlling interests tends to be smaller than in other public companies (Table 22).

The firm and stable control which the managing agency system is supposed to provide is, in fact, the perpetuation of family control. The system confers a birthright upon the managing agency family not merely to control the management of companies in the group but also to participate actively in and to direct their routine management. The technical and managerial deficiencies of hereditary management have been made up to some extent, in recent years, by the employment of professional technicians and managers, but the appointment of family members at levels superior to these professionals tends to weaken efficiency, and leads to an overlap of hierarchy in the top management of the managed companies.

There is often confusion within many managing agencies, too, for all the partners, if the managing agency is a joint venture, as well as the active family members, have the right to intervene directly in the day-to-day affairs of the managed companies.

The question of the accrual of economies of management to companies under the same management can arise only in the case of those managing agents which manage a large number of companies. As stated earlier, most managing agents manage only one or two companies each. In their case, the question of economies of management does not arise at all.

The few managing agents which manage a large number of companies cannot claim special expertise in each of the various industries in which they have a managerial interest. They are not under an obligation to provide the best managerial and technical expertise at their own cost. The cost of the expertise, when it is obtained, is almost invariably charged to the managed companies, not to the managing agents.

The rate of commission on the profits of managed companies which is charged by managing agents is independent of the number of companies managed by a single managing agent. If managing agent A, for instance, manages 10 companies, the rate of commission paid by each of these 10 companies is not any lower because the same managing agent manages nine other companies, too. The economies of management, if any, therefore, accrue to the managing agent, not to the managed companies.

As members of a group, the managed companies do share and receive many common services and facilities, but the availability of these services and facilities depends upon membership of the group, not upon a particular system of management. So long as companies A and B, for instance, belong to the same group, both are entitled to share the group facilities, whether one or both are managed by managing agents or have some other form of management.

The managing agency system is superfluous in most groups from the point of view of finance and marketing as well. The financing and marketing role of managing agents is now generally undertaken by their associates within the group, and these associates are remunerated separately for performing that role.

The managing agents are remunerated on the basis of a commission on the profits of the managed companies. The definition of profits for this purpose and the scale of remuneration to managing agents are laid down under the Companies Act, and have been elaborated further under various government decisions. The managing agents are entitled to a minimum remuneration in the absence or inadequacy of profits, but receive commission on a sliding scale as the profits increase. This system of remuneration does appear flexible as compared with the payment of relatively fixed amounts to top management, but the flexibility is superficial.

As pointed out earlier, most, if not all, of the expertise obtained for the managed companies is debited to them, not the managing agents. To the extent a commission does save on large fixed salaries to top management, it tends to be offset by the fact that the management secured in return for the commission is only part-time. The managing agents as a company, and their members as individuals, are free to have other occupations and any number of other management jobs in various capacities, even if these involve a conflict of interest.

Besides, in a protected market, the flexibility of the remuneration tends to be one way, and that is upwards.

The managing agency system is an expensive, irrational and part-time system of management. Its abolition is necessary in order to rationalise the management of public industrial companies.

The removal of this system will not make any difference to the control and management of companies by groups. It will alter only the form, status and system of remuneration of management. For some time to come, that is, till there is a fundamental change in the structure and attitudes of management, even the association of the controlling families with the routine management of companies will continue.

The reform will, over a period of time, separate the power to appoint and control management, which is bound to remain with the controlling families or their representatives, from the actual exercise of managerial functions. It will give an impetus to the building up of professional technical-cum-managerial cadres, the top members of which would be judged by their performance, not by their blood relationship and financial participation.

It would not, however, be wise to introduce this somewhat radical reform overnight. A phased programme should be drawn up for its abolition, step by step, in selected categories of companies.

The first step necessary for this purpose is to abolish the practice of banks (particularly the State Bank which started this practice) and financial institutions (that is, IFCI, ICICI, SFCs, etc.) demanding guarantees by managing agents of loans to the companies under their management. These guarantees are meaningless for, the loans are nearly always secured against the assets of the managed companies and the guarantees cannot be honoured by any managing agent, none of whom has the resources to honour them, if called upon to do so. This practice could be abolished by government and Reserve Bank directives.

Second, the prohibition of the appointment of managing agents should be extended to all private companies, companies which are subsidiaries or joint subsidiaries of other companies, public companies in which the public is not substantially interested [as defined under Section 2(18) of the Income Tax Act, 1961] and investment companies. The employment of managing agents in such companies is merely a device to get the highest possible remuneration for so-called managerial functions, over and above the dividends earned from the substantial investments made by controlling interests in these companies.

Third, no managing agent should be allowed to manage less than three companies. Under the Companies Act, an individual can be managing director of not more than two companies. Since the managing agency system is said to provide an economical form of group management, it is logical to suggest that a managing agent should manage a larger number of companies than a managing director can. This provision will also eliminate the practice of multiplying the number of managing agents within each group and giving them the formal management of only one or two companies.

The second and third steps will require appropriate amendments to the Companies Act which, in concert with related laws, prohibits the employment of managing agents only by banks, insurance companies and managing agents.

Fourth, after taking the above steps, the government should exercise its powers under Section 324 of the Companies Act to notify that, with effect from specified dates, companies the principal business of which is manufacture or processing in well-established industries like cotton, jute, paper, sugar, tea and cement will not be permitted to have managing agents. To these industries may also be added rayon, though it is not yet well established, in order to prevent cotton companies from passing as rayon. The problems of finance and management of these industries do not call for the special services which the managing agents claim to have provided so far. The technical changes and problems of marketing that they have to face require professional skill, not the part-time attention of the members of controlling families.

In all these industries, tea excepted, the managed companies are, in general, better known in their own right than the precise managing agents which manage them. The investing public, in general, evaluates the performance and prospects of individual companies and is, at best, concerned with the group to which they belong, not the particular managing agent which manages them.

The elimination of the managing agency system from these industries will not affect the control of groups over their companies for the controlling blocks in them are, in general, quite substantial.

Companies engaged in coal mining, chemicals, heavy

engineering, basic iron and steel, and power, should be permitted a longer period of grace for two reasons. First, the controlling blocks in most of the large companies in these industries are relatively small and the sudden termination of managing agencies might create dislocations. Second, the investment required in these industries is relatively large, their gestation period is long, and they have a high priority in planned investment.

Even in these industries, however, the managing agency system should be eliminated over a period of say, 15 years, for the arguments that apply to other industries ultimately apply to these industries, also.

INTER-CORPORATE INVESTMENT

The growth of inter-corporate investment is a logical and integral part of corporate growth. The liability to pay steeply progressive taxes on income during their lifetime and heavy estate duties after death induce the rich to impersonalise their shareholdings. This is done mainly through the creation of companies and trusts. The latter are not subject to taxes and combine philanthropy with control of business. Companies have perpetual existence and are legally independent of their members; beyond a certain range of income, their tax liability is appreciably smaller than that of individuals; and they can accumulate reserves.

These personal and apparently selfish motives notwithstanding, corporate enterprise is synonymous with large-scale private enterprise. Only the corporate form of organisation can mobilise the funds and personnel required for giant projects and keep them going. Whatever the nature and extent of outside participation in the raising of funds or of delegation of managerial authority, there is a decision-making power somewhere in corporate enterprise. That power is created and maintained by controlling investments. These investments have to come increasingly from companies because the controlling individuals have little personal wealth and their trusts have to confine their limited investments to a few key or principal companies only. The companies, on the other hand, can grow indefinitely; they breed other companies which ally with similar other compaines and breed further.

In recognition of this need, and its, on the whole, beneficial effect on economic growth, the governments of all countries which have private enterprise grant tax relief on income from inter-corporate investment. In India, for example, tax on inter-corporate income is now 25 per cent against the standard rate of 50 per cent for most other corporate income.

Let it be stated quite explicitly, therefore, that to accept private enterprise as socially beneficial implies the acceptance of inter-corporate investment as a corollary. You cannot have one without the other. And, if private enterprise is to be regulated in the public interest, a proposition which commands wide acceptance in this country, inter-corporate investment has also to be regulated. The purpose of the regulation has to be two-fold:

i. to prevent anti-social uses of the opportunities available; and
ii. to direct or redirect investments in accordance with the plan.

Inter-corporate investment is a powerful instrument in the hands of those who control corporate activity. It was pointed out earlier, for instance, that the total share capital of the 20 inner circles studied expanded by Rs. 93 crores between 1951 and 1958. The individuals who constituted the ultimate controlling interests of these groups contributed only a little more than Rs. 1 crore towards this expansion, their trusts put in roughly Rs. 4 crores, and the companies controlled by them put in as much as Rs. 24 crores, making a total of Rs. 29 crores. Against Rs. 1 crore provided by the controlling individuals, other individuals, for example, the investing public, subscribed Rs. 37 crores. This single example (leave aside the increase in the concentration of economic power) shows how important both inter-corporate investment and public participation in share capital have become. If both have to grow, the powerful instrument of control has to be kept free of abuses.

Most of the inter-corporate investment found in the course of this study was unexceptionable Some rather glaring abuses were also, however, noticed. To put it in mild terms, several companies, including industrial enterprises, have been found to hold shares in other companies, apparently not so much for investment nor even for the advancement of their own business, as for taking advantage of capital market situations or for serving the purposes of their controlling interest. In some cases, it can be clearly perceived that inter-corporate investments (and loans) enable some groups to set up companies the existence of which as working entities appears doubtful, and to help companies to purchase their own shares indirectly, transfer profits and losses, and to enter into transactions of a similar nature.

There can be little doubt that these are motivated largely by the desire to reduce tax burdens rather than to evade the provisions of the Companies Act. Since the problems connected with taxation are beyond the scope of this study, attention is confined here to the checking of abuses within the Companies Act.

Section 372 of the Companies Act, 1956 deals with inter-corporate investments. Under this section, the amount invested in the shares of any other company within the same group, as defined under Section 370, could not ordinarily exceed 10 per cent of the subscribed capital of the other company, and the total amount invested in companies in the same group could not exceed 20 per cent of the subscribed capital of the investing company. Investments above these limits required the approval of the shareholders of the investing company, and of the central government. These restrictions did not apply to banking and insurance companies (which are regulated by special legislation), investment companies, private companies, and to holding companies in respect of their existing subsidiaries. Nor did they apply to investments by managing agents and secretaries and treasurers in companies under their management.

The definition of companies in the same group proved too narrow and easy to evade, according to the Company Law Administration

The Companies Amendment Act, 1960 widened the scope of Section 372 considerably. Briefly, the amended section permits a company to invest in the shares of any other company up to 10 per cent of the latter's subscribed capital, provided the aggregate investment of the company in the shares and debentures of other companies, whether in the same group or not, does not exceed 30 per cent of the company's own subscribed capital; out of this, not more than two-thirds should be in companies in the same group. Any investment above these limits requires the consent of the shareholders of the investing company, as also the approval of the government. The list of exemptions is practically the same as in the principal Act, except that the amended section also applies to investment companies, which are, however, not subject to the aggregate limit on investments of 30 per cent of their subscribed capital. Read with the new Section 43A, the new Section 372 also applies to those private companies which may be deemed to be public companies.

These amendments should enable the government to regulate inter-corporate investment more effectively and to impose some checks on the operations of investment companies which, in spite of their importance as investors on behalf of controlling interests and as speculators on stock exchanges, have been practically unregulated hitherto.

In 1960-61, the Company Law Department formulated certain guiding principles for considering applications from companies under Section 372, and tightened up the rules for their enforcement.[4] Briefiy, these principles are:

a. industrial and trading companies will be allowed to make trade investments[5] in other companies, if the latter are vertically related to the former;
b. the investing company should have adequate liquid resources and its working capital should not be unduly depleted as a result of the proposed investments;
c. the investing company should not borrow funds on its own account for the purpose of making an investment other than a trade investment;
d. inter-corporate investments would not be permitted for purposes of speculation or cornering of the shares of other companies;
e. the proposed investment should be acquired at a reasonable price, promise a reasonable return and satisfy other requirements of a sound investment.

It is too early to assess the impact of the new legislation and its mplementation, largely, because most of the substantial inter-corporate investments which were found to exist in 1958 were made before the passing of the Companies Act in 1956, and were practically beyond the scope of Section 372 which covers new investments only.

The data presented earlier on the pattern of inter-industrial corporate holdings indicate that pre-1956 investments by industrial companies in technically unrelated companies are rather significant. Partly, on empirical grounds and, partly, because public attention has always been focussed on the managing agency system rather than on inter-corporate investment, the Companies Act has left these investments in unrelated enterprises untouched. This legal abstinence was rather curious for the Act did call for a number of immediate changes in the structure and working of companies.

It is true that some hardship might be caused if industrial companies are called upon to sell off their investments in companies having an altogether different business. The sale of these investments in the open market might depress their value and tend to disrupt group control. If they are transferred privately to non-industrial companies within the group, there is scope for manipulation of prices. Some companies might also contend that these old investments represent a remunerative outlet for liquid funds. These arguments notwithstanding, there is no justification, in principle, for allowing such investments to remain undisturbed, unless they fulfil the objectives of planned development. If some companies are embarrassed with liquid funds, they must either be induced to invest in accordance with plan priorities (referred to below) or required to put the funds in government securities. In the late forties and early fifties, industrial companies used to hold a significant amount of government securities but such investments have practically disappeared since then.[6]

No industrial company should be permitted, in any event, to hold any shares in managing agency, investment, finance, banking and insurance companies. Such investments tend to become circular for, the funds return to the starting points, directly or indirectly, and enable the companies concerned to purchase their own shares. These investments are made primarily to serve the purposes of controlling interests, are seldom justified by the returns they fetch, and have, in general, no market value. If the groups are keen to have non-industrial companies, the controlling investments in them should come from other non-industrial companies. The working capital of industrial companies should not be allowed to be depleted, whatever the amount involved, for making investments of this nature. An amendment to Section 372 of the Companies Act will be necessary to bring about the disinvestment of such holdings.

As regards inter-corporate investments between industrial companies *inter se*, the problem is akin to diversification within industrial companies, to which we turn now.

DIVERSIFICATION OF INDUSTRIAL COMPANIES

Broadly speaking, the diversification of an industrial company can take three forms. The simplest of them is observed when a company offers a wider variety of products than what it manufactures already. A cotton mill, for example, may decide to add finer fabrics and more 'popular' sorts to its range of products either in response to changes in demand or because its management wants to have them for reasons of prestige. In new industries like chemicals and heavy engineering, diversification of the product is an integral feature of growth.

Vertical integration is a second form of diversification. This occurs when a single unit combines the production of some raw materials and components of a product with its manufacture and subsequent processing. Strictly speaking, however, vertical integration is not a form of diversification because it merely integrates different stages of production of a single product or group of products and does not increase the number of final products produced or sold. In some cases, nevertheless, vertical integration does throw up a saleable surplus of some components and by-products, which augment the number of products sold.

The form of diversification to which specific attention is drawn here concerns the entry or intended entry of some industrial, especially cotton, jute and sugar companies, into the manufacture of products which are in no way related to the products which they manufacture at present.

The Company Law Department is known to oppose such diversification but has never stated its arguments in full officially. The only public statement issued by the Department in this connection implied that, in its view, the setting up of new technically unrelated units within existing companies constituted an evasion of Section 332 of the Companies Act. This section lays down that the number of companies under the same managing agency, as defined by the Act, should not exceed 10.

The Department also held the view that the setting up of new units in this form was a misuse of the incentives like tax holiday, liberal depreciation allowance and development rebate, since the tax liability on the income from the older divisions of existing companies could be offset against the initial losses of the new units.

Two other reasons for the Department's dislike of diversified companies, probably, were: (i) that the accounts of such companies do not give a true and fair picture of the operations of each of their divisions separately, and (ii) that the new projects benefit only the existing managements and shareholders, and do not help in widening the ranks of management and ownership.

From the opposite side, it could be pointed out that heterogeneity of industrial interests has been a major characteristic of groups in India since their inception. Whether the groups chose to have one or more companies for each of their industrial interests or combined all or several of them in one or more companies is a matter of historic accident or deliberate choice and convenience. Diversification of individual companies, too, is not a new phenomenon. Leading diversified companies like Delhi Cloth Mills and Rohtas Industries have done extremely well. Government action to prevent other companies from following their example would constitute unfair discrimination.

Moreover, every industrial company is, quite legitimately, interested in maximising its profits and the value of its assets. If that cannot be done within its existing business (which may be particularly true of cotton and jute companies), then, it should go into other industries. Expansion into technically allied fields may not be adequately remunerative and, therefore, cotton and jute companies go in for such an odd assortment of industries as rayon, chemicals, engineering, cement, etc. New plants within an existing company strengthen the earning capacity of the company and, simultaneously, reduce the tax liability of the company as a whole. This raises the value of the company's shares and increases the inducement to invest, by holding out prospects of higher dividends, large capital gains and a reduction of the risk involved in depending upon one industry alone.

The setting up of new projects under new companies necessitates a number of complex preliminaries including, in some cases, an application to the government for approval of inter-corporate investments under Section 372 of the Companies Act. In cases of inter-corporate investment, the shareholders of the investing companies do not get the full benefit of the investment in the new and more profitable projects, owing to a number of reasons. The new projects take time to make profits and pay dividends. The income from them is taxed first in the hands of the new company, then in the hands of the investing company, and, finally, in the hands of the shareholders. The capital value of the shareholdings, moreover, appreciates less than it would if the new projects were set up within the existing companies.

The establishment of new companies for new projects within the same group would not lead to a wider dispersion of economic power. It might widen the ranks of shareholders by attracting new investors but a new project augments the economic power of a group in any event, whether the project is within an old company or under a new company.

Section 332 of the Companies Act is not really meant to restrict the number of companies under the same management. Its primary, though indirect, purpose is to reduce the remuneration of those managing agents which manage more than 10 companies. The Act itself provides an escape clause by allowing managing agents to become secretaries and treasurers (who are remunerated on a relatively lower scale) of any number of companies, besides the companies of which they are managing agents. Moreover, the Act neither imposes a ceiling on the size of managed companies nor does it restrict their choice of occupation. The number of companies managed by boards of directors under the same control is not restricted at all.

As regards the non-availability of the accounts of each division separately in the annual reports of diversified companies, the government can, either by statutory amendment or by persuasion, require such companies to disclose the operational results of each division. Such disclosure has its limitations because overhead expenses can be distributed arbitrarily between divisions and inter-divisional transfers can be made to suit the convenience of management. Limitations of this kind, however, are inherent in all financial statements, including those of undiversified companies.

So far as the misuse of tax incentives is concerned, the diversified companies can contend that every project involving capital expenditure of more than Rs. 10 lakhs[7] proposed by them requires a licence under the Industries Development and Regulation Act, as well as various other sanctions from the government. Far from misusing the tax concessions, the companies are utilising them for the officially approved projects.

The last point is the heart of the matter for the officially approved pattern was, till recently, hardly consistent with the needs of planned development. Almost every sizeable industrial project in the Plan was presumed to be of more or less equal importance. A general homage was paid to priorities but, in actual implementation, licences were given for nearly all projects which satisfied certain criteria of secondary importance like foreign collaboration, import substitution, etc., but which bore little relationship to desired priorities.

Take the prominent case of rayon, for instance. This is a highly capital-intensive industry with little employment potential and a very large foreign exchange component for the installation of equipment as well as the procurement of raw materials. Nevertheless, the growth of this industry has been encouraged by the imposition of severe restrictions on the expansion of cotton mill output, in the belief that we would never be able to grow enough cotton to feed our cotton mills. A number of new rayon units were sanctioned and old units allowed to expand during the Second Plan period, though some of these programmes were not included in the original Plan, and were not part of the so-called hard core. This was done at a time when it was difficult to secure foreign exchange for such essential requirements as power expansion and new machinery for export-oriented cotton and jute mills. Since rayon and the chemical and other plants ancillary to it offered much higher returns than textiles, it is hardly surprising that many cotton and jute mills, which had funds to spare, diversified into rayon and chemicals.

Most of the diversification in recent years has been initiated by cotton, jute, sugar, and tea companies. They have diversified or intend to diversify, because, due to various reasons, they do not expect an adequate and competitive return from the expansion or large-scale modernisation of their traditional business. In cotton, the reasons, in brief, were that government did not allow the industry to expand and modernise at a sufficiently rapid pace, and the domestic and export markets did not offer opportunities for expansion comparable with those offered by other industries. The position in jute is broadly similar, though here the difficulties of export and wide fluctuations in raw material prices add their own complications. Cotton is a relatively stable business, thanks to the large home market and the fact that human beings must inevitably buy some cloth some time. Jute, on the other hand, is a far more risky business because it depends predominantly upon exports and faces severe competition from substitutes and bulk handling. The two industries are none too prosperous if taken as a whole but many units within them, especially those controlled by certain leading groups, have excess financial and managerial capacity. A similar situation has arisen in the tea and sugar industries also.

What are the prosperous companies in these industries to do with such excess capacity? It is wasteful for them as well as the country to let it remain idle.

It has been suggested that the spare funds of companies should be compulsorily deposited with government. Mr. T.T. Krishnamachari tried this experiment in 1956 unsuccessfully. It was later suspended, and finally withdrawn. This solution is inadvisable because the excess financial capacity of a company cannot be measured in quantitative terms, especially when the corporate private sector as a whole is relying increasingly upon loan finance for expansion. Most industrial companies are so heavily indebted that logically they cannot have spare funds. Those who have spare funds do not keep them in the form of cash, as some people imagine, but use them as working capital, or conceal them by under-valuing assets. A company's accounts, moreover, can hardly give an adequate idea of its potential financial capacity, including its ability to raise loans and share capital. Compulsory deposits with government or investments in gilt-edgeds will not, in any event, prevent diversification so long as companies can secure industrial licences for diversification.

In my opinion, government policy on diversification has to be part of an overall policy which lays down differential priorities for various industries.

Industries and individual companies which are export-oriented, directly or indirectly, should have the first claim on domestic and foreign exchange resources over the next 10 years. All possible means should, therefore, be adopted to maximise the investment in the modernisation of their equipment and expansion of their exports. The past policy of denying foreign exchange and other assistance to the older industries for modernisation and helping them in various forms if they wanted to produce high cost import substitutes would have to end.

Companies engaged in the production of such major export items as cotton and jute textiles and tea must, first of all, be induced to maximise investment in the modernisation of their equipment and the consolidation of their export markets through the improvement of products, marketing organisations, etc. If they are unable to do this for justifiable reasons, or, after making such investments, still have some financial capacity to spare, they should be allowed to diversify into or make inter-corporate investments in projects which have a large export potential or a high priority on other grounds.

This re-direction of investment cannot be brought about by mere compulsion or exhortation. It has to be induced through discriminatory tax and price incentives, supported by adequate releases of foreign exchange and scarce domestic resources, all of which require a clear re-definition of the order of priorities for investments and a firm resolve to maintain those priorities in the process of implementation.

In other words, the desire to diversify and to make fresh inter-corporate investments in technically unrelated industries can be turned to national advantage through a judicious combination of planned allocations and the use of the market mechanism. A shift of funds and enterprise from the old to the new industries is inevitable but it must not be left to the mercy of either free market forces or haphazard licensing policies.

NOMINEE HOLDINGS

Coming back to the question of regulating corporate affairs proper, some measures have to be taken to make shareholders' list more true and reliable. The principal sources of their inadequacy and unreliability are two:

i. transactions in shares with the help of blank transfer forms, and

ii. registration of shareholdings in the namse of persons other than the beneficial owners.

Contrary to the popular impression, these two problems are, conceptually and otherwise, distinct from each other, in spite of some common ground between them.

A blank transfer form means a form in which only the name of the transferor is specified and the name of the transferee is not mentioned. The date on which the transferor signed the form is invariably missing. The blank form facilitates and speeds transfer from hand to hand. It avoids the payment of stamp duty and transfer fee, as well as the delay involved in lodging the shares with the companies for registration of transfer. Exceptional cases apart, however, the transfers are registered before the dividends fall due. The greater negotiability thus achieved makes it easy to obtain credit against shares. When shares are pledged against bank loans, for example, the banks take the signature of the pledgor as the transferor on a blank transfer form and retain the right to sell off the shares in case of default.

A nominee holding may or may not involve a blank transfer. Its distinguishing feature is that the holding is registered for a long period, sometimes indefinitely, in the name of a person, other than the actual owner who arranges to collect the dividend, etc., from the nominee. To prevent the nominee from running away with the shares, the actual owner may retain the shares in his possession after obtaining a blank transfer signed by the nominee. If the nominee is a bank, however, the shares normally remain in the possession of the bank, which credits the dividends, etc., received to the account of the beneficial owner; this is a common practice when banks give large advances against shares or when certain shareholders do not wish to let their names appear in shareholders' lists. Such holdings are generally described as *benami* holdings and the registered holder is called a *benamidar*.

The blank transfers which circulate in the market relate only to the floating stock of the shares, a stock which is nearly always a marginal quantity compared to the total share capital of a company. Their circulation is limited to the period between the payment of consecutive dividends, generally a year. Nominee holdings, on the other hand, are a more or less permanent phenomenon and are closely tied up, among other things, with (i) the procedure for advancing bank credit against shares, (ii) the statutory bar against registration of trusts as shareholders (Section 153 of Companies Act), (iii) the facility of registering shares belonging to certain categories of companies in the names of executives, other companies, etc. (Section 49), and (iv) the bringing out of income and wealth which have not been disclosed to the revenue authorities.

The problem of blank transfers was discussed at considerable length by the Gorwala Committee on stock exchange regulation in 1951.[8] The members of the Committee failed to agree among themselves on this issue. The official members wanted a complete abolition of blank transfers on the ground that they help tax evasion and unhealthy speculation and make shareholders' lists inaccurate. Failing abolition, they suggested that the validity of a blank transfer should be restricted to six months from the date of the first transfer stamped upon the form but that a special provision may be allowed in favour of banks. The non-official members were uncompromising in their opposition to such a step They argued, *inter alia*, that some form of blank transfer was used in all capital markets, that its abolition would disrupt the working of the market by reducing the floating stock of shares, and that blank transfers were not the only or the most common instrument for tax evasion.

More recently, in 1963, it appeared that the stock exchange authorities at various centres were almost reconciled to limiting the validity of blank transfers to a period of six months. But no step in this direction was actually taken.[9] Such a restriction is necessary in order to curb excessive speculation by anonymous operators but it would obviously not have a significant impact upon the validity and common practice of nominee holdings.

Banks are registered as large shareholders in many companies, including some private and very narrowly owned public companies. In the aggregate, banks and their executor and trustee subsidiaries owned 5.2 per cent of the total share capital of the 988 sample companies in 1951; the proportion rose to 6.4 per cent in 1958 in the 1,079 sample companies. In absolute terms, the amounts involved came to nearly Rs. 13 crores in 1951 and Rs. 24 crores in 1958. It is a well-known fact that more than 90 per cent of such holdings do not belong to banks as beneficial owners but are held by them in the capacity of pledgees, trustees and nominees.

As stated earlier, banks prefer, as a matter of tradition and security, to have the shares registered in their own names when they give large advances against them to clients. They also act as trustees and nominees for the holding of shares and collection of dividends on them on behalf of clients (companies, trusts and individuals both at home and abroad) who do not wish to undertake this trouble or who desire to remain anonymous. The arrangement is part of the investment service provided by banks. It saves the companies from dealing with a large number of shareholders and earns commission for the banks.

The result, nevertheless, is that the shareholders' lists of some companies particularly cease to show the true pattern of ownership. The practice may conceal the nature and extent of the controlling interest and/or its partners and financiers. It can also conceal the identity of those waiting for a suitable opportunity to take over the control of a company. While recognising that the practice has some utility, it should also be emphasised that it is not a practice which should be allowed to continue unchecked. The public interest requires, as in the case of the balance sheet and profit and loss account, that the shareholders' list of every company should present a true and fair picture of its ownership, not one which is indefinitely distorted by anonymous holdings in the names of banks. Regulation of such holdings would help the controlling interests also, especially when the managing agency system is abolished as suggested here and the power of the controlling interests to control the day-to-day management of companies is, consequently, somewhat diluted. They can always seek the protection of the government against cornerers under Section 409 of the Companies Act but the contingency can be avoided, if they have timely warning of the identity of large beneficial but anonymous shareholders, and the government also has proof of cornering activity by undesirable persons.

The only restriction on shareholding by banks in operation at present is under Section 19(2) of the Banking Companies Act, which limits their holdings in individual companies to 30 per cent of the paid-up capital of these companies, or 30 per cent of the paid-up capital and reserves of the bank concerned, whichever is less, in the capacity of pledgees, mortgagees or absolute owners. The Reserve Bank has powers under Section 36(1)(a) of the above Act to regulate the holdings of banks as nominees or trustees, but has not exercised these powers so far. It could, as a preliminary step, discourage such holdings through moral persuasion and by calling for returns under Section 36(1)(a) of the Banking Companies Act. This could be followed, at a later stage, by a ceiling on bank holdings on behalf of their clients in any capacity. An operationally feasible ceiling may be placed at 1 per cent of a company's paid up share capital in all cases where a bank is not the beneficial owner. This limit should also cover the executor and trustee subsidiaries of banking companies.

Section 153 of the Companies Act, 1956 lays down that "No notice of any trust, express, implied or constructive, shall be entered on the register of members or of debenture holders, or be receivable by the Registrar." A provision to the same effect existed in the previous Companies Act also. Consequently, the shareholdings of trusts were generally registered in the names of the individual trustees, singly or jointly, or in the names of banks. The provision also covered the shareholdings of minors, partnership firms, Hindu undivided families, and of any other persons who were the beneficial but not the registered owners (for instance, under Section 49, which allows investment companies to register their holdings in the names of others, and permits all companies to have some investments registered in the names of nominees in specified cases).

The 1963 Amendment inserts a new Section 153A which lays down that the trustees of a trust created by an instrument in writing which holds more than a specified value of shares must make a declaration of their holdings to the Registrar and send a copy of the declaration to the company concerned. The purpose of this amendment is to take away the voting power of trusts. It does not require that the declaration of trust be formally entered on the register of shareholders, and it certainly does not affect other kinds of implied or constructive trust holdings.

The new Section 153A, therefore, leaves the problem of nominee holdings untouched—as it must for *benami* ownership is recognised as valid in principle and in fact, under various other laws and in a number of court judgements. It is, no doubt, true that this widely prevalent practice[10] helps tax evasion to a considerable extent, but the remedy for it does not lie within the Companies Act. It is a matter which requires the attention of experts in various other branches of law.

The last suggestion relates to the statutory liability of companies to file their shareholders' lists every year with the Registrar.

The number of shareholders in leading public companies like Tata Steel, A.C.C., Hindusthan Motors, etc., is increasing rapidly. There are many other companies which also have a large number of shareholders. The Companies Act allows companies to file a complete list of their shareholders once in three years, and to file only a list of transfers in the other two years. If the shareholders' lists of companies with a large number of shareholders are complete, they are very bulky and difficult to scrutinise. If, on the other hand, they are merely a record of transfers, it is difficult to find out the ownership and control of companies in two years out of three. To enable the government and other interested parties to have compact and comprehensive data on the ownership and control of companies, an arrangement on the following lines may be suggested. Companies with less than 5,000 shareholders must submit a complete list of their shareholders every year. Those with a larger number of shareholders need submit only a list of transfers in two years out of three, on condition that they file every year a list of their top 100 shareholders, giving their names and addresses and the full extent of their shareholdings.

This arrangement would require amendment of Section 159, and Part II of Schedule V of the Companies Act.

REFERENCES

1. The Swedish Government did take over the Kruger group in the thirties but that was done in extraordinary circumstances. Kruger committed suicide after his world-wide speculation was discovered. No buyer could be found for his international empire, shrunk though it was after salvage operations.
2. Subject, of course, to the availability of foreign exchange, local resources and various kinds of licences, etc., the distribution of which is admittedly biased in favour of the larger groups.

3. The number of managing agents and the companies managed by them has declined to some extent since the passage of the Companies Act, 1956. In 1954-55, companies managed by managing agents accounted for 54 per cent of the share capital of all companies, excluding government, banking, and insurance companies. The ratio for public companies alone in that year was 71 per cent. In 1960-61, the proportion for all companies, public and private, declined to about 36 per cent, inclusive of companies managed by secretaries and treasurers (see *Company News and Notes*, Vol. I, No. 23, September 2, 1963, pp. 31-40). Comparable data for public companies are not available for 1960-61; the ratio for them would exceed 50 per cent.
4. The Fifth Annual Report on the Working and Administration of the Companies Act for the year ended March 1961, pp. 42-43.
5. Note (1) to Part 1, Schedule VI of the Companies Act defines a trade investment as "an investment by a company in the shares or debentures of another company not being its subsidiary, for the purpose of promoting the trade or business of the first company".
6. Partly because the yield on government securities is relatively low but mainly because most companies are pressed for funds.
7. The exemption limit was raised to Rs. 25 lakhs in December 1963.
8. *Report of the Committee on Proposed Legislation for the Regulation of Stock Exchanges and Contracts in Securities*. Government of India, 1951.
9. The limitation has now been enforced through an amendment to the Companies Act.
10. It has not been proved statistically in this study and may not be capable of statistical verification,, but 'general observation' fully bears out the statement.

THE GREAT ESCAPE*

Concentration Good, Monopoly Justiciable

THE report of the Monopolies Commission cannot be treated with the indifference (or amusement) which was extended to the report of the Mahalanobis Committee.[1] Too many undertakings have been given about implementing its recommendations and a draft bill is incorporated in the report.

However, the only charitable interpretation possible for the general approach and recommendations of the Monopolies Commission is that it proved unequal to the task of reconciling the opposing logic of capitalism and socialism.

Those who had felt that the Commission should never have been set up in the first place have been proved right.

The report of the Monopolies Commission has three merits. It has been completed on schedule and released quickly to the public, without prolonging the existence of its establishment. The Commission has essayed, though with very limited success, the task of improving efficiency and business practices in a sheltered market through regulatory processes. And the principal deficiencies in its approach and recommendations have been made up in an able and comprehensive minute of dissent by, of all persons, a senior civil servant. It also marks a departure from the tradition of high power commissions: *obiter dicta* take the place of reasoned and documented analysis, the Commission's interpretation of recent history is unbalanced, the report is shoddy by any (leave aside Cambridge) standard, and there is no summary of conclusions and recommendations. Even those who expected little from this Commission have reason to be disappointed.

*Report of the Monopolies Enquiry Commission 1965, Volumes I and II. Price Rs. 6.50 or 15s 2d or $2.34. The listed prices are consistent with the Commission's devotion to petty detail. This review article appeared in *The Economic Weekly*, 18 December, 1965.

The Commission was supposed to bring its ripe wisdom to bear upon some of the basic problems of a semi-planned mixed economy. That it has failed to do. The majority chose either to wallow in British precedents or to refrain from the effort to reconcile the justifiable areas of concentration and monopoly with the socio-economic objective of broad-based economic power. They became victims of the implicit compulsion to frame legislation which, if at all seriously intended, can deal with monopolistic practices only, and a prey to the common irrational feeling that the judiciary can deliver the goods for which politicians and bureaucrats have proved inadequate. This faith in the judiciary, which some other countries repose in the army, is touching indeed; the Santhanam Committee, whose recommendations seem to have coloured what little thinking the Commission did, shared this faith, which only proves that the age of faith is not over.

TERMS OF REFERENCE

The main purpose behind the appointment of this Commission was never clear. By the time it took over the boiling pot from the Mahalanobis Committee on Distribution of Income and Wealth, public attention was already diverted to other more elemental issues. There was, perhaps, a serious intention to clear private traffic lanes but the implications of this process in the light of an increasingly sheltered market, a growing public sector and proliferating weeds of administrative regulation were not fully understood. Nobody, however, bargained for the substitution of judicial processes (that is, unforeseeable delays) in place of administrative bungling and indiscretion which are by now foreseen and are reasonably discountable factors.

The Commission appointed in May last year consisted of Justice K. C. Das Gupta of the Supreme Court (Chairman), G. R. Rajagopal (Legal Draftsman), K. R. P. Aiyangar (former Chairman of the Tariff Commission), R. C. Dutt (Chairman of the Company Law Board) and I. G. Patel (Chief Economic Adviser). Its terms of reference were as follows:

a. to enquire into the extent and effect of concentration of economic power in private hands and the prevalence of monopolistic and restrictive practices in important sectors of economic activity other than agriculture with special reference to:

i. the factors responsible for such concentration and monopolistic and restrictive practices;
ii. their social and economic consequences, and the extent to which they might work to the common detriment; and

b. to suggest such legislative and other measures that might be considered necessary in the light of such enquiry, including, in particular, any new legislation to protect essential public interests and the procedure and agency for the enforcement of such legislation.

It was further authorised to report on any other matter bearing on any aspect of the national economy or functioning of the private sector and financial institutions as well as to look into concentration in the ownership of newspapers.

The terms of reference, thus, clearly distinguished between concentration of economic power, on the one hand, and monopolistic and restrictive practices, on the other. The majority confounded both these phenomena under "concentration of economic power" and decided to handle only the latter on the ground that what it describes as countrywise concentration has proved beneficial so far and would remain so in future:

> The concentration of economic power has helped the economic betterment of the country. Even today our industrial development is far behind that in the western world or in Japan. But what little development there is owes much to the adventure and skill of a few men who have in the process succeeded also in becoming 'big business', thus concentrating in their hands a great portion of the economic power controlling and directing the production and distribution of national wealth and income. It is fair also to state that after concentrating power in their hands these men have gone on often to push forward development of further industries, which has been to the advantage of the country. It is also generally

> agreed that concentrated economic power has been responsible for the greater part of the not very high capital formation in the country. Huge profits were often earned so that even after the distribution of high rates of dividends good surpluses were left. They were utilised to add to the industrial capital, whether by way of issue of bonus shares or in the shape of reserves or by investment in fresh ventures.
>
> Although complaints were not infrequently heard that dynastic control of big business has sometimes kept professional managerial talent from coming into its own, it is fair to say that big business has generally been able to supply over the years a considerable amount of managerial skill of high quality, so that production has been high, profits have been good and failures comparatively few in number.
>
> It is important to note that big business has been able to attract and obtain foreign collaboration and such collaboration has helped the starting of many industries especially by supplying the essential machinery and technical know-how. As we have already stated when discussing the factors responsible for concentration of economic power, foreign business concerns are not likely to extend similar collaboration to small units.
>
> From its past records in the development of industries and the special advantage it has in starting and keeping up capital-intensive industries as also the bright chance of obtaining helpful foreign collaboration, it is reasonable to expect that concentrated economic power may be relied upon to make important contribution to industrial development in the crucial years to come.

This confidence in big business has greater empirical justification than the commonly held belief in the extra-territorial benefits of judicial processes. Beyond that one is constrained to remark that the Commission should have had the benefit of more tangible and analytical evidence before getting swept off its feet. This is all the more remarkable because it has not hesitated to outright condemn resale price maintenance (Report, pp. 129, 162, 178-79, and Section 28 of the Draft Bill, a condemnation which at least one of the signatories to the majority report does not recollect), presumably because it has been so treated in the U.K.

recently after acute controversy. The Commission has produced no evidence, apart from its anxious "consideration of the problem", to establish that resale price maintenance is *per se* against the public interest. In a word, the Commission has chosen, for reasons nowhere documented or elaborated in its report, to give an unqualified good certificate to concentration and to create a semi-judicial agency in the name of policing private sector traffic, which would add a new dimension to over-extended administration of industrial planning, or what goes under the label.

ANALYSIS OF HISTORY

In the Commission's analysis, technological economies of scale leading to control of large amounts of capital, and the limited supply of managerial skill have proved a fruitful source of concentration of economic power. From this it delves into history and comes up with a few gems. On the basis of a deductive interpretation of history, unalloyed by a check on facts, it comes to the conclusion that war-time expansion and transfers of companies from British to Indian control around 1947 "necessarily" caused an increase in concentration. Less exalted minds, bogged in detail, might find it difficult to understand how a less than 20 per cent expansion of industrial production between 1939 and 1945, during which period a number of new Indian groups came into prominence at the expense to some extent of British groups specialising in stagnant tea, coal and jute, and the subsequent transfer of several British companies to Indian control, would "necessarily" cause an increase in concentration. Judicially-oriented high power commissions, one understands, do not look into such niceties. Nor, in spite of the economic expertise at their disposal, do they care to observe that the demands of planned development itself, not merely food scarcity and hoarding and machinery imports, necessitate substantial trimming of imports.

For many years, government spokesmen vehemently denied that concentration had increased and was probably increasing. The Commission, one wonders how, takes growth of concentration as a proved fact, though its own catalogues of "productwise" and "countrywise" concentration relate only to March 1964. I refuse to believe that my modest effort, completed in 1961, in studying one aspect of these problems has borne this fruit. The Commission refrains from offering any proof of its hypothesis that concentration has increased over the period of planning. That need not restrain observers from asking how the Commission started with this hypothesis.

It gives five main reasons, nevertheless, for the increase in concentration:

1. Big business could raise capital easily and there was less risk of their industrial licences remaining unutilised. (Did the Commission look into the list of utilised licences between, say, 1955 and 1960, when the government began to revoke unutilised licences, to evaluate this risk?)
2. Licensing authorities have been inclined to favour the larger groups on account of their proven competence and greater resources. The Commission found no evidence of prejudice against the larger groups, rather the contrary. "We are convinced that the system of controls in the shape of industrial licensing, however necessary from other points of view, has restricted the freedom of entry into industry and so helped to produce concentration." It is implied, as emphasised in Dutt's note of dissent, that licensing alone prevented smaller men from taking up big projects and raising more money than they actually did.
3. Foreign collaborators have tended to favour the larger groups.
4. The advantage which big business has over smaller people in obtaining assistance from banks and other financial institutions i another factor.
5. Import restrictions and exchange shortage have played their part.

Productwise concentration is bound to arise and to continue for some time in every new line of production. In some cases, the supply of raw materials and/or the size of the market is limited. The law of patents has also played a role.

PRODUCT CATALOGUE

The Commission then proceeds to make a catalogue each of the two brands of concentration uncovered by it. The product-wise catalogue is based upon data provided by the Development Wing. The Commission itself makes no effort to define "product" or to look into the possibilities of substitution. The emphasis is on ratios, high, medium, low and nil; these can be handled with reasonable safety by supervisory and clerical staff. When the share of the three top producers is 75 per cent or more the ratio is high; between 60 and 75 per cent it is medium, and between 50 and 60 per cent low. Where the share is less than 50 per cent, "the concentration may be considered to be nil". There is no reference to price leadership with a much smaller share of production or to local monopoly. Of the 100 products "specially selected in view of their importance to the ordinary consumer", two-thirds have high concentration, 10 medium, 8 low and 17 nil. These, incidentally, include infant milk food, corn and wheat flakes, biscuits, chocolate, refrigerators, tooth-paste and talcum powder.

GROUP CATALOGUE

For countrywise concentration, the Commission defines a business group as comprising "all such (units) which are subject to the ultimate and decisive decision making power of the controlling interest in the group—the group master.[2] It has tried to ascertain the substance of control and has not gone merely by legal technicalities. The Commission does not follow the concept of "Outer Circle" which, it alleges, "has found favour with some authorities". The innocent reader is left to find out what this concept is, why it found favour with somebody, whether authority or nonentity, and why the Commission could not countenance it. It could not avoid coming across companies under joint control, which it decided to exclude from the list of companies in various groups. Consequently, Associated Cement and its affiliates are treated as a separate group, without any mention of their joint control by Killick, Shapoorji, Tata and Khatau. Parenthetical references are made to the Tata interest in MacNeil & Barry, the Bajoria interest in Soorajmall Nagarmull and British India Corporation, the links between Wallace and Vissanji and between Walchand and Kilachand. The Shapoorji interest in Nowrosjee Wadia is attributed to interlocking of directorates when it is known to exceed 40 per cent of share capital. There is no reference to the Indian holding in Jardine Henderson.

The Commission looked into financial journals, but it does not seem to have come across the fact that Binny and MacNeil & Barry are both subsidiaries of the Inchcape group. There are interesting references to close associates of the Birla group.

The group catalogue includes 75 groups and gives the number of companies (excluding banks), their share capital, assets (balance sheet totals?), turnover, industrial classification and role in product concentration. As of end-March 1964, these 75 groups had 1,536 companies which accounted for 44 per cent and 47 per cent of the share capital and assets, respectively, of all non-government non-banking companies. The Commission has refrained from giving the ratios for the two top groups, Tata and Birla, but a little calculation of its own data gives a ratio of about 12 per cent for them—which excludes the groups which are closely related with Birla, and the Tata interest in ACC, MacNeil & Barry and several other companies. That even a Commission is not immune to the dangers of cataloguing is obvious from the fact that Thapar's Crompton Parkinson (Works) is described as Crompton Engineering Co.

DEFINITIONS

The Commission has found instances of monopolistic exploitation of consumers and restrictive practices. These two are distinguished on a rather tenuous basis. A monopolistic practice is "every practice whether it is by action or understanding or agreement, formal or informal, to which persons enjoying monopoly power resort in exercise of the same to reap the benefits of that power and every action, understanding or agreement tending to or calculated to preserve, increase or consolidate such power". Restrictive practices are defined to mean practices other than those pursued by monopolists which obstruct the free play of competitive forces or impede the free flow of capital or resources into the stream of production or of the finished goods into the stream of distribution at any point before they reach the hands of the ultimate consumers, for example, horizontal fixation of prices, vertical fixation of price and resale maintenance, allocation of markets, discrimination between purchasers, boycott, exclusive dealing contracts and tie-up arrangements. Within the limited time at its disposal, the Commission could secure only illustrative examples of these practices but it believes them to be widespread.

What are the consequences of concentration? The common man in India, according to the Commission, regards concentrated economic power as wholly evil, a belief which it does not share, but which it regards serious enough to disturb "the mutual goodwill that is the *sine qua non* of a happy community". Its recipe for harmony is a lengthy appreciation of the past, present and future role of concentration and big business (quoted above), tempered with a realisation of certain evil effects, the most serious of which is the emergence of monopoly, control of publicity media, and keeping out of small business. As regards misdirection of investment resulting from concentration, which the Commission should have investigated, it was unable to study the matter. Unlike other matters, which also it did not study in any depth, it has not made any comments on this issue.

GENERAL RECOMMENDATIONS

Having found nothing to justify dealing with countrywise concentration, the Majority's general recommendations are, briefly:

1. Self-discipline by political parties, that is, rejection of assistance from business houses,
2. removal of corruption from administration,
3. liberalisation of licensing since it cannot be abolished and preference in favour of small business without sacrifice of efficiency,
4. insistence on proper distribution of goods imported under licence,
5. higher imports to stimulate efficiency,
6. countervailing action by public sector through public

units to prevent monopoly, and

7. Promotion of small industries and preferential government purchases from small units, strong consumer co-operatives and organised consumer resistance.

It considers the regulation of inter-company investments and loans with a view to dealing with concentration as wholly outside the scheme and purpose of the relevant sections of the Companies Act. This is not accepted by the dissenting member. The proposition was rejected by the government many years back.

Since rapid industrialisation is bound to bring with it greater concentration of economic power which would give rise to monopolistic conditions and practices, the principles of legislative policy (according to the Commission) have to be:

1. We need not strike at concentration of economic power as such but should do so only when it becomes a menace to the best production (in quality and quantity) or to fair distribution;
2. to accomplish this a constant watch must be kept by a body independent of the government to see that big business does not misuse its power;
3. monopolistic conditions in any industrial sphere are to be discouraged but without injury to the public interest; and
4 monopolistic and restrictive practices must be curbed except when they are conducive to the common good.

A permanent Commission should be established primarily to look into restrictive and monopolistic practices which are to the common detriment The proviso is not all that qualified, at least so far as resale price maintenance is concerned, because, as stated earlier, this practice has been condemned *per se*. The Chairman of the Commission is to be chosen from Supreme Court Judges or Chief Justices of High Courts. The minimum age for members should be 50.

EXPANSION AND MERGERS

All restrictive practices would have to be registered with a

Registrar and the documents concerned would be open to public inspection. Trade practices would be deemed to be against the public interest if they unreasonably increase the cost or price of goods or unreasonably reduce or limit competition or limit or prevent the supply of goods to consumers. A judicial investigation by the Commission would follow on the reference of a *prima facie* case either from its Director of Investigations or direct from the government. If the Commission gives a verdict of no detriment, nothing further would be done. If the practice is found to be against the public interest, it can issue an order to discontinue the practice. This order would be mandatory (not a recommendation to the government, as Dutt suggests on the British pattern) but subject to unqualified Supreme Court review on appeal. Punishment would be only by fines "in the circumstances of our country"; imprisonment is not considered feasible. Special provisions have been recommended to deal with hoarding, cornering and profiteering. It is proposed to empower the Commission to cancel the licences of those who refuse "to sell at the usual rate".

As regards monopolistic practices, the permanent Commission would be empowered to give a verdict on reasonable prices, regulation of production or supplies and prohibition of agreements against the public interest. When the Commission enquires into the conduct of any undertaking in this connection, the government would be debarred from investigating its management under Section 15 of the Industries Development and Regulation Act and vice versa. (This is, incidentally, the only provision which allows specific relaxation of other procedures of industrial policy.) It can examine the structure of an industry in order to combat inefficiency and obsolescence. Mergers and take-over bids involving undertakings with assets exceeding Rs. 1 crore which lead to acquisition of one-half or more of the market for a product or service would need prior clearance by the Commission, which would appraise the proposal on grounds of higher productivity, lower costs and better quality. Similarly, any "dominant undertaking" (assets exceeding Rs. 1 crore and having one-third or more of the market) proposing to expand by 25 per cent or more would have to get the Commission's approval (Patel and Dutt have dissented from this recommendation). Interlocking directorates in competing business outside the same group are to be prohibited (relatives and other associates are not debarred). All dominant undertakings and all companies with assets exceeding Rs. 5 crores would be required to file with the Commissions annual returns of organisation, business, conduct, practices, management, costs of production and connections with other undertakings according to prescribed rules. The Commission would look into the implementation of patent law.

This merciless delegation of powers to the proposed Commission is not softened by any recommendations to dilute controls elsewhere The unstated hypothesis is that judicial processes should work where the executive arm has failed.

So far as countrywise concentration is concerned, this is all a case of diversification and both are necessary evils in the economic interests of country. "We believe that by proper use of licensing and other powers vested in the government under the existing laws, the government can effectively prevent the growth of countrywise concentration wherever it is to the common detriment. We do not consider it necessary to vast the Commission with any power in this belief,'.

PRESS AND MANAGING AGENCY

The Press and managing agency system are dealt with summarily. The Commission finds that a large segment of the Press is controlled by big business, and the newspapers are prejudiced in favour of business, especially big business (though some papers have exposed business malpractices). By its own twisted logic, however, it considers the "essence of the matter" to be that "any attempt to curtail big businessmen's control over newspapers which impedes the exercise of fundamental rights (by big business) must be ruled out", but attempts should be made to encourage more indepedent journals.

The Commission has made no recommendation for abolition or control of the managing agency system because it is part of the blessings of concentration, its abolition would have no marked effect on concentration since its place would be taken by some other system of group management, and action in the field has to consider not just concentration of economic power but also the effect on industrial progress "which is hardly possible for this Commission to undertake". Other matters which the Commission handled somewhat less casually have, presumably, no effect on industrial progress.

It is hardly surprising that, in their evidence before the Commission, spokesmen of the Associated Chambers suggested this kind of approch and that since the publication of its report, the Federation of Indian Chambers of Commerce and Ineustry has expressed its dissatisfaction with the proposed adoption of one more set of controls. Members of the Associated Chambers are interested mainly in jute, coal, tea and cotton, none of which have high productwise concentration or expect a high rate of growth. FICCI has reason to be distributed because its members are relatively more monopoly and growth-oriented, and administrative or judicial delays hurt them much more.

NOTE OF DISSENT

In a lengthy well-reasoned note, Dutt has dissent from the approach and most of the recommendations of the Commission. He is more tolerant of monopoly than concentration. Dutt feels that the harmful effects of "real" concentration of economic power hove been seriously under-estimated, that the causes of concentratipn are basically different from those enumerated by the Majority, that planning is neutral in the growth of concentration, and that it is possible in some ways to strike at further concentration without endangering growth.

Dutt regards the managing agency system as an instrument, not a cause, of concentration. The alleged shortage of managerial talent cannot be one of its main justifiications for such shortage is to be expected; the system has made no attempt to meet the shortage. This instrument has to be dealt with to the extent concentration has to be discouraged. As regards the Majority's contention that licensing and controls have helped concentration and implicity the assumption that the growth of concentration would have been curbed in their absence, "There is no assurance that...the larger established industrialists would have had to yield their places to new entronts". If this expectation did exist, there would be no justification for anti-trust and monopoly laws in other countries or for many of the Mrjority's recommendations. He feels that the Commission should have recommended the extent and manner of using planning and controls to curb concentration.

CONTROL OVER RESOURCES

Without denying the significance of financial links between political parties and industrialists, he asserts that the influence of big business over politicians and administrators arises from their control over resources, production, employment, investment growth and the Press. Together with their command over unaccounted money, this power inevitably leads to malpractices. As for the contribution of concentration to economic betterment, bigness of individual industrial units should be distinguished from overall concentration "which involves inter-linking of companies for purposes of control and does not necessarily contribute to greater efficiency of any of the individual units so inter-linked, (and) has no effect on the quantum of surplus". It does not follow from the Majority's argument that the quantum of managerial skill available would have been less if there had been less of concentration; rather the contrary is possible resulting from the denial of opportunities to persons unattached to privileged families.

Dutt feels that it would be undesirable to restrict the growth of individual units till they receive the full benefits of economies of scale. Dominance in any particular industry does not by itself give power to a firm to influence the national economy as a whole, which comes from countrywide concentration. To the extent that dominance in individual products and industries is inevitable and economies of scale are desirable, it is necessary to set up a machinery which can deal with the monopolistic and unfair trade practices which are likely to arise therefrom.

DEMARCATION OF AREAS

At the same time, proliferation of large groups into different industries should be permitted only on a balance of advantages. Since a certain level and some growth of concentration might be inevitable, certain steps are necessary to provide safeguards against their harmful effects. Dutt favours some kind of demarcation of areas of concentration:

> It is possible, for instance, to reserve new units in conventional industries where the rate of growth envisaged is not very high for the new entrants or the small men. For certain other industries, where the rate of planned development envisaged is higher, but which still (do) not enjoy a very high degree of priority, established entrepreneurs of moderate means can be encouraged. For still other industries, such as fertiliser, aluminium, etc., which enjoy high priorities and which are also highly capital intensive, reliance will have to be placed on the well-established entrepreneurs even though such reliance may add to the concentration of power.

He also suggests that the public institutions which hold large blocks of shares in companies should take a more active interest in the management of these companies to help diffuse economic power "at least to the extent of preventing a greater concentration of such power than their shareholding justifies in the hands of a comparatively few persons". (He does not, however, specify the nature and extent of this more active interest.) And the state must play an active part in countervailing the power of big business, particularly in the basic industries.

SUPERFLUOUS COMMISSION

Personally, I did not see the need for setting up this Commission last year and feel there is little justification for setting up a permanent Commission in the near future. In so far as the problems of concentration are amenable to regulation, they have to be dealt with through the general economic policy and administrative mechanism of the government. Political corruption cannot be eradicated by outlawing corporate donations; they are at least over the counter. No amount of exhortation from judicial authorities would improve the moral tone of the community so long as the political and financial stakes are high and there is money around to play on them. Public opinion against monopolistic and restrictive practices can be mobilised only when effective action is taken to improve production and to reduce the influence of big business on the implementation of development policies. Turning a blind eye to concentration and summoning petty industrialists and traders to the witness box for charging a few paise more than the "usual rate" is hardly the right way to mobilise public opinion. The only charitable interpretation that one can place on the approach and recommendations of the Monopolies Commission is that it proved unequal to the difficult task of reconciling the opposing logic of capitalism and socialism. The reconciliation is the obligation of intellectuals.

REFERENCES

1. Mahalanobis committee on distribution of income and wealth.
2. Any resemblance between this definition and what appeared in my article in *The Economic Weekly*, 26 November, 1960, is a pure coincidence.

PART THREE

INDUSTRIAL PLANNING AND LICENSING POLICY*

I was appointed an Honorary Consultant in the Planning Commission in July 1966 to conduct a study of licensing under the Industries (Development and Regulation) Act, 1951. The study had two objectives:

i. To review the operation of licensing under the Industries Act broadly over the last two Plan Periods (First and Second Plans) and more closely over the last six-seven years, including the orderly phasing of licensing with reference to targets of capacity.

ii. To consider and suggest in the light of the present stage of economic development, where and in what directions modifications may be made in the licensing policy.

The precise areas of industrial planning and licensing policy on which I was to work were left to my discretion in consultation with the Industry and Minerals Division of the Planning Commission. I was informed that the broad objectives of industrial policy which were sought to be achieved through the Industries Act were the following:

a. the regulation of industrial development and canalising of

*This part reproduces Volume I of my final report on Industrial Planning and Licensing Policy submitted to Government of India, Planning Commission in September 1967. The sequence of its three parts has been altered in this presentation: "Framework and Policy" and "Recommendations" have been brought forward while "Statistical Outline" which was the opening piece in the report has been placed last. Volume II which contained the detailed statistical statements has been omitted.
I am grateful to the Planning Commission for permission to reprint this work.

resources according to Plan priorities and targets;

b. avoidance of monopoly and prevention of concentration of wealth;

c. protection of small-scale industries against undue competition from large-scale industries;

d. encouragement of new entrepreneurs to establish industries;

e. distribution of industrial development on a more widespread basis in different regions; and

f. fostering of technology and economic improvements in industries by ensuring units of economic sizes and adopting modern processes.

Though licensing under the Industries Act has been the principal official instrument of industrial planning, and the Act has been in force since 1952, the only appraisal of licensing carried out so far (by the Swaminathan Committee) has been confined to procedures and allied matters. There has been no attempt to appraise the role and purpose of industrial licensing in an industrial environment which has changed considerably since the enactment of the Industries Act or, to aggregate, classify or otherwise analyse the data provided in applications for licences. These omissions are quite apart from deficiencies in follow-up after the grant of licences.

The Industry and Minerals Division of the Planning Commission kindly placed at my disposal all the files available with them relating to the Licensing Committee and the Capital Goods Committee and intra-government correspondence on industrial policy. These are the only sources of statistical data analysed in this report.

This study was commissioned on the initiative of the late S. G. Barve, then Member (Industry), Planning Commission. I am grateful to the Industry and Minerals Division of the Planning Commission for providing me with the facilities required for this study.

FRAMEWORK AND POLICY

I deal first with the articulation and effectiveness of industrial planning. Since the analysis is based on certain views about planning in general, I shall first set out the broad outline of my thinking on the subject.

The Indian economy is an amalgam of various elements. The public sector accounts for less than 20 per cent of the national income (in around 1966) though its share in new investment is considerably larger. In 1950-51, the contribution of the public sector to the output of (organised) industrial manufactures was less then 2 per cent; this contribution rose to about 8 per cent in 1960-61 and should have exceeded 20 per cent at the end of the Third Plan. This improvement notwithstanding, the general picture is one of an economy in which the private sector (monetised and non-monetised) accounts for the bulk of output, income and savings. In other words, aside from subsistence activity, economic operations are subject in large part to the working of the market mechanism, which cannot be ignored while considering the allocation and management of economic resources.

Nobody seriously suggests that the market mechanism is or can be an exclusive or perfect means for the allocation of resources and maximisation of the growth rate. Equally, there are grave doubts, particularly in view of our past experience, about the possibility of achieving a perfect administration which would successfully and efficiently override or supplant what are usually described as market criteria or market assessment of operations Even a perfect administration in a fully centrally planned economy (which was held at one time as the planned counterpart of classical perfect competition) would need, it is now recognised, shadow prices, rates of returns, managerial flexibility, etc., for effective planning and assessment of performance.

In a mixed economy, with a relatively small but fast-growing public sector in industrial production, and a large but not so fast-growing private sector subject to various administrative controls, the allocation of resources is guided by a combination of market forces and administrative directions. Since the private sector generates the bulk of resources, which are a common pool upon which both public and private sectors draw and since economic activity takes place in a traditionally free environment, it is obvious that the market mechanism is in fact of greater import than administrative fiat.

A number of measures have been taken of late in the direction of making greater use of fiscal and monetary devices to regulate, among other things, the direction of private investment. At the same time, many direct controls on the prices, production and distribution of various commodities have been relaxed or lifted altogether. Tax concessions and credit policies have been more selective since 1964 while the prices and/or distribution of several industrial products have been decontrolled. Some industries have been delicensed pursuant to the recommendations of the Swaminathan Committee.[1] (I shall comment later on this approach to delicensing). Profitability standards have been or are proposed to be laid down and enforced for public enterprises. It is broadly accepted in principle that essential or high priority industries in the private sector, too, should make adequate profits to generate and mobilise resources.

All these, and devaluation, represent greater conscious and deliberate reliance upon the market mechanism without abandoning strategic controls (particularly on allocation of foreign exchange) and emphasis on a growing public sector. They are to be considered not as an exercise in pragmatism or an escape from tedious administrative burdens but as a move towards a more rational and effective policy.

I agree with the view that planning should make the best use of the market mechanism at the same time as it steps up the growth of public sector investment and output, and that it should depend upon fiscal, monetary and foreign exchange controls for manipulation of the market mechanism in the desired directions. In the context of industrial planning, this implies, among other things, a clear advance statement of priorities, greater reliance on relative profitability, taxation (both direct and indirect), and provision of credit and foreign exchange, rather than pre-occupation with the system and procedure of industrial licensing. Since planning is essentially the projection of entrepreneurship and management on a national scale, there has to be a clear perception of the areas which are of overwhelming importance in relation to the principal objectives and which, therefore, require planning in depth. These have to be distinguished from other areas which are of lesser significance in quantitative terms or for attainment of the principal objectives and which, therefore, require only nominal attention in planning.

Industrial planning, in the present situation, has to aim at three main interrelated objectives:

(a) minimising the net aggregate foreign exchange cost of the industrial programme and making the best available use of available foreign exchange,
(b) minimising the total (including rupee) cost of the industrial programme, and
(c) maximising the total output (especially in the priority areas) in relation to the given volume of investment and materials.

It is difficult to assess the extent to which industrial licensing (or planning in general) has so far contributed towards the fulfilment of these objectives. As emphasised earlier, the market mechanism is stronger and more pervasive than administrative fiat in channelising investment and determining output, directly, in the private sector and, indirectly, through the common pool of resources, in the public sector, too. Besides, licensing had a number of objectives which, at the time of enactment of the Industries (Development and Regulation) Act 15 years back were, perhaps, considered equal in importance to channelisation of investment. These objectives concerned balanced regional development, protection of small and cottage industries, and avoidance of concentration and monopoly. These, and discouragement of "wasteful competition", have received attention in planning and administration.

The area of significance which industrial licensing occupies is progressively shrinking.

From about one-fourth of total (large-scale) industrial investment in the First Plan, the public sector raised its share to roughly one-half in the following two Plans; the proportion would be about 60 per cent in the Fourth Plan. Formalities apart, industrial licensing does not apply to the public sector. Similarly, large private projects, which account for the bulk of proposed total private investment, are subjected to a procedure somewhat different from that for 'normal' licensing. Moreover, for some time to come, most of the expansion and diversification of output and fresh investment is expected from existing, rather than new, undertakings and, to that extent, licensing is either not required or involves considerations and problems different from those till say, 1961.

As for balanced regional development, the more diffused availability of power and what are in effect postage stamp rates for steel, cement and coal, together with the setting up of new industrial centres, mostly around public sector projects, have been a positive beneficial influence as against the rather negative bias which industrial licensing has.

It can also be suggested that licensing (though, perhaps, to a lesser extent than the foreign exchange crisis) has been one of the successful instruments of the policy during the Second Plan period to create the urge to industrialise. This urge was reinforced, among other things, by the implicit assurance of more or less monopolistic (or non-competitive) positions which licensees expected to occupy, with the help of foreign collaborators who initiated them into new industries. Now, the urge is there (perhaps, not so much owing to as inspite of the foreign exchange crisis) and there is a greater degree of familiarity with new technology. The extent to which additional output comes from existing rather than new units makes things somewhat easier. Correspondingly, the need to assure monopolistic positions is, to put it mildly, less pressing. More output, at less cost, has become more important than licensing of additional capacity *per se*.

OBJECTIVES OF LICENSING

The main objectives of the Industries (Development and Regulation) Act were to:

1. Provide for government control over the location, expansion and setting up of private industrial undertakings with a view *inter alia* to channel investments into the desired directions, promote balanced regional development, protect small and cottage industries, and prevent concentration of ownership and control to the common detriment;
2. Take over or transfer the management of those undertakings which are being conducted in a manner detrimental to the industry or the public interest; and
3. Set up Development Councils, one for each major industry, to act as some kind of industrial planning and development organisations.

Leaving aside (2) and (3), which I deem to be outside my terms of reference, the major assumption implicit in the Act is that growth and allocation of resources should be looked after wholly or mainly by administrative guidance, promotion and control, and hardly at all by the market mechanism. This assumption was justified up to a point for, left to itself, the market mechanism could not deliver the goods, especially in the absence of an adequate infrastructure, direct government participation in industry and trade, and the planned manifestation of inter-dependent growth of various sectors. The scale and complexity of the effort undertaken subsequently by both public and private sectors and acute continuing shortage of foreign exchange could barely be foreseen in the early fifties.

As Plan programmes for industry acquired significance, the essentially negative instrument of licensing assumed the positive role of being the principal administrative instrument and sanction for projecting the installation of capacity up to or around the targets laid down in the Plan. Licensing was not, however, concerned with the actual fulfilment of these capacity targets or the output resulting from additional capacity or the (foreign exchange and domestic) cost of additional capacity and output. It paid homage to import substitution, often regardless of the rupee cost per unit of foreign exchange saved, and the "urge to industrialise".

Since 1957, licensing has also sought (more at the Capital Goods Committee than the Licensing Committee stage) to keep the volume of projected investment within the available resources of foreign exchange and/or to utilise available foreign credits.

This wide variety of objectives, between which conflict is inherent when key resources become acutely scarce, has imposed a strain on licensing, which has been relieved only marginally by recent procedural adjustments and relaxations.

It is a well-established and admitted fact that, since the First Plan, shortfalls in investment and output have been large and persistent mainly in basic industries, notably steel, cement, machinery and fertilisers. The gains in terms of balanced regional development and wider distribution of entrepreneurship are, at best, moderate. That licensing has served to channelise investment appears to be extremely doubtful.

Within official circles, the following factors are by now

recognised as defects in the licensing system :

a. Licensing is only one among the first of the many hurdles that have to be crossed by a private entrepreneur, so that a licence does not automatically provide a package sanction or clearance.

b. The issue of licences tends to give an exaggerated picture of industrial capacity which sometimes scares away genuine entrepreneurs who might be chronologically late, at the same time as it encourages foreclosure of licensed capacity by influential groups and sitting tight on unimplemented licences.

c. Licences are normally or, in most cases, issued for a capacity 10 to 25 per cent above the target for the end-Plan year and that, too, mostly around the beginning of a Plan period. An excessive—though quantitatively unverifiable—pressure is thus exerted on the available foreign exchange and possible collaborators and also on domestic suppliers. This leads to bottlenecks and delays, apart from adversely affecting the terms of negotiation with foreign and domestic suppliers and creditors.

d. The process of consideration and reconsideration of applications at various levels and at various times contributes to delays and higher costs, without improving the feasibility of the project concerned.

e. There is very little follow-up of licensing to see that the approved projects fructify in a satisfactory phased schedule. Even the authorities concerned are not fully aware of the total investment and foreign exchange commitments of licences issued or those under implementation at any particular period of time.

ANALYSIS OF DEFICIENCIES

The above failures and deficiencies are not less important because they are obvious and admitted. These were inherent in the licensing system as it was conceived and made to function. They were bound to arise because the Planning Commission laid no guidelines and there was no official insistence or market pressure on entrepreneurs to prepare thorough feasibility studies.

Licensing has proceeded on the assumption that capacity targets for individual industries are the only constants in a changing economic situation.[2] No attempt has been made to synchronise or adjust the pace of licensing and revocation to the actual trends in capacity and output in relation to emerging demand. The Planning Commission has never, on its own, set out the criteria for fixation of priorities or listed the priority industries/ projects which should receive preferential allocation of foreign exchange and other scarce inputs. Nor has it, at any time, given clear guidelines about how precisely the various conflicting objectives of licensing should be reconciled on an industrywise, projectwise, or applicantwise basis. There has also been no quantitative indication from the Planning Commission to the executive ministries (or licensing authorities) of the effect of lags in the fulfilment of various targets from time to time on the requirements of additional capacity or output in inter-linked sectors of industry. To my knowledge, no exercise has been undertaken to assess the relative costs of securing additional output from existing against fresh investment or of domestic manufacture against imports. Setting and licensing of physical targets have not been reinforced with considerations of unit costs and overall financing.

At the entrepreneurial end, the desire to be at the head of the queue and to foreclose as much of the target as possible is not matched by adequate homework and vetting of projects. This tendency has been encouraged by the practice of issuing licences or, more recently, letters of intent, somewhat liberally in the belief that the proposals would in any case be closely scrutinised at the CGC and/or indigenous clearance stage and, subsequently, by financial institutions in many cases. Deficient entrepreneurial homework was, perhaps, inevitable to some extent so long as there was an overwhelming dependence upon the foreign collaborator to vet projects and give specifications of equipment. With the establishment of greater know-how within the country and reliance upon existing rather than new undertakings, this deficiency is no longer wholly excusable or incurable.

I would spell out the principal shortcomings of industrial planning and licensing as follows:

a. There have been no overall policy guidelines to reinforce and supplement the plan targets, which indicate the capacity and output to be achieved at the end of each five-year period. The Planning Commission has not indicated the precise areas in which investment plans are to be encouraged or discouraged and how this encouragement or discouragement is to be carried out with reference to available foreign exchange and other factors.

b. In the absence of well-ordered priorities and flexibility of interrelated programmes at various levels of performance, there has been a tendency to rely upon various *ad hoc* criteria. One of these has been the policy of licensing projects, the foreign exchange costs of which on capital and/or maintenance account are covered by available credits and/or foreign collaboration and/or export obligations. It can be said in defence of this policy that there has been no resulting distortion of planning or industrial development because the projects so approved are, in nearly all cases, included in the plan. That does not, however, answer the basic argument that this is a reversal or inversion of what is implied in planning. A project must first of all be intrinsically feasible and occupy a high place in the list of priorities before it can be considered for the allotment of scarce resources, especially foreign exchange. Just because a project is, or can be, made amenable to availability of foreign exchange should not qualify it for approval.

c. In attempting to cover almost the whole range of large-scale industrial development, licensing inevitably loses sight of the relative importance of different projects and/or products. The licensing authority and the departments which services it are loaded at any one time with hundreds or thousands of proposals, without clear and definite criteria to appraise their worth in terms of relative costs and the attainment of targets in related, particularly basic, industries/projects.

d. The maintenance or reshuffling of three lists, rejection, merit and relatively free, which passes under the euphemistic title of industrial licensing policy, has nothing to do with priorities or their fulfilment or actual fructification of licences. These lists are based on the historical or contrived accident of the pace of previous licensing in relation to end-plan targets.

e. The basic idea of a licence was, and has to be, that it represents a social sanction for drawing scarce resources from the national pool, for a project of significant size. To the extent to which licences or letters of intent have not in fact been utilised implies that licensing has not performed this function. At the same time, those licensees who seriously intend to utilise them find that they are no more than formal passports which have to be shown to various authorities for clearances in due course. A large floating population of licences inevitably reduces the utility of a licence for placing indents upon scarce resources for priority projects.

These deficiencies are so fundamental that they cannot be overcome by procedural or administrative changes. They indicate the need for better and more effective planning by the government and the entrepreneur, recasting of the scope and working of the licensing system, conscious use of the market mechanism, supported by appropriate modifications in tax and credit policies.

RECOMMENDATIONS

I would say emphatically that there can be no improvement in the licensing system unless there is a basic change in the scope and drawing up of industrial programmes in the Planning Commission. The role of the Planning Commission in this context should not comprise merely laying down of end-Plan targets, representation on the Licensing and Capital Goods Committees, and *ad hoc* intervention on certain issues.

The industrial programmes of the Five Year Plans must separate the grain from the chaff. One must know which targets are compulsive and have to be fulfilled, as distinct from those which are merely indicative and have no major impact upon income generation or crucial investment. In a word, priorities have to be clearly distinguished from posteriorities.

Practical observation and the blessings of literacy have made the elite familiar with the concept and working of interdependence but only a planning body can establish the precise location and magnitude of such interdependence where it exists and/or its insignificance where it does not.

The Planning Commission has to lay down the criteria for fixing priorities, specify the major priority areas and suggest from time to time the broad policies on taxation, credit, prices and allocation of foreign exchange required to fulfil the targets set for these areas. The selection of priority areas has to be in terms not just of consumer vs. producer or capital goods but of deriving the maximum benefit of income and net foreign exchange saving per rupee of investment. While it is understandably difficult to have uniform priority lists for various purposes, there should, in principle, be a close relationship between priority lists in the Plan, and those maintained for taxes and tax concessions, import licensing[3] or tariffs, credit policies and, finally (though, for individual units, it is essentially an entrepreneurial responsibility) for alignment of relative profitability.

Earlier Fourth Plan projections were based on the assumption, *inter alia*, of certain growth rates and estimates of foreign aid. These would now be revised in keeping with the changed situation, and fresh estimates of aggregate, sectoral and industrywise requirements, consistent with the overall plan and availability of resourees, would be derived. It is not merely worthwhile but essential that these estimates, in so far as they relate to priority and inter-dependent areas, should be worked out for various alternative levels of realisable or expected performance.

This exercise would enable the Planning Commission to know in advance the implications of various lags and leads in different areas and thereby to suggest the corrective action that is necessary and/or to modify the individual targets. Imbalances or distortions would, with the help of these exercises, be treated within the strategy of the Plan instead of remaining external to it and creating further imbalances and distortions. The industrial aggregations which find expression in the Plan have to be periodically reconciled with developments at the level of individual firms or groups of interrelated projects. The targets computed on a macro-economic basis have to be made consistent with projections of capacity, output and returns of major individual programmes and projects.

Having indicated the priorities and selected a few industries/projects which qualify for them, government should undertake to pre-empt foreign exchange and (where necessary) rupee resources, and arrange to provide key physical resources, such as power, transport and land for their benefit. Out of the given available foreign exchange or whatever is in sight, it should be possible to reserve block allocations in favour of these industries/projects, even if this means exhausting the entire available quantum or transitional locking up of foreign exchange at the expense of other sectors of the economy.

During the Third Plan period, total CGC approvals (excluding releases by the *ad hoc* Committee and the Textile sub-committee since April 1955) amounted to Rs. 688 crores (Table 1) while licences were issued for Rs. 396 crores only (including a bare

TABLE 1: **CGC releases in Third Plan by years**

(*Rs. crores*)

Year	Approved	Licensed
Grand total	687.83	395.67
1961-62	158.64	134.34
1962-63	133.35	102.69
1963-64	207.68	111.87
1964-65	114.74	38.29
1965-66	73.42	8.48

Rs. 8 crores during 1965-66). Actual payments against the licences are apparently not known to anybody. Of the total licences issued, cash licences against official credits/trade agreements amounted to Rs. 227 crores and licences against IFC/ICICI sub-loans to Rs. 55 crores, making a total of Rs. 280 crores or 70 per cent of aggregate licensing (Table 2). This 70 per cent, together with small amounts from other sources at least, is reasonably amenable to pre-emption, if the remaining 25 per cent or 27 per cent, which comes from direct foreign credits/investments and deferred payments, is not.

There are, it is true, significant lags between allocations, licensing and actual payment, so that in the mechanics of opera-

TABLE 2: **CGC releases in Third Plan by sources***

(*Rs. crores*)

Source	Approved	Licensed
Grand total	687.83	395.67
1. U.S.A.	170.06	107.00
2. West Germany	17.60	10.62
3. U.K.	14.89	12.58
4. Japan	40.49	19.69
5. France	43.78	23.67
6. Belgium	6.99	3.88
7. Canada	5.14	1.93
8. Austria	2.01	1.25
9. Holland	7.46	6.01
10. Italy	11.42	6.46
11. Switzerland	7.21	5.39
12. Denmark	1.20	0.67
13. Sweden	0.55	—
Sub-total 1 to 13	328.80	199.15
14. Poland	0.74	0.74
15. Yugoslavia	7.64	5.95
16. Hungary	1.27	1.27
17. Czechoslovakia	0.54	—
Sub-total 14 to 17	10.19	7.96
18. Rupee payment	38.07	18.71
19. IFC/ICICI	123.13	53.10
20. Free resources	4.62	3.08
21. IDA	0.94	0.80
Sub-total 18 to 21	166.76	75.69
22. Export earnings	3.67	1.38
23. STC link	3.60	2.77
Sub-total 22+23	7.27	4.15
24. Foreign share capital	80.45	53.75
25. Loans from principals	47.34	28.71
26. C.D.F.C.	11.69	6.09
27 IFC Washington	12.75	1.49
28. Deferred payments	22.60	18.70
Sub-total 24 to 28	174.83	108.74

Source for Tables 1 to 4: Economic Adviser, Ministry of Industry.
*Excluding releases by CG textile sub-committee since April 1963 and *ad hoc* committee.

tion, pre-emption is not as clear-cut or easy as it sounds. Pre-emption, obviously, can apply only to allocation and licensing, not payments, once the earlier stages are gone through. I understand that no insuperable difficulties are expected with the introduction of pre-emption, in spite of the problems thrown up by these lags.

For more than five years now, the policy of the government has been to allow the private sector to import capital goods only against credits, investments or similar facilities. (A rather similar principle is applied to the public sector also but its demands are, on an average, substantially larger). To give an example as will be observed from Table 2, a nominal approval of Rs. 5 crores and licences worth Rs. 3 crores were given against free resources during the entire Third Plan period. Most of this amount went to iron and steel companies. This policy was justified, to a considerable extent, by the extreme shortage of foreign exchange and the project bias of foreign aid and investment. While the foreign exchange shortage continues, non-project credits currently, however, account for two-thirds or three-fourths of fresh assistance.

There is no special virtue in continuing to adhere steadfastly to this rule of allowing capital goods imports against credits/investments only. Increasing domestic manufacture of machinery and availability of foreign exchange for importing machinery components are helping—or should help—to improve our bargaining position in the procurement of capital goods out of country-tied credits. This process can be reinforced by some increase in the allocation of free exchange. In absolute terms, the amounts required would be small.

It would be worthwhile to allocate an additional Rs. 5 crores per year to select priority projects, on condition that (i) sub-allocations are in lieu of specified multiples of the equivalent in country-tied allocations and (ii) no single applicant or industrial house gets more than a specified amount.

Correspondingly, the industries or projects which are not included in the priority lists should know in unambiguous terms that (a) foreign exchange allocation to them over a period on account of both capital goods and maintenance would be either within a specified ceiling or on merits after the needs of the priority sectors have been fulfilled and (b) their progress is left to the operation of market forces and they should expect little or no assistance from the government.

For consideration on merits, the principal factor should be the extent to which the proposals save foreign exchange for the priority industries/projects rather than vaguely for the country as a whole. The other factors which may be kept in mind for consideration on merits should be:

a. does the project utilise by-products or industrial wastes and thereby contribute to value added on a scale disproportionately large in relation to the initial investment? and
b. technical institutions or laboratories may be allowed to import proto-type plants for promoting subsequent fabrication without foreign collaboration and according to Indian specifications.

Better and more effective use can be made of the technical servicing capacity of DGTD. At present, one gets the impression that this organisation is used several times over for scrutinising a large number of amorphous proposals through the various stages of their progress (or lack of it).

The DGTD should publish a regular bulletin giving information on the indigenous availability, present and future, of engineering and chemical products, and test house/ISI/national laboratory reports on the quality, etc., of relatively new products. The bulletin should also publish regularly information on the prices of domestic engineering and chemical products, especially intermediates, and compare them with the landed cost or international prices of comparable products, together with the import duties levied on them.

It should also be possible for DGTD to give positive advice by publicising the areas in which it would be economical to produce components for various industrial goods, and the minimum economic capacity, investment and foreign exchange required for their production, as also the possibility of manufacturing these items with domestic collaboration.

I now come to the related objectives which industrial planning has to subserve. These are balanced regional development, promotion of small industries and reduction of monopoly and concentration of economic power.

The industrial programmes should specify in advance the

industries in which setting up of fresh capacity or substantial expansion in output from existing capacity is amenable to regional allocation. The industries which are not so allocable on grounds of techno-economic feasibility should be developed regardless of regional considerations and the programmes must say so.

Subject to considerations of economic size and foreign exchange costs, regional allocations of capacity and output can be indicated at the beginning of each Plan period for the 'allocable' industries. The allocations should be reviewed every two years or so in the light of actual developments.

One of the advantages of long-term planning is that programmes of development and even major individual projects can be contemplated, their feasibility assessed and preliminaries undertaken well in advance of the actual implementation. Provided this central effort is backed up by local initiative and preparation, it should be possible to assure each region of a fair and reasonable share in development, consistent with the overall availability of resources and the economics of location.

The government should also indicate in advance the industries and/or products which are to be either wholly reserved for small units or in which a specified percentage of projected output is to be reserved for small units over a specified period and/or in which large units would not as a rule be permitted to set up competitive plants. These lists can be reviewed every two years or so in the light of various, including technological, developments.

It might be worthwhile for the centre to allocate foreign exchange quotas to state directors of industries, on an agency basis, for disbursement of import licences to industrial units with assets of less than Rs. 7.5 lakhs. If the experiment is successful, it can be extended to units with assets of up to Rs. 25 lakhs. Such units have to obtain, at present, essentiality certificates from states and then apply for an import licence to the centre. The suggested decentralisation would reduce administrative delays and applicants' difficulties in dealing with a remote centre. This limited foreign exchange quota would be a small fraction of the total resources annually transferred from the centre to the states and, since it would be handled on an agency basis, the centre would continue to have control over foreign exchange matters.

As a matter of policy, the government should declare that certain traditional industrial activities shall be closed in future to the specified 10 or 15 largest industrial houses and their associates. This would imply that the large houses already established in these activities shall not be permitted to expand in these areas, which would henceforth be reserved for small houses and independent businessmen.

In the event of a change in the coverage of industrial licensing or its practical abolition, the large houses should not receive any capital goods import clearance or assistance from financial institutions for expansion of investment within the traditional industries; facilities for modernisation should not, however, be denied. It should also be stated at the same time that the large houses would be welcome in areas of new technology and where there are economic possibilities of large exports.

I am, thus, not in favour of imposing a complete embargo on the expansion and diversification of large industrial houses, where these are techno-economically feasible, and where other dependable promoters might not be available. Even between the large houses, it should be possible to give preference, other things being equal, to relatively smaller as against the larger houses. Going by conventional yardsticks, there is little or no substance in the belief that the largest houses are the most efficient or most dependable for growth; several medium-sized houses have a creditable record of achievement.[4]

The government should be reasonably clear in its mind at the outset regarding the industries in which competition can and should be fostered and others in which, on account of technological and economic compulsions, there is no alternative to some degree of monopoly. In the latter group of cases, it is obviously better to tolerate monopoly—though not monopolistic abuses—than to pursue *ad hoc* anti-monopoly licensing practices, which encourage uneconomically small plants.

In fiscal policy, the major tax concessions such as development rebate and tax holiday should be (a) selective, matched with Plan priorities, and granted accordingly with a larger differential than given at present, and (b) related directly to larger output, lower cost and higher profits, instead of conferring a bounty on the amount of investment *per se*. This principle would help to match priorities with relative profitability, and incentives with output performance rather than mere investment.

Excise duties can be used to mop up excess profitability where it is not consistent with priorities in order to prevent mis-allocation of resources. This device, together with denial of foreign exchange, would be more useful than having a 'banned list' for further industrial licensing which has no relevance to priorities but rests exclusively on the accident of past licensing.

Over a period of time, import policy should be liberalised in respect of those products where the cost differential between domestic production and imports is so adverse (which involves spending, say, more than Rs. 11 to save $ 1) as to make domestic production uneconomical. The schedule of import duties should be closely related to the programmes and priorities of industrial development, informed with the net benefit calculus of import substitution.

Credit planning is one of the main areas which has been left unexplored in the search for instruments to make planning more effective. Planned allocation of credit should, henceforth, assume the role of the principal strategic control for guidance of investment in both fixed assets and inventories, in place of the diffused variety of direct controls which have been in operation till recently. A number of measures would be required to make the flow of credit consistent with Plan priorities and the objective of reducing concentration of economic power. Some of these are indicated below.

A specified small but progressively increasing percentage of commercial bank deposits should be statutorily deposited with the Industrial Development Bank, at a rate of interest equivalent to the prevailing bank rate. Each percentage point of such deposits would, at present levels, fetch nearly Rs 30 crores into IDB and thereby (a) reduce the draft on government finances, and (b) make for more priority-based utilisation of public deposits with banks.

Second, a credit-deposit ratio should be laid down for commercial banks lending in the aggregate to priority sectors like agriculture, small industries, export, hire-purchase or sale on deferred payment of commercial vehicles and domestic machinery items; within this ratio, individual banks should be free to decide the particular areas in which they are specially interested.

Third, for all individual short-term credit limits above Rs. 1 crore (whether with one or more banks), which account for a large proportion of total bank credit, a constant check must be maintained not just on the security against the loan but the purpose for which the credit limit is utilised. Large borrowers should be required in principle to have a higher ratio of equity to debt and, also wherever possible, to have a shorter period of repayment.

Fourth, since the bulk of bank credit is extended against inventories, appraisal of such cash outflow from the banking system should be an essential part of annual planning. Financing of priority sector inventories should be considered almost as important as financing of fixed investment, even if this means denial of credit elsewhere.

These measures would change the traditional pattern of bank credit and, perhaps, reduce the availability of credit to a few sectors, which is unavoidable, given the total available volume of resources.

For new projects the promoter's equity is normally about 10 per cent of the total project cost. New or smaller or professional entrepreneurs often find the raising of this 10 per cent equity a difficult proposition, especially when they venture into relatively large projects and have, simultaneously, to protect their controlling interest. It should be worthwhile for public financial institutions to lend, on special terms, to such entrepreneurs a reasonable part of the promoter's equity requirements, repayable, for instance, in monthly instalments out of the managing director's emoluments. Correspondingly, for projects undertaken by large houses, financial institutions should insist on a larger proportion of promoter's equity as well as of total equity to debt: if public participation in share capital is consequently lower it would reduce and not increase concentration of economic power for the large promoter would be compelled to find more resources himself.

This principle of grading the proportion of a promoter's equity can be usefully applied on an industrywise basis also. If, say, cement has a higher priority than cotton, the promoter's equity in cement can be tolerated at a lower level than in cotton.

At the risk of over-stepping my terms of reference, I should express my doubts about the viability of carrying through the above suggestions so long as many of the major credit institutions are under the direct control and/or influence of those who might suffer under the suggested arrangements. It would be difficult to undertake credit planning unless the linked control of industry and banks in the same hands is snapped by nationalisation of banks.

PROJECT PREPARATION

The licensing system does not place adequate emphasis upon entrepreneurial homework. It favours chronological precedence instead of stressing the preparation of feasibility—and project—reports. Even at the CGC stage, leave aside the letter of intent stage, there is no firm basis for accepting the feasibility (including its import component) of a project to qualify it for the allocation of the most scarce input, namely, foreign exchange.

It might be argued (as it has been) that the expense and effort involved in this preparatory work is worthwhile only if a licence is assured and there is a reasonable assurance of other clearances. This argument reflects the extent to which the licensing system has discouraged the performance of intrinsically entrepreneurial functions and the length to which plan fulfilment has been made to depend upon a long-drawn-out scrutiny of inadequately prepared proposals.

Any project with a total fixed investment of Rs. 1 crore and above or having a capital goods import component of Rs. 25 lakhs and above should be considered for approval by the government only if it is supported by a thorough feasibility report, certified by a recognised (preferably domestic) consultant.

The feasibility reports should contain at least the following:

a. Promoter's background and interconnected undertakings.
b. Total investment, scheme of financing, import requirements on capital and maintenance accounts.
c. Market prospects and selling prices for each product line and expected profitability.
d. Phased programme of import substitution and/or exports.
e. Terms of foreign technical and/or financial collaboration,

if any.

f. Capacity of each product line, number of shifts to be operated and manufacturing process.

g. Requirements, availability and prices of major physical inputs.

h. Location and transport.

These feasibility reports should be appraised by *ad hoc* committees, one each for a group of projects, consisting of persons from DGTD, financial institutions, ministries concerned and approved consultancy firms or technical institutions.

This requirement would ensure that every project of reasonable size, which makes a draft upon national resources, is intrinsically feasible and eligible for priority rating, and not just waiting to jump the queue because it is amenable to availability of foreign credits or collaboration. Projects with an investment of Rs. 1 crore and above account for more than two-thirds of total private investment but their number each year is less than 100 (on the basis of approvals in 1964-66). The scrutiny involved would, therefore, cover relatively few projects but the major part of investment. This would be a feasible and worthwhile exercise.

It has been suggested that this requirement would handicap the smaller industrialists wishing to take up large projects. I feel, on the contrary, that prior establishment of feasibility is even more necessary in their case in order to safeguard them against greater risks; it is better to spend a lakh or two for this purpose rather than jeopardise a crore.

COVERAGE OF LICENSING

Given action on the above lines, the policy that is adopted for modification of the scope and mechanism of licensing is a relatively secondary matter. I hold this view because most of the defects of licensing policy appear to have arisen from planning deficiencies though administrative complications, too, have made their contribution. The suggestions made below on the scope of licensing are consistent with the planning approach suggested earlier, namely, that if one puts aside the public sector as being in fact outside the scope of licensing, the problem is one of laying down priorities and selecting a few top priority areas for planning in depth, and leaving the rest of the economy to look after itself within a framework of indicative targets and drastically restricted availability of foreign exchange.

Recent changes in the licensing policy fall under two broad heads. Some industries/products have been delicensed on the ground that they require little or no foreign exchange on capital and maintenance account and/or they have a large export or agricultural growth potential. Besides, in October 1966, the government revised the definition of 'substantial expansion' from 10 per cent to 25 per cent of existing licensed capacity and gave freedom to manufacture new articles (that is, to diversify), subject to a 'no entry' small industry list of 71 products, no additional expenditure of foreign exchange, installation if any of only minor indigenous balancing equipment and a diversification ceiling of 25 per cent on total production.

These relaxations confirm the view that licensing and its ancillary sanctions are concerned primarily with conservation and (some kind of) allocation of foreign exchange, rather than with channelisation of investment which was the original purpose of the Industries Act. True, a channelisation purpose is implied in the relaxations and that is in the direction of indigenous procurement of machinery and materials, and away from foreign goods. At the same time, delicensing and freedom to expand and diversify imply that regulation of the level and pace of investment in specified industries, balancing of demand for and supply of individual products, location and size of plants is being left to the market mechanism, regulated by fiscal and credit policies, in so far as there is no direct foreign exchange burden.

Consistent with the statistical analysis and approach here, I do not appreciate the basis of delicensing by industries or, more correctly, products, as recommended by the Swaminathan Committee. The industries or products concerned are a mixed bag of high and low priority items, requiring widely varying amounts of investment and number of units, and having, I suspect, widely disparate indirect import components. Some require a degree of planning in depth; others merely indicative targets or no targets at all.

The liberalisation of policy on substantial expansion and diversification is a move in the right direction, provided the preliminary essentials of industrial planning, referred to earlier, have been firmly grasped. These would imply, in brief, the selection of a few top-priority areas for planning in depth, pre-emption of foreign exchange and complementary domestic resources for them, a systematic use of fiscal and credit policies to encourage or discourage investment/production where held desirable and continued and growing emphasis upon public sector expansion and returns on investment. Matching of priorities and relative profitability, of planning objectives and techniques with market criteria and tests, should be the main instrument of industrial planning and policy. Social channelisation of investment cannot be achieved by reliance upon one instrument alone, be it industrial licensing, taxation, market mechanism or any other. Elements of all these and other techniques have to be used in concert.

Whether or not industrial licensing is retained, it is clear that the government has, in some way or the other, to look after the bulk of private investment for it has a close bearing on national objectives and the resource position. This, it should be emphasised, is not the same as regulating the bulk of investment proposals for, most of the investment is concentrated in a relatively few projects.

In 1964-June 1966, applications for the manufacture of new articles with an investment in capital equipment of less than Rs. 25 lakhs accounted for 72 per cent of such applications but only 21 per cent of the proposed investment under this head. In the case of substantial expansion, similarly, proposals of less than Rs. 25 lakhs accounted for 57 per cent of applications but only 10 per cent of total investment. For new undertakings during the same period, if Rs. 1 crore is adopted as the dividing line, applications for less than that amount were 80 per cent of total applications but would have absorbed only 25 per cent of total investment.

I am unable to find a meaningful or purposive distinction between 'substantial expansion' and 'new article'. Licensing is a futile exercise if the latter involves little or no investment, and represents more effective utilisation of investment already undertaken. In fact, freedom to produce new articles would help to make the market competitive and give room for managerial flexibility, too. If, on the other hand, the manufacture of a new article requires substantial investment, then, it is really a case of substantial expansion and ought to be treated on that basis.

Furthermore, substantial expansion itself should be defined in terms of investment, which is a readily ascertainable and quantifiable amount, than licensed capacity for a physical volume of production which is a vague and somewhat misleading concept.

The purpose of licensing, in short, should be to regulate investment, not productwise capacity or production. Taking these dividing lines, namely, Rs. 25 lakhs for substantial expansion and Rs. 1 crore for new undertakings, applications above these limits would leave the industrial policy administration with less than a quarter of the present number of applications but about three-fourths of proposed investment in capital equipment, assuming that the broad distribution pattern of 1964-June 1966 continues to hold good. The number of new undertakings to be 'looked after' would be less than 100 per year which is a reasonable number for worthwhile follow-up in detail.

I recommend that, if licensing is retained, the exempt limit for new undertakings should be raised from Rs. 25 lakhs to Rs. 1 crore, and that for substantial expansion should be Rs. 25 lakhs or 25 per cent of existing investment in capital equipment. The category 'new article' should be abolished. In substantial expansion, there should be no restriction on the installation of domestically produced equipment, and no percentage ceiling on diversified production within the total production.

The issue of a licence in the priority sectors must assure the entrepreneur concerned full assistance from the government in securing such major inputs as foreign exchange, rupee resources, power, transport and land. In the non-priority sectors, such assistance, if any, should be minimal.

The entrepreneur must, in return, undertake to commission the project within an agreed period of time. A licence should be valid for a maximum period of two years and, if not implemented till then, should lapse automatically without any formalities. Implementation should mean the fulfilment of all of the following conditions:

a. Raising of more than 50 per cent of the share capital and/or loans required for the project;

b. Acquisition (whether by purchase or lease) of the necessary land and erection of more than 50 per cent of the factory building;
c. Completion of foreign collaboration arrangments, if any; and
d. Clearance by CGC of at least two-thirds of the value of imported capital goods or, alternatively, opening of letters of credit for at least two-thirds of the plant and machinery required.

Given the feasibility reports, demand estimates and decisions on the number of units to be licensed, the licensing process would be somewhat analogous to inviting tenders, from which a selection can be made (and a waiting list maintained) on the basis of the lowest foreign exchange cost, inclusive of collaboration servicing payments, if any, and maintenance imports over a specified period. While making this selection, the licensing authority must be quite clear about whether the projects covered are to be set up at any cost or, with reference to international costs and the possibility of reaching parity with them in the foreseeable future, taking, where necessary, import duties into account.

The parties which fail to make adequate progress in the implementation of licences should be penalised by transferring their feasibility reports, licences and preliminary clearances to an alternative agency for completion of the project and its subsequent management.

There appears to be some evidence that a few influential houses make a deliberate attempt to foreclose licensable capacity by putting in multiple applications and taking out several licences for the same product. I understand that quite often there is considerable delay, that is, if there is any progress in the utilisation of such multiple licences—even after CGC approval. The freedom to set up small and medium sized undertakings and to expand and diversify production with little or no investment, suggested earlier, would take away much of the inducement for foreclosure. For major products requiring substantial investment and foreign exchange, where these market checks might not exist, not more than one licence and/or CGC clearance for a single product should, as a rule, be issued to a single firm or industrial house, unless there is a demonstrable cost advantage in favour of that firm or house.

Applicants should not be required to seek approval of a change of location within the state specified originally, or from one state to another in case the industry falls outside the list of industries for which a regional angle has been accepted. The clearance of proposals by state governments should be restricted to the availability of power and land only. Assuring or arranging the supply of domestic raw materials and water is and should be the concern of the entrepreneur.

I see no benefit or advantage in getting the opinion of a large number of departments, so long as the projects conform to the criteria of clearance set out in advance by these departments, etc., and the projects are cleared by DGTD after a thorough techno-economic appraisal.

As of January 1964 (for which the latest data are available), 751 applications for foreign exchange equivalent to Rs. 231 crores (pre-devaluation) were pending with CGC for more than one year. Applications received in 1961 and earlier, that is, pending for more than two years, were 182, and these indented foreign exchange of Rs. 173 crores (Table 4).

There is no justification for allowing cases to remain before CGC for more than two years for, by then, much of the perspective changes altogether. An application to CGC should be deemed to lapse automatically if it is not approved within two years.

It would be worthwhile to revoke all licences issued before 31 December, 1964, with reference to which implementation as defined earlier has not taken place. This would give industrial programmes a reasonably clean slate to begin with.

Steps should also be taken to revoke CGC approvals/licences if the applicants fail to make adequate and rapid progress to utilise them. Data are not available on the extent of unutilised CGC approvals and import licences due to causes other than the normal lag in shipments but one suspects that this non-utilisation is not negligible.

Broad indicative targets should be laid down by the Planning Commission, more for information than government involvement, for industries/projects which are not included in the priority lists or which are not covered by licensing. The fears that this so-called relaxation would lead to a distortion of the

TABLE 3: **CGC releases April 1961-September 1964 by industries***

(*Rs. crores*)

Industry	Total	Of which					
		Foreign share capital	Local Institutions and principals	Rupee payment	Deferred payment	STC link and export	Free and IDA
A. Total licensed	322.92	46.06	69.09	15.04	14.19	4.12	3.69
B. Total approved	559.42	67.96	147.81	25.44	20.81	6.69	5.22
Of B:							
1. Automobiles	77.47	8.36	10.82	1.20	—	0.28	0.69
2. Bicycles	0.77	0.18	0.12	0.21	—	0.04	0.05
3. Electricals	27.53	5.97	11.14	1.56	0.26	0.27	0.47
4. Engineering	69.13	8.96	21.93	6.93	0.04	1.23	1.27
5. Heavy electricals	3.56	1.37	0.26	—	1.08	0.16	0.06
6. Iron and steel	93.28	10.96	37.47	3.34	1.81	1.07	0.29
7. Other metals	28.61	2.03	12.22	0.07	—	1.16	0.21
8. Cement	21.37	0.36	5.82	2.80	—	0.05	0.40
9. Ceramics	3.56	0.29	1.81	1.30	—	—	—
10. Chemicals	90.24	13.31	19.03	0.95	3.40	0.46	0.80
11. Glass	6.69	1.77	1.87	0.18	—	—	—
12. Industrial gases	4.90	0.41	2.13	0.91	—	—	0.01
13. Paper and pulp	32.69	2.21	6.60	—	2.59	0.03	0.15

14. Refractory	2.99	—	1.01	0.20	—	—	—
15. Rubber	12.08	5.31	4.09	0.38	0.06	—	0.01
16. Cotton textiles up to March '63	28.97	—	—	2.25	10.30	1.05	0.26
17. Non-cotton textiles	39.00	4.32	5.35	2.19	1.05	—	0.10
18. Miscellaneous	16.58	2.33	6.12	0.96	0.21	1.00	0.43

*As corrected up to 12 January, 1965.
Figures include amounts on waiting list.

TABLE 4: **Industrial licences not covered by foreign exchange clearance as on 1 January, 1964***

(Foreign exchange amounts in Rs. lakhs)

Sr. No.	Product	Item	Year of issue of industrial licence					
			1962	1961	1960	1959	Before 1959	Total
1.	Alloy tool and special steel	No.	1	5	—	—	—	6
		Th. tonnes	15	90	—	—	—	105
		F. ex.	17	648	—	—	—	655
2.	Pig iron	No.	1	—	—	—	—	1
		Th. tonnes	100	—	—	—	—	100
		F. ex.	200	—	—	—	—	200
3.	Ferro manganese	No.	—	—	—	—	1	1
		Th. tonnes	—	—	—	—	44	44
		F. ex.	—	—	—	—	150	150
4.	Steel wire	No.	1	—	1	—	—	2
		Th. tonnes	1050	—	700	—	—	1750
		F. ex.	5	—	1	—	—	6
5.	Tinplate	No.	—	—	1	—	—	1
		Th. tonnes	—	—	90	—	—	90
		F. ex.	—	—	675	—	—	675
6.	Steel forgings	No.	1	1	4	—	—	6
		Th. tonnes	3	3	14	—	—	20
		F. ex.	7	2	41	—	—	48
7.	Steel forgings	No.	3	4	3	—	1	11
		Th. tonnes	8	12	10	—	5	35
		F. ex.	35	181	17	—	22	255

8.	Grey iron castings	No.	3	6	3	—	—	12
		Th. tonnes	27	18	22	—	—	67
		F. ex.	20	25	25	—	—	70
9.	M I castings	No.	6	7	3	1	—	17
		Th. tonnes	12	16	8	1	—	37
		F. ex.	57	49	59	neg.	—	165
10.	C I spun pipes	No.	—	8	2	—	3	13
		Th. tonnes	—	230	85	—	56	371
		F. ex.	—	281	52	—	101	434
11.	Steel pipes and tubes	No.	—	7	4	—	—	11
		Th. tonnes	—	408	83	—	—	491
		F. ex.	—	1240	207	—	—	1447
12.	Steel wire ropes	No.	4	—	1	—	—	5
		Th. tonnes	12	—	3	—	—	15
		F. ex.	131	—	45	—	—	176
13.	Paper mill machinery	No.	—	2	—	—	—	2
		Rs. lakhs	—	840	—	—	—	840
		F. ex.	—	93	—	—	—	93
14.	Ball and roller bearings	No.	2	2	2	—	—	6
		Lakh nos.	5	21	22	—	—	48
		F. ex.	98	99	231	—	—	428
15.	Aluminium	No.	—	—	1	—	—	1
		Th. tonnes	—	—	20	—	—	20
		F. ex.	—	—	900	—	—	900
16.	Clocks, watches, time pieces	No.	2	2	2	—	—	6
		Th. nos.	270	400	155	—	—	825
		F. ex.	9	38	6	—	—	53

TABLE 4 (*Contd*)

17.	Cables, VIR, PVC	No.	—	—	3	1	—	4
		Mn. yds.	—	—	36@	n.a.	—	36@
		F. ex.	—	—	n.a.	n.a.	—	n.a.
18.	Winding wires, B and C	No.	5	—	2	—	—	7
		Tonnes	1680	—	500@@	—	—	2180
		F. ex.	9**	—	19	—	—	28
19.	Electric fans	No.	—	—	—	—	2†	2
		Th. nos.	—	—	—	—	52	52
		F. ex.	—	—	—	—	14	14
20.	House service meters	No.	—	3	3	—	1	7
		Th. nos.	—	147	138	—	15	300
		F. ex.	—	31	14	—	3	48
21.	Fertilisers, nitrogen	No.	4	3	—	—	—	7
		Th. tonnes	262	224	—	—	—	486
		F. ex.	4279	3180	—	—	—	7459
22.	Fertilisers, phosphate	No.	2	3	2	—	—	7
		Th. tonnes	66	107	9	—	—	182
		F. ex.	L	4***	32	—	—	36
23.	Sulphuric acid	No.	1	3	3	2	—	9
		Th. tonnes	165	326	59	17	—	567
		F. ex.	L	15	10	6	—	31
24.	Caustic soda	No.	—	3	—	—	1	4
		Th. tonnes	—	32	—	—	33	65
		F. ex.	—	265	—	—	L	265
25.	Soda ash	No.	—	—	1	—	1	2
		Th. tonnes	—	—	33	—	132	165
		F. ex.	—	—	50	—	460	510

26.	Paper and paper board	No.	—	5	6	—	—	11
		Th. tonnes	—	133	66	—	—	199
		F. ex.	—	1485	1147	—	—	2632
27.	Newsprint	No.	—	2	1	—	—	3
		Th. tonnes	—	120	30	—	—	150
		F. ex.	—	1150	550	—	—	1700
28.	Cement	No.	4	2	—	—	2	8
		Lakh tonnes	7.7	2.7	—	—	4.5	14.9
		F. ex.	180	90	—	—	90	360
29.	Refractories	No.	6	—	5	—	1	12
		Th. tonnes	68	—	157	—	102	327
		F. ex.	51	—	200	—	n.a.	251
30.	Insulators, LT and HT	No.	4	3	1	—	—	8
		Th. tonnes	4.7	4.2	1.4	—	—	10.3
		F. ex.	60	84	16	—	—	160
31.	Pulp, rayon grade	No.	—	2	1	—	—	3
		Th. tonnes	—	52	60	—	—	112
		F. ex.	—	1034	650	—	—	1684

TABLE 4 (*Contd.*)

32.	Other products	No.	19	16	17	—	4	56
		F. ex.	629	688	795	—	19	2131
	Grand total	No.	69	89	72	4	17	251
		F. ex.	5787	10680	5742	6	859	23079

Source: Economic Adviser, Ministry of Industry.
*Licences issued in 1963 are excluded.
L Linked with other products.
@For one licence only; capacity of other two not available.
@@For one licence only.
**Two licences only.
†Both 1955.
***Linked with other products.

pattern of investment, misallocation of resources and excessive pressure on available foreign exchange are, in my opinion, highly exaggerated. The bulk of industrial investment and allocation of foreign exchange would be in the public sector and the priority/licensed area of the private sector, both of which would be within the ambit of planning in depth. If any misallocation of resources threatens to take place, it can be squeezed back into the desired shape by fiscal and credit measures and denial of foreign exchange. It should also be emphasised that the production of luxury goods would be effectively limited by the small size of the market for them. If the goods have a net export potential, both investment and production would certainly be worthwhile.

In the context of the above scheme, it would be neither necessary nor logical to retain the present distinction between the free, merit and banned lists of industrial licensing. These are based essentially on the historical or contrived accident of the pace of past licensing and have little to do with the realities of the situation at any particular time.

Once ceilings are set on foreign exchange allocations to certain industries and the issue of import licences to individual units is related to their actual production performance, the abolition of the banned list (except for small industry reservation) will not place any additional strain on available foreign exchange. Such ceilings and performance-based allocation of foreign exchange will liberate industrial and import licensing from the historical pre-occupation with installed capacity, base period quotas, number of units to be licensed and the production targets for each of those units.

If investments in certain directions are to be discouraged, there are other and more effective ways of doing so. Licensing by itself, one suspects from past experience, is not an economical or very effective instrument for discouraging what may be considered from the planning viewpoint as the wrong kind of investment.

STATISTICAL OUTLINE

This outline analyses the data on applications, investment in capital equipment and its estimated import component collected from the agenda papers and minutes of the Licensing Committee. The outline covers the distribution of applications (net of those deferred) and approvals for licences from 1959 through June 1966 by

a. products,
b. size of investment in capital equipment,
c. type of proposal, that is, new article, substantial expansion and new undertaking,
d. foreign collaboration,
e. location in various states, and
f. industrial houses (including co-operatives and government).

The data suffer from severe limitations, as set out later. Briefly the data are:

a. partial, because items on the free list are excluded altogether,
b. incomplete, because information on investment is not available in some cases, and
c. not fully reliable, because the information given in applications for licences is preliminary and tentative.

They should be taken as rough indicators of magnitudes, not precise amounts.

The peak of initial investment intentions, as indicated by investment applied for, was reached in 1960-62 (calendar years). It has clearly faltered since then (Table 5). Investment approved, which is the next stage of investment but far from the ultimate achievement, was highest in 1960 but has fluctuated considerably each year since then around reduced levels, which would be lower still if recast in constant prices. Investment applied for (to the extent data are available) averaged Rs. 342 crores in 1959-60, Rs. 403 crores in 1962-63, and Rs. 341 crores in 1964-June 1966. Investment approved was Rs. 250 crores, Rs. 245 crores and Rs. 284 crores, respectively; these roughly constant figures indicate a decline in real terms since they are not adjusted for price increases. The number of applications and approvals has, on the whole, tended to decline.

TABLE 5: **Licensing—A synoptic view (1959-June 1966)**

	1959	1960	1961	1962	1963	1964	1965	1966 (up to June)	Total
*Applied**									
1. Number/data not available	466	392	355	505	461	563	781	265	4053
2. Number/data available	916	988	758	820	713	709	530	164	5598
3. Investment of (2) Rs. Cr.	220	463	462	453	296	393	373	87	2748
4. Import component of (3) Rs. Cr.	170	368	327	274	168	245	239	60	1852
5. (4) as % of (3)	77.3	79.5	70.8	60.5	56.8	62.3	64.1	69.0	67.4
Approved									
1. Number data not available	336	239	258	220	228	211	287	104	1883
2. Number data available	698	685	422	471	512	534	448	142	3912
3. Investment of (2) Rs. Cr.	159	341	178	328	228	318	314	78	1945
4. Import component of (3) Rs. Cr.	119	267	122	197	130	196	199	54	1284
5. (4) as % of (3)	74.4	78.3	68.7	59.9	56.8	61.7	63.2	69.2	66.0

*Net of applications deferred for reconsideration.

It must be remembered, however, that a significant part of licensing in 1959 and 1960 remained infructuous, and the exemption limit for licensing of new undertakings was raised from Rs. 5 lakhs to Rs. 10 lakhs in 1960 and further to Rs. 25 lakhs in 1964.

The import component of investment in capital equipment averaged two-thirds over the period; it was fractionally lower for approvals as compared with applications. It has declined from about three-fourths at the beginning to roughly two-thirds at the end of the period though it dipped lower in 1962-63. The data on import component here are as estimated initially by applicants before finalisation of projects and thorough scrutiny, among others, by the Directorate General of Technical Development. The addition of new capital intensive industries constantly offsets the import substitution achieved in older industries. The fact remains, nevertheless, that the import component of capital equipment, as estimated by entrepreneurs, still exceeds 60 per cent. This level does not represent a distinct gain in import substitution.

The predominant part of approvals, both number and investment, has been for products other than consumer goods[5] (Table 6). True, some of the proposed investment in other products can also be imputed to consumer goods because it ultimately gets embodied in them, and the rough categorisation essayed in Table 6 is not altogether immune against objections. The overall trend is, however, so predominantly away from consumer goods that it would not be substantially altered by any sophisticated adjustments.

This trend cannot, at the same time, be attributed wholly or even largely to the existence and operation of the industrial licensing mechanism. It represents, in the main, a common feature of industrialisation, and the working of the arithmetic of growth. As income increases and the needs of the economy diversify, the demand for intermediate, producer and capital goods increases much faster than for consumer goods even in a poor country. Massive growth can take place only under conditions of progressive reduction of dependence upon the processing of natural materials. Even the demand for consumer goods arises from income generation and their supply requires technological inputs from industry.

TABLE 6: **Approvals by product groups (1959-June 1966)**

Product groups	Product code Nos.	Number data available	%	Investment Rs. Cr.	%	Import component Rs. Cr.	%	(7) as % of (5)
1	2	3	4	5	6	7	8	9
Grand total	001-200	3912	100.0	1945	100.0	1284	100.0	66.0
1. Consumer goods	(010-013, 016, 020-023, 045, 050, 067, 084, 085)	446	11.4	153	7.9	101	7.8	66.0
2. Other consumer goods	(015, 018, 019, 024-025, 029, 051, 052, 101, 105-107, 122, 166-168, 180-183)	249	6.3	50	2.6	34	2.6	68.0
3. Chemicals	(009, 014, 031-039, 056, 057, 068-083, 086-091, 100)	647	16.5	386	19.9	272	21.2	70.5
4. Engineering n.e.c.	(108-121, 123-139)	841	21.5	475	24.4	325	25.3	68.4
5. Machinery and components	(140-159, 177-179, 185, 190-192, 195)	722	18.5	170	8.7	115	9.9	67.7
6. Transport equipment	(160-165, 169-175)	242	6.3	155	8.0	115	9.0	74.2

TABLE 6: (*Contd.*)

7. Minerals and processing	(005-008, 092, 186-187, 193)	107	2.7	209	10.7	101	7.9	48.3
8. Other	(001-003, 026-028, 030, 040-043, 053-055, 060-066, 093-099, 102-103, 184, 188, 194, 196, 200)	658	16.8	346	17.9	220	17.2	63.6

For details, see Volume II, Statements VII to X, and Volume I (summary) of original report.
Product code at end.

The import component of investment in consumer goods as a whole is only fractionally lower than in engineering and chemicals. Import saving can hardly, therefore, be an argument in favour of substantially larger investment in consumer goods.

It is impossible to assess whether the product pattern of approved investment has been consistent with the Plans for the simple reason that the Plans specify capacity projections and not the amounts of investment involved. In broad terms, nevertheless, I do not find the pattern of approved investment to be inconsistent with the strategy of development which underlies the plans. I should point out specifically, however, that in spite of the progress in literacy and media of communication, manufacture of printing machinery does not seem to have made any progress.

Taking the period as a whole, investment proposals of Rs. 1 crore and above each account for about one-tenth of the total number of applications but three-fourths of total investment and import component (Table 7). Between 1959-60 and 1964-66, the number of proposals above Rs. 1 crore each increased considerably but their share in total investment remained practically constant at two-thirds. The size of new investments is becoming larger. This cannot be attributed wholly to higher prices for there is a substantial increase in the number of large investment proposals. There was no significant difference in the import component between the various size groups. All of them had an import component of about two-thirds.

Roughly one-half of the applications (for which investment data are available) were for new undertakings and the rest were almost equally divided between substantial expansion and new articles. (All other kinds of licences are excluded in this study). The share in total investment and import component was skewed even more in favour of new undertakings, while substantial expansion accounted for most of the balance (Table 8).

The ratio of approvals to applications has been more favourable to substantial expansion and new articles than to new undertakings. As between 1959-60 and 1964-66, new articles have acquired more significance in both applications and approvals, number as well as investment. The share of new undertakings has declined in numbers but gone up in investment. Substantial expansion has become less significant in both number and

TABLE 7: **Size distribution** @

Size (Rs. lakhs)	Period	Number	%	Investment	%	Import component	%
			Applications*				
Total	1959-66	5598	100.0	2748	100.0	1852	100.0
-10		2099	37.5	101	3.7	61	3.3
10-24		1543	27.6	232	8.4	158	9.6
25-49		893	16.0	295	10.7	202	10.9
50-99		484	8.6	322	11.7	221	11.9
100-499		491	8.8	977	35.6	660	35.7
500-999		67	1.2	431	15.7	302	16.3
1000 and above		21	0.4	390	14.2	249	13.4
Total	1959-60	1904	100.0	683	100.0	539	100.0
-10		10007	52.9	40	5.9	30	5.6
10-24		465	24.4	68	9.9	54	10.0
25-49		208	10.9	69	10.1	54	10.0
50-99		101	5.3	70	10.2	54	10.0
100-499		125	6.6	251	36.7	212	39.3
500-999		12	0.9	73	10.7	58	10.8
1000 and above		6	0.3	114	16.7	75	13.9
Total	1964-66	1403	100.0	853	100.0	544	100.0
-10		367	26.1	17	1.9	11	2.0
10-24		368	26.2	60	7.0	38	6.9
25-49		323	23.0	107	12.3	68	12.3
50-99		164	11.7	106	12.4	71	13.1
100-499		151	10.8	305	35.8	180	33.1
500-999		26	1.9	176	20.6	116	21.3
1000 and above		4	0.3	84	9.8	62	11.4

			Approvals				
Total	1959-66	3912	100.0	1945	100.0	1284	100.0
-10		1557	39.8	67	2.4	44	3.4
10-24		1044	26.7	157	8.1	107	8.3
25-49		611	15.6	202	10.4	138	10.7
50-99		299	7.6	200	10.3	133	10.4
100-499		339	8.7	690	35.5	445	34.7
500-999		46	1.8	300	15.4	208	16.2
1000 and above		16	0.4	328	16.9	208	16.2
Total	1959-60	1383	100.0	500	100.0	386	100.0
-10		746	53.9	30	9.6	23	6.1
10-24		337	24.4	50	10.0	39	10.1
25-49		140	10.1	46	9.9	37	9 6
50-99		61	4.4	41	8.2	32	8.3
100-499		84	5.1	165	33.0	138	35.8
500-999		9	0.7	54	10.8	42	10 9
1000 and above		6	0.4	114	22.8	75	19.4
Total	1964-66	1124	100.0	710	100.0	449	100.0
-10		310	27.6	14	2.0	8	1.7
10-24		288	25.6	47	6.6	29	6.5
25-49		256	22.8	84	11.8	53	11.8
50-99		120	10.7	79	11.1	53	11.8
100-499		124	11.0	256	36.1	144	32.1
500-999		22	2.0	147	20.7	100	22.3
1000 and above		4	0.4	84	11.8	62	13.8

@Excluding applications and approvals for which investment data are not available.

*Net of deferred.

TABLE 8: Type distribution

(Amount in Rs. crores)

Type	Period	Number data not available	%	Number data available	%	Investment	%	Import component	%
				Applications*					
Total	1959-66	3788	100.0	5598	100.0	2748	100.0	1852	100.0
NU		1705	45.0	2953	52.8	1752	63.7	1196	64.6
SE		1081	28.5	1413	25.2	660	24.0	439	24.1
NA		1002	26.5	1232	22.8	336	12.2	217	11.7
Total	1959-60	858	100.0	1904	100.0	683	100.0	539	100.0
NU		349	40.7	1086	57.1	406	59.4	330	61.2
SE		302	35.2	628	33.0	226	33.1	168	31.2
NA		207	24.1	208	10.9	51	7.5	41	7.6
Total	1964-66	1609	100.0	1403	100.0	853	100.0	544	100.0
NU		775	48.2	633	45.1	554	64.9	360	66.2
SE		367	22.8	314	22.4	180	21.1	110	20.2
NA		467	29.0	456	32.5	119	14.0	75	13.8

				Approvals					
Total	1959-66	1883	100.0	3912	100.0	1945	100.0	1284	100.0
NU		627	33.3	1827	46.7	1133	58.3	755	58.8
SE		730	38.8	1153	29.5	575	29.6	374	29.1
NA		526	27.9	932	23.8	237	12.2	155	12.1
Total	1959-60	575	100.0	1383	100.0	500	100.0	386	100.0
NU		219	38.1	742	53.7	276	55.2	223	57.8
SE		208	36.2	509	36.8	186	37.2	134	34.7
NA		148	25.7	132	9.5	38	7.6	29	7.5
Total	1964-66	602	100.0	1124	100.0	710	100.0	449	100.0
NU		181	30.1	447	39.8	442	62.3	284	63.3
SE		219	36.4	287	25.5	174	24.5	107	23.8
NA		202	33.6	390	34.7	94	13.2	58	12.9

*Net of deferred.
NU New Undertakings.
SE Substantial Expansion
NA New Articles.

TABLE 9: **Size distribution by type of applications***
(1964-June 1966)

(Percentages)

Type	Size (Rs. lakhs)	Number	Investment	Import component
NU	- 10	9.3	0.5	0.6
	10- 24	25.3	4.6	4.6
	25- 49	29.7	9.7	9.8
	50- 99	16.1	10.1	10.4
	100-499	15.1	31.7	29.6
	500-999	3.3	22.6	24.0
	1000 and above	1.2	20.8	21.0
	Total	100.0	100.0	100.0
SE	- 10	30.7	2.5	2.5
	10- 24	26.2	7.7	7.6
	25- 49	20.2	12.4	12.7
	50- 99	10.1	12.8	13.6
	100-499	11.2	40.8	37.3
	500-999	1.6	23.8	26.3
	1000 and above	0.0	0.0	0.0
	Total	100.0	100.0	100.0
NA	- 10	46.6	7.8	7.9
	10- 24	25.6	13.5	13.6
	25- 49	15.2	18.4	17.0
	50- 99	7.3	17.0	19.3
	100-499	4.5	27.0	29.6
	500-999	0.8	16.3	12.6
	1000 and above	0.0	0.0	0.0
	Total	100.0	100.0	100.0

*Net of deferred, and excluding applications for which investment data are not available.

investment. This trend, perhaps, indicates greater diversification, in preference to growth in established lines. The import component of all the three types of licences approved was roughly the same at about two-thirds. (Table 9)

The relative frequency of proposals with foreign collaboration declined significantly between 1959-60 and 1964-66. So far as the proposals for which investment data are available, however, the share in investment and import component of those with collaboration recorded a considerable increase (Table 10).

Out of 5,774 applications for licences in the four and a half years (1959-60 and 1964-66), 1,529 proposed to have foreign collaboration. Out of 3,684 approvals granted in these years, 1,186 involved collaboration (this is not the same as approval of collaboration itself which is handled separately from licensing).

In 1959-60, the major proportion of the number of approvals for all the three types of licences did not involve foreign collaboration; the same position held for investment in new undertakings and new articles but not, strangely enough, for substantial expansion. The position was reversed in 1964-66; collaboration became less significant for substantial expansion but more significant for new undertakings and new articles (Table 11).

It is difficult to say how far this analysis would require modification to allow for the proposals whose investment data are not available. In their case, the frequency of those not involving collaboration was much greater.

The bulk of approved investment during 1959-66 has been in Maharashtra, West Bengal, Madras, U.P., Bihar, M.P., Andhra Pradesh and Gujarat, in that order, with Maharashtra way up on top. Curiously enough, the share of Maharashtra, West Bengal and Gujarat in the number of approvals was much larger than in the amount of investment (Table 12).

The yearwise trends are somewhat erratic. As compared with the initial years, the share of approvals of Maharashtra, Mysore, U.P. and West Bengal has declined (the decline in Delhi could be due to the shift of industry out of the Territory's narrow limits). About 46 per cent of the approved investment in 1959-66 was in the three top states, Maharashtra, West Bengal and Madras.

The share of Maharashtra and West Bengal in substantial expansion and new articles is, as may be expected, larger than in new undertakings; this is also true of Gujarat. The less advanced states have secured understandably a larger share of new undertakings (Table 13).

The approved investment for new undertakings in West Bengal during 1959-66 was Rs. 100 crores only, against Rs. 171 crores in Maharashtra, Rs. 128 crores in Madras, Rs. 117 crores in

TABLE 10: Distribution by foreign collaboration

(Amount in Rs. crores)

	Period	Number data not available	%	Number data available	%	Investment of (5)	%	Import compo-nent of (7)	%
1	2	3	4	5	6	7	8	9	10
			Applications*						
Total	1959-60	858	100.0	1904	100.0	683	100.0	539	100.0
With collaboration		98	11.4	547	28.7	311	45.5	236	43.8
Without collaboration		760	88.6	1357	71.3	373	54.5	303	56.2
Total	1964-66	1609	100.0	1403	100.0	853	100.0	554	100.0
With collaboration		154	9.6	730	52.1	476	55.8	321	57.9
Without collaboration		1455	90.4	673	47.9	377	44.2	233	42.1
			Approvals						
Total	1959-60	575	100.0	1383	100.0	500	100.0	386	100.0
With collaboration		70	12.2	413	29.9	255	51.0	188	48.7
Without collaboration		505	87.8	970	70.1	246	49.0	198	51.3
Total	1964-66	602	100.0	1124	100.0	710	100.0	449	100.0
With collaboration		106	17.6	597	53.1	412	58.0	280	62.4
Without collaboration		496	82.4	527	46.9	298	42.0	169	37.6

*Net of deferred.

Note: Data for 1961-63 were not received.

TABLE 11: **Collaboration by type of licence approved (1959-60 and 1964-66)**

Type	Period	Number data not available		Number data available		Investment (Rs. crores)		Import (Rs. crores)	
						(5)	(6)	(7)	(8)
		C	NC	C	NC	C	NC	C	NC
1	2	3	4	5	6	7	8	9	10
Total	1959-60	70	505	413	970	255	246	188	198
	%	12.2	87.8	29.9	70.1	51.0	49.0	48.7	51.3
NU		19	200	211	531	130	146	104	119
	%	8.7	91.3	28.4	71.6	47.1	52.9	46.6	53.4
SE		27	181	149	360	113	73	77	57
	%	13.0	87.0	29.3	70.7	60.8	39.2	57.5	42.5
NA		24	124	53	79	11	27	7	23
	%	16.2	83.8	40.2	59.8	28.9	71.1	24.1	75.9
Total	1964-66	106	496	597	527	412	298	280	169
	%	17.6	82.4	53.1	46.9	58.0	42.0	62.4	37.6
NU		17	164	269	178	275	167	195	89
	%	9.4	90.6	60.2	39.8	62.2	37.8	68.7	31.3
SE		26	193	109	178	78	96	48	60
	%	11.9	88.1	38.0	62.0	44.8	55.2	44.9	55.1
NA		63	139	219	171	60	34	38	20
	%	31.1	68.9	56.2	43.8	63.8	36.2	65.5	34.5

Note: Percentages are in terms of total approvals.
C: Collaboration NC: No collaboration.

TABLE 12: **Approvals* by states (1959-June 1966)**

(Percentages)

State		1959	1960	1961	1962	1963	1964	1965	1966	Total
Grand Total	No.	100.00	100.00	100.00	100.00	100.00	100.00	100.00	100.00	100.00
	Investment	100.00	100.00	100.00	100.00	100.00	100.00	100.00	100.00	100.00
Andhra Pradesh	No.	2.29	3.06	3.79	2.76	2.73	3.37	4.46	2.12	3.09
	Investment	2.64	4.89	6.79	9.13	5.62	3.94	3.06	7.73	5.40
Assam	No.	1.14	1.60	1.65	0.64	0.59	0.00	0.00	0.00	0.82
	Investment	0.47	1.76	5.66	2.20	0.23	0.00	0.00	0.00	1.27
Bihar	No.	1.86	2.77	2.84	4.03	4.10	2.62	5.13	2.81	3.19
	Investment	5.94	3.44	2.11	4.57	6.39	9.42	17.10	1.97	7.52
Delhi	No.	5.73	5.83	2.36	2.54	0.39	2.06	1.12	4.23	2.10
	Investment	2.62	8.27	0.75	0.78	0.11	0.71	0.34	1.05	2.09
Jammu and Kashmir	No.	0.00	0.00	0.00	0.00	0.58	1.87	0.00	0.00	0.10
	Investment	0.00	0.00	0.00	0.00	0.34	0.07	0.00	0.00	0.05
Gujarat	No.	5.01	5.83	10.88	8.70	7.22	8.24	8.03	9.15	7.46
	Investment	2.65	2.55	8.24	2.96	5.23	8.54	4.72	7.04	4.95
Kerala	No.	2.15	2.04	3.55	2.55	2.15	0.94	2.23	2.11	2.17
	Investment	2.09	1.54	2.97	2.57	4.87	2.22	0.81	1.25	0.26
Madhya Pradesh	No.	1.60	8.20	2.66	4.05	4.90	1.30	3.35	1.41	3.94
	Investment	10.12	1.30	1.31	13.56	18.67	8.29	5.89	0.48	7.20
Madras	No.	7.74	8.18	7.11	8.70	7.42	8.43	9.60	9.15	8.18
	Investment	7.86	7.07	12.40	6.09	6.57	13.75	8.80	41.03	10.14
Maharashtra	No.	35.37	31.39	32.46	31.42	31.05	32.77	26.79	33.10	31.90
	Investment	23.57	20.36	29.97	28.88	15.77	18.42	18.51	12.28	21.46
Mysore	No.	5.01	2.63	2.84	3.82	3.71	3.56	3.57	4.23	3.66
	Investment	7.76	4.01	2.61	1.44	6.53	6.58	4.96	6.69	4.73

Orissa	No.	0.72	1.02	0.24	2.76	1.37	1.69	0.45	1.41	1.18
	Investment	1.00	0.75	0.07	6.83	1.80	3.75	1.45	1.43	2.49
Punjab, Haryana and	No.	5.16	5.55	6.16	7.22	8.40	7.87	10.49	6.34	7.03
Himachal Pradesh	Investment	2.45	4.16	5.04	2.09	6.71	5.47	5.24	2.07	4.36
Rajasthan	No.	1.00	1.02	3.55	2.34	1.17	1.12	2.46	0.00	1.61
	Investment	0.33	0.74	2.51	1.52	1.10	1.27	14.06	0.00	3.25
U.P.	No.	3.87	6.42	4.27	4.25	3.91	5.81	8.48	5.63	5.27
	Investment	11.08	18.32	4.82	2.70	6.93	4.18	5.49	3.19	7.94
West Bengal	No.	21.35	20.88	15.40	14.01	19.53	17.79	13.17	18.31	17.97
	Investment	19.42	20.76	14.49	14.68	11.20	13.05	9.24	13.79	14.53
Other	No.	0.00	0.15	0.24	0.21	0.78	0.56	0.67	0.00	0.33
	Investment	0.00	0.08	0.26	0.00	1.93	0.34	0.33	0.00	0.36

*Excluding those for which investment data are not available.

TABLE 13: **Approvals by states and types (1959-June 1966)**

(Amount in Rs. crores)

State	NU				SE				NA			
	Number data available	%	Investment	%	Number data available	%	Investment	%	Number data available	%	Investment	%
Grand total	1827	100.00	1133	100.00	1153	100.00	575	100.00	932	100.00	237	100.00
Andhra Pradesh	64	3.50	66	5.83	29	2.52	32	5.57	28	3.00	6	2.53
Assam	25	1.36	24	2.12	5	0.43	neg.	0.00	2	0.21	1	0.42
Bihar	70	3.84	117	10.33	38	3.30	20	3.48	17	1.82	9	3.80
Delhi	66	3.61	34	3.00	30	2.60	4	0.70	30	3.22	3	1.27
Jammu and Kashmir	1	0.05	neg.	0.00	3	0.26	1	0.17	—	0.00	—	0.00
Gujarat	140	7.66	49	4.32	78	6.76	31	5.39	74	7.94	17	7.17
Kerala	47	2.57	32	2.82	26	2.25	11	1.91	12	1.29	2	0.84
M.P.	77	4.21	116	10.24	21	1.82	15	2.61	12	1.29	10	4.22
Madras	170	9.30	128	11.30	91	7.89	50	8.69	59	6.33	19	8.02
Maharashtra	501	27.44	171	15.10	402	34.87	171	29.74	345	37.03	74	31.22
Mysore	51	2.79	49	4.32	63	5.48	35	6.09	29	3.11	8	3.38
Orissa	32	1.75	44	3.88	8	0.69	1	0.17	6	0.64	3	1.27
Punjab, Haryana and Himachal Pradesh	157	8.59	64	5.65	40	3.47	9	1.56	78	8.37	12	5.06
Rajasthan	44	2.41	53	4.67	8	0.69	5	0.87	11	1.18	5	2.11
U.P.	121	6.62	83	7.33	45	3.90	56	9.74	40	4.29	16	6.75
West Bengal	252	13.81	100	8.83	263	22.81	130	22.61	188	20.17	52	21.94
Other	9	0.49	3	0.26	3	0.26	4	0.70	1	0.11	neg.	0.00

Bihar, Rs. 116 crores in Madhya Pradesh, Rs. 83 crores in U.P., Rs. 66 crores in Andhra Pradesh, Rs. 64 crores in Punjab-Haryana-Himachal Pradesh and Rs. 53 crores in Rajasthan. This unsatisfactory performance in West Bengal was partially relieved by fairly large investment in substantial expansion and new articles but it could hardly have provided the stimulus which comes from fresh starts.

Communitywise, the Marwaris are, by far, at the top. Their share in approved investment during 1959-66 was 24 per cent, followed by Gujaratis 15 per cent, Southern 8 per cent, Punjabis 5 per cent and Parsis 4 per cent. The share of Marwaris and Gujaratis might be slightly larger than is indicated by the above figures for, in case of doubt and ignorance, the relevant licensees are classified under 'Other Indian' (Table 14). This classification is subject to some degree of error but that would not invalidate the general picture.

Domiciled foreign houses accounted for only 1 per cent of approved investment but international combines were way up at 7 per cent. Among international combines, those originating in the U.K. had nearly 4 per cent of approved investment, followed by the U.S.A. 2 per cent. West Germany, Switzerland and Sweden were the other countries of origin of some significance (Table 15).

The government sector got nearly 16 per cent, which is a severe under estimate because most of the larger investment proposals from this sector do not come before the Licensing Committee (Table 14). Out of this, the bulk, 13 per cent, went to government companies and the rest was thinly distributed, mainly between Andhra Pradesh, Punjab, Orissa and U.P.

Co-operatives accounted for less than 1 per cent of approved investment and of this, those in the Western States accounted for one-half.

Approved Marwari investment has taken place in all states except Jammu and Kashmir. The bulk of this investment was in West Bengal, U.P., Maharashtra, M.P., and Bihar (Table 16). Gujarati investment was mainly in Maharashtra, Gujarat, Madras and U.P. Southern houses were practically confined to the Southern States, Madras, Andhra Pradesh and Mysore, but there was a significant investment in Maharashtra, too. Punjabi investment was mainly in the Punjab-Delhi region but was also found in Maharashtra, West Bengal, M.P., Bihar and Madras. Parsi

TABLE 14: **Distribution of approvals by categories of applicants (1959-June 1966)**

Classification of licenses	Industrial house code nos.	Number data not available	Number data available	Investment of (4) (Rs. cr.)	Import component of (5) (Rs. cr.)
1	2	3	4	5	6
Grand total	01-99	1883	3912	1945	1284
%		(100.0)	(100.0)	(100.0)	(100.0)
A Marwaris	01-19	320	670	477	315
%		16.5	17.1	24.4	24.5
B Gujarati	30-39, 47	339	654	284	196
%		18.0	16.7	14.9	15.3
C Punjabi	29, 49-54	118	315	90	67
%		6.4	8.1	4.6	5.2
D Parsi	20, 27, 48, 56	46	97	68	44
%		2.5	2.5	3.5	3.4
E Bengali	21, 26, 58	43	95	34	18
%		2.4	2.4	1.6	1.4
F Maharashtrian	24, 57	35	103	43	28
%		2.0	2.6	2.1	2.2
G Southern	40-45	218	350	153	103
%		11.6	9.0	7.8	8.1
H Other Indian	22, 23, 25, 28, 46, 55, 59	479	1067	325	229
%		25.5	27.3	16.9	17.8
Sub-total A to H		1599	3351	1474	1000
%		84.9	85.7	75.8	77.9
I Domiciled foreign	60-69	49	77	20	14
%		2.6	1.9	1.0	1.1

J International combines	70-79	148	285	133	85
%		7.9	7.3	6.9	6.6
Sub-total I+J	60-79	195	362	153	99
%		10.4	9.2	7.9	7.7
Total: Private sector A to J	01-79	1794	3713	1627	1099
%		95.3	94.9	83.7	85.6
K Cooperative	80-83	40	34	16	8
%		2.1	0.9	0.8	0.6
L Government	90-99	50	165	302	177
%		2.6	4.2	15.5	13.8
Total: Public sector K+L	80-99	90	199	318	185
%		4.7	5.1	16.3	14.4

TABLE 15: **Distribution of approvals to international combines (1959-June 1966)**

Country of origin	Industrial house code nos.	Number data not available	Number data available	Investment of (4) (Rs. cr.)	Import component of (5) (Rs. cr.)
International combines (Total)	70-79	148	285	133	85
%		7.9	7.3	6.9	6.6
U.K.	70	77	141	71	42
%		4.1	3.6	3.7	3.3
U.S.A.	71	30	56	38	28
%		1.7	1.4	2.0	2.1
W. Germany	72	10	21	8	6
%		0.5	0.5	0.4	0.5
Switzerland	73	6	14	6	3
%		0.3	0.4	0.3	0.2
Sweden	74	2	14	5	3
%		0.1	0.4	0.3	0.2
Netherlands	75	6	24	2	2
%		0.3	0.6	0.1	0.2
Denmark	76	6	3	Neg.	Neg.
%		0.3	0.1	0.0	0.0
France	77	3	4	Neg.	Neg.
%		0.2	0.1	0.0	0.0
Italy	78	2	0	0	0
%		0.1	0.0	0.0	0.0
Other	79	6	8	1	1
%		0.3	0.2	0.1	0.1

Note: Percentages are in terms of total approvals.

investment was mainly in Maharashtra and Bihar. The investment of domiciled foreign houses was restricted to the old presidency areas, West Bengal, Madras, Assam, Maharashtra, and Bihar. International combines dispersed their investment a little more widely but in their case, too, the old presidency areas were predominant. Government investment was more widely dispersed than that of any other category. It was highest in M.P., followed by Andhra Pradesh, Bihar, Madras, Mysore, Orissa, Kerala, Delhi, and West Bengal.

During the period 1959-June 1966, 28 Indian industrial houses applied for licences for investment exceeding Rs. 10 crores each, net of those applications which were deferred for reconsideration

(Table 17). These 28 houses made 1,961 applications (21 per cent of all applications) of which investment data are available for 1,178. These 1,178 applications involved an investment in capital equipment of Rs. 1,627 crores (59 per cent of total applied) with an import component of Rs. 704 crores (38 per cent). Approval was granted for 1,233 applications (21 per cent of all approvals), of which investment data are available for 832. These 832 approvals involved an investment in capital equipment of Rs. 740 crores (38 per cent of total approved) with an import component of Rs. 490 crores (38 per cent again).

The shares of the top four houses in total applications (net of deferred) and approvals during 1959-June 1966 are given below. The Birla share is strikingly high in application and approval, number and investment.

Share of the top four houses in total applications and approvals

(Percentage of total)

Houses		Number data not available	Number data available	Investment of (4)	Import component of (5)
1. Birla	Applied	7.4	7.2	14.1	13.8
	Approved	5.8	6.5	14.1	14.4
2. J.K.	Applied	1.0	0.9	2.5	2.7
	Approved	0.8	0.9	2.5	2.5
3. Tata	Applied	1.1	1.3	2.0	1.9
	Approved	1.8	1.5	2.4	2.3
4. Shri Ram	Applied	0.5	0.6	1.9	2.6
	Approved	0.6	0.6	2.4	3.5

Source: Derived from Table 17.

The largest number of applications were made by Birla, Tata, J.K., and Amichand Pyarelall, in that order. The last mentioned house ranks thirteenth in the amount of investment approved in so far as investment data are available.

It is somewhat difficult to compare the beginning and the end of the period to assess the changes in the shares of houses for investment behaviour (which alone is really analysed here), as distinct from assets formation, is not spread continuously over time. The task can be risked nevertheless. The share of these 28 houses in total approved investment declined from 46 per

TABLE 16 : **Distribution of approved investment by states and**

		Marwaris	Gujaratis	Punjabis	Parsis	Bengalis
Grand total	Amount	477	284	90	68	34
	%	100.00	100.00	100.00	100.00	100.00
Andhra Pradesh	Amount	9	5	0	—	5
	%	1.89	1.76	0.00	—	14.70
Assam	Amount	16	0	0	—	0
	%	3.35	0.00	0.00	—	0.00
Bihar	Amount	45	0	3	29	8
	%	9.43	0.00	3.33	42.65	23.59
Delhi	Amount	1	1	7	—	0
	%	0.21	0.35	7.77	—	0.00
Jammu and Kashmir	Amount	0	0	0	—	—
	%	0.00	0.00	0.00	—	—
Gujarat	Amount	8	68	0	4	0
	%	1.68	24.29	0.00	5.88	0.00
Kerala	Amount	6	1	0	0	0
	%	1.26	0.35	0.00	0.00	0.00
M.P.	Amount	50	5	3	1	2
	%	10.48	1.76	3.33	1.47	5.88
Madras	Amount	18	30	2	0	—
	%	3.77	10.56	2.22	0.00	—
Maharashtra	Amount	62	153	18	33	0
	%	12.99	53.87	20.00	48.52	0.00
Mysore	Amount	5	1	0	0	0
	%	1.04	0.35	0.00	0.00	0.00
Orissa	Amount	6	0	0	1	5
	%	1.26	0.00	0.00	1.47	14.70
Punjab, Haryana and Himachal Pradesh	Amount	8	4	45	—	—
	%	1.68	1.41	50.00	—	—
Rajasthan	Amount	23	0	0	—	—
	%	4.82	0.00	0.00	—	—
U.P.	Amount	88	15	2	1	—
	%	18.45	5.28	2.22	1.47	—
West Bengal	Amount	132	1	9	1	14
	%	27.67	0.35	10.00	1.47	41.18
Other	Amount	0	0	—	—	—
	%	0.00	0.00	—	—	—

'—' stands for negligible.

categories of applicants (1959-June 1966)

(Amount in Rs. crores)

Maha-rashtrians	Southern	Other Indian	Domiciled foreign	Inter-national combines	Total : Private sector	Co-oper-atives	Govern-ment	Total : Public sector	Grand total
43	153	323	20	133	1625	16	302	318	1943
100.00	100.00	100.00	100.00	100.00	100.00	100.00	100.00	100.00	100.00
—	31	11	—	2	63	2	39	41	104
—	20.26	3.41	—	1.50	3.88	12.50	12.91	12.89	5.35
—	0	1	4	1	22	0	0	2	24
—	0.00	0.31	20.00	0.75	1.35	6.25	0.33	0.63	1.24
—	—	22	2	1	110	0	36	36	146
—	—	6.81	10.00	0.75	6.77	0.00	11.92	11.32	7.51
—	0	12	—	0	21	—	19	19	40
—	0.00	3.72	—	0.00	1.26	—	6.29	5.97	2.06
—	—	1	—	—	1	—	0	0	1
—	—	0.31	—	—	0.06	—	0.00	0.00	0.05
3	0	9	—	0	92	2	1	3	95
6.98	0.00	2.79	—	0.00	5.72	12.50	0.33	0.94	4.88
0	12	2	0	3	24	1	20	21	45
0.00	7.84	0.62	0.00	2.26	1.47	6.25	6.62	6.60	2.31
0	3	14	—	—	78	0	62	62	140
0.00	1.96	4.33	—	—	4.80	0.00	20.53	19.50	7.20
0	78	20	4	15	167	1	29	30	197
0.00	50.98	6.19	20.00	11.28	10.28	6.25	9.60	9.43	1.01
23	23	68	2	37	417	8	10	18	435
53.49	15.03	21.05	10.00	27.82	25.66	50.00	3.31	5.66	22.38
11	26	15	0	4	62	—	29	29	91
25.58	16.99	4.64	0.00	3.01	3.81	—	9.60	9.12	4.68
0	0	11	1	1	25	1	23	24	49
0.00	0.00	0.41	5.00	0.75	1.53	6.25	7.61	7.55	2.52
2	0	15	0	1	75	0	9	9	84
4.65	0.00	4.64	0.00	0.75	4.62	0.00	2.98	2.83	4.32
—	—	39	0	—	62	0	1	1	63
—	—	12.07	0.00	—	3.81	0.00	0.33	0.32	3.24
—	0	35	0	1	142	0	7	7	149
—	0.00	10.83	0.00	0.75		0.00	2.32	2.20	7.66
0	0	44	8	66	275	1	14	15	290
0.00	0.00	13.62	40.00	49.62	16.92	6.25	4.64	4.72	14.92
4	1	1	—	—	6	—	0	0	6
9.30	0.65	0.31	—	—	0.37	—	0.00	0.00	0.31

TABLE 17: **28 Houses—Applications and approvals***
(1959-June 1966)

(Amount in Rs. crores)

1	2	Number data not available 3	Number data available 4	Investment of (4) 5	Import component of (5) 6
Grand total	Applied@	3788	5598	2748	1852
	Approved	1883	3912	1945	1284
1. Birla	Applied	279	404	388	255
	Approved	109	255	272	172
2. J.K.	Applied	37	83	69	50
	Approved	16	36	48	32
3. Tata	Applied	41	71	55	36
	Approved	33	61	46	29
4. Shri Ram	Applied	20	31	52	49
	Approved	12	22	46	45
5. Walchand	Applied	12	26	39	30
	Approved	50	22	38	30
6. Sahu Jain	Applied	28	41	45	32
	Approved	10	27	26	19
7. Bangur Somani	Applied	35	46	36	21
	Approved	20	29	22	17
8. A.C.C.	Applied	18	14	19	8
	Approved	14	14	19	8
9. Kilachand	Applied	8	12	19	10
	Approved	8	8	18	8
10. V. Ramakrishna	Applied	20	20	19	10
	Approved	16	15	17	9
11. B. Patnaik	Applied	6	11	17	15
	Approved	2	11	17	15
12. Sarabhai	Applied	37	40	15	11
	Approved	21	33	15	10
13. Amichand Pyarelall	Applied	27	66	35	26
	Approved	50	36	15	11
14. Kamani	Applied	20	33	19	14
	Approved	7	21	14	10
15. Mafatlal	Applied	21	15	17	11
	Approved	16	12	14	9
16. Bajaj	Applied	11	23	14	7
	Approved	7	21	13	7
17. Kirloskar	Applied	11	39	14	10
	Approved	6	33	12	8
18. Kasturbhai	Applied	21	36	14	9
	Approved	11	30	12	8

TABLE 17 (*Contd.*)

19. Seshasayee	Applied	8	24	12	9
	Approved	6	22	11	7
20. Anantharama-krishnan	Applied	7	26	11	8
	Approved	5	24	10	7
21. Mahindra	Applied	7	18	11	9
	Approved	5	15	10	9
22. Wadia-Shapoorji	Applied	7	16	11	6
	Approved	7	12	9	5
23. Bajoria-Jalan	Applied	33	30	29	21
	Approved	18	17	9	7
24. Thapar	Applied	16	20	7	4
	Approved	10	19	7	4
25. Modi	Applied	17	14	13	12
	Approved	9	7	7	6
26. Goenka	Applied	19	28	19	10
	Approved	5	21	6	3
27. Chinai	Applied	11	11	12	9
	Approved	6	6	4	2
28. Jaipuria	Applied	6	10	15	12
	Approved	4	3	3	3
Total 1 to 28	Applied	783	1178	1127	704
	Approved	401	832	740	490

*This Table lists those individual houses which *applied for* licences for investment exceeding Rs. 10 crores during the period.
The ranking is based on the data available on investment *approved*. It is possible that rankings below 10th would be different if investment data were available for all approvals.
@Net of deferred.

cent in 1959-60 to 39 per cent in 1964-66. The share of the four top houses, Birla, J.K., Tata and Shri Ram, increased, however, from 22.4 per cent to 25.6 per cent, wholly on account of the latter three because the share of Birla actually fell (Table 18).

The houses (out of 28) which were relatively more active in 1964-66 as compared with 1959-60 were J.K., Tata, Shri Ram, A.C.C., Sarabhai, Kamani, Mafatlal, Bajaj, Kirloskar, Mahindra and Thapar. Those which became much less active in 1964-66 were Walchand, Sahu Jain, Kilachand, V. Ramakrishna, B. Patnaik, Amichand Pyarelall, Anantharamakrishnan, Wadia-Shapoorji, Chinai and Jaipuria.

The 28 houses had larger investment, as compared with the

TABLE 18: **28 Houses—Applications* and approvals (1959-60 and 1964-66)**

		1959-60 Investment (Rs. cr.)	%	1964-66 Investment (Rs. cr.)	%
1. Birla	Applied	121	17.7	116	13.5
	Approved	88	17.6	93	13.2
2. J.K.	Applied	9	1.3	27	3.2
	Approved	3	0.6	26	3.8
3. Tata	Applied	14	2.0	24	2.8
	Approved	12	2.4	24	3.4
4. Shri Ram	Applied	14	2.0	37	4.3
	Approved	9	1.8	37	5.2
5. Walchand	Applied	1	0.1	neg.	neg.
	Approved	1	0.2	neg.	neg.
6. Sahu Jain	Applied	21	3.1	10	1.2
	Approved	14	2.8	9	1.3
7. Bangur-Somani	Applied	9	1.3	9	1.1
	Approved	8	1.6	8	1.1
8. A.C.C.	Applied	neg.	neg.	11	1.3
	Approved	neg.	neg.	11	1.5
9. Kilachand	Applied	18	2.6	2	0.2
	Approved	17	3.4	1	0.1
10. V. Ramakrishna	Applied	13	1.9	1	0.1
	Approved	12	2.4	neg.	neg.
11. B. Patnaik	Applied	15	2.2	1	0.1
	Approved	15	3.0	1	0.1
12. Sarabhai	Applied	3	0.4	10	1.2
	Approved	3	0.6	10	1.4
13. Amichand Pyarelall	Applied	11	1.6	3	0.4
	Approved	6	1.2	3	0.4
14. Kamani	Applied	1	0.1	5	0.6
	Approved	1	0.2	3	0.4
15. Mafatlal	Applied	3	0.4	9	1.1
	Approved	0	0.0	9	1.3
16. Bajaj	Applied	3	0.4	6	0.7
	Approved	3	0.6	6	0.8
17. Kirloskar	Applied	3	0.4	7	0.8
	Approved	1	0.2	6	0.8
18. Kasturbhai	Applied	6	0.9	6	0.7
	Approved	6	1.2	5	0.7
19. Seshasayee	Applied	4	0.6	3	0.4
	Approved	4	0.8	3	0.4
20. Anantharama-krishnan	Applied	3	0.4	1	0.1
	Approved	3	0.6	1	0.1

TABLE 18 (*Contd.*)

21. Mahindra	Applied	2	0.3	9	1.1
	Approved	1	0.2	9	1.3
22. Wadia-Shapoorji	Applied	8	1.2	neg.	neg.
	Approved	8	1.6	neg.	neg.
23. Bajoria-Jalan	Applied	11	1.6	11	1.3
	Approved	5	1.0	3	0.4
24. Thapar	Applied	1	0.1	4	0.5
	Approved	1	0.2	4	0.6
25. Modi	Applied	3	0.4	4	0.5
	Approved	3	0.6	3	0.4
26. Goenka	Applied	2	0.3	2	0.2
	Approved	2	0.4	2	0.3
27. Chinai	Applied	8	1.2	0	0.0
	Approved	3	0.6	0	0.0
28. Jaipuria	Applied	7	1.0	2	0.2
	Approved	3	0.6	0	0.0
Total 1 to 28	Applied	312	45.5	320	37.6
	Approved	232	46.4	277	39.0
Grand total (All houses)	Applied	683	100.00	853	100.00
	Approved	500	100.00	710	100.00

*Applications are net of deferred.

Note: Applications for which investment data are not available are excluded.

aggregate, in substantial expansion and new articles, and smaller investment in new undertakings (Table 19).

Among the 28, however, there were several which had the major or predominant part of approved investment in new undertakings: J.K., Shri Ram, Sahu Jain, Bangur-Somani, A.C.C., Kilachand, V. Ramakrishna, Amichand Pyarelall, Kamani, Mafatlal, Seshasayee, Bajoria-Jalan, Modi, Goenka and Jaipuria.

Substantial expansion accounted for the bulk of investment only in Walchand, Sarabhai, Kasturbhai, Mahindra, Thapar and Chinai. New articles accounted for the major part of investment in very few houses: Patnaik, Kirloskar, and Wadia-Shapoorji. They were of considerable significance in Mafatlal, Bajaj, and Bajoria-Jalan.

Birla received approval for investment in capital equipment of Rs. 114 crores in new undertakings, Rs. 126 crores in substantial

TABLE 19: **Type distribution of approvals to 28**

Industrial house	Number data not available							
	NU	%	SE	%	NA	%	NU	%
1	2	3	4	5	6	7	8	9
1. Birla	36	33.0	47	43.1	26	23.9	100	39.2
2. J.K.	4	25.0	6	37.5	6	37.5	17	47.2
3. Tata	4	12.1	14	42.4	15	45.5	8	13.1
4. Shri Ram	1	8.3	8	66.7	3	25.0	7	31.8
5. Walchand	1	11.2	1	44.4	4	44.4	2	9.1
6. Sahu Jain	6	66.0	1	10.0	3	30.0	11	40.8
7. Bangur-Somani	8	40.0	7	35.0	5	25.0	11	37.9
8. A.C.C.	2	14.3	10	71.4	2	14.3	5	35.7
9. Kilachand	1	12.5	5	62.5	2	25.0	3	37.5
10. V. Ramakrishna	5	31.3	6	37.4	5	31.3	3	20.0
11. B. Patnaik	2	100.0	—	—	—	—	4	36.4
12. Sarabhai	—	—	11	52.4	10	47.6	2	6.1
13. Amichand Pyarelall	4	44.4	3	33.3	2	22.3	22	61.1
14. Kamani	2	28.6	1	14.3	4	57.1	13	61.9
15. Mafatlal	5	31.3	7	43.7	4	25.0	5	41.7
16. Bajaj	2	28.6	4	57.1	1	14.3	3	14.3
17 Kirloskar	—	—	3	50.0	3	50.0	3	9.0
18. Kasturbhai	1	9.0	6	54.6	4	37.4	3	10.0
19. Seshasayee	3	50.0	3	50.0	—	—	9	40.9
20. Anantharama-krishnan	2	40.0	—	—	3	60.0	9	37.5
21. Mahindra	—	—	1	20.0	4	80.0	6	40.0
22. Wadia-Shapoorji	2	28.6	4	57.1	1	14.3	4	33.3
23. Bajoria-Jalan	1	5.6	13	72.2	4	22.2	6	35.3
24. Thapar	1	10.0	3	30.0	6	60.0	3	15.8
25. Modi	—	—	5	55.6	4	44.4	4	57.1
26. Goenka	—	—	3	60.0	2	40.0	12	57.1
27. Chinai	4	66.7	2	33.3	—	—	1	16.7
28. Jaipuria	1	25.0	2	50.0	1	25.0	1	33.3
Total 1 to 28	98	24.4	179	44.7	124	30.9	277	33.3
Grand total (all houses)	627	33.3	730	38.8	526	37.9	1827	46.7

houses (1959-June 1966)

Number data available				Investment (Rs. crores)					
SE 10	% 11	NA 12	% 13	NU 14	% 15	SE 16	% 17	NA 18	% 19
94	36.9	61	23.9	114	41.9	126	46.3	32	11.8
14	38.9	5	13.9	31	64.6	12	25.0	5	10.4
24	39.3	29	47.6	23	50.0	17	37.0	6	13.0
8	36.4	7	31.8	43	93.5	2	4.4	1	2.1
13	59.1	7	31.8	neg.	0.0	37	97.4	1	2.6
8	29.6	8	29.6	17	65.4	6	23.1	3	11.5
16	55.2	2	6.9	12	54.6	10	45.4	neg.	—
5	35.7	4	28.6	13	68.4	4	21.1	2	10.5
3	37.5	2	25.0	13	72.2	3	16.7	2	11.1
3	20.0	9	60.0	13	76.5	1	5.9	3	17.6
4	36.4	3	27.2	3	17.7	1	5.8	13	76.5
22	66.6	9	27.3	1	6.7	12	80.0	2	13.3
3	8.3	11	30.6	13	86.7	neg.	—	2	13.3
2	9.5	6	28.6	12	85.7	neg.	—	2	14.3
—	—	7	58.3	8	57.1	—	—	6	42.9
12	57.1	6	28.6	5	38.5	2	15.4	6	46.1
15	45.5	15	45.5	2	16.7	4	33.3	6	50.0
19	63.3	8	26.7	1	8.3	9	75.0	2	16.7
7	31.8	6	27.3	6	54.5	4	36.4	1	9.1
10	41.7	5	20.8	4	40.0	4	40.0	2	20.0
5	33.3	4	26.7	1	10.0	8	80.0	1	10.0
5	41.7	3	35.0	3	33.3	1	11.1	5	55.6
7	41.2	4	23.5	6	66.7	1	11.1	2	22.2
12	63.1	4	21.1	2	28.6	5	71.4	neg.	—
1	14.3	2	28.6	7	100.0	neg.	—	neg.	—
3	14.3	6	28.6	5	83.3	neg.	—	1	16.7
4	66.6	1	16.7	neg.	—	4	100.0	—	—
2	66.7	—	—	3	100.0	neg.	—	—	—
321	38.6	234	28.1	361	48.8	273	36.9	106	14.3
1153	29.5	932	23.8	1133	58.2	575	29.6	237	12.2

expansion and Rs. 32 crores in new articles. These related to 100, 94 and 61 applications, respectively. In addition, there were 36, 47 and 26 approved applications, respectively, for which investment data are not available.

Some houses followed the practice of putting in a number of applications for each product. Some repeat applications are unavoidable—and welcome—over a period of seven and a half years and some are for different types of licences. The situation depicted in Table 20, however, justifies the presumption that multiple applications for the same product and for a wide, very wide indeed, variety of products are meant to foreclose licensable capacity.[6] This appears to be particularly true of Birla applications.

It is difficult to evaluate the multitude of Birla applications in almost every product without a close and complete follow-up of developments after the consideration of applications by the Licensing Committee. The data in hand indicate abiding or at least persevering interest in a tremendous variety of products, interest which at times defies several deferments or rejections of applications to attain consummation in approval, interest which seeks to overwhelm the relevant authorities with multiple proposals the moment suitable opportunities offer themselves. This performance is unrivalled, and is not to be belittled or under-estimated. Whether and, if so, to what extent, this performance actually blocks the entry of other, existing or potential, entrepreneurs is an open question.

In my interim report, I essayed a rough comparison of Licensing Committee data with CGC data to show that a large number of Birla licences did not appear to have been followed through to the CGC. I have not further pursued this line of investigation in the hope that the better equipped Licensing Enquiry (Thacker) Committee would be looking into this matter, among other things.

It is to some extent legitimate to infer, therefore, that Birla enterprise, justfiable or not in terms of ultimate performance, does tend to pre-empt licensable capacity in many industries. The sheer pressure of multiple applications for each product must be such as to yield positive results for at least two or more applications. If all the licences received do fructify or are intended to fructify, their progress, if any, before or after capital

TABLE 20: **Select products—Applications and approvals to certain houses (1959—June 1966)**
(Numbers only, applications net of deferred, but including those for which investment data are not available)

Product code no.	Product	Birla		Other houses Applied and Approved
		Applied	Approved	
005	Coal	6	4	Thapar 4 and 4
008	Other processed minerals	7	0	Bangur 2 and 2
010	Sugar	5	3	V. Ramakrishna 4 and 4, Bajoria-Jalan 4 and 4
012	Processed food	6	4	
013	Vanaspati	11	6	Shri Ram 4 and 4
018	Cosmetics	4	1	Tata 2 and 2
020	Cotton yarn	18	5	Tata 3 and 3, Bangur 3 and 1, Mafatlal 5 and 4, Kasturbhai 8 and 2, Bajoria-Jalan 4 and 2, Jaipuria 3 and 3
021	Cotton fabrics	15	13	J.K. 2 and 2, Tata 3 and 3, Kasturbhai 4 and 4, Wadia Shapoorji 3 and 3, Bajoria-Jalan 3 and 3, Modi 2 and 2, Jaipuria 2 and 1
022	Cotton yarn and fabrics	6	3	
023	Cotton other	5	4	
025	Synthetic fabrics	3	3	
026	Jute carpet and backing	5	1	

TABLE 20 (*Contd.*)

028	Textiles n.e.c.	7	2	
029	Non-woven fabrics	—	—	Tata 3 and 1
030	Rayon fibre and yarn	13	4	J.K. 5 and 2, Chinai 2 and 1
032	Polyester fibre	3	0	J.K. 2 and 0, Chinai 2 and 0
033	Polypropylene	3	0	
034	Acrylic fibre	2	1	J.K. 3 and 3
035	Tyre cord	7	3	J.K. 4 and 2, Tata 2 and 1, Shri Ram 2 and 2, Chinai 2 and 1
036	Nylon	3	3	J.K. 5 and 4, Modi 2 and 1, Jaipuria 2 and 1
037	PVA fibre	2	0	
038	Other petroleum fibres	6	0	
040	Chip and other boards	14	14	J.K. 2 and 2, Bangur 3 and 3, Mafatlal 2 and 2
041	Plywood	6	4	Sahu Jain 4 and 3
050	Paper	7	2	J.K. 3 and 1, Shri Ram 2 and 2, Sahu Jain 4 and 2, Bangur 2 and 2, Amichand 2 and 1, Bajaj 2 and 2, Seshasayee 2 and 2, Bajoria-Jalan 2 and 2
051	Paper, special finish	2	1	Kamani 2 and 0
052	Paper, film (incl. cellophone)	6	5	
053	Paper, industrial (incl. printing)	3	3	Sahu Jain 2 and 2, Bangur 5 and 5, Seshasayee 2 and 2, Bajoria-Jalan 2 and 2
057	Rayon pulp	4	1	Chinai 2 and 1

063	Rubber tyres and tubes	4	3	
064	Rubber, industrial	4	2	Kamani 3 and 3
068	Alcohol chemicals	3	0	Kilachand 2 and 2, Sarabhai 2 and 0
070	Caustic soda	21	7	J.K. 4 and 2, Shri Ram 4 and 3, Sahu Jain 4 and 1, Bangur 4 and 3, Sarabhai 3 and 2, Mafatlal 3 and 3, Kasturbhai 2 and 2, Thapar 2 and 1, Modi 4 and 1, Chinai 4 and 2
071	Soda ash	5	2	Sahu Jain 2 and 1
072	Sulphuric acid	11	5	Shri Ram 2 and 2, Kasturbhai 4 and 3
075	Petro-chemicals n.e.c.	5	1	Mafatlal 6 and 6, Goenka 3 and 0
076	Acids, n.e.c.	4	2	Kasturbhai 3 and 3
077	Carbon black	4	0	Bajoria-Jalan 2 and 0
079	Glycerine	2	2	
081	Fertilisers	6	0	J.K. 3 and 2, Kasturbhai 3 and 3
082	Insecticides	4	1	Tata 5 and
083	Resins and Plastics	17	6	Shri Ram 2 and 1, Walchand 4 and 3, Sahu Jain 2 and 1, Bangur 2 and 0, Kilachand and 1, Sarabhai 10 and 4, Anantharamakrishnan 3 and 3
088	Gases	17	6	Bajoria-Jalan and 4 and 2, Modi 5 and 3
092	Coke and carbonisation	2	1	
093	Ceramics	3	2	
094	Glass	11	7	Shri Ram 4 and 0, Amichand 2 and 0, Goenka 3 and 1
095	Refractories	2	2	
096	Cement	32	17	Sahu Jain 15 and 10, Bangur 6 and 6, A.C.C. 19 and 17, Amichand 3 and 2, Bajaj 4 and 4
097	Cement, slag	2	0	Sahu Jain 5 and 1

TABLE 20 (*Contd.*)

098	Cement, asbestos	7	7	Sahu Jain 3 and 0, Bangur 2 and 2, Ramakrishna 3 and 2, Seshasyee 2 and 2
099	Grinding Wheels	2	1	
101	Sanitary ware	3	0	Walchand 2 and 1, Kasturbhai 2 and 1 Chinai 2 and 2
108	Cold rolls	6	3	Tata 4 and 3, Amichand 2 and 1
110	Pig Iron	5	3	J.K. 2 and 0, Ramakrishna 3 and 3, Amichand 2 and 0 Kamani 3 and 1, Goenka 2 and 0
112	Structurals	4	3	Amichand 12 and 5, Kamani 3 and 3
113	Rolled Products	4	3	Amichand 3 and 2, Kamani 2 and 0
114	Sheet and flats	4	2	Tata 2 and 2, Amichand 4 and 1
116	Tinplate	2	0	Amichand 6 and 2
117	Stainless and alloy steel	9	2	Tata 3 and 2, Amichand 2 and 1
118	Containers	11	5	Tata 3 and 2, Shri Ram 5 and 3, Bajoria Jalan 2 and 2
120	Castings	8	4	Tata 4 and 4, Sahu Jain 3 and 1, Bangur 3 and 2, Ramakrishnan 4 and 2, Amichand 5 and 2, Kirloskar 3 and 2, Bajoria Jalan 2 and 1
121	Forgings	6	5	Sahu Jain 2 and 1, Amichand 2 and 2
122	Fans and sewing machines	2	2	Shri Ram 2 and 2
123	Bars and rods	3	3	Amichand 2 and 2, Wadia Sapoorji 2 and 2
124	C.I. Spun pipes	5	3	Amichand 2 and 2
125	Steel pipes	7	3	Tata 2 and 2, Patnaik 3 and 2
126	Pipes n.e.c.	3	1	
127	Steel files	2	2	
128	Pipes, industrial	7	3	Patnaik 3 and 1, Amichand 6 and 1
129	Steel wire and rope	7	3	Sahu Jain 2 and 0, Bangur 4 and 2, Seshasayee 3 and 3, Bajoria Jalan 2 and 1, Goenka 2 and 1

131	Hand and small tocls	6	5	Sahu Jain 2 and 1, Bangur 2 and 0, Amichand 2 and 2, Anantharamakrishnan 2 and 2
133	Bearings	4	3	
135	Aluminium, basic	5	5	J.K. 5 and 3
136	Aluminium products (excl. cables)	10	3	J.K. 2 and 1, Amichand 3 and 1, Kamani 3 and 1
137	Wires	4	0	Bangur 7 and 3, Kamani 6 and 1, Modi 2 and 1
138	Cables	13	10	J.K. 3 and 1, Bangur 5 and 3, Kamani 4 and 4, Seshasayee 8 and 7
141	Machinery conveying	12	8	Tata 3 and 3, A.C.C 6 and 4, Amichand 3 and 2
142	Machinery construction	—	—	Tata 4 and 4, Bajoria Jalan 5 and 4
146	Machine tools	13	11	Walchand 3 and 3, Kirloskar 4 and 3, Anantharamakrishnan 2 and 2, Mahindra 2 and 2
147	Drilling and cutting tools	8	5	Tata 5 and 2
150	Motors and generators	12	8	Shri Ram 3 and 1, Bajaj 3 and 3, Kirloskar 5 and 4
151	Switchgears and transformers	15	5	Bajaj 2 and 2, Kirloskar 3 and 3, Anantharamakrishnan 2 and 2
152	Other elcctrical machinery and components	8	6	Shri Ram 2 and 1, Kamani 2 and 1, Bajaj 3 and 2, Kirloskar 8 and 6, Thapar 4 and 3
169	Transport : electric components	8	5	
170	Transport : mechanical components	8	7	Tata 2 and 2, Walchand 2 and 2, Ramakrishnan 2 and 1 Anantharamkrishnan 9 and 8, Mahindra 2 and 2
175	Tractors and power tillers	8	3	Amichand 2 and 0, Kriloskar 3 and 0, Anantharamakrishnan 2 and 2, Mahindra 2 and 2 Bajoria 4 and 1

TABLE 20 (*Contd.*)

180	Electric lamps, starters	—	—	Bajaj 5 and 4, Goenka 4 and 4
181	Household appliances	9	5	
182	Office appliances	4	1	J.K. 4 and 2, Bajoria Jalan 2 and 0
183	Radio and components	3	2	Tata 4 and 2.

goods approval can be so adjusted or spaced as to minimise the financial and managerial burdens at any time of the group—not necessarily those of the economy as a whole. If the applications are rejected or deferred for subsequent consideration, they remain on the waiting list against future licensing, ahead of new applications from others.

LIMITATIONS OF DATA

The data are taken wholly from the agenda papers and minutes of the Licensing Committee set up under the Industries (Development and Regulation) Act. This is, I understand, the first time that investment and import component data from this source have been aggregated and classified. The applications also contain some information on the requirements of physical resources like power, railway wagons, water, raw materials, etc. I further understand that it has never been considered worthwhile to aggregate these data either; in any event, they have not been used for purposes of planning or administration.

Since 1962 the Ministry of Industry has maintaind three lists of industries which are subject to change every six months: (i) free list, in which licences are given without reference to the Licensing Committee, (ii) merit list, in which licences are given on merits after scrutiny by the Licensing Committee, and (iii) rejection list, in which applications are rejected on grounds of sufficient licensed capacity without reference to the Licensing Committee.

Applications for the free list, as it stands from time to time, do not come before the Licensing Committee. Such applications and approvals are not included in the data analysed here. It is reasonable to suppose that the number of such applications and approvals, and the investment proposed under them, are considerable.

Applications rejected on grounds of their being on the rejection list are reported to the Licensing Committee which sometimes does consider them on merit. This reporting does not normally contain any data beyond specifying the applicant's name, product applied for and the state of location. Hence the data analysed here are incomplete to that extent.

The Licensing Committee is furnished with a fairly comprehensive summary of the data only in respect of the merit list. Even in this case, the amount of proposed investment is, in many cases, not specified or the summaries as presented omit some particulars, for example, state of location, type of proposal, and so on.

There is a time lag between approval by the Licensing Committee, which is technically a recommendation to the government and the issue of a licence or, sometimes, an intra-government difference of opinion which delays confirmation of the minutes of meetings.

Since 1964, it has been the practice of the Licensing Committee to issue first a letter of intent, valid for a specified period and, after completion of various preliminaries, to give a licence. In this Report, no distinction is made between licences and letters of intent.

The same application with or without alterations is, at times, considered more than once by the Licensing Committee which may defer or reject it and then reconsider, again, sometimes more than once, at the request of the applicant or the state of location or consequent upon reopening of a whole issue.

In the analysis, applications have been taken net of deferred, but this is open to the objection that deferred applications do not always have full data when they come up for reconsideration. Some of the deferred cases are decided "on file" at a higher level and the decision is not available in the Licensing Committee papers. Some others do not return to the committee, presumably, because the applicants withdraw them.

The distinction between the three types of licences, new article, substantial expansion and new undertaking, is not always clear in the papers available. Errors of recording are somewhat common in this area.

Owing to these limitations, the data on the number of applications and approvals analysed here are not expected to tally with those released periodically by the Ministry of Industry.

Estimates of investment and import component are, in most cases, tentative and are to be taken as broad magnitudes only. For the sake of convenience, investment is identified in this analysis with capital equipment and excludes all other fixed investment. The import component is as estimated initially by the applicant.

The minimum exemption limit for licensing of new undertakings was raised from Rs. 5 lakhs to Rs. 10 lakhs in 1960 and further (with the exception of some industries) to Rs. 25 lakhs in 1964. Inter-temporal comparisons have to keep in mind the changes in exemption limits, though these would not appreciably affect the distribution of investment as distinct from the number of applications.

New articles and substantial expansion of undertakings already licensed are not covered by the exemption limit. A separate licence is required for each such proposal, even if no investment is required for the manufacture of a new article.

Substantial expansion is not defined precisely in the Industries Act but is interpreted to mean an addition of more than 10 per cent (25 per cent since end-1966) to licensed capacity. The distinction between substantial expansion and new article is not always clear.

Under the Industries Act, only the central government and specified government agencies are exempt from licensing. State governments and public sector bodies corporate have to apply for licences in the normal course. The procedure for considering proposals from such applicants is not uniform. Apparently, many of the larger investment proposals do not come before the Licensing Committee; the data of such proposals are not included here.

The classification of products is subject to the usual difficulties of such classifications, especially the difficulty of distinguishing complete plants from components and different varieties and grades of equipment and materials from one another.

The state of location refers generally to the location of the undertaking. Sometimes, however, it also refers to the state of location of the registered or liaison office, etc. It has not been possible to be absolutely accurate on this account.

The definition of industrial houses and their regional/communal origin broadly conforms to that used in my book, *The Structure of the Corporate Private Sector—A Study of Concentration, Ownership and Control.* The classification made on this basis is not infallible though care has been taken to see that it is consistent with the information available to me. In many cases, especially of private and new companies as also individuals and partnership firms, classification is difficult—and is subject to some degree of error. On the whole, however, my impression is that the errors so far as several major industrial houses, or categories are concerned, are more of omission than commission.

The data have no reference to follow up action after consideration of proposals by the Licensing Committee. To the extent licences do not fructify ultimately or, there is a time lag between sanction and actual investment or, a difference between estimated cost and actual cost, there would be a wide gap between investment intentions and fulfilment.

INDUSTRIAL HOUSE CODE

01 Birla
02 Sahu Jain
03 Dalmia
04 Bangur-Somani
05 Goenka
06 J.K.
07 Bajoria-Jalan
08 Kamani
09 Khaitan
10 Morarka
11 Bajaj
12 Modi
13 Khandelwal
14 Poddar
15 Jaipuria
16 Ruia
17 Mundhra
18
19 Other Marwari
20 Tata
21 Martin Burn
22 ACC
23 Shri Ram
24 Kirloskar
25 Srivastava
26 Sen
27 Godrej
28 Devidayal
29 Jolly
30 Mafatlal

31 Walchand
32 Kasturbhai
33 Kilachand
34 Sarabhai
35 Thackersay
36 Amin
37 Dharamsi Morarji
38 Chinai
39 Other Gujarati
40 Ananthäramakrishnan
41 Seshasayee
42 Ramakrishna
43 TVS
44
45 Other Southern
46 B. Patnaik
47 Bombay Burmah and Vissanji
48 Wadia-Shapoorji
49 Escorts
50 Thapar
51 Mahindra
52 Amichand Pyarelall
53 Harbans Lal Malhotra
54 Other Punjabi
55 Sindhi
56 Parsi n.e.c.
57 Maharashtrian n.e.c.
58 Bengali n.e.c.
59 Other n.e.c.
60 Bird Heilger
61 Andrew Yule
62 Inchcape Mackay
63 Larsen & Toubro
64 E I D Parry
65 Balmer Lawrie
66 Harvey
67 Rallis
68 Gillanders
69 Other domiciled foreign
70 International combines: UK

71 International combines: USA
72 International combines: West Germany
73 International combines: Switzerland
74 International combines: Sweden
75 International combines: Netherlands
76 International combines: Denmark
77 International combines: France
78 International combines: Italy
79 International combines: Other
80 Co-operatives: Northern States
81 Co-operatives: Eastern States
82 Co-operatives: Western States
83 Co-operatives: Southern States
90 State Govt., SIDC's: Andhra Pradesh
91 State Govt., SIDC's: Assam
92 State Govt., SIDC's: Gujarat
93 State Govt., SIDC's: Kerala
94 State Govt., SIDC's: Orissa
95 State Govt., SIDC's: Punjab
96 State Govt., SIDC's: U.P.
97 State Govt., SIDC's: Other
99 Government companies

PRODUCT CODE

001 Gum and natural resin
002 Glue and gelatin
003 Animal feed
005 Coal and lignite
006 Other mining
007 Coal washery
008 Other processed minerals
009 Salt
010 Sugar
011 Flour and confectionery
012 Processed food
013 Vanaspati and edible oil
014 Alcohol, industrial
015 Alcohol, potable
016 Soap

018 Cosmetics
019 Tobacco
020 Cotton yarn
021 Cotton fabrics
022 Cotton composite
023 Cotton other
024 Woollen (incl. carpets)
025 Synthetic fabrics
026 Jute carpet and backing (incl. tufted)
027 Jute other
028 Textiles n.e.c.
029 Non-woven fabrics
030 Rayon fibre and yarn
031 Petrochemical fibres: Intermediate
032 Polyester
033 Polypropylene
034 Acrylic
035 Tyre cord rayon/nylon
036 Nylon
037 Poly Vinyl Alcohol
038 Petro-chem other fibre
039 Cellulose n.e.c.
040 Chipboard
041 Plywood
042 Cork
043 Wood n.e.c.
045 Matches
050 Paper
051 Paper spl. finish
052 Paper film
053 Paper industrial (incl. printing)
054 Paper board
055 Newsprint
056 Pulp paper
057 Pulp rayon
060 Leather
061 Synthetic leather
062 Synthetic tanning agents
063 Rubber tyres and tubes
064 Rubber, industrial

065 Rubber synthetic
066 Rubber other
067 Contraceptives
068 Alcohol chemicals
069 Bleaching agents
070 Caustic soda
071 Soda ash
072 Sulphuric acid
073 Calcium carbide
074 Chlorine
075 Petrochemicals n.e.c.
076 Acids n.e.c.
077 Carbon black
078 PVC products
079 Glycerine
080 Dyes
081 Fertilisers
082 Insecticides
083 Resins, plastics, laminates
084 Drugs
085 Detergents
086 Paints
087 Solvents and extractions
088 Gases
089 Chemicals n.e.c.
090 Batteries
091 Electrodes
092 Coke and carbonisation
093 Ceramics
094 Glass
095 Refractories
096 Cement
097 Cement slag
098 Cement asbestos
099 Grinding wheels
100 Explosives
101 Sanitaryware
102 Vulcanised fibre
103 Fibre pipes
105 Stainless steel sheets

106 Safety razor blades
107 Utensils
108 Cold C.I. rolls
109 Iron sponge
110 Iron pig
111 Steel basic
112 Steel structurals
113 Steel rolling
114 Steel sheet and flats
115 Steel aluminised
116 Steel tinplate
117 Steel alloy and stainless
118 Steel containers
119 Ferro alloys
120 Castings
121 Forgings
122 Light engg. (fans, sewing machines, etc.)
123 Bars and rods
124 CI Spun pipes
125 Steel pipes
126 Pipes n.e.c.
127 Steel files
128 Pipes, industrial
129 Steel wire, rod, rope
130 Nuts, bolts, screws
131 Hand tools
132 Magnets
133 Bearings
134 Metals, non-ferrous non-aluminium n.e.c.
135 Aluminium basic
136 Aluminium products (excl. cables)
137 Wires
138 Cables
139 Metal products n.e.c.
140 Machinery and components: agricultural
141 Machinery and components: conveying
142 Machinery and components: construction
143 Machinery and components: mining
144 Machinery and components: industrial n.e.c.
145 Machinery and components: industrial components n.e.c.

146 Machinery and components: machine tools
147 Machinery and components: drilling and cutting tools
148 Broches
149 Printing
150 Electrical machinery: motors and generators
151 Electrical machinery: switchgear and transformers
152 Electrical machinery: other and components n.e.c.
153 Electrical machinery: turbines and turbo units
154 Electrical machinery: boilers
155 Electrical machinery: air compressors
156 Electrical machinery: furnaces
157 Electrical machinery: stampings
158 Welding and cutting equipment
159 Valves, industrial etc. (excl. radio)
160 Transport equipment: railway wagons
161 Transport equipment: railway other
164 Transport equipment: engines
165 Transport equipment: trucks, buses, jeeps
166 Transport equipment: motor cars
167 Transport equipment: motor cycles and scooters
168 Transport equipment: bicycles and components
169 Transport equipment: electrical components
170 Transport equipment: mechanical components
171 Transport equipment: aviation
172 Transport equipment: ropeways
173 Transport equipment: vessels and barges
174 Transport equipment: trailers
175 Transport equipment: tractors and power tillers
177 Heavy and special castings
179 Heavy engg. components n.e.c.
180 Electric lamps, starters
181 Household appliances
182 Office and commercial appliances
183 Tele-comm. equip. and components
184 Photo equipment and materials (incl x-ray)
185 Meters
186 Petroleum refining
187 Petroleum lubricants
188 Surgical equipment
190 Weighing machinery

191 Electronics and advanced communications equip.
192 Electronic computers
193 Titanium dioxide
194 Instruments, mechanical
195 Instruments, electrical and industrial
196 Refrigeration equipment
200 Manufacturing n.e.c.

REFERENCES

1. Eleven industries were delicensed in May 1966: (1) iron and steel castings and forgings, (2) iron and steel structurals, (3) electric motors up to 10 h.p., (4) pulp, (5) power alcohol, (6) solvent extracted oils, (7) glue and gelatin, (8) glass, (9) firebricks and furnace linings, (10) cement, gypsum and insulating boards, (11) timber products.

   The reconstituted Swaminathan Committee recommended in March 1966 that " . . . generally speaking, industries which do not involve the import of capital goods and of raw materials should be exempted from the licensing provisions of the Act . . . It should by and large be left to the economic judgement of the entrepreneur to decide whether or not he will enter the field and make an investment and to what extent. In these fields the targets laid down by the Planning Commission should serve as indicative targets and as a factor to be considered by the prospective investor in his assessment of demand and other economic data."

   In November 1966, 29 more industries were delicened on the two grounds mentioned above, plus the need to create additional Fourth Plan capacity and to exploit export potential and increase agricultural production: (1) cast iron spun pipes, (2) steel ingot billets by electric furnace, (3) non-vehicular internal/combustion engines below 50 h.p., (both diesel and petrol), (4) electric motors up to 50 h.p. (5) electric furnace without import of switchgear and transformer, (6) bicycles and components, (7) tea machinery, (8) power driven pumps, (9) agricultural sprayers (except manual) (conventional and non-conventional type with indigenous engines), (10) air and gas compressors up to 6 C.M.C., (11) fire fighting equipment, (12) coated abrasives, (13) sewing machines and components, (14) weighing machines, (15) mathematical, surveying and drawing instruments, (16) mixed fertilisers, (17) calcium carbonate, (18) barium carbonate, (19) barium chloride, (20) barium nitrate, (21) barium sulphate, (22) blane fixe, (23) activated bleaching earth, (24) activated carbon, (25) metallic stearates, (26) sodium aluminate, (27) paper board/straw board, (28) paper for packaging, (29) hard board including fibre board, chip board and particle boards.

2. In a plan, only the targets of aggregate income, consumption and investment can be considered as relatively invariant. I am unable to uncover any sanctity or utility in treating each component target as a constant, though I readily concede that some targets should be less variable than others.
3. I would like in this connection to point out, as an illustration, that in spite of the strong case made out by the Bhabha Committee, the import of electronic components has not been given priority status, which is enjoyed by many items with a much smaller potential for income generation, import substitution, export and employment.
4. See V.D. Lall: "Taxation and profitability", *Economic and Political Weekly* (Special Number), August 1967.
5. This picture would not differ significantly if applications, instead of approvals, were taken into account.

PART FIVE

PUBLIC SECTOR IN INDIA*

THE FIRST STAGES

The loud noises made by official spokesmen and in policy statements during the late 1940s and early 1950s notwithstanding, large-scale manufacture in the public sector was not seriously contemplated till the launching of the steel programme (especially the Bhilai steel plant) in 1955. The industrial policy statement of 1948 did classify large-scale industry into public and private sectors and held out the possibility of nationalisation within 10 years of private units falling in the public list. As events turned out, private steel was not nationalised nor was private coal; railways had been nationalised before and during the Second World War and the private sector was not interested in them anyway. Airlines and the Reserve Bank were the solitary instances of nationalisation in the late 1940s. The Imperial Bank was taken over in 1955, Life Insurance in 1956. Earlier the Damodar Valley Corporation was set up in 1948 on the T.V.A. model, and the states were advised to set up statutory bodies for power and road passenger transport. Preliminary (or perfunctory) negotiations for a 500,000-ton steel plant at Rourkela started around 1952, but this solitary project could not be said to have set the public sector going; it began with German equity participation and precedents for this kind of venture were not altogether lacking.

In brief, between 1947 and 1955 the public sector was almost wholly a collection of non-manufacturing enterprises taken over from private ownership. Stated alternatively, it represented the transplantation of Fabian concepts from Britain which included, in their overall perspective, mechanisms for physical and

*"The Public Sector in India" from E.A.G. Robinson and Michael Kidron (eds.): *Economic Development in South Asia—1970* (Macmillan). Reproduced by permission. This paper was written in 1969.

institutional control of private investment, price-fixing and distribution of goods and materials. Active, widespread and direct involvement of the government in manufacturing and mining in the sense of investment and management was conspicuously absent during this period, though speeches to the contrary were frequent and abundant.

Shorn of verbiage, the speeches postulated that profits were inconsistent with social priorities (if not actually anti-social), that essential goods received the first bounties of development and had, therefore, to be kept under price and distribution controls, and that the public sector would invest for priorities, not profits; but, at the same time, it was not worthwhile taking over old junk through nationalisation. During the First Plan (1951-56) the preoccupation was with food and elemental scarcities which required attention to irrigation, power and transport; two other consumer goods in short supply, cloth and sugar, were supplied by a large number of units whose nationalisation could not be contemplated on managerial grounds or consistently with the division of industries between the public and private sectors in the 1948 policy statements.

POST-1955 POLICIES

As the dire scarcities of food and cloth moderated towards the mid-1950s and the sterling balances in London were unblocked, the horizons of development widened suddenly. The demands of irrigation, power, transport and associated construction were seen to proliferate into steel, cement, machinery and engineering goods. Of course, steel and heavy engineering were deemed ideal for the public sector. Why? The most facile explanation is that 1948 policy statement said so. Had its categorisation been sacred, action on it could have been taken earlier.

Given the cardinal premise of demand generation by public expenditure, the industrial programmes that emerged after 1955 were built around two hypotheses:

(i) private investment in relatively simple goods would be prompted by shutting out imports as well as through excess demand at home, with a consequent boost to profits; and

(ii) public investment, being autonomous of profits, would take place in basic areas which had long gestation periods, low or no profits, a large foreign exchange component, complex technology and equally complex problems of co-ordination.

In other words, induced investment was to be boosted by protection, while autonomous[1] investment was justified by longer-term considerations of import substitution, building-up of capacities ahead of demand, and supply of inputs at what were expected to be low-or at least low-profit-prices. Rising public expenditure, in official parlance, assurance of increasing budgetary appropriations, was to underpin both types of investment, providing sheltered markets irrespective of traditional comparative cost limitations.

Total investment in central goverment undertakings (which excludes large chunks of investment by states in their electricity boards and transport undertakings) rose from Rs. 29 crores in 1950-51 to Rs. 81 crores in 1955-56, Rs 953 crores in 1960-61, Rs. 2,415 crores in 1965-66 and is currently estimated at Rs. 3,500 crores. Gross capital formation out of central government budgetary resources rose from 1.2 per cent of GNP in 1950-51 to 2.9 per cent in the First Plan, 5.6 per cent in the Second Plan and 7.8 per cent in the Third Plan, but declined to 6.2 per cent in 1967-68 (Table 1). The share of the public sector as a whole in the total capital stock of mining, manufacturing and transport reached 53 per cent in 1960-61 and rose to 58 per cent in 1965-66 (Table 2). In sharp contrast with this major share in capital stock, direct income generation by the public sector

TABLE 1: **Gross capital formation out of central government budgetary resources as percentage of GNP**

1950-51	1.2
Total First Plan (1951-56)	2.9
Total Second Plan (1956-61)	5.6
Total Third Plan (1961-66)	7.8
1965-66	8.3
1966-67	7.2
1967-68	6.2

Source: *Commerce*, 8 March, 1969.

TABLE 2: **Share of public sector in capital stock**

(*Percentages*)

	Mining, manufacturing and transport	All sectors
Estimated		
1960-61	53.1	25.6
1965-66	58.3	33.7
Projections		
1970-71	61.5	44.1
1975-76	64.0	51.9

Source: Planning Commission, Perspective Planning Division, *Notes on Perspective of Development India*: 1960-61 to 1975-76 (April 1964), pp. 8-9.

has been extremely low. The share of departmental and non-departmental enterprises (that is the public sector excluding government administration) in gross domestic product at current prices was 5.8 per cent in 1960-61 and 6.4 per cent in 1964-65 (Table 3). Between these two years, the share of the non-departmental public sector (that is, statutory corporations, boards and companies) in the GDP generated in large-scale manufacturing rose from 4.2 per cent to 8.8 per cent (Table 4). Apart from the fact of large investments, there is one other easily quantifiable indicator and that is the composition of output. The public sector has helped to change the industrial structure by increasing the output of basic heavy and technologically sophisticated goods

TABLE 3: **Share of public sector in GDP (at current prices)**

	Amount		Percentages	
	1960-61	1964-65	1960-61	1964-65
	(Rs. crores)			
1. Government administration	744	1,233	5.2	5.7
2. Departmental enterprises	611	891	4.3	4.1
3. Non-departmental enterprises	214	505	1.5	2.3
4. Total public sector (1)+(2)+(3)	1,569	2,629	11.0	12.1
5. Gross domestic product	14,261	21,672	100.0	100.0

Source: *Brochure on Revised Series of National Product for 1960-61 to 1964-65* (CSO, August, 1967).

TABLE 4: **Sectorwise share of the public sector (non-departmental) in gross domestic product at current prices**

Industry	1960-61			1964-65		
	Gross product of public sector (Rs. crores)	Total gross product (Rs. crores)	Percentage share of public sector	Gross product of public sector (Rs. crores)	Total gross product (Rs. crores)	Percentage share of public sector
1. Agriculture	—	6889	—	1.6	10396	neg.
2. Mining	20.5	153	13.4	34.1	224	15.2
3. Large-scale manufacturing	49.3	1188	4.2	172.1	1950	8.8
4. Construction	1.6	643	0.2	6.6	946	0.7
5. Electricity	46.6	78	59.7[a]	98.0	146	67.1[a]
6. Trading, storage, hotels and restaurants	5.0	1334	0.4	12.8	2121	0.6
7. Transport other than railways	29.8	322	9.2	64.4	502	12.3
(a) Air	12.5	15	83.3	25.0	28	89.3
(b) Water	2.4	59	4.0	5.9	90	6.3
(c) Road	14.9	248	6.0[a]	33.5	384	8.7[a]
8. Banking and finance	27.5	103	26.7	43.9	182	24.1
9. Insurance	32.9	58	56.8[a]	70.2	112	62.7[a]

Source: *Brochure on Revised Series of National Product for 1960-61 to 1964-65* (C.S.O, August 1967).

[a]The actual public sector share would be higher under these heads if departmental enterprises were also included.

and services. There has been more than a proportionate increase in the production of such goods as measured by the index of industrial production.

EVALUATION OF THE PUBLIC SECTOR

The achievements of the public sector should not be evaluated in terms of amounts invested in relation to Plan targets and/or budgetary appropriations, though this is the favoured official mode of evaluation. The difficulty is that once one moves away from this smug government accounting indicator, it is difficult to find tangible, measurable macro-criteria for evaluating the public sector as a whole. Comparisons of rates of return on public sector investment with those on private investment, for instance, are fouled up by a number of factors. First, since non-profit objectives are a much larger component of public investment, it is improper to compare the rates of return without making appropriate adjustments—which would require quantification of the non-profit objectives. Second, private sector returns have been greatly boosted by much greater protection against external competition for consumer and lighter goods generally than for capital goods, which have had to face much greater competition from imports financed by aid and foreign private investment. Third, the public sector is not merely capital-intensive and characterised by longer gestation periods; in steel, which accounts for the bulk of investment, it is also material-intensive, and to that extent its value-added component is smaller than in items like, say, chemicals. Finally, the prices of public sector products are controlled formally or informally or, what comes to the same thing, the products are sold to the government at cost-plus and, to that extent, the possibilities of making a killing on profits are generally dim. Allowing for all these factors, one can only say that the difference between capital stock and income generated in the public sector exaggerates its deficiencies. The deficiencies are there all right.

Comparative rate of return apart, the only other conventional criteria are contributions to the raising of aggregate investment, import substitution, technological development, external economies, etc. These criteria are used *en passant* quite often, but it is seldom possible to trace the net benefit accruing to the economy with the help of these measures.

To evolve a set of criteria for evaluation of public sector investment and performance, one has to go back first to the major deficiencies that have been noticed and the principal reasons for them. To begin with the beginning, the trouble starts with the investment programming. Since autonomous investments cannot possibly be appraised in the same manner as induced investments, their feasibility depends essentially upon Plan forecasts of assumed trends. To the extent that the assumed trends are not translated into reality in time, the feasibility suffers. This built-in suffering is accentuated when the entire national matrix of investment processes and income generation depends upon budgetary appropriations at home and abroad. Uncertainties about domestic budgetary appropriations could be reduced to some extent if the processes of investment depended a little more on bank (including development bank) finance rather than almost exclusively on the Treasury, but the intrinsic problem of assuring the feasibility of public investment projects would remain, particularly in the case of manufacturing, mining and construction which, unlike power and transport, are not supposed to endure excess capacity with benefit to the economy. So long as investment is considered a good thing by itself, there is a natural incentive to invest more than is strictly necessary for the desired level of production. And so long as capital funds for the public sector are provided at artificially cheap rates, and much of the equipment is procured against aid, physical, over-capitalisation is bound to be common. Things are made worse when the ruling economic philosophy requires essential goods to be sold at relatively uneconomic prices in the interest of the rest of the economy.

The solution of this basic problem is not easy; it is not impossible either. There must be a large stock of technically sound projects of various sizes out of which economic choices (including choices of size) can be made. The criteria of economic feasibility should be known and announced in advance and should include:

a. pricing of products on the basis of international prices with an initial mark-up in the form of import duties;
b. sufficient flexibility of product pattern to take advantage

of market trends;

c. optimum scheduling of investment and cash generation so as to minimise the total capitalisation (which would in many cases require starting on a relatively small scale and then expanding with the help of earlier cash generation); and

d. use of a realistic interest rate for purposes of capital rationing.

The second problem which bedevils public investment is the absence of specified objectives. Assuming that the target rate of return has been taken care of in the feasiblity assessment process (this itself is such a conventional exercise that it should offer no special difficulties)—the question really is of dealing with the non-profit or non-commercial objectives. Whether these objectives relate to strategic considerations, social benefits like townships, regional development, compulsory exports, monopolistic buying by government itself, special R and D efforts, and the like, it is not impossible to quantify their impact upon the capital-at-charge, the time stream of earnings and cash flow, and the rate of return. Rather than leave these special factors hanging in the air to cloud the issue every time the question of profitability comes up, it is reasonable to build them into the feasibility formulae and provide outer limits for the costs of these factors as reducing elements in the target rate of return.

The third factor relates to the general economic policy of keeping essential goods 'cheap' and at the same time pumping large investments into their production in the national interest. Without entering into the controversy over the Hotelling Theorem, the proposition can be advanced that such goods should be rendered cheap by maximising productivity rather than by over-capitalisation and under-pricing, and that it is safer to make the enterprises self-reliant for their financing than to make them dependent upon uncertain budgetary appropriations.

Fourth, there is the basic but inscrutable problem of intangibles which make or unmake a business. Investment has been so intensely identified with physical capacity as to reach the absurd limit of the one-product-one-factory idea on the one hand and the neglect of investment in marketing, designing and R and D on the other. This link between investment and physical capacity must be broken and replaced by a direct link between investment, value added, productivity and the rate of return. Physical capacity, it must be firmly understood, has practically no operational meaning, especially in the area of capital goods. In operational terms, capacity has reference to management and know-know, not equipment.

Finally, there is the question of autonomy and accountability. Both have to be defined in terms of performance, not archaic rules and notions. It is ridiculous to suggest in this connection that politics and politicians should have nothing to do with the public sector. Without them there would be neither motive force nor objective, nor, perhaps, markets for products. Major investments, whether public or private, cannot possibly be divorced from political considerations; even mangement decisions, as distinct from investment decisions, need a binding element in the form of political resin. Once it is conceded that public enterprises have a variety of non-commercial, non-profit objectives, it is logically impossible to avoid any local pressures for employment or the responsibilities of being a good citizen in the area of location, quite apart from wider, national-level responsibilities.

Managerial and financial autonomy and accountability in the public sector pose problems of organisational scale, technique and vision which are comparable with those faced by international companies. They have sought to get over these problems mainly through budgetary and personnel controls which keep a tight rein on capital expenditure, principal revenue items and top appointments, without intervention in day-to-day management. Accountability on a current, not historical, basis is assured through reporting systems which keep a check on deviations from budgetary norms and through frequent top-level consultations on policy directions. I submit that the public sector has a lot to learn from the control and reporting systems operated in international companies, and that these systems can be adopted, without any great difficulty independently of the political environment, so long as the decision to adopt them has been taken. Such transplantation is possible once attention is diverted from facile generalisations like maximum autonomy to managements, relaxation of audit, and forbearance from executive and parliamentary interference.

THE REMAINING HURDLES

There are at present two main hurdles in the working of the public sector. One is the lack of assured orders, the pace of which depends upon autonomous investment decisions, and the other is the absence of a modern system of financial control appropriate to large impersonal enterprises. Getting over the first hurdle requires political vision and strength. Clearing the second hurdle is a challenge to intellectual and professional discipline.

REFERENCES

1. The identification of autonomous with public, and induced with private, investment here is not meant to convey a rigid distinction.

INDEX

Accounting years, 199
Advisory Planning Board
  report, 52
Agriculture,
  Five Year Plan I, 62
Air India, 55
Aluminium Industry, 13, 39
Antony, K.A., 163-64
Atkinson-Dawson Committee
  report, 18

Backward Areas
  public sectors
    Five Year Plan II, 76
Balance Sheet, 199
  items, 200
Banks
  controlling blocks, 265*t*, 271
Bank credit
  traditional pattern, 358
Banking, 92, 283
Bhabha Committee
  recommendations, 107
Birlas, 291
  licences, 404
  occupational diversification, 217
Board of directors, 105
Bombay
  European firms, 98
  industrialists plan, 52
British capital export, 35
British Iron and Steel Industry, 8
British law and practice, 94
British manufacturers
  influence, 46
British Policy, 3
Burma
  Japanese innovations, 39

Calcutta
  companies management, 98
Capital and Producer Goods Industries
  Five Year Plan III, 82
Capital equipment
  investment, 362
  prices, 166
Capital expenditure, 34, 91
Capital Goods Committee, 340, 345
  recommendations
    industries, 366*t*-67*t*
  Third Plan Years, 351*t*
Central Government Budget
  gross capital formation, 427*t*
Central Government Undertakings, 427
Charfield Committee, 41
Chatterjee, Atul, 33
Coal Transport Committee, 53
Commercial Bank Deposits, 352
Commodities control
  British period, 39
Common Production Programme
  Five Year Plan I, 65
Companies Act, 105, 292
Companies Amendment Act, 104
Companies managed by managing agents, 11*t*, 111*t*-13*t*
  industrywise classification, 286*t*-87*t*
Companies ownership
  pattern, 202-204
Companies registered, 93
Company law, 94
Composition of complex, 198
Concentration of Economic Power, 216, 290, 297
  measurement
    selection of units, 165
  method, 145
  monopoly commission, 325
  resources, disposition of, 165
Congress National Planning

Committee, 52
Consumer Goods, 55
Constitutional Reforms, 21
Control and Remuneration, 100-102
Control over Resources, 333
Controlling Blocks, 204-207, 253-254, 255*t*-256*t*, 257
by size of companies, 262*t*-264*t*
inner circle service, 270*t*
Corporate groups
definition, 149-152
Corporate management, 148
Corporate private sector, 148
share capital, 93, 173*t*-180*t*
Corporate Sectors
Five Year Plans, 94
growth, 92-94
law, 292
physical assets, 163
Cotton
excise duty, 27
Cotton Mill Industry
world war I, 17
Credit deposit ratio, 357
Credit planning, 357
Customs revenue, 16

Dalal, Ardeshir, 41
Dalmia Sahu Jain
occupational diversification, 217
Damodar Valley Corporation, 55
Das Gupta, K.C., 321
Defence Expenditure
British Policy, 41
Deshmukh, C.D., 110
Dey, 30-31
DGSD Purchases of equipment and stores, 85
Directive Principles on Economic Power, 290
Directors
nationality, 106*t*
Displaced persons
Rehabilitation
Five Year Plan II, 75
Diversification of Industrial Companies, 308-313
Dutt, 332-333

Economic Development
industries, role of, 52
Employment, 32
British Policy, 36
Engineering Stores, 10-12
Entrepreneurial Class, 47
Entrepreneurship, 291
Essential Commodities
prices, 87
Excise Duty, 30
Expansion and Mergers, 329-331
Export companies
production, 313
Export Incentives, 87
External Capital, 33
Committee, 33

Famine Commission Report, 3
Feasibility Reports, 359-360, 364
Finance
source and uses, 201-202
Finance Companies
controlling blocks, 266*t*-267*t*
investment by industrial companies, 253*t*
Financial Assistance, 87
Financial devices
use, 341
Financial Institutions
loans, 296
Financial liabilities of Industries, 212-214
Financial protection
effects, 32
Financial Structure of Industries, 224-226
Fiscal and allied development
Five Year Plan III, 86
Fiscal Commission
protection policy, 26-27
Fiscal Commission II
report, 32-33, 55-56
Five Year Plans
corporate sectors, 94

deficiencies and defects, 78-79
investments, 343
Five Year Plan I
general priorities, 62-63
industrial policy, 61-71
Five Year Plan II
industrial policy, 71-81
objectives, 71-72
Five Year Plan III
industrial policy, 81-116
resources, 352*t*
Food prices, 80
Foreign capital, 27
Foreign collaboration, 79, 385
distribution, 380
investments, 391
types approved, 387
Foreign companies, 97*t*
Foreign controlled enterprises, 33
Foreign credits, 351
Foreign exchange, 80, 86, 92
allocation, 353, 355
control, 342
crisis, 344
Foreign Investors, 282

Gandhian Plan, 52
Gold Export, 34
Government companies, 96
Investment, 391
Government of India Resolution on Industrial Policy 1948, 119-126
Government of India Resolution on Industrial Policy 1956, 129-136
Government of India Resolution on Industrial Policy, 53

Heavy Industries
Five Year Plan III, 82
Hyderabad
mining industries, 45

Import, 324
British Policy, 8, 22
capital equipment investment, 376
capital goods, 353, 356
consumer goods, 379
duty, 15, 29
licences, 355
licensing, 294
machinery and mill work, 48*t*
policy, 90, 357
revenue, 27-28
Income
distribution, 321
per capita, 61
Indian Famine Commission
report, 6
Indian insurance companies,
Role of, 229
Industrial capacity
Five Year Plan II, 74
Industrial classification, 196-197
Industrial Commission, 19, 21, 36
tariff policy, 19-20
Industrial companies controlling
blocks, 268*t*-269*t*
Industrial countries output, 49
Industrial development
Baroda, 25
Expenditure, 22
public works deptt., Role of, 4
Industrial disputes, 53
Industrial Finance Corporations, 55
Industrial Groups
capital, 95*t*
code, 414-416
communal origin, 413
ranking method, 167
Economic power, 148 161
Industrial Management, 96-97
Industrial Planning, 339-340, 342, 362
defects, 347-349
objectives, 342-343, 345
Industrial Policy
after independence, 51
implementation, 52
pre-independence period, 5
statement 1956, 68-71
world war I, 17
Industrial priorities
Five Year Plan III, 84

Industrial Production, 38, 49*t*, 50*t*
  Five Year Plan III, 83
  index, 89*t*
  public sector, 341
Industial Products
  distribution, 242
Industrial Targets and achievements
  Five Year Plan I, 67-68
  Five Year Plan II, 77
Industrial Trust Fund
  Hyderabad, 25
Industrialisation
  Fiscal Commission II
    report, 56
  Five Year Plan II, 72
  Five Year Plan III, 83
Industries
  employment in, 51
  financial protection, 6, 31
  unbalanced and inadequate growth, 34
  world war period, 37
    role, 52
Industries Act 1951, 59-61
  licensing, 90
Industries conference, 52
Inner circle companies
  controlling Blocks, 296
Insurance Companies, 92, 283
  controlling blocks, 265*t*-271
Inter company investments, 108
Inter-corporate investment, 297, 303-308
Inter-Group variations, 257
Inter-industrial corporate holdings, 237
  change, 250*t*-251*t*
International combines, 394*t*
Interim Tariff Board
  formation, 42
  functions, 43-44
  inquiries, 44
Interwar period difficulties, 21
Investment, 48
  Five Year Plan II, 78
  fixed, 359
  initial, 374
  patterns, 373
  policy, 293
  social overheads, 3
  states, 385
  states approval, 396*t*
  utilization, 362
Iron and Steel Industry
  financial protection, 28
  store purchase policy, 7-8
Iron Industry
  purchases, 13

Joint-Stock Companies, 92
Joint subsidiaries, 276
Joint ventures, 219, 220*t*-222*t*, 223-224

Labour
  Five Year Plan II, 73
  training, 80
Laissez-Faire, 3, 5, 13
Land resolutions
  remodelling, 3
Large capital investment, 291
Large groups
  break ups, 292
  classification, 425
  controlling blocks, 261
  growth, 293
  opportunities, 295
Legislative Assembly
  budget, 23
LIC Holdings
  Govt., Role of, 232*t*-233*t*
Licences
  applicants, 385
    categories, 392*t*-393*t*
  Foreign exchange, 368*t*-372*t*
  types, 385
Licensing and capital goods committee
  recommendation, 349-351
Licensing
  synoptic view, 375*t*
  objectives, 344
  policy, 79, 296, 339, 340, 362
    changes, 361
  defects, 346-349
    deficiencies, 347
    Five Year Plan 1II, 87, 90-92

framework, 340
Industrial Act, 340
objectives, 343
priority list, 91-92
purpose, 363
system, 359
Licensing Committee, 340, 345, 411
Lokanathan, P.S., 104
Long-term finance, 47
Long-term investment, 47

Machine tools
production, 39
Machinery
import prices, 17
Madras Chamber of Commerce, 13
Mahalanobis Committee, 321
Mahalanobis draft
Plan Frame, 72, 79
Management
as tool for measurement, 147
Companies Act 1956, 106
Managers
appointment, 107
Managerial personnel
categories, 107
Managing agencies, 99, 100, 276, 277
by complex, 280*t*
by ownership, 282*t*
by share capital, 277*t*
by size, 278
combined balance sheet, 279*t*
joint ventures
as form of management, 283
mixed blessing, 102-104
multiple directorships, 105
press, link with, 331-332
share capital, 280, 281*t*, 282
system, 297-303
advantages, 298-303
Managing agency system
note of dissent, 332
Managing agency commission, 102
Managing Agents,
investment, 285
remuneration, 113-114*t*
by size 115*t*
by industry, 115*t*-116*t*
Managing directors, 113
Market mechanism, 341-342
Marketing
Fiscal Commission II, 58
Marwaris, investment, 391
Medium groups, 295
Monopoly Commission
analysis of history, 324
appointment, 321
concentration of economic power, 322
control over resources, 333
definition, 327
general recommendations, 328-329
group catalogue, 326
note of dissent, 332
product catalogue, 326
report, 320-321
Monopolistic Practices, 330
Montague-Chelmsford report, 25-27
Morley policy, 13-14
Munitions Board
function, 18
Mysore
enterprises, 45
industrial development
British policy, 5
Iron steel industry, 45

National Income
third plan period, 81-82
Nationalization of large groups, 292
Neogy, K.C., 52
Nominee Holdings, 313-318
Non-Government companies
physical assets, 165*t*
share capital, 164
Non-Government public companies
share capital, 172

Occupational diversification, 217
Ordnance factories, 13, 18
Ownership of companies, 230-231, 242, 243*t*
by industry, 244*t*-249*t*

Science [illegible]
[illegible] volume, 145, [illegible]
Sectoral [illegible], 41, 48
Sectoral and [illegible]
[illegible]
Sales products [illegible]
[illegible]
Short-term [illegible]
[illegible]
[illegible]
Short-term [illegible]
Short-term credit [illegible]
Seasonal Fluctuations, 1937 [illegible]
Small and cottage industries, 27
Small-industry products
Government purchases, 87
Small scale industries, 137
[illegible]
[illegible]
[illegible]
Statement on industrial policy
Budget, 43
[illegible]
Foreign [illegible] capital, 56
Steel [illegible]
[illegible]
[illegible]
[illegible]
Stock [illegible]
[illegible]
Subsidies, [illegible]
[illegible]
Sugar industry
Protection, [illegible]
Sukhamoy [illegible]

Swaminathan Committee on Money [illegible]
report, 47-48
Tariff Board, 27, 47, 190
political influence, 190
Tariff Policy, 28
East India Company, [illegible]
fiscal commission, 27-28
world war I, 27
Taxes, 91
occupational [illegible], 213
Tax-concessions, 81, 86
Technical considerations
Five Year Plan III, 84
Technological innovation, 14
Technical personnel, 108
Technique of control, 272, 275
Textile purchasing, 18
Traditional Industries, 284
Trade-union
industries, [illegible]
[illegible]
[illegible], 277
maintenance, [illegible]
Tyson, 29

USA
[illegible] 108, 133, 203

Village and Small Industries
Five Year Plan I, [illegible]
Five Year Plan II, [illegible]
Five Year Plan III, [illegible]
[illegible]

Virginia [illegible]

[illegible]
[illegible], 14, 24